The Peasant Land Market
in Medieval England

The Peasant Land Market in Medieval England

Edited by
P.D.A. HARVEY

CLARENDON PRESS · OXFORD
1984

Oxford University Press, Walton Street, Oxford OX2 6DP

London New York Toronto
Delhi Bombay Calcutta Madras Karachi
Kuala Lumpur Singapore Hong Kong Tokyo
Nairobi Dar es Salaam Cape Town
Melbourne Auckland

and associated companies in
Beirut Berlin Ibadan Mexico City Nicosia

Oxford is a trade mark of Oxford University Press

Published in the United States
by Oxford University Press, New York

British Library Cataloguing in Publication Data

Harvey, P.D.A.
The Peasant land market in medieval England.
1. Peasantry—England—History
2. Farms, small—England—History
I. Title
338.6'42   HD1339.G7
ISBN 0-19-822661-6

Library of Congress Cataloging in Publication Data
Main entry under title:
The Peasant land market in medieval England.
Includes index.
1. Land tenure—England—History.   2. Peasantry—
England—History.   3. Agriculture—Economic aspects—
England—History.   4. Farms, Small—England—History.
5. Real estate business—England—History.
I. Harvey, P. D. A.
HD1339.G7P42   1984   333.3'23'0942   83-23793
ISBN 0-19-822661-6

Typeset by DMB (Typesetting), Oxford
Printed in Great Britain
at the University Press, Oxford

Preface

Published here are four regional studies with, by way of introduction and conclusion, comments on some of the broader
problems that they raise. Each author's contribution stands by
itself as an independent piece of work with its own emphases,
its own insights. The book is in no sense a work of collaboration
setting out an agreed joint view; I believe it would be the poorer
for any attempt to iron out whatever minor differences of interpretation there may be between us.

On the other hand all the authors of the regional studies read
drafts of the introduction and conclusion, and so too did my
colleagues Dr C.W. Brooks and Dr M.C. Prestwich; I am
grateful for all of their very helpful comments and have taken
many of them into account in the final text while, of course,
accepting full responsibility myself. I am grateful to the four
authors too for their cheerful acceptance of strong editorial
guidance in the painful process of abridging and reordering
their work to suit it for publication in this form, as well as for
the punctilious way they met all deadlines that were set. And
I am grateful both to them and to the Oxford University Press
for much patience over my own delays in preparing the work
for the press. The authors' individual acknowledgements are
made in a note at the beginning of each regional study, but it
is proper for me to express here our thanks to the following
scholars who have allowed one or other of us to cite their unpublished work: Dr J.S. Beckerman, Dr B. Campbell, Mrs S.
Campbell, Miss E.M. Halcrow, Dr R.A. Lomas, Dr D.
Roden, and Dr P. Wade-Martins. It has unfortunately proved
impossible to trace Miss L.C. Latham, whose valuable pioneer
work on Berkshire, Hampshire, and Wiltshire in the fifteenth
century is cited in chapter III. One important relevant study,
Dr Cicely Howell's *Land, Family and Inheritance in Transition*
(Cambridge, 1983), appeared when work was too far advanced
to take it into account beyond references to some illustrative
points in chapter V. Finally I should like to express my debt to
my wife, who has corrected much clumsy expression in my own

contribution to the book and who has done so much more besides to make the work possible.

Two other points should be mentioned here. One is that throughout the book county names and boundaries are those in use before the reorganization of 1974. The other is that medieval surnames are given in standardized spellings; these have the authority of contemporary records, but the name of any particular individual may occur in the records only in variant forms.

University of Durham   P.D.A.H

Contents

Maps

Abbreviations

AgHR	*Agricultural History Review*
Agr. Hist. Eng.	*The Agrarian History of England and Wales*, ed. H.P.R. Finberg and Joan Thirsk (Cambridge, 8 vols., 1967-)
Ault, *Open-field Farming*	W.O. Ault, *Open-field Farming in Medieval England* (London, 1972)
Baker & Butlin	*Studies of Field Systems in the British Isles*, ed. A.R.H. Baker and R.A. Butlin (Cambridge, 1973)
Bean, *Percy Estates*	J.M.W. Bean, *The Estates of the Percy Family 1416-1537* (London, 1958)
Bec Documents	*Select Documents of the English Lands of the Abbey of Bec*, ed. Marjorie Chibnall (Camden 3rd Series, vol. lxxiii; 1951)
Beckerman, 'Customary Law'	J.S. Beckerman, 'Customary Law in English Manorial Courts in the Thirteenth and Fourteenth Centuries' (London University Ph.D. thesis, 1972)
Bennett, *Eng. Manor*	H.S. Bennett, *Life on the English Manor* (Cambridge, 1937)
BHRS	Bedfordshire Historical Record Society
BL	British Library (Reference Division), London
Bodl.	Bodleian Library, Oxford
Boldon Buke	*Boldon Buke*, ed. W. Greenwell (Surtees Soc., vol. xxv; 1852)
BRO	Bedford County Record Office, Bedford
Buck. Archdeaconry Cts.	*The Courts of the Archdeaconry of Buckingham 1483-1523*, ed. E.M. Elvey (Bucks. Record Soc., vol. xix; 1975)
Campbell, 'Adisham'	Sarah Campbell, 'Some Aspects of the Social and Economic History of the Manor of Adisham, *c.*1200 to the Dissolution' (University of Kent M.Phil. thesis, 1981)
Campbell, 'Field Systems in E.Norf.'	B.M.S. Campbell, 'Field Systems in Eastern Norfolk during the Middle Ages' (Cambridge University Ph.D. thesis, 1975)

Cart. Mon. Ram.	*Cartularium Monasterii de Rameseia*, ed. W.H. Hart and P.A. Lyons (Rolls Series, 3 vols., 1884-93)
Cart. Nat.	*Carte Nativorum: a Peterborough Abbey Cartulary of the Fourteenth Century*, ed. C.N.L. Brooke and M.M. Postan (Northants. Record Soc., vol. xx; 1960)
CCR	*Calendar of Close Rolls*
CFR	*Calendar of Fine Rolls*
CP	G.E.C[ockayne], *The Complete Peerage* (2nd edn., London, 13 vols., 1910-59)
CPR	*Calendar of Patent Rolls*
Danelaw Ch.	*Documents illustrative of the Social and Economic History of the Danelaw*, ed. F.M. Stenton (British Academy, Records of the Social and Economic History of England and Wales, vol. v; 1920)
Darby, *Dom. Geog. E. Eng.*	H.C. Darby, *The Domesday Geography of Eastern England* (3rd edn., Cambridge, 1971)
Davenport, *Norf. Manor*	Frances G. Davenport, *The Economic Development of a Norfolk Manor 1086-1565* (Cambridge, 1906)
DBR	Durham bishopric records, Prior's Kitchen, Durham
DCD	Dean and Chapter of Durham records, Prior's Kitchen, Durham (BA Bursar's Account, BR Bursar's Rental, HCB Halmote Court Book, HCR Halmote Court Roll, LA Livestock Account, MA Manorial Account)
Dewindt, *Holywell*	E.B. Dewindt, *Land and People in Holywell-cum-Needingworth* (Toronto, 1972)
Dodgshon, *Origin*	R.A. Dodgshon, *The Origin of British Field Systems: an Interpretation* (London, 1980)
Douglas, 'East Anglia'	D.C. Douglas, 'The Social Structure of Medieval East Anglia', *Oxford Studies in Social and Legal History*, ed. P. Vinogradoff, vol. ix (Oxford, 1927)
Du Boulay, *Canterbury*	F.R.H. Du Boulay, *The Lordship of Canterbury* (London, 1966)
Dyer, *Lords and Peasants*	C. Dyer, *Lords and Peasants in a Changing Society: the Estates of the Bishopric of Worcester, 680-1540* (Cambridge, 1980)

EcHR	*Economic History Review*
EHR	*English Historical Review*
Eynsham Cart.	*Eynsham Cartulary*, ed. H.E. Salter (Oxford Historical Soc., old ser., vols. xlix, li; 1907-8)
Feodarium	*Feodarium Prioratus Dunelmensis*, ed. W. Greenwell (Surtees Soc., vol. lviii; 1872)
Feudal Aids	*Inquisitions and Assessments relating to Feudal Aids* (London, 6 vols., 1899-1920)
Godber, *Beds.*	Joyce Godber, *History of Bedfordshire 1066-1888* (Bedford, 1969)
Goody, Thirsk, & Thompson	*Family and Inheritance: Rural Society in Western Europe, 1200-1800*, ed. J. Goody, Joan Thirsk, and E.P. Thompson (Cambridge, 1976)
Gostwicks	*The Gostwicks of Willington, and other Studies* (BHRS, vol. xxxvi; 1956)
Gray, *Copyhold*	C.M. Gray, *Copyhold, Equity, and the Common Law* (Cambridge, Mass., 1963)
Grey Valor	*The Grey of Ruthin Valor*, ed. R.I. Jack (Sydney, 1965)
Halcrow, 'Durh. Cath. Priory'	Elizabeth M. Halcrow, 'The Administration and Agrarian Policy of the Manors of Durham Cathedral Priory' (Oxford University B.Litt. thesis, 1949)
Harvey, *Oxon. Village*	P.D.A. Harvey, *A Medieval Oxfordshire Village: Cuxham 1240-1400* (London, 1965)
Harvey, *Westminster*	Barbara Harvey, *Westminster Abbey and its Estates in the Middle Ages* (Oxford, 1977)
Hatcher, *Cornwall*	J. Hatcher, *Rural Economy and Society in the Duchy of Cornwall 1300-1500* (Cambridge, 1970)
Hatfield's Survey	*Bishop Hatfield's Survey*, ed. W. Greenwell (Surtees Soc., vol. xxxii; 1857)
Hilton, *Decline*	R.H. Hilton, *The Decline of Serfdom in England* (London, 1969)
Hilton, *Eng. Peasantry*	R.H. Hilton, *The English Peasantry in the Later Middle Ages* (Oxford, 1975)
Hilton, *Leics. Estates*	R.H. Hilton, *The Economic Development of some Leicestershire Estates in the 14th and 15th Centuries* (London, 1947)

Hilton, *Medieval Society*   R.H. Hilton, *A Medieval Society: the West Midlands at the End of the Thirteenth Century* (London, 1966)

Homans, *Eng. Villagers*   G.C. Homans, *English Villagers of the Thirteenth Century* (Cambridge, Mass., 1941)

Howell, *Land, Family and Inheritance*   Cicely Howell, *Land, Family and Inheritance in Transition: Kibworth Harcourt 1280-1700* (Cambridge, 1983)

Hyams, *King, Lords, and Peasants*   P.R. Hyams, *King, Lords, and Peasants in Medieval England: the Common Law of Villeinage in the Twelfth and Thirteenth Centuries* (Oxford, 1980)

JBS   *Journal of British Studies*

Jones, 'Beds. Land Market'   A.C. Jones, 'The Customary Land Market in Bedfordshire in the Fifteenth Century' (Southampton University Ph.D. thesis, 1975)

Kerridge, *Agr. Problems*   E. Kerridge, *Agrarian Problems in the Sixteenth Century and After* (London, 1969)

King, *Peterborough*   E. King, *Peterborough Abbey 1086-1310: a Study in the Land Market* (Cambridge, 1973)

Kosminsky, *Studies*   E.A. Kosminsky, *Studies in the Agrarian History of England in the Thirteenth Century*, ed. R.H. Hilton (Oxford, 1956)

Lennard, *Rural Eng.*   R. Lennard, *Rural England 1086-1135* (Oxford, 1959)

Levett, 'Black Death'   A. Elizabeth Levett, 'The Black Death on the Estates of the See of Winchester', *Oxford Studies in Social and Legal History*, ed. P. Vinogradoff, vol. v (Oxford, 1916)

Levett, *Studies*   A. Elizabeth Levett, *Studies in Manorial History*, ed. H.M. Cam, M. Coate, and L.S. Sutherland (Oxford, 1938)

Lomas, 'Durham Cath. Priory'   R.A. Lomas, 'Durham Cathedral Priory as a Landowner and a Landlord, 1290-1540' (Durham University Ph.D. thesis, 1973)

Macfarlane, *Eng. Individualism*   A. Macfarlane, *The Origins of English Individualism: the Family, Property and Social Transition* (Oxford, 1978)

Maddicott, *Eng. Peasantry*   J.R. Maddicott, *The English Peasantry*

	and the Demands of the Crown, 1291-1341 (*P&P* Supplement i; 1975)
Maitland, *Domesday*	F.W. Maitland, *Domesday Book and Beyond* (Cambridge, 1897)
Man. Records of Cuxham	*Manorial Records of Cuxham, Oxfordshire, circa 1200-1359*, ed. P.D.A. Harvey (Historical MSS Commission, Joint Publications No. 23; Oxon. Record Soc., vol. 1; 1976)
Miller, *Ely*	E. Miller, *The Abbey and Bishopric of Ely* (Cambridge, 1951)
Milsom, *Legal Framework*	S.F.C. Milsom, *The Legal Framework of English Feudalism* (Cambridge, 1976)
MM	Merton College, Oxford, muniments
Non. Inq.	*Nonarum Inquisitiones in Curia Scaccarii, temp. Regis Edwardi III*, ed. G. Vanderzee (Record Commission, 1807)
NRO	Norfolk and Norwich Record Office, Norwich (DCN Dean and Chapter of Norwich records)
Page, *Crowland*	Frances M. Page, *The Estates of Crowland Abbey* (Cambridge, 1934)
P&P	*Past and Present*
Pollock & Maitland	F. Pollock and F.W. Maitland, *The History of English Law before the Time of Edward I* (2nd edn., Cambridge, 2 vols., 1898)
PRO	Public Record Office, London
Raftis, *Ramsey*	J.A. Raftis, *The Estates of Ramsey Abbey* (Toronto, 1957)
Raftis, *Tenure*	J.A. Raftis, *Tenure and Mobility: Studies in the Social History of the Mediaeval English Village* (Toronto, 1964)
Raftis, *Warboys*	J.A. Raftis, *Warboys: Two Hundred Years in the Life of an English Mediaeval Village* (Toronto, 1974)
Razi, *Life, Marriage and Death*	Z. Razi, *Life, Marriage and Death in a Medieval Parish: Economy, Society and Demography in Halesowen 1270-1400* (Cambridge, 1980)
Rees, *S. Wales and March*	W. Rees, *South Wales and the March 1284-1415* (London, 1924)
Roden, 'Chiltern Field Systems'	D. Roden, 'Studies in Chiltern Field Systems' (London University Ph.D. thesis, 1965)

Rowley, *Origins*	*The Origins of Open-field Agriculture*, ed. T. Rowley (London, 1981)
Saunders, *Norwich Rolls*	H.W. Saunders, *An Introduction to the Obedientiary and Manor Rolls of Norwich Cathedral Priory* (Norwich, 1930)
Searle, *Battle*	Eleanor Searle, *Lordship and Community: Battle Abbey and its Banlieu 1066-1538* (Toronto, 1974)
Select Man. Pleas	*Select Pleas in Manorial and other Seignorial Courts*, ed. F.W. Maitland (Selden Soc., vol. ii; 1889)
Somerville, *Lancaster*	R. Somerville, *History of the Duchy of Lancaster*, vol. i (London, 1953)
Tawney, *Agr. Problem*	R.H. Tawney, *The Agrarian Problem in the Sixteenth Century* (London, 1912)
Test. Records in London	*Index to Testamentary Records in the Commissary Court of London*, ed. M. Fitch, vol. i, 1374-1488 (Historical MSS Commission, Joint Publications No. 12; British Record Soc., Index Library, vol. lxxxii; 1969)
Thrupp, *Merchant Class*	Sylvia L. Thrupp, *The Merchant Class of Medieval London, 1300-1500* (Chicago, 1948)
Titow, *Eng. Rural Soc.*	J.Z. Titow, *English Rural Society 1200-1350* (London, 1969)
TRHS	*Transactions of the Royal Historical Society*
VCH	*Victoria History of the County of . . .*
WAM	Westminster Abbey, London, muniments
Williamson, 'Norf. Peasant Holdings'	Janet Williamson, 'Peasant Holdings in Medieval Norfolk' (Reading University Ph.D. thesis, 1976)
Wind.	St. George's Chapel, Windsor, muniments

I Introduction

1 METHOD AND HISTORIOGRAPHY

This book comprises four regional studies of thirteenth-, four-teenth-, and fifteenth-century England with some more general discussion by way of introduction and conclusion. Each study is by a different author, and each stands on its own as an independent, self-contained piece of work. They have not been written on a uniform pattern: each reflects the particular interests of its author, the differences between one region and another, and the different sorts of surviving record on which each is based. But all four are centred on a single topic: the lands held by the small-scale landholders, whom we call peasants, and the way these lands moved, by mutual agreement, from one living landholder to another, which we call the peasant land market.[1] All four studies have the same method of approach: detailed examination of a small number of places from which good evidence survives to discover exactly what was happening there rather than a more impressionistic picture drawing on evidence from many different places. In three of the studies these places are scattered within a single county: three in Norfolk, ten in Berkshire (one is actually just over the border in Wiltshire), and five in Bedfordshire. The fourth examines eleven places which form an almost complete block of land in the south-east corner of County Durham.

In all then, we are shown twenty-nine places lying in four quite widely separated areas of late-medieval England. In Norfolk, Berkshire, and Bedfordshire they come from the various agricultural regions within each county. The fact that in Durham the places lie in a single block is a useful check on the others: given uniformity in the local economy and geography

---

[1] In this usage, which we have adopted simply for convenience, we differ from Macfarlane, *Eng. Individualism*, where peasant is taken to imply conformity to a general model of peasant society; from P.R. Hyams, 'The Origins of a Peasant Land Market in England', *EcHR*, 2nd ser., xxiii (1970), 19, where land market is taken to mean a substantial volume of transactions; and from Cicely Howell, 'Peasant Inheritance Customs in the Midlands, 1280-1700', in Goody, Thirsk, & Thompson, p. 135, where land market is taken to exclude very small areas of land.

it is easier to see what differences arose from having one or another manorial lord. Another check is provided by the periods covered. In Berkshire we are looking at the fourteenth and fifteenth centuries, in Durham the period 1350-1500, and in Bedfordshire just the fifteenth century—but the study on Norfolk deals with the thirteenth century and as it reveals there certain phenomena which first appeared much later in the other areas it usefully forestalls us from trying to explain them by the mid-fourteenth-century plagues and their population reductions. Unavoidably the places investigated have been chosen from the few for which adequate records survive, but they are not confined to the even smaller number with really full series of late-medieval records that come mostly from the archives of the largest and richest ecclesiastical estates. We should thus have avoided any extreme bias that might arise from using the records only of one sort of landlord; and indeed the places in Berkshire and Bedfordshire were chosen partly with a view to covering a fair range of differing estates, lay and ecclesiastical, episcopal and monastic, large and middle-sized. Middle-sized, not small—for it is the small owners who have left fewest records of the running of their properties. But we meet many of these smaller landlords in the records of their larger neighbours, and we meet some at least of their tenants and sub-tenants. Overall the coverage of different types of estate is as wide as is reasonably practicable.

Choosing the places with a view to variety rather than to superb documentation has obvious advantages but it also imposes some limitations. It has not been possible to subject any of these places to the intensive study that would reconstruct the full life-histories of all the tenants, their family relationships, their age-pattern, their office-holding and the other parts they played in village life—the approach that Zvi Razi has so revealingly applied to Halesowen (Worcestershire).[2] At the same time, many of the places covered provide ample evidence for reconstructing the local tenants' landholding; behind each of the four studies lies a great deal of work, too lengthy to be published here, on the individual tenants and families, tracing in detail their landholdings and land transactions over one or

---

[2] Razi, *Life, Marriage and Death*, and 'Family, Land and the Village Community in Later Medieval England', *P&P*, xciii (1981), 3-36.

more generations—a kind of tenurial prosopography, particularly full for Coleshill (Berkshire) and Leighton Buzzard (Bedfordshire), but worked out for many of the other places as well. However, two problems that cannot be overcome without extraordinarily complete records are family relationships and variable surnames. As Zvi Razi has shown, unless one has the evidence to reconstruct entire pedigrees, some family relationships will remain hidden; as hereditary surnames, consistently used, were just spreading through the lower classes of society in the later Middle Ages, there is the risk of failing to recognize closely related persons or even a single individual who bore more than one surname. In the four areas considered here the risk is probably greatest in Durham where, as we shall see, fifteenth-century usage favoured patronymics rather than hereditary surnames; in the thirteenth century standardized surname usage was probably particularly well advanced in Norfolk, and in the fifteenth century it was certainly far more general in the south Midlands than in northern England. Given that each of the four studies distinguishes land transfers within the family primarily so as to compare one place with another, there is probably little risk that these difficulties will lead us seriously astray; it is unlikely that surname usage at a particular period varied significantly from place to place within a single county. But the risk is greater in comparing one county or one period with another, and we should bear in mind that the net effect of these shortcomings in our evidence is to conceal relationships and identities: transfers of land within the family will be underestimated rather than overestimated, and we should see the figures for intra-family transfers as minima, for inter-family transfers as maxima.

The lands of the medieval peasant—what they comprised, how they were held, how they passed from one to another— have been studied by historians for a century or more. They have been viewed from the legal standpoint, as by Vinogradoff, and from the economic standpoint, as by Postan; or in the context of estate organization, as by Levett, and of the village community, as by Homans.[3] The subject is an intricate one, with

---

[3] Where full references to works cited in this paragraph and the next are not given in the footnotes they can be found in the list of abbreviations. The works mentioned are far from being a comprehensive list of even the best published work; in addition there is much relevant research in unpublished theses.

far-reaching implications for the social and economic history of the period, and although there is an abundance of surviving evidence from the thirteenth century onwards much of it is difficult to interpret. During the past twenty-five years certain aspects of the subject have received particular attention; they are all closely related, and most of the relevant published work touches on more than one of these themes. One is the peasant land market, the transfer of land from one living individual to another: the chronology and extent of these transfers both of free land and of unfree land held by local manorial custom, the procedures followed in each case, the regulation of this traffic by manorial lords, and the effect on the landholding of the individual. Of prime importance here was the publication in 1960 of the *Carte Nativorum*, the apparently unique Peterborough Abbey register of deeds by which its unfree tenants had acquired extra lands; edited by C.N.L. Brooke, it included a stimulating and wide-ranging historical introduction by M.M. Postan. A differing interpretation of the same evidence was offered by Edmund King in 1973, but meanwhile in 1970 P.R. Hyams had raised another dissentient voice in an article that discussed the place of the thirteenth century in the general history of the local land market.[4] The reverse of this land market—what happened to a peasant's lands on his death—is another theme that has attracted attention. In an important article in 1966 Rosamond Faith showed that the manorial customs governing the inheritance of unfree land varied from place to place much more than had been supposed, and that in practice the difference between ultimogeniture and partible inheritance was less clear-cut than simple definition might suggest.[5] Other work has looked at the inheritance customs for particular regions and places: East Anglia by Barbara Dodwell in 1967, the Chilterns by David Roden in 1967, Kibworth Harcourt (Leicestershire) by Cicely Howell in 1976, Halesowen (Worcestershire) by Zvi Razi in 1980 and 1981.[6] A third theme

[4] Hyams in *EcHR*, 2nd ser., xxiii (1970), 18-31.

[5] R.J. Faith, 'Peasant Families and Inheritance Customs in Medieval England', *AgHR*, xiv (1966), 77-95.

[6] Barbara Dodwell, 'Holdings and Inheritance in Medieval East Anglia', *EcHR*, 2nd ser., xx (1967), 53-66; D. Roden, 'Inheritance Customs and Succession to Land in the Chiltern Hills in the Thirteenth and Early Fourteenth Centuries', *JBS*, vii (1967-8), 1-11; Howell in Goody, Thirsk, & Thompson, pp. 112-55; Razi in *P&P*, xciii (1981), 3-36.

has been what happened to the villein and his lands in the 150 years after the Black Death of 1348-9: the changes in his tenure, how he held his lands and what he owed for them, and the changes in his personal status, in his legal disabilities and his obligations towards the lord of his manor. Here there have been important general works by R.H. Hilton: *The Decline of Serfdom in Late Medieval England*, 1969, is centred on this theme, which is crucial too to his broader-based Ford Lectures of 1973, published in 1975. But studies of particular estates have also made significant contributions to this theme, very notably John Hatcher's work on the duchy of Cornwall in 1970 and Barbara Harvey's on the estates of Westminster Abbey in 1977, which both pay particular attention to these questions, but also the work of J.A. Raftis on Ramsey Abbey (especially his book on *Tenure and Mobility* in 1964), of Christopher Dyer on the bishopric of Worcester in 1980, and of others. So too have certain studies of particular places, as E.B. Dewindt's on Holywell-cum-Needingworth (Huntingdonshire) in 1972.

Nearly all these works bear on more than one of these three aspects of peasant landholding in the Middle Ages. Closely linked are three other topics that have likewise attracted recent work; they are very relevant to the four studies published here, while lying outside their authors' terms of reference. The most obvious of these topics is the structure of the late-medieval rural community: the economic and social relationships between villagers, their hierarchy of wealth and of local office-holding, their patterns of life and death. Here again the work of Zvi Razi and of J.A. Raftis and his associates at Toronto is particularly important, and the work too of Sylvia Thrupp in 1965 on village population,[7] of J.R. Maddicott in 1975 on the peasants' obligations to the Crown, and of R.M. Smith in 1979 on the rôles of family and community in thirteenth-century Redgrave (Suffolk);[8] more specialized work on this topic has included discussion of the historical significance of the fines for fornication and for marriage that were levied on the unfree.[9] A

[7] S.L. Thrupp, 'The Problem of Replacement-rates in Late Medieval English Population', *EcHR*, 2nd ser., xviii (1965), 101-19.

[8] R.M. Smith, 'Kin and Neighbors in a Thirteenth-century Suffolk Community', *Journal of Family History*, iv (1979), 219-56.

[9] This discussion was begun by Jean Scammell, 'Freedom and Marriage in Medieval England', *EcHR*, 2nd ser., xxvii (1974), 523-37; the most recent contributions are

second related topic is field systems, their forms and development, on which a great deal of research has been done, much of it stimulated by Joan Thirsk's seminal article in 1964 on the origin of the open fields and the debate with J.Z. Titow that stemmed from it.[10] *Studies of Field Systems*, edited by A.R.H. Baker and R.A. Butlin in 1973, was a notable milestone, bringing together and expanding a number of important pieces of local research; particularly significant work since then includes the interpretative studies of R.A. Dodgshon, brought together in a single structured argument in 1980, and the reassessment by H.S.A. Fox in 1981 of the chronology of the Midland field system.[11] The third topic is the common law which ultimately, beyond local manorial custom, determined how the peasant held his land. Notable work here includes that of C.M. Gray in 1963 on the chronology of the royal courts' protection of copyhold tenure, of S.F.C. Milsom in 1976 on the law and twelfth-century feudalism, and of P.R. Hyams in 1980 on the law of villeinage as viewed by the courts and the legal writers of the twelfth and thirteenth centuries.

This is the historiographical background to the four studies printed here. It might seem that further work had little to add. But, as P.R. Hyams has recently remarked, the subject of the medieval peasant land market 'is by no means exhausted', [12] and in fact each of the studies makes a distinctive and significant contribution to our knowledge. Each provides a great deal of hard evidence of what was really happening in particular places, evidence that can be seen as both a source and a testing-ground for more general theories of development. The four studies were produced over quite a long period: the doctoral theses on which they are based were presented in 1962 (Rosa-

by Eleanor Searle, 'Seignorial Control of Women's Marriage: the Antecedents and Function of Merchet in England', *P&P*, lxxxii (1979), 3-43, and a debate on this article, including comments by P.A. Brand, Rosamond Faith, and P.R. Hyams, in *P&P*, xcix (1983), 123-60.

[10] Joan Thirsk, 'The Common Fields', *P&P*, xxix (1964), 3-25, and 'The Origin of the Common Fields', ibid., xxxiii (1966), 142-7; J.Z. Titow, 'Medieval England and the Open Field System', ibid., xxxii (1965), 86-102. All three articles are reprinted in *Peasants, Knights and Heretics*, ed. R.H. Hilton (Cambridge, 1976), pp. 10-56.

[11] H.S.A. Fox, 'Approaches to the Adoption of the Midland System', in Rowley, *Origins*, pp. 64-111.

[12] Hyams, *King, Lords, and Peasants*, p. 40 n.

mond Faith on Berkshire), 1975 (Andrew Jones on Bedford-shire), and 1976 (Janet Williamson on Norfolk and Tim Lomas on Durham). That all four look at the same problems the same way and are all equally relevant to current debate shows how far each is firmly based on the facts as revealed by local records and also how far we still are from full understanding of the subject. Putting them side by side produces some interesting comparisons and contrasts. Although they cover not only different areas but also different periods, we are looking in each case at a time when the structure of local landholding underwent what seem to be very similar changes. Basic to these are problems connected with the standard peasant holding and the chronology of the peasant land market.

2 THE STANDARD HOLDING

In most manorial records of the thirteenth and early fourteenth centuries, and in most writings on the medieval English country-side, we find the standard peasant holding: on a manor there would be one or more groups of holdings whose tenants owed customs and services uniform for everyone in the group and which thus were presumably more or less alike in size or value. Each holding would usually consist of a dwelling, areas of arable and meadow, pasture and other rights, but its exact composition and its form—whether the arable was a single block for instance, or dispersed among common fields—varied from one place to another. The names of these holdings varied too, but on a regional basis. In the present four studies we find them called tenements in Norfolk, virgates (or yardlands) and half-virgates in Berkshire and Bedfordshire, bovates (or oxgangs) in Durham; if one of the studies had covered Kent we should have been dealing there with yokes. It was very unusual for all the tenant lands of a manor to be held in standard holdings of this sort; generally they would comprise the larger unfree hold-ings—those of the villeins rather than the cottagers—but many kinds of variation occurred.

In these studies we are particularly concerned with these standard holdings in their decay: their fragmentation and often their complete disappearance. The chronology of this varied from region to region, even from place to place. On our three

Norfolk manors the standard tenements had all but vanished from sight by the end of the thirteenth century, whereas throughout south-east Durham the bovate was still a basis of tenure two hundred years later. In fifteenth-century Bedfordshire virgates and half-virgates disappeared from Leighton Buzzard but remained the normal holdings at Shillington. How, why, and when these standard holdings broke up in each area is discussed below. But behind these discussions lies the assumption—often demonstrably true—that at an earlier date, let us say at the end of the twelfth century, it would be normal for a high proportion of a manor's tenant lands to be held in standard holdings with uniform obligations and apparently of uniform size. It is here that the problem of these standard holdings arises. Let us take two specific examples. We shall see how at Martham (Norfolk) there were, about 1220, some twenty holdings called, unusually, eruings, nearly all held as single units or in halves or quarters. These eruings were very precisely defined: each consisted of exactly 24 acres (measured by a perch of 18½ feet) made up of as many as thirty or more separate pieces which might be as small as ½ rood. By 1292, though manorial administration retained a recollection of these eruings, they were no longer effective tenurial units: they had been split into as many as ten or more portions, each held by a different tenant.[1] Our other example comes from Combe, on the borders of Berkshire and Hampshire, a manor of Bec Abbey in Normandy. A custumal of about 1230 lists thirteen tenants who held a virgate of land each for more or less identical rents and services; later versions of the same custumal, made during the next twenty years, show two or three acres of assart, newly cleared land, added to a number of these hitherto identical holdings in return for extra rents.[2] Both these cases, Martham and Combe, present the same difficulty. Either these standard holdings, these eruings and virgates, were quite recent creations in the early thirteenth century. Or a long tradition of unchanging stability was in the thirteenth century suddenly broken, at Martham by the rapid fragmentation of age-old

---

[1] Below, p.65; a good example of fragmentation is the 12-acre holding that had been Thomas Knight's, its 33 separate parcels being held in 1292 by 11 tenants (BL Stowe MS 936, fos.39ᵛ-40ᵛ.

[2] *Bec Documents*, pp. 41-5.

holdings, at Combe by the extension of the cultivated area for the first time in centuries. Both explanations invite disbelief.

And indeed, though we must always reckon with possible local peculiarities, neither explanation fits what we know about standard holdings of this sort before the thirteenth century. Certainly we cannot doubt their antiquity; we find ample evidence for them in the late, even the mid-, eleventh century. Several of their names correspond to assessment units of the Anglo-Saxon taxation system. The bovate and the virgate were regular subdivisions of, respectively, the carucate (used in eastern and northern England) and the hide (used in most other parts of the country). But even before this taxation system fell into disuse in the twelfth century[3] the virgates of the standard holdings were no longer the same as the virgates of tax assessment—if, indeed, they had ever been. It is only for Middlesex that Domesday Book regularly defines the holdings of individual manorial tenants; there it was common in 1086 for groups of villeins on a particular manor to have holdings called virgates or half-virgates, but on only about half the manors with full details does the sum of these holdings, when added to the assessment of the demesne and other lands, equal the assessment for the entire manor.[4] Domesday Book's smallest tenant holdings in Middlesex—those of the bordars and cottars—were defined not as fractions of a virgate but in acres; but these again were measures not of area but of assessment, of liability to tax, for they were fiscal acres, the smallest unit of the taxation system, of which there were thirty to the virgate, 120 to the hide.[5] Just as the villeins on any one manor often had holdings all with the same description so too did the bordars and cottars: five acres was a standard holding on many of these Middlesex manors, and it is interesting that the *Rectitudines Singularum Personarum*, a mid-eleventh-century text, remarks

[3] The last Danegeld was in 1162, but the carucage of 1194 seems to have been based on the same assessment.

[4] Maitland, *Domesday*, pp. 477-8; Lennard, *Rural Eng.*, p. 341; T.G. Pinder in *VCH Middx.*, i. 86-8, 130-2. A similar problem on the Ramsey Abbey estates is discussed by Raftis, *Ramsey*, pp. 69-71.

[5] The classic account of the three medieval meanings of the word acre—the customary (or field) acre, the measured acre, the fiscal acre—is in Maitland, *Domesday*, pp. 373-93; a summary is in *Man. Records of Cuxham*, pp. 77-8. The use of the three sorts of acre is discussed, with many examples, by A. Jones, 'Land Measurement in England, 1150-1350', *AgHR*, xxvii (1979), 10-18.

that the cottar (*kotsetla*) often holds five acres.[6] It is presumably these same fiscal acres that lie behind the standard holdings, the tenements (*tenementa*), of thirteenth-century East Anglia (at Martham, we shall see, it was not the fiscal acres of tax assessment but acres measured on the ground that were in question). There the holdings on any one manor tended to fall into groups each with the same number of acres: in Suffolk ten-acre units were frequent, in Norfolk units of twelve acres or multiples of twelve acres.[7] East Anglia had been assessed for taxation in carucates and bovates, not hides and virgates, but the fiscal acre was still the lowest unit of the system, one-120th of the carucate as well as of the hide. In Kent there was a different terminology, but again we find that units of land, much split up by the thirteenth century, had apparently been, a century earlier, standard holdings in the hands of individuals;[8] these units were called *iuga*, yokes, a name again harking back to eleventh-century tax assessment, which in Kent was returned in sulungs of four yokes each.

But it these holdings took their names from a tax-assessment system that flickered out in the twelfth century it does not follow that they then became fixed and stabilized. On the contrary, there is much evidence of flexibility and change in their structure in the course of the twelfth century. New ones might be created. At Brancaster (Norfolk) the number of twelve-acre villein units was increased in the mid-twelfth century by letting out lands from the manorial demesne.[9] At Barnetby-le-Wold (Lincolnshire) four new bovates were formed about 1160 by combining some demesne with other adjacent lands.[10] In these and other cases surviving records show us the process as it actually occurred; in many more we can infer the creation of new standard holdings from the increasing number of tenants and holdings in successive surveys. Nor were the existing holdings immutably fixed. At Theddingworth (Northamptonshire) and Keddington (Lincolnshire) we find one acre being subtracted

---

[6] Lennard, *Rural Eng.*, pp. 340-4; *Die Gesetze der Angelsachsen*, ed. F. Liebermann (3 vols., Halle, 1903-16), i. 446.

[7] Dodwell in *EcHR*, 2nd ser., xx (1967), 55-8.

[8] A.R.H. Baker in Baker & Butlin, pp. 398, 407-8.

[9] Dodwell in *EcHR*, 2nd ser., xx (1967), 58.

[10] *Danelaw Ch.*, pp. 180-2 (cf. Baker & Butlin, p. 267).

from each virgate or bovate to endow local churches.[11] Conversely where new land was brought under the plough each standard holding might be enlarged by taking a share of it; this is specifically envisaged, for instance, in a charter granting a bovate at Spaldington (Yorkshire).[12] In these cases the reduction or enlargement would apply equally to all the standard holdings in a particular manor; but this need not be so. At Kirton (Nottinghamshire) the meadow belonging to a single bovate was taken from it and granted away separately.[13] This is a useful reminder that none of the names given to these holdings—not even those defined as so many fiscal acres—carried any implication of specific size. Those of ancient origin may all at one time have owed the same amount of tax. Generally all those in a single group on any one manor owed the same rents and services to the lord. But it need not follow that even on the same manor they were more than very roughly alike in area or resources. At Gillingham (Kent) the yokes demonstrably varied in size, apparently reflecting the varying quality of soil in different parts of the manor.[14] Here the yokes can be identified on the ground, as Kentish holdings were generally compact blocks of land. But elsewhere, bovates and virgates might well be made up of scattered strips and pieces of arable and meadow, together with shared rights over wide areas of pasture. The form and composition of the standard holding varied enormously, depending on the region or the particular vill where it lay.

Given this variety of form, given their different origins, given the changes that we find occurring in these standard holdings in the course of the twelfth century, we may well wonder whether by the thirteenth century we can properly regard them as a single type of unit, a single phenomenon. Can we see the decay of twelve-acre holdings in thirteenth-century Norfolk and of virgates and half-virgates in fifteenth-century Bedfordshire as different aspects of a single process? We have seen that standard holdings were far from being new creations at the end of the twelfth century, and that they had by then already

[11] *Danelaw Ch.*, pp. lxx-lxxi, 342-3 (cf. Baker & Butlin, pp. 271-2).

[12] Homans, *Eng. Villagers*, p. 84.

[13] *Danelaw Ch.*, pp. xl, 274.

[14] Du Boulay, *Canterbury*, pp. 121-2; A.R.H. Baker, 'Open Fields and Partible Inheritance on a Kent Manor', *EcHR*, 2nd ser., xvii (1964-5), 5.

undergone much local change. We might reasonably ask whether the standard holdings of late-medieval England had any discoverable shared baseline, any common starting-point that would make it meaningful to compare or contrast their varying fortunes in different places. The answer is that they had, but that it is not to be sought in the ultimate origin of these holdings. It is to be sought rather in a process which occurred in the twelfth century and which might be called a process of territorializing the holdings of manorial tenants.

Put simply, we might say that in 1100 the lord of a manor was the lord of men who held lands of him; in 1200 he was the lord of lands that were occupied by tenants. The change is slight but significant. In 1100 the tenant's holding could be viewed simply as a standard share in the vill's resources; by 1200 it was far more likely to be viewed as precisely defined in its area of land and other rights. At most, of course, it is no more than a change of emphasis. It would be absurd to suggest that the eleventh-century manorial lord cared nothing for precisely defined lands and boundaries, or that his thirteenth-century successor was uninterested in his seignorial rights over his tenants. All the same a clear shift can be seen. Its precise manifestations varied from region to region and from place to place. As we shall see, tenurial forms differed a good deal from one manor to another in the late Middle Ages and there is no reason to assume any greater uniformity in earlier periods— indeed, Domesday Book points quite the other way, despite its bureaucratic tendency to iron out variations. Just as local conditions and forms of tenure varied, so the effects of this territorializing process were bound to vary too, but everywhere the trend was the same. It was a trend towards precise definition on the ground of the lands and territorial rights of the individual tenant, and it is this process of definition that forms the common starting-point, the basis for the comparisons and contrasts we draw in later developments.

This same trend may be compared with the changes in relationship between lord and free tenant in the twelfth century that S.F.C. Milsom has described.[15] It lies behind the view of William Rees, in 1924, on developments in south Wales and

---

[15] Milsom, *Legal Framework*, pp. 34-5, 65-6, 90.

the March[16] as well as the views of two recent writers on the development of English field systems. R.A. Dodgshon, taking up a phrase of Vinogradoff, has argued that subdivided fields originated in a tenurial structure based on shareholding by the vill's tenants rather than on specifically delimited properties.[17] And H.S.A. Fox, writing of twelfth- or early-thirteenth-century charters that describe arable holdings simply as lying in the vill's open fields (sometimes these fields are named, but without further topographical detail), asks 'might the idea behind this terminology have been to reinforce the grantee's claim to a stake in a *system* of husbandry involving the two or three great fields?'[18] It would thus not be necessary to define the holding more precisely—and indeed it might not have been possible to do so. There are indications that in some places the trend towards precise definition of holdings took the form of changing from a system of regular re-allotment of strips in the arable fields to one where all the strips were attached permanently to particular holdings. We get, for example, a possible hint of this (and of other agrarian changes as well) in an extent of Woodeaton (Oxfordshire) in 1366: the manor's twelfth-century owner had given the nuns of Littlemore one acre in an unmanured furlong, a grant since replaced by the gift of the wheat from two selions of the manorial demesne.[19]

Better documented, and probably much more widespread, was the growing tendency to define assarts, newly cultivated lands, in precisely measured acres, roods, and perches,[20] and to regard them as additions to the standard holding, not merely as realizations of potential assets that had always belonged to it. The holding was now defined and fixed, and any additions to it must be paid for in the form of extra rent. The distinction was made quite explicit in certain places in Cheshire, where

[16] Rees, *S. Wales and March*, pp. 150-1.

[17] R.A. Dodgshon, 'The Landholding Foundations of the Open-field System', *P&P*, lxvii (1975), 14-26, and Dodgshon, *Origin*, pp. 34-41, 52-3.

[18] Fox in Rowley, *Origins*, p. 78 (the reference on p. 107 to *Danelaw Ch.* should be to pp. xxxi-xxxii, 232-3).

[19] *Eynsham Cart.*, ii. 17-18 (cf. p. lxxii). The same 12th-century grantor's gift of an acre of meadow, specifically 'per assignacionem custodis manerii' but in 1366 a permanently identifiable strip (ibid., p. 17), points to the same process in the manor's meadows.

[20] This was just one aspect of increasingly precise measurement of lands in general (Jones in *AgHR*, xxvii (1979), 12-13, 15-16).

lands were referred to as either *oxgang lands*, that is the ancient holdings, or *rodelands*, the assarted lands measured in roods or by the rod.[21] In south Lincolnshire the change is very clear in the first half of the thirteenth century: until then newly reclaimed lands were held to belong to existing bovate holdings as of right, but they then start to be seen as additions to the holdings, carefully measured and defined, usually in terms of acres but on one occasion as seven-twelfths of a bovate.[22] In Durham the bovates of the bishop's local tenants scarcely changed between the Boldon Book survey of 1183 and Bishop Hatfield's survey of about 1382, but a new class of holding, exchequer lands, had appeared; these were small areas defined in acres and held by money rents and seem to have been lands newly brought under cultivation.[23] In East Anglia, where the standard holdings were themselves defined in units called acres, the distinction is less obvious, but some thirteenth-century surveys show tenants holding extra lands with very irregular acreages, suggesting that here we have assarts defined in acres of actual measurement, not the fiscal acres used for the basic holdings.[24] This does not mean that we cannot still find, as in parts in Yorkshire in the thirteenth and fourteenth centuries, new oxgangs being created from waste land, and in the fifteenth century assarts might still be divided in strict proportion between the tenants of standard holdings.[25] But at least it became a very general corollary to the stricter territorial definition of standard holdings that any additional lands should be no less strictly measured and paid for. Thus where rents for small assarts suddenly start to appear, as in the early-thirteenth-century surveys from Combe, it need not follow that cultivation was being expanded for the first time since the standard holdings had come into existence, nor that an age-old total equality of tenure was now being disrupted. The provision of the Statute of Merton (1236)

[21] G. Elliott in Baker & Butlin, p. 45.

[22] H.E. Hallam, *Settlement and Society: a Study of the Early Agrarian History of South Lincolnshire* (Cambridge, 1965), pp. 9-10, 11, 13, 15, 20, 27-8, 44, 51, 55, 61-2, 68-9, 99, 104, 110, 158-61.

[23] B. Roberts, 'Townfield Origins: the Case of Cockfield, County Durham', in Rowley, *Origins*, pp. 150, 153.

[24] Dodwell in *EcHR*, 2nd ser., xx (1967), 58-9.

[25] J.A. Sheppard in Baker & Butlin, pp. 174-5; Homans, *Eng. Villagers*, p. 425 n4; Raftis, *Tenure*, p. 29.

that asserts the manorial lord's rights over waste is almost an explicit statement of the same change as affecting free tenants' claims over common lands.

We find too that landlords were starting to apply exact measurement to the standard holdings themselves. F.M. Stenton drew attention to a grant of a bovate at Dunholme (Lincolnshire) which lists and measures each of its individual strips of arable; he dates this probably to the reign of Henry II, certainly not later than 1200, and comments that 'it would be difficult to find the record of any earlier measurement of the component parts of an open field bovate'.[26] But from about this time some landlords began to record at least the approximate acreage of the virgate or bovate on each of their manors (whether in measured acres or in field acres is seldom clear). This is information that we are given in a list of Ramsey Abbey's manors; here the virgate varied from 15½ to 44 acres, and J.A. Raftis has shown that in manors on the clay uplands it was larger than on the gravels of the valleys.[27] A register of about 1240 shows that the number of acres in a virgate was a question regularly asked when manorial surveys were drawn up on the estate of Worcester Cathedral Priory; the answers would be given in field acres or measured acres, whereas the acreages of the 1182 surveys for the bishop of Worcester's estate are simply the figures of fiscal assessment.[28]

We have seen enough of the earlier history of standard holdings to realize that on a single manor they need not all be the same size, even if measured in the somewhat loose units of field acres; and indeed we find that the 1244 survey of Ramsey Abbey's manor of Cranfield (Bedfordshire) says that some virgates there were 48 acres, some were smaller.[29] But we can see how easy it was (and still is), once the way of thinking in strictly territorial terms was adopted, to assume that, because the holdings all had the same description—a bovate, half-virgate, and

[26] *Danelaw Ch.*, p. xlvi n; Dodgshon, *Origin*, p. 40, slightly mistakes Stenton's dating of this charter and the significance he attaches to it.

[27] *Cart.Mon.Ram.*, iii. 208-15, discussed by Maitland, *Domesday*, pp. 393-5, and by Raftis, *Ramsey*, p. 68.

[28] Hilton, *Medieval Society*, pp. 115, 122; Dyer, *Lords and Peasants*, pp. 87-9. Another list of acres per virgate for various manors on an estate is supplied by Harvey, *Westminster*, pp. 208, 434.

[29] *Cart.Mon.Ram.*, i. 438, discussed, with other examples, by P. Vinogradoff, *Villainage in England* (London, 1892), p. 240.

so on—and all owed the same services to the lord of the manor, they must therefore be alike in every respect and in particular must comprise exactly the same area of land. This may well lie behind the planning of villages investigated by B.K. Roberts in Durham and June A. Sheppard in the East Riding of Yorkshire, where the length of each house-plot's street frontage seems directly related to the definition of the associated holding in terms of the bovate. It is not certain when these villages were laid out but it may well have been in the twelfth or thirteenth century in Yorkshire, though Roberts argues for a late-eleventh- or early-twelfth-century date in Durham.[30] Also in the East Riding, in Holderness, Mary Harvey has found fields set out with a regularity that seems to stem from translating standard holdings into egalitarian divisions on the ground; again, a date in the twelfth or early thirteenth century is possible.[31]

In this context let us return to the Martham survey and its group of holdings each consisting of small pieces that add up to exactly 12 acres. Historians of medieval English fields and measures have often been confused by the bewildering use of the word acre with three different meanings and have failed to distinguish clearly between fiscal acres, field acres, and measured acres. Medieval estate administrators were just as likely to fall into the same trap as we see from notes and tables which make a single system of units of measurement and of ancient tax assessment.[32] What more natural than that some official at the beginning of the thirteenth century, confronted with what were called twelve-acre holdings, should assume that they were, or had once been, or ought to be, 12 acres each? The fiscal acre could well have been entirely forgotten. In these circumstances it would seem only proper, in any reorganization of the vill's fields, to assign to each of these holdings exactly 12 acres of arable; this would do no more than restore their pristine integrity. It is very likely that some such line of argument underlies the 12-acre holdings of the Martham survey and that

---

[30] B.K. Roberts, 'Village Plans in County Durham: a Preliminary Statement', *Medieval Archaeology*, xvi (1972), 33-56; J.A. Sheppard, 'Metrological Analysis of Regular Village Plans in Yorkshire', *AgHR*, xxii (1974), 118-35; J.A. Sheppard in Baker & Butlin, pp. 183-6.

[31] Mary Harvey, 'The Origin of Planned Field Systems in Holderness', in Rowley, *Origins*, pp. 184-201.

[32] e.g. *Walter of Henley and Other Treatises*, ed. D. Oschinsky (Oxford, 1971), p. 475.

they date from some more or less thoroughgoing reallocation of the vill's arable that occurred not long before 1220, the time of the 'former' tenants referred to in the survey of 1292.[33] It is most improbable that these holdings of exactly 12 acres were already ancient in the early thirteenth century. Although they must have been based on measurement and calculation this measurement was not very precise; the areas of the pieces of land making up each holding seem to have been entered only to the nearest ½ rood (20 perches), suggesting that their basis was, at best, a rather roughly measured acre.[34] This meant the process was unrepeatable: remeasurement would not produce the same result, the same exact 12 acres in every holding. Once they had been laid out, the detailed composition of each holding and the definition of each of its component parts must have been preserved either in the memory of each tenant, in which case it is hardly possible that there would be no divergence from the exact 12-acre totals, or in the form of a written survey— but a survey of such detail and complexity that it would be unique among estate records before the thirteenth century. The reallocation of lands in exactly equal units and the construction of detailed surveys based on careful description or measurement can be seen as a part of the general move towards the precise definition of tenants' holdings; it is in this light that we should see the 12-acre holdings of thirteenth-century Martham and the early-thirteenth-century survey in which their composition was probably first recorded.

In the studies that follow we get further glimpses of this move towards precise territorial definition of holdings. In thirteenth-century Gressenhall (Norfolk) it may well have underlain the new practice of dividing holdings among heirs; if this marked a change from joint tenure by a group of heirs then the connection is clear, but if (as seems likely) it marked a change in local

[33] Although only six of the 'former' tenants held an entire eruing the subsequent fission of the eruings proceeded so fast that this need not stop us from seeing them as still fairly new in 1220.

[34] Interestingly, though the ½-rood is the smallest unit used in measuring the 12-acre holdings, the survey elsewhere defines parcels of land much more precisely: 3 perches, 1 rood 21 perches, 13 perches 6 feet, etc. This reflects the exact measurement of arable that would have become normal by 1292 (Jones in *AgHR*, xxvii (1979), 12-13, 15-16); applied to the 12-acre holdings it would almost certainly produce the wrong totals, so the older less precise computation was retained for them.

custom from impartible to partible inheritance the connection
may still be there, for the former sole heir may effectively have
supported his brothers, whose claims were simply made specific,
were defined territorially, by the change in custom.[35] In thirteenth-century Kent the division of the standard holdings, the
yokes, may well have come about through changing interpretation of the custom of partible inheritance, replacing joint
tenure by individual holdings.[36] Pursuing this thought a little
further, we may wonder whether the new emphasis on territorial definition may not have brought about in many places
the first definition of inheritance custom, the change away from
a vague claim of the family corporately to inherit and towards
an explicit, specified claim of one or more of its members—but
this is a point we shall return to later.

With more confidence we can see a connection between the
new approach to manorial tenants' lands and the emergence of
a distinction that brought many problems to the lawyers of the
thirteenth century and later, the distinction between the status
of the tenant and the status of the lands he held.[37] While the
lord of the manor was lord primarily of the tenant and only sec-
ondarily of his holding there was little scope for differentiation
between the status of the land and the status of the tenant.
Whatever was held by a villein was self-evidently villein land.
As P.R. Hyams has put it, in the twelfth century 'lordship over
men and over land were still much the same thing'.[38] But once
the lord started to look more to the land than to the tenant,
started to define precisely the holding and the rights on the
ground, it became easier to see the land apart from the tenant,
to see the land as property that might pass to new and desirable
tenants who were prepared to take over all its traditional rents
and obligations but who were not at all prepared to accept the
disabilities (themselves ever more closely defined) that were
attendant on the personal status of villeinage.

And behind it all, behind the whole process of closer definition of tenants' lands, lies the growth of population and the
looming land shortage which may have been felt in some areas

---

[35] Below, Ch. II, section 2.
[36] Du Boulay, *Canterbury*, pp. 146-8.
[37] Hyams, *King, Lords, and Peasants*, pp. 107-19.
[38] Ibid., p. 228.

by the late twelfth century and which a hundred years later was widespread and critical. It is against the same background of rising population and increasing pressure on land that we should see the development of the local land market in the thirteenth century.

3 CHRONOLOGY OF THE PEASANT LAND MARKET

There are few aspects of medieval English society for which we have more documentary evidence than we have for the local land market. Private charters that grant or sell or exchange or quit-claim or lease tiny pieces of land survive in their thousands in the muniment-rooms of estate owners, in local record offices, and in other repositories. The properties involved were all held in free tenure, not in villeinage, and nearly all the parties to these transactions were free men, not villeins, yet historians seem to have been slow to appreciate the scale of the local market in small pieces of free land at this period, or, indeed, the numerical importance of the small freeholders in rural society. In 1938 F.M. Powicke drew attention to the potential significance of the work of E.A. Kosminsky, then available only in Russian, in showing just how numerous and widespread these freeholders were in the late thirteenth century, and pointed out how interesting too their land transactions might be.[1] The English translation of Kosminsky's book appeared in 1956;[2] in 1957 W.G. Hoskins in his study of Wigston Magna (Leicestershire) showed how important the land market was to the free tenants there from the thirteenth century onwards,[3] and in 1960 further interest was aroused in the thirteenth-century local land market by M.M. Postan's important introduction to the *Carte Nativorum* register of Peterborough Abbey. This text showed that not only free men but villeins too were acquiring free land by private charter, and Postan argued that this traffic was on such a scale that it must be taken into account in

---

[1] F.M. Powicke, 'Observations on the English Freeholder in the Thirteenth Century', *Wirtschaft und Kultur: Festschrift zum 70. Geburtstag von Alfons Dopsch* (Baden bei Wien, 1938), pp. 382-93.

[2] Kosminsky, *Studies*.

[3] W.G. Hoskins, *The Midland Peasant* (London, 1957), pp. 30-53.

assessing the economic and social position of the medieval villager, whether villein or free; moreover this market in pieces of
free land, conveyed by charter, should be seen as only one
aspect of a much wider local land market, in which subletting
of tenants' lands, the leasing of parcels of demesne land, and
the transfer of customary holdings by surrender to use or other
means all contributed to producing great flexibility, even fluid-
ity, in local tenants' holdings beneath the apparent stability
suggested by many manorial surveys.

Postan saw this as no new development in the late thirteenth
century. He argued that 'the habit of selling land (and . . . also
of leasing it) had been fully formed before the date of the earliest
Curia Regis rolls or that of the earliest bailiff's account: certainly by the turn of the twelfth and thirteenth centuries'.[4]
Barbara Dodwell, writing in 1967 of the land market in East
Anglia, went further: '. . . there is no reason to suppose that the
free peasantry of the Old English period did not buy, sell, and
exchange land at will. That they did so in the twelfth century is
abundantly clear.'[5] But historians writing subsequently have
preferred to see the burgeoning of peasant charters in the
course of the thirteenth century as marking the development of
the local land market itself, not merely the application of written
documents to transactions that had long been common. Thus
P.R. Hyams in 1970, in a critique of Postan's argument, con-
cluded that 'there is no good evidence of a *general* peasant land
market in the early thirteenth century'—it should be said that
his definition of a land market demanded a substantial volume
of transactions.[6] Likewise Edmund King, writing in 1973 on
the Peterborough Abbey estates, saw 'a land market, which
began with baronial property in the early twelfth century, and
spread downwards in the social scale over the next hundred
years', so that the knights became heavily involved in it in the
last quarter of the twelfth century, and small freeholders and
villeins in the thirteenth.[7] Either way, an explanation for its
origin can be found. Postan drew attention to what had already
been observed by F.M. Page and A.E. Levett on the estates of

---

[4] *Cart. Nat.*, p. xxxix.
[5] Dodwell in *EcHR*, 2nd ser., xx (1967), 63.
[6] Hyams in *EcHR*, 2nd ser., xxiii (1970), 19; see the last paragraph of this chapter.
[7] King, *Peterborough*, p. 168.

Crowland and St. Albans Abbeys: at any one period we find some tenants consistently acquiring land to build up their holdings, others consistently shedding it. These, he argued, were 'natural' buyers and sellers, responding to the varying demands of family circumstance and changing family size, demands that could be just as compelling in earlier periods as they were in the thirteenth century.[8] On the other hand the land market could be seen as originating in the thirteenth century's rapid growth of population and consequent land shortage. In fact there is less divergence between these two interpretations than might appear at first sight. They are not mutually exclusive—indeed, Postan may himself have had population growth in mind as Hyams pointed out[9]—and both should probably be taken into account, for whether or not the local land market originated in the thirteenth century it is generally agreed that at least it expanded and changed its character then.[10]

We may wonder, in any case, whether the question has always been posed the right way. If we see the land market as comprising all temporary or permanent transfers of property between living tenants—even if we restrict it to transfers involving payment—we must take into account transactions of several sorts. All, whether they operated singly or in combination, had the same effect: they introduced greater flexibility into local landholding than appears from the formal record of manorial tenure. But from the administrative or legal standpoint they had little in common, and one consequence is that the sources of our information about them vary according to the type of transaction. The four studies that follow all show clearly how the historian of the medieval land market is at the mercy of sources that are varied and inconsistent. As the twelfth and thirteenth centuries were a period when written records were first being used in an ever-increasing number of administrative and legal processes we must also consider the date of the first appearance or survival of our evidence; this differs a good deal from one type of transaction to another.

Our main evidence for transfers of land held in free tenure is the private charter. We find charters recording the transfer of

---

[8] *Cart. Nat.*, pp. xxxiv-xxxvi.

[9] Hyams in *EcHR*, 2nd ser., xxiii (1970), 20.

[10] Thus *Cart. Nat.*, pp. xlix-l, and Dodwell in *EcHR*, 2nd ser., xx (1967), 63.

small areas—the few acres that we would expect in the local
land market—from the mid-twelfth century onwards,[11] but it
is only in the early thirteenth century that they start to become
at all common. It is unlikely to be an accident of survival that
so many of our earliest charters for small pieces of land were
grants to religious houses. Monasteries were particularly aware
of the value of the written record and led the way in ensuring
that even their smallest acquisitions of landed property had this
support; the charter would be drafted at the monastery's behest,
even in the monastery itself.[12] This underlines the risk of using
charters as a guide to the chronology or scale of the market in
free land. If an early-thirteenth-century freeholder who sold a
couple of acres to a neighbouring religious house had this recorded in a charter it did not follow that a charter would
accompany his sale of another piece of land to a fellow villager.
Still less would we expect a charter to record the freeholder's
lease of small areas of his lands to a sub-tenant; such documents
are extremely rare at any date, though subletting can have
been the only practicable way of running the scattered properties that many freeholders were acquiring.[13] Generally speaking, the smaller the area of land, the humbler the recipient, and
the shorter the term of a transfer, the later the date will be
when we can expect a transaction to have a written charter to
confirm it—for this is all the charter would do: conveyance was
by public ceremony to which the charter, in form and probably
in the early thirteenth century still in fact, merely bore witness.
How early we have charters for transfers of free land to (and
on occasion from) villeins is not certain, but whenever this
occurred—and it certainly was not later than the mid-thirteenth
century[14]—it should probably be seen as an extension of the
use of written records rather than as an extension of the local
land market.

[11] Cf. *Danelaw Ch.*, pp. xlviii-l.

[12] This could probably be formally demonstrated from the recurrence of distinctive
phrases in grants to a single monastery from various grantors; it is a point that de-
serves investigation. A good example is the specific provision for exchange in case of
failure of warranty that occurs in a number of mid-13th-century grants to Beaulieu
Abbey (*The Beaulieu Cartulary*, ed. S.F. Hockey (Southampton Records Series, vol.
xvii; 1974), Nos. 86, 117, 122, etc.).

[13] Kosminsky, *Studies*, p. 220; Harvey, *Oxon. Village*, pp. 115-17.

[14] *Cart. Nat.*, p. xlii, citing the references to charters in the 1239 court roll from
Brancaster (Norf.) in *Cart. Mon. Ram.*, i. 423-8.

For villeins' dealings in free land charters are not our only evidence—indeed of themselves they are sadly uninformative, for they never specify that a party to a transaction was a villein. We learn far more from the manorial lords' own records. Peterborough Abbey's *Carte Nativorum* register, with its copies of the charters that villein tenants acquired with their freeholdings, seems to be unique, but manorial court rolls are numerous and here we see villeins reporting their acquisitions and showing their charters to the steward, or getting permission to buy or sell free land, or being amerced for doing it without permission.[15] These records show marked differences between manorial lords in the amount of surveillance, control, or restriction that they exercised over these transactions in the late thirteenth and early fourteenth centuries, and Postan suggested a tendency towards increasing strictness as time went on.[16] But manorial court rolls appear quite late on the scene. The earliest from which copied extracts survive dates from 1237, our earliest original court roll is of 1246, and they do not seem to have been a very common form of record until the 1270s.[17] Significantly, we find references in them to villeins' transactions in free land right from the start; it is not a question of the gradual emergence of entries of this sort. However, we have one earlier record of proceedings in manorial courts. This consists of entries on certain manorial accounts of the profits from local courts, entries which do not (as was usual later) give just the total proceeds from the court of each manor, but give the reason for every payment imposed by the court—each amercement, each entry fine, and so on. The enrolled accounts of the bishop of Winchester's estates from 1208-9 onwards are our only substantial series of such accounts before the mid-thirteenth century. Postan drew attention to the number of entries we find there of villein tenants' payments for permission to sublet parts of the lands they held, and used this to support his argument that in the development of the local market in customary land widespread leasing paved the way to general acceptance of the

---

[15] Ramsey Abbey seems to have required even its free tenants to produce in the manorial court their charters for any newly acquired properties (Raftis, *Tenure*, pp. 82-3)

[16] *Cart. Nat.*, p. xlv.

[17] *Man. Records of Cuxham*, pp. 79-80.

principle that villein tenants could effectively sell or otherwise dispose of their holdings.[18] This suggested progression from leasing to alienation has been accepted by Hyams as plausible, if unprovable;[19] however, the entries on the Winchester accounts as well as Postan's other corroborative evidence show at least that subletting of villein holdings was a normal practice at as early a date as we could possibly expect to know anything about it. Once we have manorial court rolls we have no lack of widespread evidence for subletting of lands held in villeinage, and here again how far manorial lords sought to control or restrict this varied a good deal from one estate to another. In subletting, just as in villein acquisitions of free land, we can never be sure that the court rolls tell us the whole story; the extent of 1352 that gives full details of subletting at Havering (Essex) is a most unusual record, more unusual probably than the complex structure of sub-tenancies that it reveals.[20] Even when controls were strictest on a particular manor there may have been successful evasions and concealments, and clearly some manorial lords' surveillance—or indeed, their interest in these transactions—was weak or non-existent. The same is true of tenants' exchanges of small pieces of customary land that we sometimes find recorded on court rolls.[21]

Looking at the permanent transfer of entire villein holdings from one tenant to another we find rather different problems, though our most informative source is again manorial court rolls. Here there can be no question of concealment or evasion, nor even of the evidence being affected by different policies from one manor to another. Everywhere land in customary tenure could technically pass only between lord and tenant; transfer from one tenant to the next could be effected only by returning the holding to the manorial lord, who would then hand it over to the new tenant. Evasion of this procedure was hardly possible: the new tenant would be responsible for the rents and services, so the transfer could not be concealed. The

[18] *Cart. Nat.*, pp. xxxvii-xxxviii, lii-liii.

[19] Hyams in *EcHR*, 2nd ser., xxiii (1970), 19, 28-31.

[20] M.K. McIntosh, 'Land, Tenure, and Population in the Royal Manor of Havering, Essex, 1251-1352/3', *EcHR*, 2nd ser., xxxiii (1980), 20-5.

[21] A court roll of 1296 for the Cambridgeshire manors of Crowland Abbey shows neatly how permission for certain exchanges of land brought to light a group of other exchanges that had been made illicitly (Page, *Crowland*, p. 336).

amounts of the entry fines due from incoming tenants were always entered on the court rolls, which in any case seem from the start to have been meant to record all surrenders and entries of customary holdings. We can be fairly certain that a complete series of court rolls will give us a complete picture of all changes of customary tenants on a particular manor. But what they do not necessarily tell us is who chose the incoming tenant. Sometimes the outgoing tenant surrendered the holding 'for the use' (*ad opus*) of a named person who would then be admitted to it; sometimes a father surrendered a holding in favour of his son, with a maintenance agreement entered on the court roll which makes the relationship clear. But we cannot safely equate the growth of surrenders specifically *ad opus* with the growth of a market in customary holdings on a particular manor, for they are as likely to reflect simply the increasing detail and formality of manorial court rolls. Earlier admissions to holdings surrendered without the *ad opus* formula may just as well have been made on the initiative of the outgoing tenant, who will have nominated his successor in return for payment or other favours or as part of a change of responsibilities within the family. The origin of the local market in entire customary holdings is hidden from us.

The same is true of part holdings. We shall see how from the thirteenth century onwards the market in portions of standard holdings varied from region to region, even from place to place; some manors still maintained intact into the sixteenth century a system of standard holdings that on some others had vanished through fragmentation two hundred years earlier. From what we have seen of the history of standard holdings in the twelfth century we should not be deceived by their apparent uniformity. If villeins in the early twelfth century simply had a share in the manor's resources rather than precisely defined lands and rights, then in an age when neither estate administrator nor historian supposed that holdings with identical names must be of identical size there was plenty of scope for flexibility, for permanent as well as temporary transfers of small portions of holdings—of part claims on these shares—from one villein to another. Rights in assarts may have been particularly susceptible to this. What interested the manorial lord was his tenants and their obligations, not the specific details of what they held

of him. It is by no means impossible that we see the workings of
a land market in the division of virgates into half-virgates,
quarter-virgates, or even cotlands,[22] though an alternative,
perhaps more likely, explanation is that this occurred when
partible inheritance by joint tenure was replaced by partible
inheritance by division, to be replaced in turn (if the fission
stopped there) by impartible inheritance.[23]

The leasing to local tenants of small portions of manorial
demesne lies outside the peasant land market as we have defined
it, for the transfers were from lord to tenant, but it certainly
contributed a good deal to the flexibility of the individual tenant's holding and at least we can trace its chronology with
confidence. Manorial court rolls and, particularly, accounts
show clearly that leases of this sort were unusual in the age of
demesne farming, the thirteenth and early fourteenth centuries,
when landlords had local officers, reeves and bailiffs, to manage their demesne lands. From the mid-fourteenth century onwards these small-scale leases were a common prelude to letting
the demesne *en bloc* to a single farmer, whereupon they would
cease.[24] But the leasing of manors in the fourteenth century
was not a new phenomenon; it was simply a return to the system that had prevailed before the end of the twelfth century.
The manorial farmer of this earlier period was only broadly
analogous to his late-medieval successor; we cannot rule out
the possibility that local circumstances may sometimes have
made it practicable or profitable for him to let out portions of
the demesne to local tenants. Domesday Book, after all, records
a number of cases where the villeins themselves held the farm
of a full manor.[25]

In the four studies that follow we see all these aspects of the
peasant land market in late-medieval England—the buying

---

[22] As, for example, on the estates of Ramsey and Westminster Abbeys (Raftis,
Tenure, p. 17; Dewindt, *Holywell*, p. 31; Harvey, *Westminster*, pp. 299-300) and,
probably, at Weston Underwood (Bucks.), where in the 13th century three cottage
holdings were the equivalent of one virgate (Powicke in *Wirtschaft und Kultur: Festschrift
zum 70. Geburtstag von Alfons Dopsch*, p. 389).

[23] Below, p. 355; note how at Warboys (Hunts.) in 1251 there was a clear distinction
between a full virgate held by two tenants and a half-virgate held by one (Raftis,
Warboys, p. 155).

[24] e.g. Rees, *South Wales and March*, pp. 182-3; Hilton, *Leics. Estates*, pp. 88-90, 117;
Raftis, *Ramsey*, pp. 273-4; Dyer, *Lords and Peasants*, p. 123.

[25] Lennard, *Rural Eng.*, pp. 153-4.

and selling of both free and customary land, subletting and division of holdings, leasing of portions of demesne. But the character of the market, just which aspect predominated, varied a great deal—from one period to another as well as from place to place. So too did the sheer volume of the market: in some places over long periods there was little or no transfer of properties in this way, while others had long traditions of an active local land market. We can hardly suppose that there would be any less diversity in whatever local land market there may have been before it produced written records. Was there such a land market? We do not know, but it seems very likely on grounds of general probability as well as in view of the demonstrable activity of each form of the market from the very point when we first have records that could tell us of it. Historians are rightly suspicious of postulated patterns of change which see developments occurring coincidentally with the first appearance of the written records that tell us about them or which assume a falling off from a regulated, ordered structure that existed in some previous, barely recorded age. To be suspicious is not to be dismissive: the development of land transfers of this sort may at least have helped to bring into being the types of written document that record them, while regularities of one sort or another are now known to have occurred in a way we would have doubted thirty years ago and may have been less exceptional than appears. But whatever peasant land market there may have been before the thirteenth century we can be fairly sure it will have differed from what we find then. We may suppose, for example, that leasing played a much larger part in it than permanent alienation and that the further we go back the more likely it will be that payments were in produce or labour rather than in money. And almost certainly it will have been at a lower level overall: there is no need to doubt that growing population pressure and land shortage produced a rapid growth of the local land market in the thirteenth century.

In his article of 1970 P.R. Hyams takes the land market to be 'the buying and selling of land for money . . . on a large enough scale to constitute something like a "market" in the sense in which the word is used by economists'. While seeing no evidence for a general peasant land market of this sort in the early thirteenth century, he suggests that 'it is likely that the

peasant land market developed earlier in East Anglia (or perhaps more generally over eastern England) than elsewhere'.[26]
This is particularly interesting in view of other differences that
seem to distinguish eastern England at just this period: there
are some signs that it lagged behind in the change from manorial leasing to demesne farming, and that manorial court rolls
came into use faster here than elsewhere.[27] In support of his
contention Hyams puts forward two pieces of evidence. One is
that East Anglia is the origin of nearly all the cases that can be
brought in support of Bracton's doctrine of implied manumissions (that is, a lord's enfeoffment of a villein with land to
be held freely to himself and his heirs constituted manumission
of the villein). The other is that all seven references before 1240
to the writ *per villanum* (for the lord whose tenant had sold or
leased land in villeinage to a stranger without permission)
relate to East Anglia or the Home Counties.[28] Certainly both
pieces of evidence suggest that the land market developed early
in East Anglia, though they might plausibly be held to point
only to greater uncertainty over the status of land and tenants
there than elsewhere. By the late thirteenth century holdings
were fragmented in other parts of eastern England—in the
Chilterns, in Kent—just as in East Anglia.[29] We do not find
this fragmentation in other regions, though it may be that
the local land market (on a broader definition than Hyams's)
took different forms there. At any rate, of the importance of the
land market in thirteenth-century East Anglia we can be in no
doubt. It is demonstrated clearly in the study that follows of
three Norfolk villages: Gressenhall, Martham, and Sedgeford.

[26] Hyams in *EcHR*, 2nd ser., xxiii (1970), 19.

[27] P.D.A. Harvey, 'The Pipe Rolls and the Adoption of Demesne Farming in
England', *EcHR*, 2nd ser., xxvii (1974), 353-4; *Man. Records of Cuxham*, p. 79.

[28] Hyams in *EcHR*, 2nd ser., xxiii (1970), 24-5.

[29] D. Roden and A.R.H. Baker in Baker & Butlin, pp. 333, 407-8.

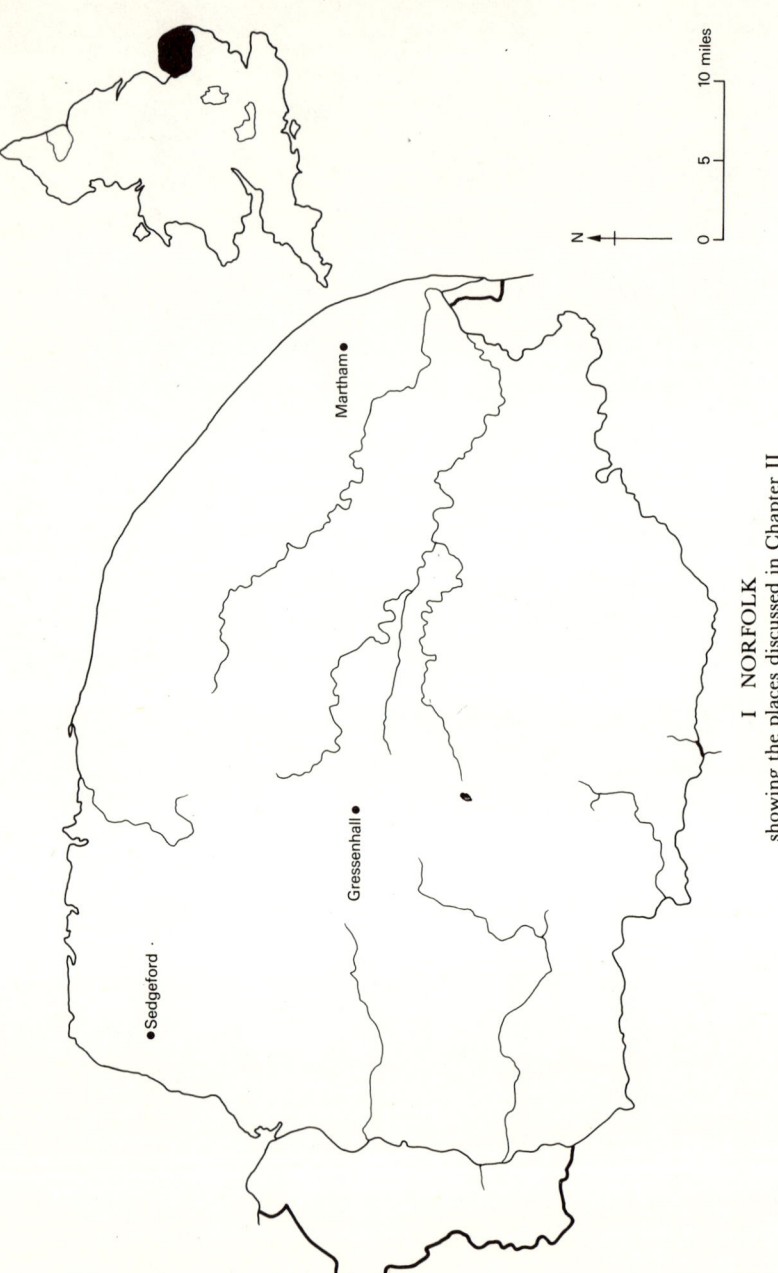

10 miles

5

0

N

I NORFOLK

showing the places discussed in Chapter II

Martham ●

Gressenhall ●

● Sedgeford

II Norfolk: Thirteenth Century*

1 THE THREE MANORS

The modern historian, unlike D.C. Douglas in 1927, need no longer feel it necessary to offer an apologia for the study of local history. Douglas believed that 'an examination of local conditions prevailing in different parts of the country is essential before further wide generalizations can be made',[1] yet Douglas himself may have been guilty of premature generalization in his assumption that there existed—in East Anglia or elsewhere—a body of custom that could be studied both as being uniform in itself and as differing significantly from that in other socially discrete areas of medieval England. It has become increasingly clear that, just as Douglas believed a study of local conditions must necessarily precede any generalizations on national terms, so a detailed examination of individual village conditions is necessary before it is possible to speculate on the source or effects of a locally peculiar 'body of custom'.

Norfolk, with its substantial free peasantry and widespread partible inheritance, is an obvious area for such an inquiry. Specifically, this study will examine individual manors to determine the effects of different inheritance customs on the patterns of land distribution among the peasantry and the contribution of inheritance customs to the development of the peasant land market. The work will look particularly at three Norfolk manors which present a wide range of surviving evidence and which can also be considered as broadly representative of medieval Norfolk as any three manors are likely to be. Each of the vills lies in a different land-use area of the county. Gressenhall is at the edge of the mid-Norfolk region, an area of clay soil

* This chapter is based on J. Williamson, 'Peasant Holdings in Medieval Norfolk: a Detailed Investigation into the Holdings of the Peasantry in three Norfolk Villages in the Thirteenth Century' (Reading University Ph.D. thesis, 1976). The thesis gives throughout additional evidence and illustrations of the points discussed here. I would like to recognize my indebtedness to Miss B. Dodwell for her invaluable help with this work.
[1] Douglas, 'East Anglia', pp. 1-16.

of reasonable fertility; Sedgeford is firmly in the good-sand region of the north-west, the sandy soil of which gave good yields only with the introduction of eighteenth-century agricultural improvements; and Martham is in the loam region, an area of glacial drift with soil more fertile than the clay found in the middle of the county.[2] The agriculture of the villages naturally reflected the differences in their soils, with Gressenhall practising wood-pasture and Sedgeford sheep-corn husbandry;[3] Martham's agriculture was adapted to its position on an island of the Broads. Following the fertility of the soil, Martham was in an area of unusually dense population in 1086, while the population of Gressenhall was average and that of Sedgeford low. The principal manor in Martham and in Sedgeford was ecclesiastical, while that in Gressenhall was lay. The three manors offer a contrast in inheritance customs: partible inheritance at Gressenhall and Martham, impartible at Sedgeford. In two respects, however, the three manors studied were not typical of Norfolk. First, in each case the single manor encompassed most of the village land; all three manors were large ones, and even Gressenhall, the smallest, was large for a lay manor in Norfolk. Second, villein holdings on all three manors were comparatively lightly burdened. Whether either of these facts was significant should emerge in the course of the study.

On the surface, then, these three manors provide sufficient points of similarity and difference to make their contrast and comparison valuable. This study concentrates on the thirteenth century, a period of acute pressure on existing arable resources and hence a critical period in the development of peasant holdings. The peasants in Gressenhall, Martham, and Sedgeford were operating in different agricultural and social contexts, and their responses—and those of their landlords—to common stimuli should help us to see how important those differences were.

[2] P. Wade-Martins, 'The Development of the Landscape and Human Settlement in West Norfolk' (Leicester University Ph.D. thesis, 1971), p. 23.

[3] M. Postgate in Baker & Butlin, pp. 281-3.

2 GRESSENHALL

The manor and its records

Gressenhall is a village in central Norfolk approximately 3 miles north-west of East Dereham.[1] It is in the hundred of Launditch, largely an area of boulder clay lying between 150 and 250 feet above sea level. The soil of Gressenhall is loam and clay, with a subsoil of clay and gravel. The village lies on the edge of what Allison described as the wood-pasture region of Norfolk, where the soil is heavier and more fertile than in the sheep-corn region to the north and thus did not need extensive sheep-dunging to maintain its productivity. Heaths and commons were less in evidence in the wood-pasture than in the sheep-corn region, but there was, not surprisingly, a higher proportion of woodland. Although barley was the predominant crop throughout Norfolk, wheat was relatively more important in the mid-Norfolk area than on the more sandy soil of the north. The general prosperity of the district at the time of Domesday Book, as indicated by plough teams and population, was average for the county as a whole. The entire area was probably wooded at one time, accounting for the still substantial amount of woodland recorded in Domesday Book.

The Domesday Book entry of the lands of William de Warenne lists Gressenhall with one berewick (Scarning),[2] but by the end of the twelfth century Gressenhall had become the head manor of a holding of nine knights' fees stretching over eight villages in the hundred.[3] Throughout most of the thirteenth century the Gressenhall honour was held of the king by the Earls Warenne, and of the Warennes by first the Stuteville and then the Foliot families.[4] The Stutevilles and their successors were not the only landholders in the Gressenhall complex of manors or in the village of Gressenhall itself. Because the name of the head manor

---

[1] This paragraph is drawn from *Kelly's Directory of Norfolk* (London, 1937), pp. 171-2; Darby, *Dom. Geog. E. Eng.*, p. 147; and K.T. Allison, 'The Sheep-Corn Husbandry of Norfolk in the Sixteenth and Seventeenth Centuries', *AgHR*, v (1957), 14.

[2] *VCH Norf.*, ii. 87.

[3] Gressenhall, Scarning, Hoe, Bittering, Stanfield, Brisley, Bilney, and Horningtoft (NRO MR 79).

[4] G.A. Carthew, *The Hundred of Launditch and Deanery of Brisley* (Norwich, 3 vols., 1877-9), i. 189-93.

was often applied to the whole complex, it is difficult to determine whether landholders mentioned in connection with Gressenhall held land there or in one of the other villages associated
with it. Both Wendling Abbey and Castle Acre Priory certainly
had small holdings in Gressenhall itself.[5] There is evidence for
only one large secular landholder apart from the Foliots in late-
thirteenth-century Gressenhall, and that is the Herford family.
In the last decades of the century, Warin de Herford had a house
and mill in Gressenhall and claimed the right of fold and the
right to hold court for his tenants.[6]

All the evidence surviving from medieval Gressenhall concerns the Stuteville-Foliot holding. A large proportion of this
evidence is in the form of extents, rentals, and surveys dating
from the late thirteenth century up through the fifteenth century. A complete and detailed early extent—and, incidently,
one of the few dated ones—occurs in the inquisition post-mortem
taken after the death of Jordan Foliot in 1299.[7] The inquisition
describes Foliot's demesne in Gressenhall then gives a list of his
tenants with the sizes of their individual holdings and the rents
and services due. Probably the most useful extent is an undated
one of about 1282 which is fuller in its details of tenant holdings; the details of the demesne, however, are largely illegible.[8]
There are also four other late-thirteenth- and early-fourteenth-
century documents which, being incomplete, are more useful
in throwing light on the two complete extents than for any independent information contained within them. These are a list
of tenants in a number of manors of the Gressenhall complex,
along with their holdings and the value of their rents and services;[9] a 1299 list of Foliot tenants in several manors in the
complex;[10] an early-fourteenth-century custumal giving the
holdings and services of Gressenhall tenants and the rents of
tenants in Bittering;[11] and an early-fourteenth-century survey

[5] *Taxatio Ecclesiastica Angliae et Walliae auctoritate P. Nicholai IV, circa A.D. 1291*
(Record Commission, 1802), p. 98.

[6] NRO ING 8, 5 May 1287, 7 June 1288, 23 Nov. 1289, 3 Oct. 1290; PRO JUST
1/575, fo. 108.

[7] PRO C 133/90(1), mm. 8-9. The inquisition is transcribed, occasionally incor-
rectly, in Carthew, op. cit., i. 202-7.

[8] NRO 21187.

[9] NRO ING 198a, 207. It is the second and third rotulets which survive.

[10] NRO MR 1.

[11] NRO ING 209.

(about 1315) of the Gressenhall complex that is unusual in being written in English.[12] A large number of late-fourteenth- and early-fifteenth-century terriers and rentals of Gressenhall and its associated manors also survive; these are of value in confirming trends suggested by the earlier material.

Gressenhall is unusual in having not only extant surveys but also an almost unbroken series of court rolls from 1275 to 1307 and beyond.[13] In contrast, few early Gressenhall charters survive; only sixteen can be found among the L'Estrange family collection in the Norfolk Record Office.[14] Finally, there are a number of miscellaneous documents relating to medieval Gressenhall which can be useful in connection with other evidence, among them a fourteenth-century leet roll[15] and a reeve's account for the manor of Gressenhall dated 1280.[16] Although this study is meant to cover just the manor of Gressenhall and not the entire complex that had Gressenhall as its head manor, the evidence often makes such a distinction difficult. The Gressenhall complex was divided into two sokes, the North Soke (Stanfield, Brisley, Bilney, and Horningtoft) and the South Soke (Gressenhall, Scarning, Hoe, and Bittering).[17] The name Gressenhall is applied in documents variously to the manor itself, to the South Soke, and to the entire honour. The court for the Foliot tenants of all eight manors was held at Gressenhall, and only in the case of leet courts is any consistent distinction made between North Soke and South Soke tenants. Occasionally the location of land involved in a dispute or transfer is recorded, but this is the exception rather than the rule.[18] The election of officials and assize infractions are both recorded by soke, but litigation seldom records the village of plaintiff or defendant, so that distinguishing the cases involving Gressenhall tenants becomes impossible. Surveys and extents present similar problems. Thus, while an attempt has been made to restrict

[12] NRO MR 55, 56, 58; ING 208, 214. The survey was deposited in the record office in fragments, and each was given a separate number.

[13] NRO ING 1-78, MR 1.

[14] NRO L'Estrange N and NA.

[15] NRO L'Estrange N2.

[16] NRO ING 186.

[17] NRO MR 79; cf. F. Blomefield and C. Parkin, *An Essay towards a Topographical History of the County of Norfolk* (Lynn, 5 vols., 1739-75), v. 1014.

[18] e.g. NRO ING 28, 1 May 1307, where out of five land transfers only one is assigned a location.

discussion to the village of Gressenhall, the frequent inclusion
of material from the other associated villages is inevitable.

The most accurate evidence for the size of the Stuteville-
Foliot manor in Gressenhall is in the 1282 extent, which gives a
figure for the entire holding in Gressenhall of 1,038 acres excluding pasture.[19] These 1,038 acres comprised a 6-acre demesne messuage, 192 acres of demesne arable, 160 acres of
woodland, 12 acres of meadow, and 668 acres of tenant land.
Pasture and common would probably have increased the size
significantly. It must be emphasized that these acres are not
necessarily statute acres; we do not know the size of the perch
used at Gressenhall. What evidence there is of the Herford
holding confirms that the Stuteville-Foliot manor was larger
and held more tenants.

Apart from eight free holdings, the 1282 extent lists ninety-
nine holdings totalling 560¼ acres. We can distinguish ten
villeinage holdings of standard size from the other miscellaneous
holdings. That these standard holdings were of 24 acres is
proved by the 1299 inquisition post-mortem, in which the listing of Gressenhall village tenants begins with the statement
that 'there are there ten villeins of which each holds one messuage with 24 acres of land'.[20] This statement is followed by a
list of the common services attached to each holding, which
include three days hoeing, three days mowing, thirty-six
autumn works, the ploughing of one acre, carting dung, and
the rendering of one hen, five eggs, one capon, and 2 bushels of
oats. There was obviously strong pressure at the manorial level
to retain these standard holdings as units; they occur in extents
and surveys as late as the fifteenth century, and by this period
the names of the thirteenth-century tenants had been transferred to the tenements themselves.[21] The 1282 extent is the
earliest evidence of the 24-acre holdings and the names of their
tenants.[22] An early-fourteenth-century survey gives ten 24-acre
holdings plus that of Simon Palmer doing identical services,

[19] NRO 21187.

[20] Carthew, op. cit., i. 206.

[21] As e.g. in NRO ING 198.

[22] The names in order of occurrence are Palmer (24 a.), Neuman (20 a.), Backe and
Rodland (24 a.), Avenaunt and Granger (12 a.), Body and son of Matilda (24 a.), son
of William (24 a.), son of Richard and Martyn (12 a.), Frost (24 a.), Sparewe and
Proudfot (24 a.), son of William (24 a.), and Erl (24 a.).

many of the tenants having the same surnames as those of the 1282 extent.[23] The number of standard villeinage tenements returns to ten in a rental dated 1343.[24] In this rental, the 24-acre tenement previously described as that of Richard son of William is called *tenementum Richardson*, presumably from the next generation. Again, the 24 acres held jointly by Henry Sparewe and John Proudfot in the late thirteenth century, and by Walter Sparewe and his parceners in the early fourteenth, appears from 1343 onwards as *tenementum Proudfot*, although there were by that time neither Sparewes nor Proudfots associated with it. As late as the fifteenth century, the *tenementa* survive as units, with names basically unchanged.[25] It is tempting to connect these ten 24-acre villeinage holdings with the ten villeins of Gressenhall's Domesday population. In view of the conservatism which preserved the *tenementa* through the fifteenth century, their survival from the eleventh century cannot be considered unlikely.

Excluding from the 1282 extent the standard holdings, the remaining eighty-seven non-free Gressenhall holdings total only 324¼ acres, giving an average size of only slightly under 3¾ acres.[26] Most of the holdings of ½ acre or less were cottages without any attached arable land.[27] Among holdings of over an acre we find that holdings of 4, 6, 8, and 12 acres predominate, which may indicate that at one time even those apparently irregular holdings derived from a 24-acre standard. Eight free tenants in Gressenhall are listed in the 1282 extent, their holdings ranging in size from Warin de Herford's 40 acres

---

[23] NRO ING 209. The tenants are Palmer, Neuman, Backe and Rodland, Gode and Balle, son of Richard, Martyn and le Neve, Frost, Fite, Sparewe, Erl, and Sencler, all with 24 a. each.

[24] NRO MR 54, the first survey to describe the holdings as *tenementum Pawmer*, etc. The surnames are Palmer (24 a.), Neuman (12 a.), Backe and Rodland (24 a.), Body (24 a.), Martyn (12 a.), Richardson (24 a.), Frost (24 a.), Proudfot (24 a.), Fite (24 a.), Erles (24 a.), atte Gate (24 a.).

[25] NRO ING 198. The *tenementa* are described· as Palmer, Backe, Martyn, Richardysson, Frost, Proudfot, Fyte, Rafattegate (corresponding to the 1343 *tenementum Radulfi atte Gate*), Neuman, and Erles; Martyn and Neuman are 12 a., the others 24 a. each.

[26] This is a good illustration of why the concept of average holdings must be considered of dubious value (Hilton, *Eng. Peasantry*, p. 39). The average holding is introduced here only for comparison.

[27] Of the 27 such holdings, only 5 were arable holdings of ½ acre each; 22 were of cottages alone.

with messuage to the cottage of Henry Chaplain. Their average size is 12½ acres, but this figure conceals the wide gulf between the two holdings of 40 acres each, and other holdings of 12 acres, 6 acres, 2 acres, 1 rood, a messuage, and a cottage respectively. Two of the free tenants—Warin de Herford and Alexander de Gressenhall—may be found witnessing Foliot charters,[28] but none of the smaller free tenants ever appears. There is no distinction among Gressenhall tenants in the 1282 extent or in the 1299 inquisition apart from that between free and unfree. The early-fourteenth-century custumal, however, distinguishes between villeins holding the 24-acre standard holding, mondaymen, molmen, and free tenants.[29] The mondaymen correspond to the first twenty-one tenants in the 1282 extent, the molmen to the tenants who follow the 24-acre holdings with significantly lighter services. Any difference in the personal status of villeins, mondaymen, and molmen is impossible to discover, as these classifications are based on their tenurial status alone. Apart from one court-roll entry concerning the obligation of mondaymen to provide their own vessels for water-carrying services,[30] the one custumal is the only evidence of the distinction between mondaymen and molmen in medieval Gressenhall.

Thus far, tenant holdings in the manor have been discussed primarily with reference to the 1282 extent. The 1299 inquisition can add little to our knowledge of the free tenants, since it is difficult to determine which were at Gressenhall as against other villages in the complex. There is a large discrepancy between the eighty-eight unfree holdings listed in the extent and the forty-six in the inquisition post-mortem, although the amount of land described is comparable.[31] This means that the average holding in the inquisition, including the ten 24-acre holdings, is about 7½ acres—over twice the average of the extent. One explanation is that the inquisition seems to disregard cottage holdings. Only one cottage and three messuages are listed without attached land, with the result that there are more holdings of 24 acres each than of 1 acre or less. A great

[28] Warin de Herford: NRO L'Estrange N15, 16; L'Estrange NA10, 20, 25. Alexander de Gressenhall: NRO L'Estrange N15.
[29] NRO ING 209.
[30] NRO ING 3, 29 June 1310.
[31] The inquisition has 45 a. less tenant land than the extent.

deal of consolidation of holdings can also be seen when the extent is compared with the inquisition. For example, in the extent Thomas Winkel holds a messuage and 11 acres and Richard Winkel a messuage and 2 acres; the inquisition has William Winkel and William son of Richard Winkel holding jointly two messuages and 13 acres of land. In almost every case where the inquisition names more than one tenant for a holding, the earlier extent enters two or more apparently independent holdings. The consolidation of holdings between the extent and the inquisition illustrates the difficulties involved in relying on administratively based evidence for the individual tenant's economic situation.

The 1282 extent reveals at least one of the forces working towards the breakup of the holdings which the lord of the manor was obviously working to preserve—the force of partible inheritance. Thirty-one of the 107 holdings listed have at least two tenants. Three of these joint holdings name only one tenant with his parceners, and ten of them name two tenants with different surnames, possibly not closely related. The remaining eighteen holdings, however, are held jointly by two or more brothers or sisters—in one case six sisters, and in another five brothers. The unusually complete court rolls from Gressenhall allow one to examine the opposing forces of change and conservatism working on the holdings towards the end of the thirteenth century and show how—in one village, at least—balance was eventually achieved.

Inheritance and the land market

Most of the surviving Gressenhall extents and surveys give the impression that the majority of holdings in the manor were held by only one tenant, joint tenure being uncommon though not unknown. The fact that partible inheritance was practised in Gressenhall makes this unlikely. The evidence for partible inheritance lies in the number of cases in which two or more brothers pay heriot or relief to enter their father's land and the number of disputes over the division of hereditary land. It is common in the Gressenhall court rolls to find brothers entering their father's land as heirs after his death. For example, in the entries of heriot and relief taken over two arbitrarily chosen

years (1282-3 and 1283-4) 40 per cent were paid by two or more
heirs, and none of these cases involved daughters in default of
sons.[32] Of course, this figure represents all the manors in the
complex and not Gressenhall alone. But with one exception,
there is no indication in the surviving court rolls that inheritance
customs differed significantly among the eight villages.[33]
However, the assumption of partible inheritance in Gressenhall
does not rest on such negative arguments alone. The evidence
of joint holdings in the 1282 survey has already been mentioned: fourteen were held by brothers or other tenants with the
same surname.[34] A number of examples of joint entry into
patrimony occur among tenants who can be associated with
Gressenhall in other sources.[35] It can be confidently asserted
that partible inheritance was the practice in Gressenhall, in
the late thirteenth century in any case.

An example of the way in which partible inheritance could
rapidly break down a holding can be found in the surviving court
rolls, where one 6-acre holding with messuage in Gressenhall
went from one to five tenants over a period of four years. At the
beginning of 1284, the tenement was held by Peter Cupere. By
March of that year, two successful suits had been brought, first
against Peter for half the land, then against Peter and the successful suitor for a third of the land.[36] Both suits were based on
hereditary rights that had descended from the two brothers of
Peter's grandfather, rights that had not been taken up by their
immediate heirs. Peter died in December 1287, and his remaining property—2 acres and one-third of a messuage—was
entered by his three sons.[37] Two aspects of this extended case

[32] NRO ING 8. Of 20 entries into the land of deceased tenants, 12 were by one heir,
5 by two heirs, 2 by three heirs, and 1 by four heirs. This is strikingly like the incidence
of partible inheritance in 13th-century Coltishall as computed by Campbell, 'Field
Systems in E. Norf.', p. 235.

[33] NRO ING 8, 23 June 1287, where a dispute suggests that land in Stanfield may
have been impartible.

[34] NRO 21187. Of the 14 holdings, 5 are held by two brothers, 3 by two tenants
with the same surname, 3 by three brothers, 1 by two brothers and a third tenant with
the same surname, 1 by a man with his four (unnamed) brothers and a sixth tenant,
and 1 by a man with an unspecified number of brothers.

[35] To take two Gressenhall tenants named in NRO 21187, the land of Peter Cupere
was entered by three sons on 8 Dec. 1287 (NRO ING 8), and the land of Stephen
Prikel by three sons on 2 Dec. 1297 (NRO ING 19).

[36] NRO ING 8, 3 Feb. 1284, 16 Mar. 1284.

[37] Ibid., 8 Dec. 1287.

seem contradictory, and it is this contradiction which makes it both interesting and significant. First, the property was clearly considered partible at the end of the thirteenth century; in both court cases partibility was upheld, and Peter Cupere's land went to all three of his sons on his death. But second, the land involved was not divided even in theory until 1284, despite the fact that a tenant three generations earlier had had three sons. The messuage and 6 acres, held as a single tenement for three generations, was divided among five related tenants in only four years.

The custom of partible inheritance was of course not the only force that divided tenements in thirteenth-century Gressenhall. Like the other two Norfolk manors in this study, Gressenhall had an active land market at the end of the century. In 1283-4, for example, there were 103 land transactions recorded in the courts, transfers ranging in size from ⅛ rood to a whole tenement of unspecified size and averaging less than ½ acre per transaction.[38] The year was not an unusual one in either the number or the nature of the land transfers. There was rationalization of individual holdings, probably prompting the exchange of ¼ rood and ¾ rood between John Proudfot and Henry Sparewe, and certainly prompting the two successful suitors for Peter Cupere's land to surrender all rights in a messuage to Peter Cupere in exchange for ½ acre and ¼ rood of land.[39] There were family arrangements: Thomas son of William rendered 1 rood into the lord's hands for the use of his brother Walter.[40] There were simple buyers and sellers: Henry Makefare disposed of 2 acres and ¾ rood in six transactions, while Peter de Kirtling acquired 1 acre and ¾ rood in three.[41] All of these tenants can be identified as Gressenhall tenants.

Although no information is available on Gressenhall specifically, there does not seem to have been much restriction on the freedom of Foliot tenants in the honour generally to hold or transfer land. There is no evidence of any regulation or prohibition of the holding of free land by villeins or of villein land by freemen. A court decision of 1284 established that a villein could

---

[38] Ibid., 1283-4 *passim*.
[39] Ibid., 3 Feb. 1284, 17 May 1284.
[40] Ibid., 16 Mar. 1284.
[41] Ibid., *passim*.

transfer free land without the lord's licence.[42] Jurors declared in
1303 that 'the custom of this court is that villeins [*nativi*] of the
lord can sell their tenements to free men by licence of the
lord',[43] and there are examples in the court rolls of a free man
holding villein land and of a villein leasing villein land to a free
man.[44] An inquiry of 1309 listed ten 'free tenants of the lord's
villeinage' in Gressenhall, with holdings varying from 1 rood to
7 acres in size.[45] Villein land was taken into the lord's hands
only if it was claimed to be held freely,[46] not if it was simply
held by a free man. It is not possible to discover at what time
the distinction between free and villeinage land was made, but
a case in the surviving court rolls indicates that a change in the
status of land was not impossible.[47] Nevertheless, most land in
the Gressenhall manors had a defined status which did not
change according to the status of its tenants, and neither the
status of the land nor that of the tenant restricted its sale, lease,
or exchange.

The way inheritance functioned in Gressenhall and its associated manors was greatly complicated by the land market.
In a court in 1305 a villein was prevented from selling ½ acre
of free land in Brisley 'because such a surrender would be to
the disinheritance of the heirs'[48] but nowhere else in the surviving rolls is this given as a reason to restrict or prevent land
transactions. Most recorded disputes about hereditary land are
disputes not over partibility but over prior sales and surrenders
that affected its eventual disposal. More than once, the partibility of a specific piece of land is denied by the defendent on
the basis of a prior transaction in the courts. In 1283, for example, Walter Blickling countered his brother's action to recover a 'reasonable part' of 11 acres of land by claiming that he
had received the land by the gift of their father and not by descent after his death.[49] Thus, land transfer could be used to

---

[42] Ibid., 3 Feb. 1284.
[43] NRO ING 25, 21 Mar. 1303.
[44] Ibid., 28 Feb. 1303, 12 Nov. 1303.
[45] NRO ING 31, 13 Oct. 1309.
[46] e.g. NRO ING 8, 31 July 1286; ING 31, 22 Sept. 1309.
[47] NRO ING 8, 5 Apr. 1283.
[48] NRO ING 26, 1 Mar. 1305.
[49] NRO ING 8, 13 Jan. 1283; the decision was for the plaintiff. The Blickling
family was based in the village of Gressenhall (NRO 21187).

forestall the division of a tenant's land among his heirs. In 1282 William son of Gilbert Godwyne sought against his brother Roger an acre of land 'which was his by hereditary right after the death of Gilbert his father because the land is partible among brothers'.[50] However, the decision was for Roger, the court accepting his contention that Gilbert had come into court before his death and surrendered all rights in his holdings to his son Roger and Roger's heirs. There was clearly no concept here of inviolable patrimony subject to customary rules of inheritance; partible inheritance worked only on the land of which a tenant died seised. Such cases illustrate the need, felt even by tenants who could buy and sell free land without the court's licence, to have a record of land sales and purchases that could be easily consulted. The court rolls themselves were obviously the most efficient such record.

It is clear that the practice of partible inheritance alone would not lead to the division of every tenement in every generation, but it is interesting to discover in the court rolls examples of tenements retaining their integrity despite their theoretical partibility. As the tenement of Peter Cupere shows, not every heir with the right to a 'reasonable part' of land claimed that right, at least not immediately after the death of the previous tenant. In fact, court-roll evidence suggests that it was not uncommon for land to be entered by only one of a number of heirs who had rights in it. There are numerous entries in thirteenth-century rolls in which one or more men pay 6*d*. to have entry in a 'reasonable part' of their inheritance.[51] It is significant that the sum was paid for entry not into an entire tenement but only into a 'reasonable part', suggesting that other heirs in the tenement were already seised of the entire holding. This suggestion is confirmed by the example of the Pistor holding. In 1289 John son of Walter Pistor paid a heriot for his father's land.[52] Two years later Edmund son of Walter Pistor paid 6*d*. 'for his portion of the tenement of his father'.[53] There is no evidence that

---

[50] NRO ING 43, 12 Jan. 1282.

[51] e.g. NRO ING 9, 2 Mar 1289, in which Henry Dase and his brother Roger paid for licence to have the 'reasonable part of the tenement that was their father's'.

[52] NRO ING 9, 23 July 1289.

[53] NRO ING 8, 14 June 1291. A Henry son of Walter Pistor appears in a court-roll entry of 1284 acquiring land (ibid., 3 Aug. 1284), so that there may well have been a third brother with a claim to a share of Walter's land.

Edmund was a minor or otherwise debarred from entering his inheritance on his father's death, nor is there anything in the surviving court rolls to suggest that Edmund had to sue his brother John for his right to a share of their father's land. On the contrary, it appears that Edmund simply waited to claim his inheritance for several years after his father's death. Such delay does not seem to have been unusual, and suggests that there were legally partible tenements in which not all heirs claimed their share, either in the original payment of heriot or relief or afterwards. The position of the heirs of original entry must have been that of Geoffrey son of Thomas, who in 1286 paid 12*d.* for licence to have the whole tenement of Thomas Mercator until Geoffrey's brother Simon might come and give satisfaction for his portion. If Simon did not come, Geoffrey was to hold it entire in perpetuity.[54]

Division of hereditary land among heirs could thus be postponed or neglected entirely as a result of the inactivity of one or more of the heirs concerned. Such inactivity may well reflect prior agreement. For example, ½ acre of villein land held by Robert Brode was partible, and on his death should have been divided among his four sons. In fact, however, the two eldest sons occupied the whole of the land during their lifetimes, and on their deaths it descended to their two younger brothers.[55] Manorial regulations preventing the inheritance of land by bastards also reduced the division of holdings. The possible effects of the prohibition are illustrated in the case of one Godwin, who had four sons. When, on Godwin's death, the four brothers came into court to receive their patrimony, the two eldest were adjudged by the court to be bastards, so that only the two youngest paid heriot to enter the land.[56] One died without direct heirs, and his share of the land eventually descended to his brother's only son. Thus, where Godwin's holding might have been divided among four heirs at his death, in fact it descended to one of his grandsons intact, without any land transfer or quitclaim.

Although the land market in Gressenhall contributed to the fragmentation of tenements, it also prevented holdings from

[54] Ibid., 3 Jan. 1286.
[55] NRO ING 3, 24 July 1329.
[56] NRO ING 8, 8 July 1288.

fragmenting beyond a certain level by facilitating the disposal of sub-subsistence holdings. The land market could be used to redistribute the shares of a hereditary holding. For every tenant like John son of Walter Chaplain, who surrendered land for the use of his daughter and two sisters before surrendering his remaining holding to his son,[57] there was probably a Richard Astel, who surrendered all rights in his father's land or any other land in Bilney to his brothers Geoffrey and John.[58] In the former case, a holding was divided which the hereditary custom alone would have preserved intact, while in the latter the hereditary division of a holding was at least partially prevented by agreement. Surrenders or quitclaims did not only concern the smallest holdings; the 24-acre Erl tenement remained undivided for one generation because three brothers quitclaimed their rights in the land to a fourth, the youngest.[59] Leasing land provided an alternative to dividing it, particularly if division would result in holdings too small for subsistence. In 1293 John, Walter, and Geoffrey Gille paid a heriot for the land of their father Henry, and Walter had his brother Geoffrey's entire tenement for a period of twelve years.[60] A particularly striking illustration of the way in which the land market could occasionally offset the effects of partible inheritance occurs in a court-roll entry of 1302, in which four brothers—Nicholas, William, John, and Robert Jordan—quitclaimed their messuage and 4 acres to one William atte Strete, who was already a tenant in Gressenhall.[61] In this case the total number of tenements was reduced by one instead of being increased by three.

Despite the opportunities available to minimize the divisive effects of partible inheritance, much partition of holdings inevitably took place. Only three holdings in the 1282 extent are said to be held by a tenant with his parceners, but the number of times that parceners (*parcenarii*) and 'fellows' (*socii*) appear in the court rolls suggests that they were much more prevalent in Gressenhall than the extent reveals. There are a number of

---

[57] NRO ING 5, 9 Dec. 1314.
[58] NRO ING 8, 15 Mar. 1288. This is another example of the delayed appearance of a coheir: Geoffrey and John paid a heriot for their father's land three years earlier (ibid., 1 Feb. 1285), and there is no mention of Richard at that time.
[59] Ibid., 10 Apr. 1284. The tenant gave one of his brothers 40*s.* for a quitclaim.
[60] NRO ING 12, 9 Nov. 1293.
[61] NRO ING 23, 11 Sept. 1302.

cases in the surviving rolls, particularly connected with default of rent or services, in which a number of related and unrelated tenants can be seen acting together by virtue of their holdings in a single tenement. Roger Overfeld and his parceners, tenants of the Belleward tenement, were attached in 1283 for non-payment of rent; the parceners included Henry atte Gatesende and Thomas Faber, from whom cows were taken as surety for the rent.[62] Similarly, although Henry Gille had only three sons who entered his land on his death in 1293,[63] twelve tenants 'of the land that was Henry Gille's' were amerced in 1302 for failing to perform a day's harvest work.[64]

The existence of tenemental parceners acting together in rendering services and rent need not imply a subdivided tenement. Thus, Simon, Adam, and Roger Leche, who withheld 17½*d*. from the lord's collector of rents, were probably jointly working a patrimony.[65] One of the most interesting aspects of the Gressenhall court rolls, however, is the number of cases in which one can see the physical division of tenements and the apportionment of rents and services among parceners. The point of physical division is clear because a fine of 6*d*. or 12*d*. was paid for licence to divide. Between 1274 and 1307 twenty-four such applications for division were recorded in the surviving court rolls, although the wording suggests that the extent of division may have varied. In a number of cases, one tenant pays the 6*d*. fine 'for the apportioning of his land',[66] sometimes specifically 'between himself and his parceners'[67] suggesting prior entry into the land. Ralph Corbin in 1293 paid 6*d*. 'to have a reasonable part of the land of his father and just division so that he can have entire seisin';[68] Adam Corbin had died in 1286, and this wording seems to differentiate between Ralph's demand for his reasonable share of his father's land and the actual physical division of that land. In many cases the wording on the court roll unquestionably points to the physical division

---

[62] NRO ING 8, 29 Mar. 1283, 5 Apr. 1283.   [64] NRO ING 23, 9 Oct. 1302.

[63] Above, p. 45.   [65] NRO ING 8, 19 July 1324.

[66] e.g. '6*d*. Rogerus Neuman dat domino pro licencia proportionandi terram suam' (NRO ING 30, 24 Sept. 1309).

[67] e.g. '3*d*. Willelmus Leffe dat domine ad porcionandam terram suam quam tenet de domina inter se et parcenarios suos' (NRO ING 27, 31 Oct. 1306).

[68] NRO ING 12, 15 Aug. 1293.

of a tenement. In five cases the fine is paid 'for the limiting and apportioning of land'[69] and once 'for the measuring and apportioning of land',[70] so that some adjustment of holdings on the ground was taking place. The apportionment of tenemental land among parceners need not have meant that each parcener's land became an individual holding; it was possibly only the tenant paying a fine for apportionment who thereby separated his land from the joint holding. An entry of 1307 may represent the division of a tenement between two groups of parceners: William Backe, Roger Cupere, and Cristiana atte Grange paid 'to limit and apportion land between themselves and Richard Martyn and other parceners'.[71] Whatever the mechanics of tenemental division, the Gressenhall court rolls make it clear that division was not necessarily attendant on the transfer of a holding—whether by sale or by inheritance—to more than one tenant.

The formal apportionment of a tenement's obligations may or may not have accompanied physical division of the land, but that such apportionment did take place is apparent from a number of court-roll entries. In 1298 Henry Aylmer, Juliana Aylmer, Robert son of Richard, and their parceners paid 'because their lands should be apportioned with regard to a reasonable division of rent (*secundum rationabilem portionem in redditu)*'.[72] Rent in such a case may include services; services were certainly divided among parceners in 1288 at the request of Thomas Bonesey, who paid 6*d.* 'so that services and rents may be equally divided among the tenants of the Bonesey tenement'. Ten tenants are listed holding only 7 roods of land in all, and how the services were to be divided amongst them is not indicated.[73] A later entry concerning another tenement sets out the principle that 'each acre should be equally apportioned with the others in doing all customs'.[74] In what way services such as the hen due from four tenants of the land of Alice Winkel[75] were apportioned will be discussed later.

[69] e.g. NRO ING 18, 1 Oct. 1297; ING 78, 29 Aug. 1304.

[70] NRO ING 17.

[71] NRO ING 18, 20 Feb. 1307.

[72] NRO ING 19, 8 Nov. 1298.

[73] NRO ING 9, 4 Dec. 1288. In this case, the stimulus to divide the tenement may have come from its retention in the lord's hands earlier for failure to render services (NRO ING 8, 8 July 1288).

[74] NRO ING 6, 29 Mar. 1316.   [75] NRO ING 8, 14 Jan. 1283.

The difficulties—both for the individuals concerned and for manorial administration—of tenements held by a number of parceners are fairly obvious. It cannot always have been easy to determine the tenant of a given piece of land: Walter Blickling sued Henry Deneman in 1284 for taking ½ acre from him, only to be amerced for a false plea when Henry replied that he was not the tenant of the land in question. The next entry on the roll shows Walter suing Henry son of Geoffrey Pistor for the same land.[76] But these are difficulties of minor importance compared with the problem of knowing what services and rent were due from parceners. The court rolls frequently record payments for inquiries into services owed from individual tenants or tenements, and some of the uncertainty may well have resulted from the formal apportionment of the land. For example, Adam Brunger paid 6*d.* in 1287 to determine whether his holding owed one boon-work or two.[77] Tenure by more than one tenant undoubtedly presented an obstacle to the sale or exchange of land, made the definition of individual holdings difficult, and even after formal division created confusion over which tenant was responsible for each portion of the rent and services. Administrative resistance to tenemental division appears only in the minor obstacle of licence fines. A brother delaying entrance into his patrimony was required to go into court for licence to receive his 'reasonable portion'; with such a system inactivity amounted to quitclaim. Similarly, the physical division of tenements apparently required the initiative of one tenant prepared to appear in court and pay the requisite fine.

On the whole, the lord of Gressenhall and his officers sought to minimize the administrative difficulties of fragmented tenements rather than to prevent or obstruct the division itself. They coped with the fragmentation of holdings in two ways: first by preserving the tenemental unit in extents and surveys, and second by maintaining the concept of a single set of customs due from a single tenemental unit wherever their value justified this. Four documents illustrate this administrative conservatism: the 1282 extent, the 1299 inquisition post-mortem, the English survey, and the 1343 rental. The 1282 extent is the earliest complete list of Gressenhall tenants with their holdings;

---

[76] Ibid., 3 Feb. 1284.
[77] Ibid., 18 Feb. 1292, 5 May 1287.

it gives by far the greatest number of tenant names and the smallest average size of holding of any extant Gressenhall survey. Although some of the single tenant names probably conceal joint holdings of unrelated parceners, the fact that parceners are specifically named for a number of holdings, and the relatively small average holding size, suggest that most of these holdings were in fact single holdings, held, if not by one tenant, at least by only a small number of tenants as an immediate or extended family. This is the more likely in that in more than half the cases where parceners are named (seventeen out of thirty-one) they consist of an immediate family—a tenant with brothers or sisters. We have already seen how the 1299 inquisition post-mortem simplified the enumeration of holdings. Not only are the holdings of two or more tenants that are listed separately in 1282 often entered as single holdings in the inquisition,[78] but the inquisition gives no indication that any of these holdings are shared, whether by brothers or by unrelated tenants. The inquisition records only one of the eight cases in which the land of a 1282 tenant was inherited by more than one son: John Blickling and parceners held the land previously held by Walter Blickling.[79] In the other seven cases only one son is named in the inquisition as tenant of the entire holding, although there is no evidence that any of the heirs either quitclaimed or died between the time of inheritance and 1299. Thus, for example, the land of Peter Cupere was entered by his three sons—Roger, Richard, and Adam—in 1287, but only Roger occurs as a tenant in the inquisition. An inquisition postmortem has of course a different purpose from a manorial survey, but a comparison of the inquisition with the slightly earlier extent demonstrates one way of simplifying the structure of holdings for administrative purposes. The rental of 1343 shows the Gressenhall *tenementa* in their final form: administrative

---

[78] Often arbitrarily, it seems. In the extent Adam and Henry Corbin hold 24 a. and William Picher holds two messuages and 12 a. with five other tenants. In the 1299 inquisition Richard Corbin and William Picher hold two messuages and 26 a.— presumably the 24-a. Corbin holding plus Picher's share of the 12-a. holding.

[79] John, Ralph, and Theobald Blickling paid a heriot for their father's land on 20 Feb. 1290 (NRO ING 8). In fact, Walter held only a messuage and 6 a. in the extent, so the holding of 'Johannes Blickling et parcenarii' in the inquisition (a messuage and 8 a.) may also have included the 2-a. holding of Gilbert Blickling that follows Walter's holding in the extent.

units splintered among a large number of unrelated tenants.[80]
The *tenementa* are identified by the surnames of their former
tenants, possibly taken from the 1282 extent. Where a Christian name as well as a surname is attached to a 1343 *tenementum*,
those Christian names usually correspond with the 1282 tenants. Thus, for example, the rental lists *tenementum Henrici de
Wisbeche* (4½ acres), *tenementum Rogeri Simondisson* (4 acres),
tenementum Jordani Smyth (4 acres), and *tenementum Galfridi atte
Strete* (1½ acres), while the 1282 tenants were Henry of Wisbech
(6 acres), Roger son of Simon (4 acres), Jordan Faber (4 acres),
and William son of Geoffrey del Strete (1 acre). Cottages and
messuages as well as arable holdings were identified in 1343 by
the names of late-thirteenth-century tenants. The conclusion
must be that in 1343 the *tenementa* are fossilized relics of the late
thirteenth century.

Tenure and its obligations

The primary purpose of maintaining the tenemental units was
undoubtedly to simplify as far as possible the collection and account of rents and services due. Two court-roll entries and a
unique survey from Gressenhall show how the rendering of services due from a tenement was organized among its tenants.
Curiously, both of the relevant court-roll entries occur in the
court of 1 August 1300.[81] That court records:

It is agreed between William Lithfot and his parceners that Richard
brother of the said William will give to William ¾ *d.* annually at the
feast of St. Michael. And the said William will give every quarter-
year one hen for the whole tenement that was of Elias le Longe. And
Edmund Faber will give to the said William every year ½ *d.* at the
feast of St. Michael. And the said William will do every other year
half of one autumn boon-work for himself and his parceners.

The agreement is not complete; it is said in the margin of the
roll to be 'finished on another roll', but the conclusion has not
survived. Nevertheless, the entry as it stands clearly demonstrates one among a number of parceners being paid money by
the others for assuming the responsibility for all the services
due from the tenement. The lord need pursue William alone

for default of services, and William likewise has legal recourse should his parceners default. That the arrangement put a legal obligation on the parceners and was thus more binding than an informal agreement, is shown in another entry in the same court:

Geoffrey atte Hil was attached to answer John Elser in a plea of detention of rent. John says that the said Geoffrey unjustly withheld from him a quarter part of 2¼d. of rent and a quarter part of 1d. for ploughing rent which he ought to render (to John) for the portion of the tenement which was once of the fee of the ancestor of the said John.

In this case John (who entered his father's holding with his brother Nicholas in 1286[82]) appears to be the responsible head of a divided Elser holding, able to charge Geoffrey atte Hil with detention of rent.

The English survey of about 1315 further illuminates the process by which individual holdings of 1282 became the *tenementa* of 1343. This survey is not organized by *tenementa*, but in nineteen cases it shows services organized on the lines just described, with one tenant wholly responsible for them and with parceners making him annual payments for undertaking this responsibility. The evidence of the Palmer holding shows that these nineteen holdings had not yet become the indivisible *tenementa* of 1343. In 1282 the first 24-acre villein holding described was that of the brothers Robert and Elfred Palmer. In the English survey their respective successors, Simon and Peter Palmer, each had a holding of half a messuage, 4 acres, and ½ rood. The services for which each was responsible were half those of a standard 24-acre villein holding; Peter had ten tenants paying him 'to the werkes' and Simon had eleven. In the 1343 rental and afterwards, however, there was only one *tenementum Palmer* of 24 acres. It is significant that of the nineteen holdings in the English survey which retain the same tenemental cohesion as the two Palmer holdings, fourteen are villein holdings; not surprisingly, it was the most heavily burdened holdings which the administration tried to keep as single units. This survey, then, represents a transitional stage between the single-family holdings of the early thirteenth century and the

---

[82] NRO ING 8, 31 Oct. 1286.

tenementa of the mid-fourteenth, and it demonstrates one form of compromise between the administrative desire to maintain single-tenant responsibility for services and the inevitable process of tenemental division.

Just as the services once due from individual holdings became attached to named tenements, so the obligation to fill manorial offices seems to have evolved from an individual to a tenemental liability. Because the Gressenhall complex extended over eight manors, the number of manorial officials needed in the thirteenth century was quite large. In most years from which court rolls survive five officials were elected annually: one reeve, three haywards (one each for Gressenhall, Scarning, and the North Soke), and one rent collector. That by the middle of the fourteenth century manorial officials were chosen by tenement is proved by the 1343 rental, which shows that single or combined tenements of 18 or 36 acres were responsible for providing a reeve and tenements of 9 acres a hayward. The fact that the responsibility to fill office was tied to tenements in 1343 at once raises the question whether in the late thirteenth century tenants were elected to office as individuals or as representatives of a tenement. In most cases before 1300, there is no indication that election to office involved anything more than the choice of an individual; the record of most elections gives only the name of the tenant chosen. There are enough exceptions, however, to suggest that already by the end of the thirteenth century election to office was often by tenement rather than by individual. In 1284, for example, the 'tenants of Henry Choue' were elected rent collector and the 'tenants of John Vincent' the hayward for Scarning.[83] In 1291 the office of reeve was held by 'Henry Trinmere and his parceners'.[84] In 1283 William Picher was elected hayward but did not actually take up office because 'he and his parceners gave Walter de Grisehawe 8*s*. to take the burden from them for the whole year';[85] not only were William Picher's parceners joined with him in the payment to discharge the office, but the burden of the office was said to be not his but theirs. It is possible, then, that in many more instances the apparent election of a single tenant to

[83] NRO ING 8, 20 July 1284.
[84] Ibid., 28 July 1291.
[85] Ibid., 4 Aug. 1283.

a manorial office is in reality the election of a holding he has
been chosen to represent. This view is supported by a court-roll
entry of 1302 involving the election of officers in Bittering.[86]
Jurors of Gressenhall and the North Soke stated that the
Bittering tenants 'ought to elect their reeve by tenement and
not by who is best to occupy the office'. The burden of manorial
office could be heavy, and for this reason there were safeguards
against the burden lying too heavily on any single tenement.
The fairly constant period of eight to ten years between the
repetitions of individuals in lists of officials is evidence that
tenements responsible for providing officials were rotated over
a period, so that one holding need not accept the burden more
often than about once a decade.[87] The liability to fill manorial
offices was an obligation as closely tied to the holding as the rents
and services due from it. It seems likely that this liability, as other
tenemental obligations, went through an evolutionary adjustment as the tenements on which it was based began to break
down. Already by the end of the thirteenth century there is
evidence that the responsibility for providing an official was
more frequently that of a holding of parceners than that of a
single tenant or single-tenant holding. There is no evidence
before 1343 of an association of particular sizes of holding with
particular manorial offices, but it is not difficult to envisage a
more rigid organization of offices accompanying the restruc-
turing of tenements which undoubtedly took place before that
date.

If, as seems probable, the fragmentation of holdings was
more advanced in the late thirteenth century than surviving
extents indicate, then the average size of holding must have
been much smaller than the 5½ acres of the 1282 extent. Given
the land market, a tenant with a holding too small for subsistence could always either sell it or buy more land to supplement
it; the sale of 'whole tenements' of unspecified size is not uncommon in the court rolls. For many, however, leasing provided
a more attractive alternative. Renting land required less outlay
from the lessee than purchase and represented for the lessor a

---

[86] NRO ING 23, 4 Feb. 1302.

[87] Unlike Forncett, where no elections of manorial officials were recorded in the
13th century and the officers were held by the same persons in successive years
(Davenport, *Norf. Manor*, p. 25n).

more temporary arrangement than sale. A great deal of leasing was apparently done privately (and illicitly) without going through the court for a licence, so that it is difficult to tell how often land was being leased. Henry ad Pontem's leasing of his entire tenement, for example, appeared in the court rolls only when the tenement was taken into the lord's hands for having been let without licence.[88] The size of Henry's tenement is not given, but the leasing of a sub-subsistence holding can be clearly seen in the case of Ascelia Hoog, who inherited 3 roods from her mother in 1310 and in the same court leased the land to Roger Gallon for eleven years.[89] Cases of tenants withholding rent they owe for leased land occur occasionally in the court rolls, reinforcing the impression that the renting of land was a common method of overcoming the problems of a small holding.[90] At least one pair of brothers, Robert and William Winkel, took lands on lease on an extensive scale; an inquiry made in 1284 listed eleven lessors who had rented to them, from 1 rood to 1 acre 1 rood, for periods ranging from two to twelve years.[91] The average parcel size was ⅔ acre and the average term of lease almost seven years. The total amount of land leased by the Winkels in 1284 was 7 acres 1 rood, a substantial addition to their existing holding. Unquestionably leasing was an important way of adjusting the size of a holding, one ignored by surviving extents because of its peripheral importance to the lord of the manor. It would be interesting to know whether in the purchase and lease of lands individuals were concentrating their holdings in one area of the village fields, but this is impossible to discover. No surviving extent or survey before the sixteenth century gives the locations of holdings in the fields. There are very few charters mentioning tenant names in connection with specific fields, and court-roll entries involving land transactions seldom mention the village concerned, let alone where the land lay within the fields.

It is important to remember in this context that a peasant's arable land was not his sole source of subsistence, nor did arable

[88] NRO ING 8, 4 Aug. 1292.

[89] NRO ING 2, 12 Jan. 1310.

[90] e.g. Alexander and Martin Leche were amerced for detaining 2½ d. rent from Agnes Holbek in 1290 and 2¾ d. rent from Roger of Ingringhowe in 1293 (NRO ING 8, 7 Aug. 1290; ING 12, 20 July 1293).

[91] NRO ING 8, 24 Feb. 1284.

land represent a peasant's entire holding. Livestock was often part of a holding, and sheep, for example, could provide income in the sale of lambs or wool.[92] Many tenants undoubtedly owned cows, either individually or shared with another tenant,[93] and extant statements of services suggest that horses were not uncommon. In Gressenhall some tenants held woodland as well as arable,[94] and at least one mill was held by tenants, some having shares as small as one forty-eighth of the whole mill.[95] All the Gressenhall tenants had fishing rights in the river from the mill of Warin of Herford to the house of Ralph son of Walter.[96] An illegal but undoubtedly popular resource for supplementing income was the poaching of hares which technically belonged to the lord; in 1299 there was an inquiry concerning hares taken in the lord's warren and sold in the market at Dereham.[97] There were some opportunities to earn money by doing work on the larger holdings. For example, Hugh Clutere accused Margaret Gurre of withholding from him 22*d*. payment for harvest work in 1306.[98] Most arable holdings in Gressenhall were undoubtedly small, but tenants of arable holdings that appear smaller than necessary for subsistence need not have been tenants with insufficient resources to support life.

It is unfortunate that in Gressenhall, where the manorial complex stretched over a number of villages, it is difficult to examine inter-village activities because of the lack of information on the tenants' village of residence. However, there is no evidence that individual holdings commonly comprised arable land in more than one of the manors of the complex.[99] Whenever the court rolls give the location of land involved in a transfer, Gressenhall tenants can usually be observed buying, selling, and leasing Gressenhall land.[100] There were undoubtedly

[92] e.g. NRO ING 24 lists tenants who paid *faldagium* to have their sheep outside the lord's fold.

[93] NRO ING 8, 16 Mar. 1287, 21 Apr. 1292.

[94] NRO ING 19, 5 May 1298.

[95] NRO ING 8, 21 Apr. 1292, 21 Nov. 1286, 8 June 1284.

[96] Ibid., 5 May 1287.

[97] NRO ING 20, 19 Oct. 1299.

[98] NRO ING 27, 14 Nov. 1306.

[99] Thomas Langland, a Gressenhall tenant who held 1 a. in Bittering, appears to have been an exception (NRO 21187).

[100] The Winkel brothers, mentioned above, leased all their land from Gressenhall tenants.

social and contractual arrangements between residents of neighbouring villages, through both the Gressenhall courts and the market at East Dereham,[101] but the information available suggests that a tenant's resources within this manorial complex were limited to his village of residence. That is not to say that they were limited to the Stuteville-Foliot manor in the village, but any involvement in the Herford manor or other independent holdings in Gressenhall must remain conjectural.

Conclusion

It is only on the 24-acre villein holdings that we find evidence in the Gressenhall extents and surveys of administrative pressure to retain tenement integrity. At the same time, the only sign in the 1282 extent of partible inheritance in the village is the numerous cases of joint tenure by brothers; there is certainly no evidence that partible inheritance had been practised over a long period of time. There are no cases in 1282, as there are forty years later, of two tenants with the same surname having equal areas of land as a result of holding division. Why does the fragmentation of holdings appear so much more pronounced in 1315 than in 1282? There are several explanations that can be offered. Perhaps the most obvious is that the administrative pressure against the physical division of patrimony may have been lifted at the end of the thirteenth century with a decreasing dependence on labour services for demesne cultivation. A second explanation is that partible inheritance in fact occurred so infrequently that it took some centuries for it to affect the pattern of peasant holdings. However, it is difficult to believe that the application of partible inheritance over two centuries of population expansion would result in only a threefold increase in the number of tenants from Domesday Book to 1282.[102] A third explanation lies in the internal pressures on a family unit to maintain the family holding. Work on modern peasant societies—always accepting the limitations of comparison imposed by the time difference of 700 years—has shown that, although partible inheritance may be practised in theory,

---

[101] Disputes in the Gressenhall courts arising from contracts made in East Dereham are not uncommon (e.g. NRO ING 8, 31 Mar. 1292, 27 Oct. 1292).

[102] Only a twofold increase if one includes the Domesday bordars as tenants.

it is common for the domestic group of an extended family to retain its integrity for generations, the partible inheritance of land and goods remaining potential rather than actual.[103] The optimum size of such a domestic group is defined by the amount of labour required to work the holding and the problems of internal governance of the unit. When the unit grows too large to function communally, or to support itself from its communal resources, members of the group will take the initiative to make the partibility of the holding real rather than potential. In this way the initiator gains total control of his portion of the communal resources either to work independently (possibly with the hope of increased efficiency and increased yield) or to sell or lease his share. If there were sufficient land available for assart in Gressenhall to absorb the energies of an expanding family group—and the number of molmen in 1282 as well as the position of the village in a heavily wooded area supports this hypothesis—then the impetus for the actual division of family holdings could well have been delayed until the late thirteenth century, after which time the breakup of holdings would have been swift and progressive. The last explanation not only fits the evidence available from the last quarter of the century but also explains such cases as the Cupere family holding, which was not divided until 1284 even though a tenant three generations earlier had had at least three sons.

However, the explanations of historical processes are seldom so simple, and a court-roll entry of 1287 suggests that the partibility of inherited land in Gressenhall may have been a positive change in custom. In August 1287 an inquiry was made concerning the partibility of the land of Hugh Stoppewrytte, half of whose holding was sought by one of his grandsons against another. The plaintiff's case, upheld by the jury, was based on his claim that a change in the inheritance of the holding had taken place at the time of William de Stuteville (*c.* 1216-59)[104] as a result of a deliberate change in administrative policy:

And Peter says that in no time of his ancestors were tenements partible in Gressenhall but always held whole until a certain G. Crowe steward of the lord William de Stuteville, with the consent of the lord

103 E. Wolfe, *Peasants* (New Jersey, 1966), p. 74.
104 W. Farrer, *Honors and Knights' Fees* (London and Manchester, 3 vols., 1923-5), iii. 397-8.

and the whole court, ruled that always in future the tenement should be partible between brothers because he wished to have more tenants.[105]

Although the entry does not specifically state that this decision was an important change of policy applicable more generally than just to the tenement under litigation, such an extension is suggested by two aspects of the defence: the implication that the consent of the 'whole court' was necessary to the judgement and the general statement that the decision was motivated by the desire of the lord and his steward 'to have more tenants'. Examples of changes in local inheritance custom from primogeniture to ultimogeniture or from ultimogeniture to primogeniture as a result of the judgement of a lord's steward have been discovered from the early fourteenth century, showing that inheritance customs were not impervious to change.[106]

One court-roll entry is not sufficient to prove a general change in inheritance customs in Gressenhall in the mid-thirteenth century, but the argument is strongly supported by the very neatness with which it fits the late-thirteenth-century conditions in the village. It certainly explains three of the most puzzling aspects of the evidence: the limited amount of division by 1282, the number of delayed entries into patrimonial holdings, and the almost total lack of administrative pressure to maintain traditional holdings before the 1343 rental. The small amount of fragmentation in 1282 and the number of cases in surviving court rolls in which ancient holdings were clearly being apportioned for the first time in the late thirteenth century appear as anomalies requiring explanation in a village of traditional partible inheritance but are at once explicable if the division of holdings did not begin until the mid-thirteenth century, either in theory or in practice. The pattern of the delayed entry of heirs into their patrimony then becomes a logical way of adjusting the traditional pattern of inheritance to effect an administratively motivated change; by the mid-thirteenth century the administration gave a higher priority to acquiring more tenants than to ease of collecting their rents and services. However, a decision by the lord and his steward to change their attitude to division of patrimony was not necessarily an auth-

---

[105] NRO ING 8, 10 Aug. 1287.   [106] Homans, *Eng. Villagers*, pp. 126-7.

oritarian decision made without regard to the tenants' own wishes. It might be that in the early thirteenth century tenements were considered family holdings, with non-inheriting sons having rights of subsistence in the holding but possibly without any specifically defined rights of tenancy; pressure towards the middle of the century to realize the potential rights of non-inheriting sons may well have lain behind the administrative decision in favour of partibility. Such a hypothesis closely fits the available evidence. At any rate, partible inheritance seems to have had little effect on peasant holdings in Gressenhall before the middle of the thirteenth century, when the removal of administrative restraint resulted in rapid fragmentation of holdings.

Leasing was undoubtedly the easiest method of adjusting the holdings to family size, but once holdings began to fragment, an increase in the amount of land permanently alienated through the land market was inevitable. The manorial administration in Gressenhall did not seem to place any restrictions on selling or leasing land beyond the requirement that all such transactions not concerned solely with free land should go through the lord's court. There is no question of land transfers through the court being only for the lifetime of the recipient and therefore temporary,[107] because the common form of transfer was that land was surrendered into the lord's hands for the use (*ad opus*) of the recipient and his heirs.[108] The land market was thus closely associated with partible inheritance. By offering a profitable means of disposing of sub-subsistence holdings the market encouraged the physical division of patrimony, while such division in turn stimulated the activity of the market. The land market may also have been responsible for the formal arrangements for rendering the services of a holding; land which could be easily transferred had to have its communal obligations defined, so that their accomplishment did not require fresh negotiation with every new tenant.

The rôle of population increases in the impact of social and economic forces of peasant holdings in Gressenhall has so far

[107] As suggested in *Cart. Nat.*, p. lii.

[108] In fact, a change of form took place between 1281-2 and 1282-3; in the earlier rolls, transfers were recorded as sales, but from 11 Edward I they were recorded as surrenders *ad opus*. There is no evidence that there were any changes in the conditions by which the transferred land was held.

only been implied. There can be no doubt that the population of Gressenhall was increasing up to the end of the thirteenth century. To take two numerical indicators of population movement, in a stationary population only some 60 per cent of heriots or reliefs will be paid by male heirs in a direct line,[109] while the replacement rate will be 1.0—that is, every male tenant who dies will be succeeded by only one other male tenant in a direct line of inheritance.[110] At Gressenhall in the two years 1282-3 and 1283-4, there was an 80 per cent entry of sons into land[111] and a replacement rate of almost 1.6.[112] The forces of partible inheritance and the land market were applied to an increasing population, and one reason for their impact must lie in their being the only way peasant holdings could be adjusted to absorb the population increase, short of administrative redistribution of land. In Gressenhall the prolonged period of population increase, once the opportunities for extending the arable had been exhausted, brought theoretically partible holdings to physical division in the middle of the thirteenth century, and suggested to the administration the profitability of encouraging an increase in the total number of tenants.

3   MARTHAM

The manor

Martham is a village on the Norfolk Broads, about 8 miles north-west of Great Yarmouth. The evidence which has survived from medieval Martham is in many respects more complete and its interpretation more straightforward than for either Gressenhall or Sedgeford; it is also the only one of the three on which considerable work has already been done.[1] Despite the

[109] Campbell, 'Field Systems in E. Norf.', p. 227.

[110] S. Thrupp, 'The Problem of Replacement Rates in Late Medieval English Population', *EcHR*, 2nd ser., xviii (1965), 105-6.

[111] Of the 20 entries, only two were by daughters and two by collateral heirs.

[112] The 16 male tenants who died were collectively replaced by 25 direct male heirs.

[1] W. Hudson, 'Traces of Primitive Agricultural Organisation as suggested by a Survey of the Manor of Martham, Norfolk', *TRHS*, 4th ser., i (1918), 28-58; W. Hudson, 'The Anglo-Danish Village Community of Martham, Norfolk', *Norfolk Archaeology*, xx (1921), 273-316; Campbell, 'Field Systems in E. Norf.', pp 20-150.

amount already written on medieval Martham, there remain aspects of the evidence which have not yet been discussed, in particular the light it sheds on the mechanics of partible inheritance in the manor.

The seven Domesday Book entries concerning Martham are evidence that even in the eleventh century it was a well populated village divided among a multiplicity of major and minor landholders, many of whom were based in neighbouring villages. Domesday Book describes Martham with its neighbouring hamlet, Sco, as having 90½ tenants divided among six landlords.[2] By the thirteenth century the largest Domesday Book holding—that of the bishop of Thetford—had been divided between Norwich Cathedral Priory and a military sub-tenant, the Gunton family. The priory had by far the largest part of the bishop's land in Martham, and thus in the thirteenth century held the largest manor in the village. Most of the information on thirteenth-century Martham comes from the priory's records, so that of necessity it is the priory's lands with which this study is primarily concerned. Throughout, it is important to remember that many, if not most, of the priory's tenants probably held land of other lords and owed them services; there is certainly one example of a tenant who held socage land of the prior and free land of the Gunton fee at the beginning of the thirteenth century.[3] A long history of gifts, leases, sales, and exchanges among the various tenants and landlords in Martham and surrounding villages must have resulted by the end of the thirteenth century in an extremely complex pattern of landholding.[4] The clearest evidence of the difficulties to which such transactions led is to be found in an indenture made between the priory and Laurence of Huntingfield in 1322.[5] Recognizing that each had the right to exact annually from certain of the other's villeins 'boon-works, harvest works, ploughings, hens, and eggs' and that such exactions had become

---

[2] *VCH Norf.*, ii. 43-4, 58, 72, 118, 123, 140, 195.

[3] Thomas de Syk, discussed below (p. 81).

[4] For example, when Robert son of Warin gave the priory 10 a. 7 p. in exchange for 9 a. 2 r. 29 p., three of the parcels of land in Robert's gift—of ½ a., 39 p., and 35 p.—had to be confirmed by Robert son of Elinode of Rollesby as being part of his fee (NRO DCN Register I, fo. 218).

[5] Ibid., fo. 225r,v. Confirmation of the agreement by the wife and son of Bartholomew de Burle follow.

'irrational and without justice', they finally agreed to quitclaim to one another all such rights so that each lord's villeins would be free of distraint or molestation by the other. They also agreed to share equally the fines and profits from the common pasture, saving to each all profits that were exclusively his by ancient right. The indenture was an attempt to rationalize a state of affairs which had obviously by that time become too involved for efficient administration on either part.

Martham is located on the island of the Broads which comprises the hundreds of East and West Flegg; most of this area at the present time lies less than 60 feet above sea level.[6] The island's soil is a very fertile medium loam, particularly suitable for barley, and presumably because of this the island has, from the eleventh century at least, supported a large population closely settled in numerous villages.[7] In the Domesday survey the densities of population and plough teams in the two Flegg hundreds are among the highest in Norfolk, a fact that is particularly striking when the large amount of marshy alluvium in the area is taken into consideration. There was little wood in the area, though it was abundantly provided with meadow. Salt-making was an important industry in the area although there is no evidence of it at Martham, where the turbaries seem to have been a more important source of income. The proportion of land to water was probably slightly higher at the time of Domesday and until the late thirteenth century, as the water table of the area definitely rose over the period. Complaints of flooding are recorded in the thirteenth century, and by the late fourteenth century most of the turbaries that had been worked a century earlier were under water.[8]

The early thirteenth century

A survey of 1292 finds Norwich Cathedral Priory holding approximately 1,033 acres of arable land in the village and 65 acres of pasture, meadow, and turbary.[9] The priory used a perch of 18½ feet in Martham, which means that the priory's

---

[6] Most of the following information is taken from Darby, *Dom. Geog. E. Eng.*, p. 149.

[7] Most of these villages, unlike Martham, have Danish names.

[8] J. Lambert and others, *The Making of the Broads* (Royal Geographical Soc. Research Series, vol. iii; 1960), pp. 91-4.

[9] BL Stowe MS 936.

arable was approximately 1,300 statute acres. There are several court rolls from the priory's manor court, three of which date from the last decade of the thirteenth century.[10] Grants made to the priory have been recorded in a series of registers, one of which also contains a survey of land held separately by the priory cellarer in Martham.[11] Finally, and undoubtedly most important, there is an exceptionally full extent of the priory's lands and tenants in the vill, made in 1292 as part of a general survey of the priory's estates.

The 1292 survey provides evidence for the state of the priory's manor of Martham both in 1292 and in the early thirteenth century, although the evidence for the earlier date is incomplete and the date itself uncertain. Though Martham was by no means the most extensive of the priory's manors, for some reason its survey is by far the most detailed. In the manuscript nine of the priory's manors are surveyed in the first 36 folios;[12] the survey of Martham follows on fo. 37 and continues for 78 folios to the end of the manuscript, being alone more than twice as long as the other nine surveys collectively. After describing the manorial demesne, the survey lists 107 tenant holdings. Three are identified only by the name of the contemporary tenant, but for the other 104 the names of former tenants are given. In each case the survey first sets down the rents and customary services due from the holding, followed by the names of the contemporary tenants and a detailed description of each tenant's land. The land was held by the 1292 tenants in small strips of variable size, and each strip is described by the field in which it lies, the name of the tenant whose land it adjoins on one long side, and the name of the tenant (or road) on which it abuts on one short side. The former tenants' land is recorded as either villeinage (or *werklond*) or socage (or *mollond*), with a large number of holdings composed of both types of land. Villeinage tenements are expressly stated to be 22¼ in number, the standard tenement being 12 acres and known as an eruing.[13] Among the former tenants there were only seven who

10 NRO DCN 4970, 4971.   11 NRO DCN Registers I-VIII.

12 The first survey, for Hindringham, is incomplete, the beginning of the manuscript having been lost.

13 The history of the eruing and its distribution are discussed in Douglas, 'East Anglia', p. 48, and G. C. Homans, 'The Frisians in East Anglia', *EcHR*, 2nd ser., x (1957-8), 190-201.

held a full eruing, most of the villeinage holdings being only a fraction of the standard 12 acres.[14] After a summary of rents and services at the end of the survey, there is a list of turbaries and abuttals (probably small pieces of arable) and the description of a tenement 'formerly of Simon de Len' with its contemporary tenants. The survey concludes with two free holdings, only one of which is given a former tenant, and four (presumably free) abuttals, the rent of two of which is said to have been unjustly received by Roger Bavent.

Every writer who has studied the Martham survey has attempted to assign a date to the former tenants, but none of the arguments has settled the question. Several threads of evidence, none conclusive in itself, together argue strongly for a date about 1220.[15] The assumption has been made throughout this study that the 104 former tenants named in the 1292 survey were coeval, which seems likely in that all these threads of evidence point to a date at the beginning of the thirteenth century; this can hardly be coincidental. Far from relying on popular memory for the former tenants' names, the prior probably took them from an earlier rental or survey. Analogies from other estates as well as common sense support this explanation.[16]

Thirty-eight of the former tenants had their primary holding in villeinage, described as a portion of the 12-acre eruing with proportionate eruing services. Of these thirty-eight eruing-men,[17] thirty-three also held land in socage, in eleven cases the socage holding being at least as large as the respective villeinage holding. There were twenty-seven sokemen who held from 3 to 22½ acres and who are said to do services as Roger de Hil, the first sokeman to have his holding described; three of these Hil

---

[14] Two characteristic entries from the survey and a summary of the former tenants and their holdings are given by W. Hudson in *TRHS*, 4th ser., i (1918), pp. 34-6, 55-8.

[15] A fuller discussion of the argument is in Williamson, 'Norf. Peasant Holdings', pp. 130-3.

[16] e.g. the Gressenhall survey of 1434-5 (NRO ING 205) or the 1284 rental of Bexley (Kent), described in F.R.H. DuBoulay, *Medieval Bexley* (Bexley, 1961), pp. 19-25.

[17] Those tenants whose first described holding was villeinage land will be termed eruingmen rather than villeins in order to distinguish between their personal and tenurial status.

sokemen also held portions of a villeinage eruing. Finally, there were thirty-nine tenants holding miscellaneous pieces of land from 3 roods to 16 acres in size, the average being considerably smaller than that of a Hil sokeman. None of these miscellaneous sokemen held any villeinage land. The average holding size for the former tenants was 8 acres; for the eruingmen it was just under 10 acres, for the Hil sokemen almost 10½ acres, and for the miscellaneous sokemen 4½ acres.

The 1292 survey defines the eruing, the standard villein holding in Martham, as 12 acres, with the explicit statement that there were in the manor 22 eruings and 3 acres of villeinage.[18] The 12 acres of an eruing were measured rather than customary acres, based on the 18½-foot perch. The parcels which comprise the individual 1292 holdings are described in the survey in some detail after the former tenant and his services, and in 72 per cent of the tenements the sum of the measured parcels corresponds to the amount of land held by the former tenant. The twenty-nine tenements in which there are discrepancies are almost without exception tenements with a large number of tenants in 1292, so that the discrepancies can reasonably be attributed to scribal error. Eruing is an ancient word and suggests an ancient origin for these standard villeinage holdings, although the number of eruings bears no relation to the number of villeins in the village at the time of the Domesday survey (seven). Twelve acres is not a large standard holding, but even so there were among the former tenants only seven holdings of the full 12 acres. By far the most common holding was the 6-acre half-eruing (eighteen holdings), and there were as many quarter-eruing holdings as full eruings. The average holding of villeinage land for the eruingmen was under 6 acres, but most of them also held land in socage, and many of these socage holdings were of considerable size. Thirty-three of the eruingmen held a total of 141 acres of land in socage, the holdings varying from ½ acre to 20 acres. The average additional holding is just under 4½ acres, which, when added to the eruing holdings, brings the average holding of eruingmen among the former tenants to slightly less than 10 acres.

---

[18] In fact, there are only 20⅝ eruings so designated in the survey, but there are five irregular villeinage holdings of 3¾ a. each; this brings the total villeinage land close to 22¼ eruings.

It is very likely that there had been a standard holding among the Hil sokemen. The twenty-seven socage tenements described as owing the services of Roger de Hil are by this very uniformity more likely to represent traditional holdings than those socage lands more variously burdened. A predominance of both 10-acre holdings (six of the twenty-seven) and holdings of simple fractions of 12 acres (thirteen)[19] suggests either a 10-acre or a 12-acre standard holding. Two other pieces of evidence, however, point to the 10-acre standard holding: the fact that Roger de Hil himself held 10 acres and the fact that in the fourteenth century 10-acre holdings as well as 12-acre ones (the eruings) were taken as the basis for electing manorial officials,[20] suggesting that both may have had a rôle in the distribution of ancient tenements.[21] Only three of the twenty-seven Hil sokemen held any villeinage land, and they had only quarter-eruings. There is no indication what personal distinctions existed between a Hil sokeman with 4 acres in socage and 3 acres in villeinage and the eruingman with a quarter-eruing and 4 additional acres of land held in socage. In fact, as we shall see, the eruingman was probably the more lightly burdened.

There remain those former tenants who were neither eruing-men nor Hil sokemen but who held miscellaneous pieces of socage land variously burdened. The sokemen who are not said to do the same services as Roger de Hil number thirty-nine, and their holdings varied widely, from as little as 3 roods to as much as 16 acres. The average size of these tenants' holdings was only 4½ acres of land; twelve of the thirty-nine had less than 1½ acres and only fourteen had more than 5 acres. None of these sokemen held any land in villeinage. The standard services required from most of these miscellaneous sokemen were rent, aid, three boon-works, one hen, and five eggs, although the last three elements occasionally varied. A few of the holdings were held by rent alone. Land which was not held

[19] One holding of 12 a., five of 6 a., three of 4 a., four of 3 a.
[20] NRO NNAS 5924.
[21] Miss B. Dodwell points out how an old tenemental unit could serve as the basis for the selection of manorial officials long after the tenement itself had disintegrated ('Holdings and Inheritance in Medieval East Anglia', *EcHR*, 2nd ser., xx (1967), 66). In both Gressenhall and Forncett, the election of manorial officials in the 14th century was based on an older tenemental tradition, using in Gressenhall a duodecimal and in Forncett a decimal base (above, pp. 52-3, and Davenport, *Norf. Manor*, pp. 50-1).

for boon-works often paid a higher rent instead. The holding of Richard Gemere, for example, included one 5½-acre socage holding for 11½*d*. rent, 6*d*. aid, three boon-works, one hen, and five eggs (total value 23½*d*.) and another socage holding of the same size for 21*d*. rent, 6½*d*. aid, one hen, and five eggs (total value 29*d*.).[22] This was not always the case, however; Peter Vosse held 1 acre of socage land for 2*d*. rent and 1¼*d*. aid (total 3¼*d*.), while Yware son of Geoffrey held another for 4*d*. rent, 1¼*d*. aid, three boon-works, one hen, and five eggs (total value 11¼*d*.). The Hil sokemen owed, on average, services worth 6*d*. per acre, while the miscellaneous socage land carried an average burden of 4¼*d*. per acre. This suggests that the latter may have been of lower quality, perhaps assart or former demesne. Many of the miscellaneous socage tenants had more than one holding; for example, Richard Tusard held two of 1 acre each and one of ½ acre. The rents due from each holding are given separately, so they have been treated as independent holdings. The burdens of both the Hil socage land and the other pieces varied between 3*d*. and 11*d*. per acre. The miscellaneous socage land certainly included both the most lightly and the most heavily burdened, but the variation is not significantly greater than that of the Hil sokemen.

There are two holdings which have not been considered in this summary because of their special nature. One is a free holding whose former tenant, Thomas de Syk, is also named as a former tenant of socage land.[23] The other is a tenement which is set apart in the survey, listed after the rest and introduced as the 'tenement once of Simon de Len', consisting of both villeinage and socage land; five former tenants holding a total of 20½ acres are then named along with the 1292 tenants Both holdings were relatively recent additions to the priory's manor of Martham, coming from a grant by Bartholomew of Caister in 1281 after having been given to him by Simon and Katherine his wife, the daughter of Roger de Gunton.[24]

The 1292 survey describes the former tenants as having a

---

[22] Commuted values for boon-works, hens, and eggs are given in the survey.

[23] That the two former tenants are the same man can be inferred from the fact that in 1292 he had mostly the same successors in both the free holding and the socage land.

[24] NRO DCN Register I, fo. 220ᵛ. For the date of the grant, see NRO Rye MS 3 (A. Norris, 'An History of the Hundreds of East and West Flegg in the county of Norfolk'), i. 13.

total of 266 acres 1½ roods held in villeinage, 141 acres of socage land held by eruingmen, 235¼ acres held by the Hil sokemen, and 184 acres 20 perches held by the other sokemen in the survey; that is, a total of 560 acres 1½ roods of socage land in Martham. The impression is one of customary eruingmen and sokemen with average holdings of over 10 acres, and miscellaneous sokemen with average holdings of less than 5 acres, most holdings being distributed unevenly over a number of the village fields. Services attached to each holding were presumably the responsibility of the former tenant whose name appears in the survey, whether he was in fact a single tenant or only representative, as the head of a household. Given that in the late thirteenth century Martham, like Gressenhall, was a village of partible inheritance, the lack of any evidence of partibility among the former tenants is striking. Only four of the 104 holdings were shared by two tenants in the early thirteenth century, none by more than two. In one instance the joint tenants have no surnames, in two they have the same surname, and in the remaining instance the two tenants have different surnames.[25] In none of the 104 tenements are unnamed siblings or parceners mentioned with the former tenant. While such predominance of single tenants can be paralleled in surveys of other manors with partible inheritance, it is certainly unusual.[26] Of course, former tenants may have been heads of households rather than sole tenants, and as such represented extended family holdings; this will be discussed later. It is also possible that holdings were physically divided before the time of the former tenants, although there is no evidence of such division in the size and distribution of holdings.

[25] Godwyne and Goda; John and Osbert Steward and Roger and William de Hendegord; Osbert Blaking and Roger Elser (BL Stowe MS 936, fos. 101ᵛ-102ʳ, 105ᵛ-106ʳ, 103ʳ-104ʳ, 66ᵛ-68ʳ respectively).

[26] Among the manors of the abbey of Ely in the 13th century, most of the villages where partible inheritance was practised (e.g. in Norfolk, Terrington and Walton) simply credit the tenant of a standard holding with *participes* (Homans, *Eng. Villagers*, pp. 114-15). On the archbishop of Canterbury's manor of Bexley (Kent), a survey of 1284 was organized much as that of Martham in 1292, by *iuga* with their present and former tenants; the former tenants probably date from 1207-14, and of the 22 former holdings only 10 then had single tenants (DuBoulay, op.cit., p. 18).

The survey of 1292

By 1292 most of the holdings of the former tenants in Martham had become fragmented beyond all but administrative recognition. The 104 tenements of the early thirteenth century were broken up into over 900 smaller units. Fifteen of the 104 tenements were from one former tenant to fifteen or more tenants in 1292, the most fragmented being the full eruing holding of Nicholas Godrich, now divided among twenty-three tenants.[27] In contrast, only eleven of the former tenements were held in 1292 by one or two tenants. Five of the eight former holdings which remained intact under single tenancy until 1292 were 1½ acres or less and presumably resisted further fragmentation only by their small size. Only one of the holdings surviving as an integral unit in 1292 was a socage holding of moderate size: the 6-acre tenement owing Hil services held formerly by Matilda Coleman and now by Thomas Toyt.[28] With nine times as many units of land as before, most of the former tenements were so fragmented that it would be impossible to reconstruct the standard eruing or Hil holding without the particular structuring of the survey—a valuable example of the way the historian is at the mercy of survey techniques.

Although there were 900 holdings in 1292, there were far from 900 tenants. Only half of them had land from only one of the former holdings; the other half had land from two or more. Almost 10 per cent of the 1292 tenants had land in more than five of the former holdings, the greatest number being the fourteen in which Robert Stannard's name is found. Variations in surnames present some problems of identification,[29] but there seem to have been just under 370 tenants holding land in Martham of the priory in 1292. There are 153 family surnames among these tenants, and 63 of these can be found among the early-thirteenth-century tenants as well. We find the distribution of land among family members that we would expect in a village of partible inheritance; that is, brothers of the same generation usually have equal areas of land. Certain families, however, had become prominent by 1292—the Syks, the

---

[27] BL Stowe MS 936, fos. 84ᵛ-85ᵛ.
[28] Ibid., fo. 66ʳ.
[29] As e.g. the Sco family, alternatively surnamed De Belaghe.

Stannards, and the Gemeres, for example—as having holdings
larger than average, although in at least one case, the Stannards,
the holding of the former tenant of the same surname (6 acres
in socage) was no larger than average.

Only three 1292 holdings are not associated in the survey
with a former tenant: two contiguous toft holdings of 1 acre
each, and a holding of 1 ½ acres in Westfeld.[30] These may have
been holdings created since the early thirteenth century; if so,
this was the only increase in the area of arable. Obviously, with
almost four times as many tenants in 1292 as there had been a
century earlier, and with practically no increase in the total
area of tenant land, holdings were on average a great deal
smaller. Table I shows how the pattern of landholding changed
between the early thirteenth century and 1292. The average
holding dropped from 8 acres to 2¼ acres, and in 1292 over
two-thirds of the holdings were below average size. Whereas
almost half of the former tenements had comprised from 6 to 10
acres of land, over half of the 1292 tenants held less than 1½
acres of land, and there were only eight who held over 10 acres
compared with twenty-six in the early thirteenth century; taken
as a proportion of the landholding population this seems a

Table I

Total holdings of tenants in Martham, c.1220 and 1292

Description of holding	c.1220		1292	
	Number of tenants	Percentage	Number of tenants	Percentage
Under 1 a.	9	9	118	32
1 a.-under 2 a.	9	9	102	28
2 a.-under 5 a.	17	16	95	26
5 a.-under 10 a.	45	43	39	11
10 a.-under 20 a.	20	19	10	3
20 a. and over	4	4	0	0
Total	104	100	364	100

[30] The tofts held in 1292 by William Godrich and Margaret Kilderous, the Westfeld
holding jointly held by John Hil and John Keneman (BL Stowe MS 936, fos. 85r,v,
112r).

dramatic change in land distribution. Table I also graphically illustrates how the apparently rapid breakup of the former tenements had obliterated any traces of standard holdings—of 12 acres or otherwise—by 1292.

In the plethora of small holdings in 1292 the distinction between villeinage and socage seems to have been largely forgotten. We have already seen that on many tenements comprising both socage and villeinage land in the early thirteenth century the two types of land were no longer distinguished in the 1292 survey. Most of the holdings of less than 1 acre in 1292 were probably exclusively socage or villeinage land—but not all: a 2½-rood holding of Margaret Tusard comprised 1½ roods of socage land from Richard Tusard's former holding and 1 rood of villeinage land from Richard Gemere's. In most of the larger holdings in 1292 there is the expected predominance of socage land (which did after all account for 68 per cent of the total tenant acreage) but here also there are exceptions. The land of Robert Webbestere, for example, totalled 3 acres 3 roods 30 perches and came from nine of the former tenements; five of his pieces were villeinage land (2 acres 2 roods 30 perches), and the rest was socage land. Robert Faldgate, in contrast, in a 6½-acre holding that derived from seven of the former tenements, held at most only 2 roods of villeinage land. Almost three-quarters of the 126 holdings which were over 2 acres included at least a small amount of villeinage land, so that the distinction between eruingmen and sokemen cannot be maintained in the late thirteenth century.

There can be little doubt that one of the chief reasons that the standard holding in Martham broke down was the practice of partible inheritance. Evidence for partible inheritance on the manor abounds. In the three surviving thirteenth-century court rolls there are a number of examples of brothers jointly entering land that had belonged to their father or mother.[31] References to immediate heirs in the court rolls are always in the plural, assuming the likelihood of multiple heirs. And tenants whom the court rolls show to be brothers can be seen in the 1292 survey holding equal amounts of one or more former tenements.[32] All this demonstrates the existence of partible

[31] e.g. NRO DCN 4970, 26 July 1291; DCN 4971, 7 July 1300.
[32] e.g. the Alexanders and the Elsys, discussed below.

inheritance in Martham, at least for some time before 1292. This custom applied to socage land as well as to villeinage land. In seventeen of the former tenements no distinction was made in 1292 between socage and villeinage land, suggesting that there had been no distinction made in the process of division.

The survey evidence also suggests that the joint inheritance of land by two or more brothers was usually accompanied by a real division of the property on the ground. Relatively few joint holdings are listed: only 18 of over 900 tenemental units had more than one tenant in 1292. On two holdings a single named tenant is said to have parceners—1½ roods of William Court- man and 3 roods of Roger Avant[33] (in neither case was this his only holding). On most of the other sixteen joint holdings the tenants were probably related, and they are in a few instances specifically stated to be brothers or sisters; there is only one case of joint tenants of a piece of land having different sur- names.[34] Not all the jointly held land was in small units. The largest joint holding was 10½ acres of a former 11-acre tene- ment, held in 1292 by the three brothers Geoffrey, John, and Roger Alexander.[35] It seems to have been left to the joint ten- ants to decide whether or not to divide a holding formally, though it is difficult to discover what the basis for the decision might have been. In Table II we see the example of the Elsy brothers. John, Roger, and Robert Elsy held 3 acres of vil- leinage land as joint tenants, and John and Roger also jointly held 2 roods of socage land.[36] A 6-acre holding of villeinage land, however, seems to have been divided equally among the three brothers (Table III), as also 4 acres 1 rood of a former socage holding.[37] In addition, John and Robert each held 1 rood of socage land, and the fact that the two roods were contiguous points to the division of a 2-rood holding.[38] It is possible that some of the jointly held land was acquired other than by inheri- tance. In examining the mechanics of partible inheritance in Martham it is important to remember how the active market in land might complicate the picture. Nevertheless, it is clear that

---

[33] BL Stowe MS 936, fos. 72[v], 110[r].

[34] Bartholomew Hare and William Dane jointly held 1 a. in 1292 (BL Stowe MS 936, fo. 105[r]).

[35] Ibid., fos. 98[v]-99[r].

[36] Ibid., fos. 90[v], 101[r].

[37] Ibid., fo. 90[r,v].

[38] Ibid., fo. 77[r].

Table II
Holdings of the Elsy brothers in Martham, 1292

Tenants c.1220	Tenants in 1292		
	John Elsy (a.r.p.)	Robert Elsy (a.r.p.)	Roger Elsy (a.r.p.)
Socage land			
John Sunnof	0.0.30	0.1.0	0.1.30
Emma Pecke		0.2.0	—
Robert le Longe	1.1.27	1.1.26	1.1.27
Villeinage land			
Bartholomew son of Matilda		3.0.0	
John Wymere	2.0.0	2.0.0	2.0.0
Uncertain			
William le Archere	0.1.0	0.1.0	—
Total	5.0.17	4.3.26	5.0.17

Table III
Divison of a former 6-acre holding in Martham, 1292

Location	Tenant		
	John Elsy	Robert Elsy	Roger Elsy
	(a.r.)	(a.r.)	(a.r.)
Toft	0.2	—	0.2
Estfeld	0.2	0.2	0.2
Suthfeld	0.2	0.2	0.2
Tomeres	0.2	1.0	0.2
Total	2.0	2.0	2.0

in the thirteenth century land was usually formally divided among multiple heirs and not shared as a single joint holding.

With the detailed description of each parcel of land in the 1292 survey, it is possible to discover something of the practical mechanics of the division of land among brothers. In the first place, it is evident that land was usually equally divided among all the heirs; there was no custom whereby one brother, either eldest or youngest, got a larger share than the others. It is true that occasionally more land may have been transferred to one brother than to another in the course of the father's lifetime, but this was in order to circumvent custom, not to implement it. Given the fact that most holdings were physically divided on the tenant's death among his immediate heirs, one would like to know by what rules the division of the land was accomplished. All that can be said is that while equal division parcel by parcel was probably the rule, variation was not only possible but frequent. We see an example in Table III, which shows how the three Elsy brothers divided what had once been the half-eruing of John Wymere. It would be following common sense to suppose that division of the smaller pieces of an inheritance was avoided as far as possible. The number of parcels in which land was held had already so multiplied by 1292 that it is difficult to believe that strict equality would not often be balanced by considerations of practicality.

It is clear, then, that the socage and villeinage land of which a tenant died seised was divided equally among his immediate heirs; whether they then held the land jointly, divided each parcel individually, or divided the holding as a whole seems to have been a question less of custom than of internal agreement among themselves, although the second arrangement was the most common. The conservative forces acting to hold the tenements together even within a system of partible inheritance have already been discussed in the case of Gressenhall,[39] and these forces were of course also acting to minimize the effects of partible inheritance in Martham. Twenty-one of the 104 former tenements had less than four tenants in 1292, so that while the majority of the former tenements were unrecognizable by that date, this was by no means invariably the case. Twelve of

[39] Cf. also A.R.H. Baker, 'Some Fields and Farms in Medieval Kent', *Archaeologia Cantiana*, lxxx (1965), 62-3.

these twenty-one holdings were of 2 acres or less; division may
have been avoided when the resultant holdings would have
been uneconomic. On the other hand, the lack of subdivision
could also have been caused by the recurrence of single heirs in
successive generations, as happened for at least three generations on the Dekene holding.[40] A holding once divided might be
partially reconstructed after the death of one of the coheirs
without immediate heirs of his own.[41] A tenant without immediate heirs might also transfer land to one or more of his siblings before his death, often with the understanding that he
would continue to be supported throughout his life.[42]

By 1292, largely as a result of the common practice of dividing
each parcel of an inheritance evenly among the coheirs, land in
Martham was held by the priory's tenants in over 2,100 parcels
of an average size of just over 1½ roods. This physical breakup
of holdings as well as their division, often to sub-subsistence
level, undoubtedly contributed to the growth of a land market
among the prior's tenants in the village. The late-thirteenth-
century court rolls record a great many transfers between tenants. At five courts in 1290-1 there were 37 transfers, at five
courts in 1291-2 there were 34, and at four courts in 1299-1300
there were 21, excluding in each case leases from one tenant to
another.[43] Many of these were transfers to sons or brothers as
heirs, the donor explicitly retaining a life interest in the land or
at least being assured of support during his life.[44] Others were
gifts of small pieces of land to a daughter or sister for the term
of life, reverting after death to the male heir or heirs.[45] Others
too were gifts on the marriage of a daughter. However, transfers of land within a family account for less than 20 per cent of

[40] NRO DCN 4970, 7 Feb. 1291.

[41] e.g. when Matilda Litelgod took over her two brothers' land on their deaths
(NRO DCN 4970, 29 Jan. 1292).

[42] e.g. James Knight, who transferred his half share of his father's land to his
brother Matthew (NRO DCN 4970, 6 Nov. 1298).

[43] NRO DCN 4970, 4971.

[44] e.g. Cecilia Hil's gift of ½ a. to her son Robert in 1299; Cecilia then held the land
of Robert for the term of his life (NRO DCN 4971, 14 Oct. 1299). The ½ a. was
Cecilia's entire holding of the priory in 1292 (BL Stowe MS 936, fo. 104ᵛ).

[45] In the same court at which John and Nicholas Herbert paid a heriot to enter their
father's land, they gave the use of a *cotagium* 6 perches in length and 3 perches less 3
feet in width to Matilda and Cecilia Herbert and 20 perches of land to Alice Herbert
for the terms of their lives (NRO DCN 4970, 26 July 1291).

recorded transfers: among the total of 92 transfers in the three years, 18 were within an immediate family and the remaining 74 were sales or exchanges between two apparently unrelated villagers. The amounts of land involved were small: apart from two transfers of over 2 acres each to heirs and an exchange of 1½ acres, the land involved was never more than ½ acre and in most cases was expressed in perches. Indeed, one exchange was of only 15 feet square, and ten sales were of 10 perches or less.

Not enough court rolls survive from thirteenth-century Martham to allow many conclusions to be drawn about the regulation of the land market there. It can be assumed that the form of transfers between tenants (one tenant surrendering land into the lord's hands for the use of another) usually masks the sale of land. The fact that so many of the former eruingmen held socage land as well as villeinage land suggests that there was no ancient prohibition in Martham against villeins holding land in socage. Undoubtedly all socage land in Martham could be transferred freely, and it was only villeinage land that had to be transferred through the lord's court.

Clearly in Martham as in Gressenhall the workings of the land market must have contributed to the breakup of the standard holding. It would be interesting if the numerous small sales and exchanges of land in Martham could also be shown to have led to the rationalization of holdings, as tenants used the market to consolidate their lands or expand existing holdings into adjacent areas. As even the early-thirteenth-century tenements were not regularly distributed among the fields, the only possible sign of any trend towards consolidating holdings would be in the number of the 1292 holdings which were located in single fields. This number is not large; only twenty-one of the 240 tenants whose land was held in more than one parcel had all their pieces of land in a single field. Of these twenty-one tenants, only nine held more than 1 acre of land. The existence of holdings of less than 1 acre in one field can easily be attributed to chance, so it is only in holdings of more than an acre that any policy could be discerned. Two of these larger holdings were undivided holdings, where the former tenement lay mostly in one field. The other seven tenants, however, each held land from several former tenements but with all their pieces in the

same field. This at least suggests that convenience of cultivation was one reason for the exchanges of minute pieces of
land that are recorded in the court rolls.

The landholding pattern in Martham as described in the
1292 survey is a complex one, with single tenants having land
in a multiplicity of former holdings and therefore presumably
being responsible for a proportion of the rent and services due
from each; nevertheless, there are tenurial relationships that
are concealed in the survey. Leases of land between tenants,
for example, took place in Martham as in Gressenhall. The
court rolls reveal something of this activity. In the three years
for which they survive, seventeen leases of land were arranged,
the area involved varying from 1 rood to 1 acre and the term of
lease averaging about four years. During these three years four
tenants who held less than an acre can be seen renting out their
entire holdings.[46] There are also examples of tenants with small
holdings in the survey supplementing them with leased land.[47]
The amount of inter-tenant leasing that occurred in Martham
is liable to be underestimated for reasons already discussed: the
court rolls more often record the discovery of clandestine leasing
than the payment of fines in advance for licence. The extent of
illicit leasing as compared with sale or exchange is illustrated
by two courts of 1291, in which an unusually large number of
parcels of land were taken into the lord's hands for being sold,
leased, or exchanged without licence.[48] Of the twenty parcels of
land so sequestered, only three were seized for illicit sale, three
for illicit exchange, and the remaining fourteen for illicit leasing. Another tenurial relationship that may be concealed in the
survey is that of sub-tenancy among the priory's tenants, but the
only evidence for this is in a court-roll entry of 1291: Cecilia
Hare offered the lord 6*d.* so that she might hold her land not of
Robert Dekene but in chief of the prior.[49] She is in fact listed as
one of the priory's tenants in the survey.[50]

The form of the 1292 survey suggests that services and rents
were regarded as obligations on the tenement rather than on

[46] e.g. Robert Aleyn (½ a.) and Gunnilda Dekene (3 r.) (NRO DCN 4970, 19 July
1290 and 27 Nov. 1291).
[47] e.g. Richard Horn (NRO DCN 4971, 14 Oct. 1299).
[48] NRO DCN 4970, 26 July 1291, 6 Nov. 1291. These illicit transfers may have
been discovered in compiling the 1292 survey.
[49] NRO DCN 4970, 21 June 1291.   [50] BL Stowe MS 936, fo. 81ᵛ.

the tenant, and the increase in the number of tenants with shares in each tenement which apparently took place in the thirteenth century must have necessitated some communal organization of services. There are few indications in the survey and none in the surviving court rolls as to how services were divided among the many 1292 tenants of a former single tenement. It is possible that, unlike the Foliots in Gressenhall, the priory was concerned only with the collection of total rents and services and that the tenants arranged among themselves how payment was ensured. The very silence of the records supports this view, as does the maintenance of the former tenements as administrative units. After describing Thomas Knight's former tenement, the survey reads 'and all these tenants render services for the full eruing as Thomas Knight did in his time', and it makes similar statements in the entries of the former tenements of Roger de Hil and Yware son of Geoffrey.[51] This implies that there was no formal arrangement recognized by the priory for apportioning the responsibilities among individual tenants. On the other hand, one reference in the survey suggests that in Martham, as in Gressenhall, one tenant would be responsible for organizing the services due from an entire former tenement: the five tenants of 2 acres called Stocklondgore are said to owe services 'as the tenants of Robert Blakyng for the land of Gunild Frone',[52] implying that one of the two Robert Blakings with shares in the Frone tenement acted in some way as the primary tenant of the holding. It is unlikely that the other occupants of the holding were literally Robert's tenants, because in this case it would be difficult to see why the survey mentioned them at all. This is the only reference which gives any hint of the lord's view of the many tenants of a former holding. It is probably on this basis that the priory received both rents in kind and services from its tenants in Martham in the late thirteenth century.[53] One tenant of each former tenement was responsible for them, so that the arrangements resembled those at Gressenhall, even if they were made among the tenants themselves and not by the lord of the manor.

Another problem likely to arise from the changes in thirteenth-

[51] Ibid., fos. 39ᵛ, 40ᵛ, 55ʳ.
[52] Ibid., fo. 112ʳ.
[53] NRO DCN 5208.

century Martham was in the arrangements for cultivation, the problem of how sowing and reaping were organized among so many tenants with tiny pieces of land often widely dispersed among the village fields. On the priory demesne at Martham there was no regular fallowing in the thirteenth century, and yields were among the highest recorded from English demesnes of the period.[54] Cultivation need not have followed the same pattern on the tenant lands as on the demesne, but if it did this would have lowered the minimum area of arable needed for a family's subsistence in Martham from the 10 acres postulated for villages with a three-field system[55] down to some 6 or 7 acres; this would help explain the plethora of apparently sub-subsistence holdings in the late thirteenth century. One cannot imagine that a practical farming community, even in a period of acute land shortage, would have rigidly applied partible inheritance to the point at which the majority of holdings were uneconomic. If throughout the Martham fields there was no fallow course this would enormously assist the cultivation of minutely fragmented holdings; the need for arrangements to enable the fallow to be used for grazing would have been eliminated.

It must be emphasized that at Martham as at Gressenhall a tenant's resources—even his arable resources—were not restricted to the land he held of the one manor. At the end of a court roll of 1291 is a list of Martham tenants fined at the leet of Bartholomew of Fleg at Somerton; among them are Geoffrey Gele, William Blakeman, and Richard Anger, all of whom held land of the priory in Martham.[56] At least three of the priory's tenants with small holdings in 1292—Robert de Martham (1 acre 1 rood 22 perches), John de Camera (1½ roods), and Geoffrey Brunstan (1 acre 1 rood)—were probably freemen with substantial holdings in Martham outside the priory's manor. The 1292 survey names all three as holding lands adjoining the priory tenants' parcels more often than the size of their holdings of the priory would warrant, and all three appear as

---

[54] Campbell, 'Field Systems in E. Norf.', pp. 86-7.

[55] Titow, *Eng. Rural Soc.*, p. 89.

[56] NRO DCN 4970, 'Leta Bartholomei de Fleg apud Somerton'. There is no explanation why the list is given, since it seems to include other people beside the priory tenants.

witnesses of charters involving land in Martham.[57] Even tenants without additional arable holdings probably had many of the same alternative sources of income as the Gressenhall tenants, though as so few court rolls survive from Martham this can only be conjecture. The absence of large tenant holdings would mean very little opportunity for employment there, but the demesne certainly made use of hired labour.[58] There was unquestionably livestock at Martham, and the marsh provided abundance of grazing, which will have made up for any lack of grazing on fallow. There were no foldage requirements outlined in the 1292 survey, although the priory received 4*s*. 0*d*. 'from grazing rights let' (*de faldagio dimisso*) in 1262.[59] Holdings on the priory manor of Martham were small, but the smaller the arable holding the more significant are those aspects of peasant economy which seldom emerge in the manorial records.

Conclusion

The most striking difference between the early-thirteenth-century tenants and those of 1292 is the increase in the number of tenants and the corresponding decrease in the average size of holding. The parcels of land comprising individual holdings were also of smaller average size in 1292 (1 ½ roods per parcel), largely through the physical division of parcels of land following inheritance by coheirs. The distinction between villeinage land and socage land is not consistently maintained in the survey, although the status of land was important in determining whether its transfer took place through the manorial court. It is impossible by 1292 to divide the tenants into eruingmen and sokemen, and the only meaningful division is between those with small holdings that lay in only a few of the former tenements and those with large holdings that extended into many tenements; the latter were probably the result of systematic acquisition by marriage or purchase.

How far did the apparent changes in the landholding pattern between 1200 and 1292 reflect real changes in the organization

---

[57] NRO DCN Register I, fos. 219-21.

[58] In 1262 the priory paid 2*s*. 10½*d*. for labour for three weeks and two days from 8 Sept. and 38*s*. 6*d*. for labour from 29 Sept. to 1 Aug. following (NRO DCN 4941).

[59] NRO DCN 4941.

and administration of the tenements? This question hinges on the exact position of the former tenants: whether they were in fact single tenants or simply the nominal or legal heads of extended-family holdings. The way the descent of the holdings to the 1292 tenants can be reconstructed suggests that the early-thirteenth-century tenants were single tenants from whom all the 1292 tenants descended. In only one case can this be formally demonstrated: the former holding of Thomas de Syk. Bartholomew of Caister gave the priory, along with other lands and tenants, the services and 18*d.* annual rent of the heir of Thomas de Syk.[60] These were due from a free holding of 2½ acres, held in 1292 in five equal shares of ½ acre each. There is no doubt that this was the same Thomas de Syk who appears in the survey as the early-thirteenth-century tenant of a 22½-acre socage holding, since the same 1292 tenants are entered for his socage land as for his free holding, and each tenant has almost the same proportion of both. In one sense at least, Thomas de Syk was considered the single tenant of his 22½-acre former holding, from whom the 1292 tenants derived their hereditary rights in the land. Nevertheless, to see them all as his immediate heirs may be to over-simplify their relationship to him. It is difficult to believe that the 104 named tenants represent the entire tenantry of the early-thirteenth-century village—only a 35 per cent increase in tenant population since the time of the Domesday survey. It is far more likely that these tenants were the responsible heads of collective family holdings, who for all practical administrative purposes were single tenants. The very form of the 1292 survey demonstrates the strength of administrative pressure in Martham for the maintenance of both villeinage and socage tenements intact, a pressure that was clearly more systematically applied by Norwich Cathedral Priory in Martham than by the Foliots in Gressenhall. The unusually detailed enumeration of tenants and their lands in 1292 may reflect a change of administrative policy in recognizing and accepting the physical division of tenements on the entry of coheirs, but the form of the survey is uncompromising in recording the division of land without implying any division of its rents or services. Indeed, the few specific references to the performance

---

[60] NRO DCN Register I, fo. 220ᵛ.

of services—that they were done by 'all together' or, in the case of the Blakings, by all under the administrative leadership of one—suggest that the priory was not concerned with the private arrangements made by tenants for dividing the services among themselves. On the other hand, this apparent disregard for the practical difficulties of getting services due from a fragmented tenement may be simply a result of the form of survey; without contemporary court rolls to complete the picture one cannot judge how far the administrative theory approached reality.

One reason for maintaining the tenemental structure against pressure from hereditary and economic forces must have been to facilitate the efficient collection of services, but there is no obvious explanation why this should have operated at Martham and not at Gressenhall. The proportion of demesne to tenant arable was not significantly higher in Martham; in fact, comparison with the 1282 extent for Gressenhall shows the same proportion of arable (about 20 per cent) in demesne in both villages, although the Martham demesne may have been more intensively cultivated. A possible reason for the administrative conservatism in Martham is the higher proportion of tenements owing customary services (other than boon-works). At Gressenhall the tenements most subject to administrative pressure were the 24-acre standard villein holdings and the holdings of the mondaymen, which owed various customary services. It may be that with a larger proportion of tenant land owing services, there was a stronger incentive at Martham than at Gressenhall to resist the fragmentation of tenements.

The strength of the opposite pressure in thirteenth-century Martham, particularly from partible inheritance, is obvious in the 1292 survey. What is not clear is whether customary division of holdings had been a feature of land tenure in Martham from the time of the Domesday survey or whether, as at Gressenhall, it was a new development in the thirteenth century. On the whole, the former seems the more likely. Population was already high at Martham in 1086, as in most villages in the Flegg hundreds, and the amount of marsh, as well as the area's general density of settlement, points to fewer opportunities for assart than there were at Gressenhall. Some such opportunities there certainly were, probably producing the small tofts, but there was certainly no significant expansion of arable after the early thirteenth century. The 12-acre standard holding in Martham was not large, even for an area of unusually high fertility,[61] and the predominance of half- and quarter-eruing holdings in the early thirteenth century suggests that some division of holdings (possibly accompanied by redistribution of land) had already taken place, thereby temporarily relieving pressure for division. All this suggests that the 1292 survey's list of 104 former tenants was an administrative simplification of the actual position in the village; division of holdings among coheirs was probably not a thirteenth-century innovation in Martham, although the priory's recognition of it may have been.

The few surviving court rolls show the land market in Martham performing much the same functions as in Gressenhall. It made possible some rationalization of holdings after physical partition had taken place. The court rolls of 1290-2 record ten exchanges of land, varying in size from 15 feet square to 1½ acres;[62] mutual convenience of cultivation must have been the reason for at least some of them. The land market also provided for the disposal of sub-subsistence holdings and, at the other end of the scale, for the acquisition of land by those who wished to expand their holdings. Finally, it provided a means of modifying the customary descent of land.

Particularly in a village such as Martham, where many holdings in 1292 must have been just at or below subsistence level, the primary function of the land market was to enable holdings to be adjusted to the physical requirements of subsistence. In Martham, as in Gressenhall, the land market broke down tenements by facilitating the transfer of land out of a family holding, but it also served to maintain average holding size nearer subsistence level. Again as in Gressenhall, we see a close relationship between partible inheritance and the land market: among the tenants of 1292 many tenants who are apparently newcomers clearly have their land through the sale of an inherited share or through marriage.

Assuming that at one time the former tenements had been

[61] The priory's demesne land at Martham and in the neighbouring village of Hemsby was consistently given the highest valuation—3s. per acre—of all the priory's demesne lands in the calculation of manorial profits (Saunders, *Norwich Rolls*, p. 56).
[62] NRO DCN 4970.

single-tenant holdings, even if not in the early thirteenth century, population increase in Martham is clear from the decrease in average holding size from 8 to just over 2 acres.[63] If fallowing could be eliminated on the tenant lands, as it seems to have been on the priory's demesne at Martham, the productivity of the available land could be increased and the size of subsistence holdings reduced.[64] In default of opportunities for increasing the arable by assart in the thirteenth century, continued population increase in Martham seems to have produced division of holdings, even below subsistence level, and then to have encouraged redistribution through the land market. It was only the demands of administration that prevented the ancient standard holdings from being all but lost to memory.

4 SEDGEFORD

The manors

Sedgeford is a village in north-west Norfolk, 12 miles north-east of King's Lynn. The village is in Smithdon hundred within the area termed the Good Sand region by Arthur Young.[1] This region lies between 150 and 300 feet above sea level, and the soil is a light loam with a subsoil principally chalk. Although Young called the area the Good Sand region in contrast to the more sandy and infertile Breckland to the south, the region became 'good' only with the introduction of eighteenth-century agricultural improvements such as marling or claying and the cultivation of root crops. In the thirteenth century the soil was naturally infertile and required sheep and their dung to make arable cultivation productive. Thus the landscape of the region was dominated by great stretches of heaths and sheep-walks.

Part of what is now Sedgeford had a separate identity in the

---

[63] This is illustrated by a comparison of 13th-century conditions in Martham with those in the late 14th and early 15th centuries when, although partible inheritance was still practised, there was little fragmentation of holdings (Campbell, 'Field Systems in E. Norf.', pp. 119-23).

[64] Ibid., p. 86

[1] The geographical information on Sedgeford is taken from Darby, *Dom. Geog. E. Eng.*, pp. 150-1; M. Postgate in Baker & Butlin, p. 282; and Allison in *AgHR*, v (1957), 12-14.

eleventh century: Gnatingdon or Nettington was held by Godwin Haldein, one of few Englishmen to retain his independence after the Conquest.[2] It was a small holding, assessed at 1 carucate, with two bordars and a sokeman who held only 1 acre. In 1086 the bishop of Thetford held most of the land in Sedgeford and received the commendation of the eight freemen who held the remaining land.[3] Within the next 200 years, however, the number of independent landholders in the village multiplied. In the late thirteenth century, Norwich Cathedral Priory and the Sedgeford family were the major landholders there; the priory probably held at least three-quarters of the land of the village, with most of the Breydeston half-fee in the hands of the priory by the middle of the century.[4] The Hackford family possibly held some land in Sedgeford as part of their manor of Fring, apart from what they held of the priory, and the only other independent landholder of any importance was the Ingoldisthorpe family, of whom we hear nothing before the end of the century.[5]

In the thirteenth century, and for at least the next 300 years, the priory holding in Sedgeford was divided between Easthall (the Gnatingdon of Domesday Book) and Westhall. Although the priory thus had two manors in Sedgeford and two sets of manorial officials it held only one court;[6] separate courts would have been impractical because the tenants of the two manors were largely identical. In a 1282 survey almost every tenant owes rent to both Easthall and Westhall, and the lands of each are not distinguished but given as a single total area. It is certain, however, that Easthall and Westhall were kept distinct in fact as well as in name. The practice of electing two sets of officials continued at least to the end of the fourteenth century,[7] and the rents due to the two halls were collected and accounted for separately: a 1282 rental, when compared with the 1282 survey, is clearly a rental of Westhall alone.[8] Westhall was

---

[2] *VCH Norf.*, ii. 194.

[3] Ibid., ii. 116.

[4] NRO DCN 4242.

[5] NRO DCN Register V, fo. 137ᵛ; Register I, fos. 117-18.

[6] Apart from the election of officials, the only reference to either Easthall or Westhall in the surviving court rolls is in the record of a view of frankpledge held at Easthall on 17 June 1259 (NRO DCN 5282).

[7] NRO DCN 5293.   [8] NRO DCN 4438.

always the principal manor of Sedgeford, the hall itself being close to the church in what was (and is still) the most populous part of the village.

The tenants and their holdings

Any analysis of peasant holdings in a manor must clearly begin with the number of tenants and the sizes of their holdings. But in Sedgeford even this information is not easy to obtain. The earliest list of the priory tenants and their holdings which is unquestionably complete dates from the early fifteenth century.[9] For a working list of the priory tenants in Sedgeford towards the end of the thirteenth century one must rely on two surveys and one rental which are nearly contemporary and which, although none of them is certainly complete, can be used to complement one another. These three sources are a survey of about 1279 of the 'tenements of Easthall and of Walter son of Roger' (possibly incomplete),[10] a rental of about 1282 of Westhall (probably incomplete),[11] and a survey also of about 1282 of Easthall and Westhall (certainly incomplete.)[12] Clearly, a list obtained by comparing these three sources can hardly be considered definitive, but it can provide a useful starting-point. The main problem in the comparison is identifying names. Only twenty-one tenants unquestionably appear in all three sources, but the sources closely correspond in what is said about these tenants, showing that the sources are substantially accurate and that the information missing from one can be tentatively taken from another. Allowing for cases where the same person clearly appears on more than one of the documents, the three together list 231 different names. While this cannot be taken as the exact number of tenants, given the likelihood of omissions and of tenants being known by more than one surname, it does at least make it likely that around 1280 the priory's tenants in Sedgeford numbered between 200 and 250.

[9] NRO DCN 4437.

[10] NRO DCN 4241. The survey does not seem to include any Westhall land.

[11] NRO DCN 4438. There is no total of rents, and names continue to the bottom of both sides of the membrane, suggesting that an additional membrane has been lost.

[12] BL Add. MS 57975. This Sedgeford portion was separated from the rest of the surveys in BL Stowe MS 936 (above, p. 63), and it is clear that some folios are missing.

Unfortunately, even when we know the tenants' names we do not always know the size of their holdings. Thirty-eight names appear only in the Westhall rental, which tells us nothing of the amount of land they held. For the remaining 193 tenants, either the 1279 or the 1282 survey gives the sizes of their holdings; in all they held about 1,925 acres,[13] making the average holding just about 10 acres. It is important to remember that the land in the area was not particularly fertile in the thirteenth century—the manorial accounts consistently give the Sedgeford and Gnatingdon demesne land the lowest valuation of any on the priory's estates[14]—so that the size of a subsistence holding must have been significantly larger than in the more fertile areas of Gressenhall or Martham. The smallest holdings found in either survey are the cottages without arable held by Beatrix Escelyn and John Hert, and the largest the 54 acres of Walter Hulyn. Small holdings predominated but, unlike Gressenhall and Martham, holdings of over 25 acres were not unusual. Fifty holdings, or just over a quarter of those listed, contained less than 3 acres of arable, but sixty-five holdings, just over a third, were over 10 acres; seventy-eight tenants held between 3 and 10 acres.

Most of what we know about the personal or tenurial status of the priory tenants in Sedgeford has to be discovered from the surveys by inference. None of them mentions free tenants. In the 1279 survey the tenants with their holdings are introduced as villeins (*villani*). In the 1282 survey the only information on status is that three otherwise undistinguished tenants hold their land in villeinage;[15] it is difficult to believe that we are told this

---

[13] 1,925 a. is a maximum figure: some holdings, with tenants who cannot be positively identified as the same in the 1279 and 1282 surveys, have almost certainly been counted twice. Two later hands have independently totalled the tenant land in the 1282 survey as 1,605 a. 6½ p. and 1,509 a. 2 r. 36 p.; given the missing folios it is impossible to check which, if either, is right. Neither total would include the land of the Breydeston fee, approximately 350 a.

[14] Although by the end of the century the valuations may have been more traditional than realistic, the low valuation of Sedgeford and Gnatingdon (8*d.* per acre in contrast to Martham's 3*s.* 0*d.*) must reflect a much lower anticipated yield (Saunders, *Norwich Rolls*, p. 56, and E. Stone, 'Profit and Loss Accountancy at Norwich Cathedral Priory', *TRHS*, 5th ser., xii (1962), 34-5).

[15] In fact, two tenants are said to hold land in villeinage—William atte Howe (one messuage with 14 a. 3½ r.) and Robert la Ducke (4 a. 1 r.)— and the third, Geoffrey son of Walter Palmer, is said to hold 5 a. *in landsetagio* (NRO DCN 4241, fos. 3ʳ, 17ᵛ, 12ᵛ).

because such tenure was unusual, nor can it have been to distinguish villeinage land from soke or free land of the same
tenant, since in two cases the villeinage land was the entire
holding. That there were free tenants of the priory's manor of
Sedgeford is in fact certain. In 1265 William Cornel and his
brother Henry gave ½ mark in the manorial court for an
inquiry whether they were of villein or free status.[16] Unfortunately, the result of the inquiry does not appear in the surviving
rolls, but both William and Henry are more than once mentioned as tenants of free land.[17] In 1281 Gilbert Caly son of
Roger Caly 'became [*devenit*] a free man of the priory' as tenant
of the whole tenement which John son of Robert Caly had held
freely.[18] Of the 114 tenants listed in the Westhall rental, ten
pay from ½ *d.* to 5*d.* annually for suit to the hundred court. As
this was an obligation of free tenants,[19] we may suppose that
these ten were free; one of them, John Palmer, is mentioned as
a free man in a court-roll entry of 1278.[20] Ten seems a small
number of identifiable free tenants on the priory's Sedgeford
manors. However, few of the tenants appear as charter witnesses, and those who do are all among those who owed suit to
the hundred court or who are mentioned as free in the court
rolls.

A later thirteenth-century document naming those of the
priory's villeins in Sedgeford who had acquired free land confirms that most of the prominent families who appear in the
surviving Sedgeford records were in fact villein.[21] In naming
those from whom the villeins had acquired land, this document, together with the charters, also reveals a class of free
landholders in Sedgeford who did not hold land of the priory
manor. Some of the free land acquired by the priory's villeins
came from five men who can be identified as free tenants of the
priory manors; Richard Palmer, father of the John Palmer
already mentioned, granted (*dimisit*) a total of 6 acres 3 roods to
six villeins. But the list names a further eighteen apparently

[16] NRO DCN 5282, 16 Apr. 1265.

[17] William is one of the Sedgeford tenants who let free land to the priory's villeins
(NRO DCN 5274), and both William and Henry each gave 1 r. of land by charter to
the prior and convent (NRO DCN Register I, fos. 115ʳ, 116ᵛ).

[18] NRO DCN 5284, 21 Oct. 1281.　　　　[20] NRO DCN 5284, 9 Mar. 1278.

[19] Pollock & Maitland, i. 530.　　　　[21] NRO DCN 5274.

independent landholders who granted considerable amounts of land to the priory's villeins, suggesting that their own holdings were probably large: Ralph son of Alan of Thorpe granted almost 29 acres, George of Birlingham 27 acres, Roger son of Ralph Mareschal 11 acres, and Albin of Stanford almost 10 acres. All these four appear as witnesses to charters involving land in Sedgeford,[22] and one of them, Roger Mareschal, is described as 'of Sedgeford'.[23] Albin of Stanford was for a time the priory's steward in Sedgeford.[24] Many of the eighteen landholders also appear in charters as grantors or recipients of land in Sedgeford, sometimes in considerable amounts—as Albin of Stanford, who in five charters acquired a total of 27½ acres of land and the homage and service of one man.[25] These are examples of the free landholders, intermediate between the major manorial lords and their tenants, who were undoubtedly common in medieval Norfolk but about whom little evidence survives. In most cases we do not know whether they were free tenants of manorial lords or themselves tenants-in-chief. Such tenants may have been closely associated with both manorial lords and their tenants, as these apparently were, but unless they owed suit to the manorial court any record of their activity depends on the evidence of charters.[26]

It seems likely, then, that almost all of the priory's tenants in Sedgeford were villeins, with a small number of free tenants who can be recognized by their suit to the hundred court of Smithdon. As at Gressenhall and Martham, even if most of the tenants were villeins it by no means followed that all their land

[22] George of Birlingham: NRO DCN 420, 501, 1129, Register I, fo. 113[v]. Albin of Stanford: NRO DCN 1, 477, Register I, fos. 112[v], 113[r,v], 126[r]. Alan of Thorpe: NRO DCN Register VII, fo. 61[v]. Roger Mareschal: NRO DCN 329, 429, Register I, fo. 124[v]. Walter Pavely, who granted only 5 r. to a villein, is also a frequent witness: NRO DCN 1, 393, 423, 441, 510, 3295, and others.

[23] NRO DCN Register I, fo. 123[r].

[24] NRO DCN 5284, 24 Sept. 1277.

[25] NRO DCN 349, 415, 510, 1124, 3293. Richard son of Albin of Stanford gave the priory a total of 89 a. in Sedgeford (NRO DCN 392, Register I, fos. 119[v]-120[r]). Other examples of these independent landholders granting or selling land in Sedgeford are Roger Mirigong (NRO DCN Register I, fos. 122[v]-123[r]) and Geoffrey Bolle (NRO DCN 510).

[26] 'It follows from the nature of the extant material that the freeholder of small estate is most clearly revealed to us through his power of disposing of his land by charter' (F.M. Stenton in *Danelaw Ch.*, pp. cix-cx).

was held in villeinage. Most of the priory's villeins in Sedgeford had land held for money rent as well as land held for services, and that some at least of the former was free land is proved
by the late-thirteenth-century list of free lands acquired by villeins. The purpose of this list was to set out the 'new increments' of rent, varying from ¼*d.* to 5*d.* according to the
amount of land, imposed by the priory on 'free land acquired
by villeins of Sedgeford'. Forty-three villeins are listed, along
with the amount of land acquired and its source; at the end of
each entry is the new increment of rent and the sum paid to the
priory for the release of the land, which had been taken into the
lord's hands. Free land, even when held by villeins, could be
freely transferred by charter without licence from the lord. The
priory was clearly not concerned with regulating the transfer of
free land; it was a question of discovering what free land the
villeins held so that additional rent could be charged for it.[27]

None of the ten tenants who owed suit to the hundred court
held any land for services other than boon works; that is, none
of them seems to have held any villeinage land. Isolated entries
in the surviving court rolls suggest that, although there was no
prohibition against villeins holding free land, free men were
not permitted to hold the priory's villeinage land at Sedgeford.
Thus in 1278 John Palmer gave the priory ½ mark to enter a
messuage with 4 acres and 3 roods that had belonged to his
nephew Peter Fish 'and because the said John is a free man he
gives the land to Olive his daughter who will hold it and who
will be a villein of the lord'.[28] This makes it all the more likely
that the ten tenants who owed suit to the hundred court were in
fact the only free men listed on the surveys.

Thus far, villeinage land has been discussed without any
mention of standard villein holdings. Unlike the Gressenhall
and Martham surveys, none of the surviving Sedgeford surveys
explicitly refers to any sort of full holding or standard villein
services. Analysis of the size of villeinage holdings in 1282 only
suggests that there may once have been a standard duodeci-
mally based holding of either 12 or possibly 24 acres. Nevertheless, the concept of a villein tenement as opposed to villein land

[27] NRO DCN 5284, 24 Sept. 1277. Cf. *Cart. Nat.*, pp. xlvi-xlviii.
[28] NRO DCN 5284, 9 Mar. 1278. Similar transfers are in NRO DCN 5281,
12 Mar. 1263; DCN 5284, 22 Oct. 1285.

was certainly maintained in Sedgeford at the end of the thirteenth century; we see this in a court-roll entry of 1277, which stated that a holding that had belonged to one Alan Turpin had been transferred, at some date in the past, 'because the lord would not permit Alan to hold at the same time two villeinage tenements'.[29] Certainly of the eighty tenants with villeinage land listed in the 1282 survey, only seven had more than one parcel of land from which services were due, and in three of these seven cases the second holding was held jointly by the tenant and his wife. The concept of the single villeinage holding—often as small as 1 acre or less—is the more striking when one considers the large amount of free land many of these villeins, such as Alan Turpin himself, had managed to acquire. Finally, even if the 1282 survey does not point with certainty to a standard size of villeinage holdings, it reveals a set of services that were clearly standard. Almost every villeinage holding rendered the whole or an even proportion (a half, a quarter, or in one case an eighth) of a set of services which included commuted winter works, hens and eggs, harvest work, carrying services, and Monday works.[30] The size of the holdings from which these services were due supports a theory of a 12-acre standard holding. Of the ten tenants whose villeinage holdings owed the full set of services, only one held 12 acres, but six more held between 11 and 13 acres.[31]

Both free and villeinage land in Sedgeford theoretically descended impartibly to a single son or next closest male relative; failing male heirs, land was divided among female heirs of the same degree. In the surviving court rolls the land of a deceased tenant is never taken up by more than one male heir, although in several cases it can be shown that the heir had brothers who were engaged in independent land transactions.[32] Nowhere in extant court rolls is there a case where land is judged to be partible by custom, although in several cases a plaintiff

---

[29] NRO DCN 5284, 24 Sept. 1277.

[30] The actual services were 4*d*. for commuted winter works, one hen and one loaf at Christmas, ten eggs and a loaf at Easter, one man to work through the harvest, the carriage of three hurdles and three woolfells, and eight Monday works.

[31] The remaining three held 1 a. 3 r., 2½ a., and 22½ a. respectively.

[32] For example, Adam Ruheued inherited the land of his father in 1281 (NRO DCN 5284, 16 Dec. 1281); his brother William was buying land as late at 1288 (ibid., 11 May 1288).

made that claim. In the one instance when, in 1279, a father's land was divided between his two sons, the division was made by the 'special grace' of the prior and on the specific understanding that it would not create a precedent;[33] we do not know why the prior agreed to division on this one occasion, but he was clearly anxious it should never occur again.

As it is so difficult to reconstruct standard holdings in Sedgeford from late-thirteenth-century records, impartible inheritance obviously did not mean that tenements were invariably inherited intact, remaining unchanged as they passed from generation to generation. As at Gressenhall and Martham, the inheritance custom applied only to the land of which a tenant died seised, placing little restriction upon what he did with his land during his lifetime. Thus, in Sedgeford the land that the tenant had when he died went impartibly to a single heir, but he might permanently alienate either free land or villeinage land from his holding before his death. The land market in the village made it possible for those with the necessary capital resources to acquire land, and the distinction between a tenant's patrimony and his other acquisitions seems to have been carefully maintained in the thirteenth century. In 1279, when Ralph son of Geoffrey Alan took over land that had belonged to his uncle Ralph Raven, he entered 14½ acres of patrimony, 12¾ acres of other land held of the priory, and 5½ acres of the fee of Breydeston.[34] The 1282 survey clearly distinguishes inherited land from other acquisitions, occasionally explicitly[35] but in most cases simply by listing the inherited land first.

Tenants can often be seen transferring land during their lives to their non-inheriting sons, and there is some evidence that this might include land they had themselves inherited. One of the most straightforward examples of a father providing for a number of his sons is Robert son of Matilda. In 1282 he surrendered into the lord's hands 9 acres: 3 acres for the use of each of

---

[33] NRO DCN 5284, 5 Aug. 1279. A messuage and 36 a. belonging to Godfrey Hervey was the land involved. The whole of the land had been taken over by Richard Hervey in 1273 and now was divided between him and his brother Roger (ibid., 6 Dec. 1273).

[34] Ibid., 6 Oct. 1279.

[35] e.g. Elyas Bustard, who held a messuage and 16 a. 'de hereditate suo' plus 3 a. 10 p., or Thomas Tulte, who held a messuage and 3 a. 'de hereditate suo' plus 10 a. 1 r.

three sons, Ralph, William, and Thomas. Three months later a fourth son, Walter, took over the messuage and 21 acres of which his father had died seised.[36] Both Walter's inheritance of his father's land and the transfers to Ralph, William, and Thomas appear in the 1282 survey. This shows that Thomas's 3 acres had been acquired by Robert from Ralph atte Howe and Geoffrey of Norwich, and that William's 3 acres came from his father's holding in the Breydeston fee; Ralph's 3 acres, on the other hand, were specifically described as villeinage land when they were inherited by his son Walter in 1285.[37] Given the prohibition against a tenant holding two villeinage tenements, it is unlikely that Robert, with his own 12 acres of villeinage land, could have acquired additional villeinage land to give to his son Ralph; it seems most likely that he gave Ralph 3 acres of land from his hereditary villeinage holding. Likewise the 7½ acres that Geoffrey of Norwich gave his three sons probably also included part of his inherited holding: the 4*d.* due from one son for winter works and the eight Monday works owed by another complement the services due from Geoffrey himself in the 1282 survey to make up the standard set of services that have been associated with an original 12-acre holding.[38] It seems, then, as if inherited villeinage tenements as well as other lands could be permanently alienated during the lifetime of the tenant. Daughters as well as non-inheriting sons might be provided with gifts of land during the parent's lifetime;[39] widows of course kept their dower land, and land was usually transferred with a daughter in marriage. Nor was it only the parents who provided for those who would not inherit lands; there are many cases in the court rolls of tenants transferring land to brothers or sisters, though often only for the recipient's lifetime.[40] In all, the economic position of non-inheriting sons or daughters in Sedgeford was not as

[36] NRO DCN 5284, 21 Nov. 1282, 8 Feb. 1283.

[37] Ibid., 22 Jan. 1285.

[38] Ibid., 14 Feb. 1284.

[39] e.g. Muriel Colin, who gave an acre of land to each of two daughters in 1264 (NRO DCN 5282, 25 June 1264). Her son took over the remainder of her land ten years later (NRO DCN 5284, 1 June 1274).

[40] e.g. Robert Caly, who gave 5 a. to each of two brothers (NRO DCN 5284, 16 Dec. 1281). He had two other brothers: Richard bought land and was given 1½ a. by Robert (ibid.), and Gilbert took over a free tenement of 5 a. formerly held by his uncle (ibid., 21 Oct. 1281).

difficult as one might expect under a system of impartible inheritance.

The surviving court rolls from Sedgeford thus reveal the priory's tenants participating in a land market which enabled them to provide for their non-inheriting offspring. Although some of the land bought, sold, or exchanged was undoubtedly villeinage land, most of it seems to have been free land held by villeins; we would expect the court rolls to give us a far from complete record of the transfer of such free land, for it has already been shown that free land in Sedgeford, even when held by villeins, could be freely transferred by charter without licence from the lord. On the other hand, getting licence and thereby recording a transfer in the priory's court roll may well have been a less expensive and more convenient procedure than transfer by charter. The thirteenth-century Sedgeford rolls show an average of over twenty-two transactions a year involving the sale, purchase, exchange, or grant of parcels of land that seldom exceeded 2 acres, but there is no way of knowing what proportion of the total land market this represents.

One would like to know which tenants were most prominent in this land market, as this might throw light on its stimulus and effects. An analysis of the transactions in the court rolls reveals that very few of those involved both bought and sold land, while the number of exchanges averages less than one per year. It seems, therefore, that what lay behind the land market was not the consolidation or improvement of holdings but rather the desire for additional land. The motives of those who acquired it were, as one might expect, varied. In a few cases, fathers can be seen specifically buying land for their sons, or at least transferring land recently acquired to them.[41] There are also cases of non-inheriting sons acquiring land apparently independently of their fathers.[42] Geoffrey and Nicholas, sons of Walter Hulyn, are an example of two non-inheriting brothers acting together; they bought a total of 4½ acres in two transactions in 1278-9 and in each case it was stated that the land

---

[41] e.g. the 6½ a. given by Martin Suvel to his two sons (NRO DCN 5284, 8 Feb. 1285; cf. Williamson, 'Norf. Peasant Holdings', p. 249), or the 1 a. 3 r. bought by John Ruheued (NRO DCN 5284, 23 Oct. 1283).

[42] e.g. Gilbert Neuman, who gradually acquired 12 a. over the 24 years 1260-84 (NRO DCN 5281-6 *passim*).

would remain with the survivor when either of the brothers died, whether with or without other heirs.[43] However, if many of those buying land in Sedgeford simply wished to bring their holdings up to subsistence level, there were certainly many others who acquired land to expand their already substantial holdings. Martin Suvel, besides providing for his sons, managed to build up his own 3-acre patrimony to a holding of over 35 acres by 1282.[44] William in the Pit took over a messuage and 11 acres of his father's land in 1264; by 1282 he held two messuages and almost 25 acres.[45] In 1279 Alan Turpin, who had inherited a holding from his father, held of the priory a messuage and 32 acres, of which he had acquired at least 20½ acres between 1259 and 1276.[46] Such tenants used the land market in Sedgeford to expand their own holdings considerably while also acquiring land to provide for their sons.

The vendors of land in Sedgeford stand out less clearly than the purchasers. Many tenants appear once in a court-roll entry selling land and then disappear from all records; many of these must have been non-inheriting sons who had decided to dispose of a small paternal grant instead of using the land market to increase it. This probably accounted for a large proportion of the land fed into the market. There are examples, however, of entire holdings being sold off piecemeal, possibly for want of an heir. Between 1259 and her death in 1276 Beatrix Stute gradually sold her entire patrimonial holding of a messuage and over 13 acres of villeinage land; she clearly had no heirs, for the last piece of the holding—1½ roods—was sold from the lord's hands in 1276.[47] Similarly, Nicholas Buterman sold his 11½-acre villeinage holding in twelve transactions over a period of nine years.[48] It is harder to explain the activities of Ralph Leche, who between 1273 and 1285 sold 11 acres of land; he was not without heirs, as at least 1 acre was sold with the consent of his son Walter.[49] In no case is poverty or necessity ever mentioned as the reason for selling land. Probably the

---

[43] NRO DCN 5284, 9 Mar. 1278, 5 Aug. 1279.

[44] Williamson, 'Norf. Peasant Holdings', p. 399.

[45] NRO DCN 5282, 21 June 1265. Of the land William acquired 2 a. 3½ r. was free (DCN 5274); the purchase of 7 a. 2½ r. can be traced in four transactions in the court rolls of 1273-8.

[46] NRO DCN 5282-3 *passim.*

[47] NRO DCN 5281-6 *passim.*

[48] 1275-84. Ibid., *passim.*

[49] NRO DCN 5284, 23 Apr. 1285.

motives for selling land were as varied as the motives for buying.

We have already seen that the division and transfer of villeinage land in Sedgeford was usually accompanied by the division of the services due. Thus, Geoffrey Kelman took over the eight Monday works of the family tenement when he entered 2 acres of land alienated from it.[50] The permanent division of standard services is occasionally revealed in the 1282 survey, when the services due from consecutive holdings are clearly the result of such division. The services due from the holdings of Alan Skeppe and Geoffrey Elverith, for example, add up to the standard set, Alan owing one third (1*d.* for winter works, one-third of a hen and one-third of a loaf at Christmas, three eggs at Easter, one man working through one-third of the harvest, and the carriage of one hurdle and one woolfell) and Geoffrey two-thirds (3*d.* for winter works, two-thirds of a hen and two-thirds of a loaf at Christmas, seven eggs at Easter, one man to work through two-thirds of the harvest, the carriage of two hurdles and two woolfells). Cases such as this suggest, incidentally, that hens, eggs, and loaves were no longer rendered in kind. Perhaps the best example of the division of services comes from the piecemeal sale of the messuage and 13 acres ¾ rood of Beatrix Stute, which owed the standard services; by 1276 the property was in the hands of eight tenants who each answered for a portion of the total services due.[51] In contrast to both Gressenhall and Martham, the division of villeinage land in Sedgeford was accompanied by the formal division of services, and the form of the 1282 survey certainly does not suggest that the priory was concerned to have one tenant responsible for all the services due from a single original tenement. The prohibition against having more than one villeinage holding prevented any one tenant from being liable for a portion of the services due from more than one original tenement; the formal division of services at Sedgeford was thus less complicated in its results

[50] Ibid., 6 Dec. 1273; BL Add. MS 57975, fo. 6ᵛ.

[51] The actual division of the services was: Sarlo Ruheued (3½ r.) 2*d.*; Beatrix Rice (2½ r.) 1¾*d.*; Gilbert Neuman (2 a.) 5½*d.*; Alan Stepper (1¾ r.) 2*d.*; Gilbert Chese (messuage and 4½ a.) man to work through half of harvest, every other year ten eggs, a hen and a loaf, two Monday works, 6*d.*; Richard Blome (3 a.) four Monday works; Agnes Winter (3 r.) two Monday works; Robert Stepper (1 a. 1 r.) half of harvest work, every other year ten eggs, a hen and a loaf, 1¾*d.* The total rent was 19*d.* of which 4*d.* is aid and 4*d.* for winter works. (NRO DCN 5284, 12 Oct. 1275).

than it would have been at Gressenhall or Martham. However, it is also true that the villeinage land in Sedgeford was comparatively lightly burdened.

Finally, it must again be emphasized that although the priory held by far the largest part of the village arable, its tenants' holdings were by no means confined to the land on the priory manor. The priory's acquistion of the Breydeston half-fee reveals the additional holdings, which might otherwise have remained conjectural, of such tenants as Robert son of Matilda and Ralph Raven—and many more could be cited. The involvement of other freeholders with the priory's tenants in the village land market has been shown by the unusual document that lists the increments of rent claimed by the priory for lands acquired from them. The priory tenants must also have held land directly of these prosperous freemen; at least one of them, Albin of Stanford, had some of the priory's villeins as sub-tenants, for his son Richard gave the priory 14½ d. rent owed to him for lands in Sedgeford which the priory's villeins held of him.[52] The number of independent landholders of whom a single tenant could hold land is demonstrated in a charter of John Bintree in which he gave to the priory all the land he held in Sedgeford with the exception of a capital messuage with 2½ acres which he held of Adam of Birlingham, 11 acres which he held of Geoffrey of Wisbech, 4 acres which he held of Alan of Thorpe, 1 acre which he held of Hervy Clerk, and 1 acre which he held of Simon of Lenn.[53] There is no reason to believe that the priory's tenants, particularly the more prosperous among them, were any more restricted in the number of landholders of whom they in turn could have held land.

Conclusion

To summarize briefly what is known of the peasant holdings in Sedgeford around 1280: on the priory's two manors of Westhall and Easthall (or Sedgeford and Gnatingdon) there were between 200 and 250 tenants with holdings of about 10 acres on average. There is little direct evidence of a standard villein holding, although from the 1282 survey there seems to have been a standard set of villein services which may once have

[52] NRO DCN Register I, fo. 119ᵛ.   [53] NRO DCN 417.

been due from a 12-acre tenement. By the late thirteenth century there was wide variation in tenant holdings, ranging from the cottages and subsistence holdings granted to non-inheriting sons and daughters to the 30-, 40-, and 50-acre holdings which could be amassed in a single lifetime by prosperous tenants using the market in free land. Two particular aspects of the situation around 1280 seem significant: first, the apparent fragmentation of former standard villein holdings in a village of impartible inheritance, and second, the apparent redistribution of both villein and free land to create great differences in the economic status of tenants.

In contrast to the policy they adopted at Martham, the priory and its officials exerted little if any administrative pressure to preserve the standard tenements at Sedgeford. Not only did the priory make no attempt to hinder the division of villein holdings theoretically impartible (except in so far as it avoided in the case of the sons of Godfrey Hervey setting a precedent for the partible inheritance of the land) but it must have acquiesced in the division of services among tenants when part of a villein holding was alienated. The only evidence of administrative pressure on the villein holdings in Sedgeford is in the two prohibitions debarring freemen from villein land and preventing villeins from having more than one villein holding of whatever size. The first prohibition is not uncommon on medieval manors,[54] although it was certainly not in force at Gressenhall and there is no sign of it at Martham. The second, while it clearly did not prevent the fragmentation of villein tenements, prevented single villeins from having a share in the land and services of more than one original tenement, and thus must have simplified the collection of services; it may also have restricted the division of holdings by reducing the potential market for villein land. This second prohibition ensured the villein land remained widely distributed, as shown by Alan Turpin having to give up his second tenement to a relative. The priory's lack of concern to have a single tenant responsible for the services due from each original tenement was not because the services had been commuted; winter works were invariably commuted for 4*d.*, but harvest works and boon-

---

[54] *Cart. Nat.*, p. xxxiii; Raftis, *Tenure*, pp. 68-9.

works were as invariably taken as services and were so entered in both the Sedgeford and the Gnatingdon accounts.[55] However, the services of the priory's tenants on the Sedgeford manors can hardly have been significant in cultivating the demesne, where over 800 acres were sown yearly. The Westhall and Easthall villeins were lightly burdened, and as an indication of the additional labour needed for the demesne cultivation, thirteenth-century manorial accounts for Sedgeford and Gnatingdon record payments for both regular and seasonal labour. Both manors usually kept, among other servants, a carter or harrower and eight ploughmen for the whole year.[56] As many as seventy-four workers might be hired for the five weeks of harvest on the two manors, as in 1296 when they included ten carters, two stackers, and sixteen reapers at Sedgeford and ten carters, two stackers, and fifteen reapers at Gnatingdon.[57]

Nor does there seem to have been any strong communal pressure in Sedgeford to keep villein holdings intact, given cases like Robert son of Matilda, who apparently gave part of his villein lands to his son although he also had free land to give.[58] One reason for communal pressure to maintain holdings intact would be to help in enforcing communal regulations, particularly those concerning cultivation. The individual tenant at Sedgeford, however, must have been relatively free in cultivating his land, despite the demands of the *hirdgongs*, areas regularly kept fallow to be grazed and dunged by sheep.[59] Arrangements must have been made to rationalize the cultivation of contiguous holdings, but this was probably done privately between individuals. That the individual was in principle free to cultivate his land as he wished is borne out by the 1282 survey, which refers to rent allowances when an area of tenant land was under *hirdgong* or fallow. If the fallowing and grazing had been elements of an ancient pattern of holding distribution

[55] NRO DCN 5208. Manorial accounts from Sedgeford and Gnatingdon, in listing the costs of food for the harvest workers, record among the hired labour a number of reapers 'cum operariis ville', confirming that harvest works were not commuted (e.g. NRO DCN 4629, 5233: accounts for 1272-3).

[56] NRO DCN 4626, 4627 (Gnatingdon); DCN 5236, 5237 (Sedgeford).

[57] NRO DCN 4633, 5241.

[58] Above, pp. 92-3.

[59] For sheep and their importance in Sedgeford see Williamson, 'Norf. Peasant Holdings', pp. 272-301.

and crop rotation, no allowance would have been necessary; tenants were apparently being compensated for the sacrifice of their freedom of action and the temporary loss of land which they would otherwise have been free to cultivate.

The custom of impartible inheritance at Sedgeford did less to prevent the division of holdings than might be expected. There was always the possibility of division in that if there was no male heir land would be divided among female heirs of the same degree of kinship. Nevertheless, a great deal of the fragmentation of holdings that can be traced through the thirteenth-century court rolls and surveys was the result of the transfer of land by tenants in order to provide for non-inheriting sons or daughters. Impartible inheritance undoubtedly helped to keep holdings together by passing the initiative for division to the individual tenant, who also had to pay a fine in the lord's court for licence to bring it about. On the other hand, there are enough cases of fathers providing for non-inheriting sons and daughters to show that social custom encouraged tenants to divide their holdings so as to provide subsistence for as many members of the immediate family as possible. Unfortunately, the nature of the court-roll evidence makes it impossible to gauge how far this was normal practice. However, the fragmentation of villein land and the duplication of surnames among tenants suggest that such provision for non-inheriting offspring was not uncommon.[60] Certainly in combining impartible inheritance with fragmentation of holdings Sedgeford was not unique; the similar fragmentation in thirteenth-century Hevingham, also in Norfolk, led B.M.S. Campbell to postulate an earlier change in custom from partible to impartible inheritance.[61] The Sedgeford evidence shows that the freedom to transfer land was all that was needed to make a system of impartible inheritance scarcely different from one of partible inheritance in its effect on holdings. Given this freedom of action, social pressure apparently worked either within or with-

---

[60] For example, the surviving folios of 1282 survey record eight tenants surnamed Neuman, seven Suvel, six Ruheued, six Hert, five Starlyng, five Profete, four Palmer, four Norwich, four Atte Howe, four Fish, and four Berry in a list of only 104 tenants. Their relationship can be assumed from the fact that in most cases tenants with the same surname occur together under the same *gate*, suggesting neighbouring messuages.

[61] Campbell, 'Field Systems in E. Norf.', pp. 282-300.

out the inheritance customs to encourage the distribution of tenant land among as many members of the family as possible.

The function of the land market in Sedgeford in producing a form of *de facto* partible inheritance has been emphasized because it was perhaps unexpected, but this should not obscure its other function of enabling tenants to accumulate large holdings. A few tenants, such as Alan Turpin, Sarlo le Riche, and Martin Suvel, are particularly prominent in this respect; their patrimonies were relatively small, and it was through the land market that their holdings were built up. However, there is no evidence of a family systematically accumulating land over more than one generation. Many of these amassed holdings reflect the rôle in the land market of a group of free landholders, intermediate in economic and social position between the manorial lords (the priory, the Hackfords, the Ingoldisthorpes) and their tenants. They were apparently prosperous enough to let land to tenants, and to participate in a market in free land by both buying and selling. The Sedgeford evidence thus confirms that the opportunities of the manorial tenants to acquire or dispose of land were not limited to their own manors.

Without the evidence (which partible inheritance would provide) of the record of all surviving sons' entry into a patrimonial holding, it is difficult to estimate the increase of population in Sedgeford during the thirteenth century. Certainly the population was doing more than replacing itself during the latter part of the century. At Sedgeford, of the 73 male tenants whose deaths are recorded in the surviving court rolls, 50 (69 per cent) were succeeded by their sons, and only 10 (14 per cent) had no heirs in the direct line.[62] There was probably land available for assart in Sedgeford at least until the early thirteenth century, and this would have absorbed some of the population increase; the relative infertility of the soil, on the other hand, in itself limited population since a larger holding than elsewhere would be needed for subsistence. Some tenant land may have been converted from demesne. The Sedgeford account roll for 1300-1 records 90 acres 30 roods of 'herbage let at Westhall' to eighteen tenants in pieces ranging from 1 acre to 11 acres,[63] and a

---

[62] The remaining 13 entries were by one or more daughters.
[63] NRO DCN 5242.

court-roll entry of 1288 lists ten tenants who held from 1 acre to 4 ½ acres of land 'once in demesne'.[64] There were, then, some opportunities even in the thirteenth century for expanding the tenant arable, and the existing arable may in the course of the century have been more intensively manured and cultivated. Nevertheless, population growth at Sedgeford must have led to increased demand for land, a demand that was largely met through the land market. It has already been suggested that the physical division of tenements hitherto only potentially divisible was one effect of population pressure: the land market—with the acquiescence of the lord of the manor—apparently produced a *de facto* change of inheritance customs to meet population growth.

5   CONCLUSION

When we compare the three villages, one fact becomes immediately clear: differing seignorial policy in the matter of keeping tenements intact cannot be explained as a difference between lay and ecclesiastical lordship, since the manors where the difference was greatest—Martham and Sedgeford—were both under the lordship of Norwich Cathedral Priory. Nor did it reflect local inheritance customs, for there is a sharp contrast between Gressenhall and Martham, the two villages of partible inheritance. A more likely explanation lies in the rôle of tenant services in demesne cultivation. The three villages differed in the size of their demesnes and the labour services owed by their tenants. In both Martham and Gressenhall about one-fifth or the manorial arable was in demesne, but it was probably more intensively cultivated at Martham. Customary labour services were similar at Gressenhall and Martham, but the proportion of tenements owing them varied from 63 per cent in early-thirteenth-century Martham to 29 per cent at Gressenhall in 1282. The labour services at Sedgeford were unusually light, and in view of the size of the demesne they can hardly have contributed significantly to its cultivation. It seems then that, as might be expected, the lords' insistence on keeping tenements intact probably varied with the importance of their ser-

[64] NRO DCN 5284, 11 May 1288.

vices to demesne cultivation. Certainly at Martham, with its intensively cultivated demesne and high proportion of burdened tenements, there was more reason to retain the tenemental structure than at Sedgeford, where demesne cultivation necessarily demanded a great deal of hired labour.

Turning to social customs, the obvious distinction is between the two villages of partible and the one village of impartible inheritance. But in their effects on peasant holdings there was less difference between partible and impartible inheritance in the thirteenth century than a bare description of the two systems would suggest. Both systems included a number of common customs—for example, the partible inheritance of land by daughters in default of a male heir or the provision of land as dowry on a daughter's marriage—and these customs introduced an element of fragmentation into both systems. Whatever the letter of the local inheritance law, tenants generally seem to have used their land to provide for as many of their immediate family as possible. Given the many tenants at Sedgeford who transferred both inherited and other land to non-inheriting sons, the fact that holdings in Sedgeford were significantly larger on average than in Gressenhall and Martham probably reflects the relatively poor soil there as much as the custom of impartible inheritance; tenants were practical farmers, and whatever the inheritance system they were unlikely to allow holdings to fragment to the point at which they became uneconomic. In the transfer of land from one generation to the next the chief difference between the two villages of partible and the one village of impartible inheritance was that in the latter the provision for offspring was more arbitrary. Although social pressure clearly encouraged the provision of land for non-inheriting sons, there were no customary rules—as in the system of partible inheritance—to say how much they should be given, nor was there any way they could assert rights in the patrimony if such provision was not made voluntarily. But even partible inheritance did not guarantee the equal division of patrimony among surviving sons, as at least one tenant in both Gressenhall and Martham transferred the greater part of his holding to one of two sons before his death. Partible inheritance undoubtedly offered the individual the security of legal rights in a patrimony, but the social pressure for the division of impartibly inherited land provided a degree of security in itself.

The impact of the land market on holdings—its contribution to the division and redistribution of tenements—cannot be assessed without the survival of a sufficient number of court rolls. Similarly, the movement of free land among tenants within and without the manor can only be glimpsed in the relatively few surviving charters. The most important function of the land market must have been to enable land to be permanently alienated from a family holding. It undoubtedly encouraged the physical division of tenements by offering tenants of sub-subsistence holdings the opportunity to sell or lease. Were there no means of profitably disposing of a patrimonial holding too small for subsistence, many claims would probably have been neglected; the land would remain in the family and the claimant would either take part in joint cultivation or else would seek an alternative livelihood. With a land market, on the other hand, sub-subsistence shares of a patrimony could provide their tenants with some capital or a small money rent. The Martham evidence shows how temporary agreements such as leases might be made outside the manorial court and thus, like the transfer of free land, beyond the knowledge of the historian.

In villages of partible inheritance the land market served, by redistribution, to adjust the result of that inheritance to the physical needs of subsistence; at Sedgeford it seems to have performed much the same function by permanently alienating land to non-inheriting sons. It thus probably played a more active part in breaking up traditional tenements there than at Martham and Gressenhall, where inheritance custom effected the first partition. In all three villages the land market served to reinforce the impulses of social custom rather than to oppose them. In many ways, it gave a greater flexibility than the customary practices by offering an alternative to communal cultivation or sub-subsistence division. The land market in the thirteenth-century was used not only to accumulate large holdings but also to adjust holding size to economic realities under the pressure of continued population increase.

Evidence from other Norfolk manors shows that what happened at Gressenhall, Martham, and Sedgeford was not peculiar to these three villages. However, the responses of these three villages were clearly not the only responses to population pressure to be found in thirteenth-century Norfolk; the whole-sale redistribution of land which may have occurred at Pulham was one alternative,[1] and another was the modification of in-heritance laws that seems to have taken place at Northwold and Hindringham.[2] The redistribution of land through the land market, on the other hand, brought the lord considerable and continuing financial benefit in fines for entry, fines for licence to sell or lease, and even (as at Sedgeford) in increments of rent. Gressenhall, Martham, and Sedgeford show three different ways of organizing services from fragmented tenements, but in all three cases the lord's profits from the process of fragmen-tation must have fully compensated for the administrative in-convenience.

By the thirteenth century in Norfolk, the pressure on land had become acute and in most cases required institutional ad-justment to minimize its effects. In manorial records, this institutional adjustment can be seen only in the lord's accepting the breakup of tenements; that this was such a late develop-ment implies earlier administrative resistance. The thirteenth century was a period of stress and adjustment in the three vil-lages studied here, as on most other Norfolk manors. The stresses were general, the adjustments particular.

[1] The 1222 and 1251 surveys of Pulham were organized by *letes* similar to the Sedgeford *gates*. The total amount of land held by the tenants in each *lete* was almost the same, a regularity which suggests recent redistribution.

[2] Patrimony was partible in Hindringham, but neither acquired land nor let-off demesne was considered partible (NRO DCN Hindringham court roll 3, 19 July 1268). A similar arrangement was used at Wighton (NRO H 154).

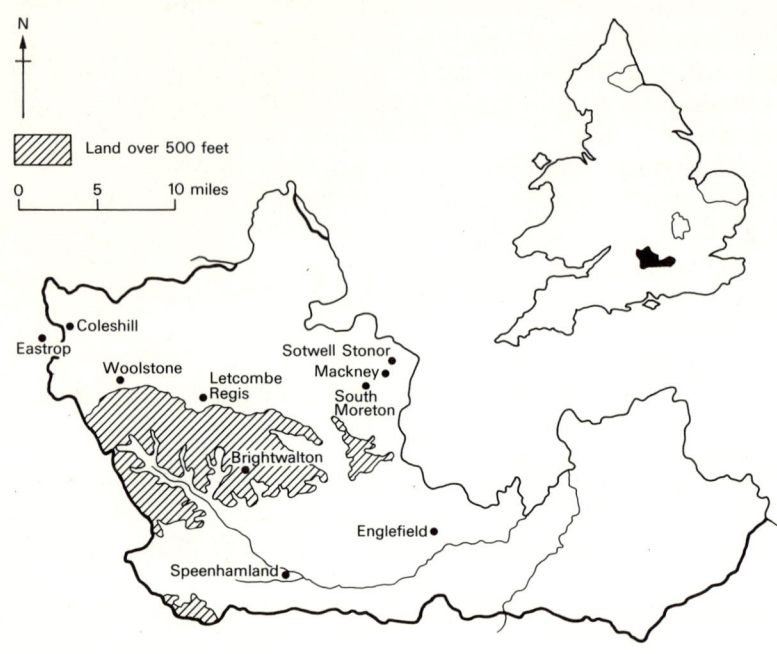

II BERKSHIRE
showing the places discussed in Chapter III

III Berkshire: Fourteenth and Fifteenth Centuries*

1 THE MANORIAL SETTING

The ten manors

This study is based on a group of nine manors in Berkshire and one in Wiltshire for which there is a plentiful supply of four- teenth- and fifteenth-century court rolls and a good series of rentals or surveys. Inasmuch as they were chosen for study on the basis of their surviving records, these manors are a random sample. Fortunately, they are distributed among the main regions of the county and are to that extent representative. Woolstone, Brightwalton, and Letcombe Regis are villages of the chalk downlands, the foremost sheep-producing area of the county in the Middle Ages.[1] Mackney, Coleshill, Sotwell Stonor, and South Moreton are all in the flat plain known as the Vale of the White Horse, then a dairying and mixed farming region. Speenhamland and Englefield both lie in the Kennet valley. The village of Eastrop, near Highworth, lies just over the Wiltshire border. It has been included because it was in the same geographical region as Coleshill and part of the same estate, and because the two villages were in many ways closely connected. As far as ownership is concerned, these manors are also a fairly representative sample. Five were held by ecclesi- astical corporations: Eastrop and Coleshill by Edington Priory, Woolstone by the cathedral priory of St. Swithin's, Win- chester, Letcombe Regis first by Cluny and then by Westmin- ster Abbey, Brightwalton by Battle Abbey. Speenhamland was

---

* This chapter is based on R.J. Faith, 'The Peasant Land-Market in Berkshire in the Later Middle Ages' (Leicester University Ph.D. thesis, 1962), which includes much further material on the land transactions of individual peasant families. Since it was written changes in county boundaries have moved the following villages studied from Berkshire to Oxfordshire: Coleshill, Letcombe Regis, Mackney, Sotwell Stonor, South Moreton, Woolstone.

[1] Woolstone and Letcombe Regis are both long narrow parishes with some land in the Vale but most of their acreage on the downs.

held by an important noble family, the Despencers; Sotwell Stonor, South Moreton, Englefield, and Mackney by a succession of lesser lay landlords. Of course, as these villages only included a small fraction of the total peasant population of the county their development in the later Middle Ages cannot be taken to be representative of the Berkshire peasantry as a whole, even though many elements seem to have been common to all of them. Moreover, in concentrating on the villein land market, it has been necessary to look very cursorily, or not at all, at much interesting material and many important subjects. Nothing is said here, for instance, about the legal status of copyholders in the royal courts. Nor has it been possible to deal at all thoroughly with the land transactions of freeholders who may have been of similar economic standing to their villein neighbours. Peasant agriculture is only touched on in so far as it affected landholding and social structure. As this study is principally based on the evidence of manorial court rolls and surveys its limits are set by the boundaries of the manor, not the village, and only when the two are coterminous can we make any meaningful statements about developments in village society.

Labour services and demesne leasing

During the fourteenth and fifteenth centuries two changes in the economy of manorial lords profoundly affected the economy of their dependent peasantry: the commutation of labour services and the leasing of demesnes. It is impossible to give a firm date for the final commutation of labour services on all of the manors we are concerned with here. In many cases our evidence consists solely of rentals, custumals, and court rolls, which are not reliable evidence in this respect. Moreover, the commutation of services was a gradual process and one which could be reversed. At Brightwalton, for instance, the population fall due to the Black Death temporarily increased the ratio of hired to customary labour but works were reimposed from the 1350s, while at Woolstone the plague led to many permanent conversions of tenure from labour to money rent. At Coleshill, where the amount of demesne arable diminished by two-thirds between 1316 and 1421, labour services were finally commuted

between 1385 and 1421, probably in connection with the leasing
of the demesne. For the other manors we have very little information. Several fifteenth-century rentals list services owed by
tenants—as indeed some of the Coleshill documents do after
1421—but there is no means of knowing what proportion of the
services owed to the lord were ever performed. Although we
cannot give a final date for its extinction the fact remains that
in Berkshire, as elsewhere, the labour-service system was
obsolescent from the mid-fourteenth century at latest. The process of demesne leasing is easier to date for, even when we lack
the evidence of ministers' accounts, court-roll references to
farmers (*firmarii*) give us dates by which it had begun. These
farmers may have leased only a part of the demesne, and of
course incidental references to them seldom show at what point
the demesne was first leased, although in one case the farmer's
lease is recorded on the court roll.[2] It is certain that all or part
of the demesne was leased at Coleshill by 1422, at Eastrop by
1423, at Woolstone by 1423, at Brightwalton by 1428, at
Sotwell Stonor by 1430, at South Moreton by 1452, at Mackney
by 1471, and at Englefield by 1486-7. At Letcombe Regis the
demesne was at farm to a group of peasants, possibly as representatives of the village as a whole, in the thirteenth century.[3]
It is quite possible, of course, that the farming of these manors
in the fifteenth century was not a new development but merely
a resumption of a much earlier policy. In general, our evidence
confirms the conclusion reached by L.C. Latham, that on the
average Berkshire manor the bulk of the manorial demesne was
being leased out by about the mid-fifteenth century.[4]

The commutation of labour services 'meant that one great
force making for equality between the holdings of different
tenants was removed'.[5] Rents could easily be divided among
tenants or added together as a charge on a single tenant as the

[2] PRO SC 2/154/62, m. 7, 19 Oct. 1430.

[3] Coleshill, PRO SC 6/743/14; Eastrop, PRO SC 2/208/53, m. 2, 21 Oct. 1423;
Woolstone, PRO SC 6/757/5; Brightwalton, PRO SC 2/153/72, m. 7, 27 July 1428;
Sotwell Stonor, PRO SC 2/154/62, m. 7, 19 Oct. 1430; South Moreton, PRO SC
12/5/52; Mackney, PRO SC 2/154/40, m. 3, 29 Nov. 1471; Englefield, PRO SC
2/154/23, m. 9 [1486-7]; Letcombe Regis, PRO SC 2/154/35, m. 4, 4d, 25 Oct. 1269.

[4] L.C. Latham, 'The Decay of the Manorial System during the first half of the
Fifteenth Century, with special reference to the Decline of Villeinage' (London
University M.A. thesis, 1926), pp. 150-65.

[5] Tawney, *Agr. Problem*, p. 92.

tenements themselves were divided and recombined. Rents and tenants, not works and villeins, were the properties which interested lords now. The sources reflect this change of emphasis, not only in their terminology but in their character: rentals become more common than custumals, and their layout itself changes, ranking tenants by the amount of their rent and omitting all but the most summary description of their land.[6]

If the lord was no longer interested in the integrity of tenements, even less so was the farmer when he came to take his place between the village community and the seignorial authority. His rôle was not simply that of the most important villager economically: he had a certain authority of his own. At Woolstone the farmer leased half the profits of the manorial court and presumably attended it with an eye to these profits.[7] At Coleshill the farmer had previously been the lord's rent collector. At Brightwalton in 1433 the farmer was engaged in leasing land to other tenants without the cognizance of the manorial court.[8] At Eastrop his counterpart clearly had the ear of the lord's *supervisor* and interceded with him to obtain special concessions for his relatives.[9]

Changes in agricultural policy led to changes in seignorial attitudes. Not only did the lord no longer have an interest in keeping tenements intact and in restricting alienation; he now had a positive interest in regulating and profiting from such alienation. Our records do not enable us to say anything about seignorial policy towards peasant land transfers during the thirteenth century. M.M. Postan considered that by the turn of the thirteenth and fourteenth centuries lords were often successfully regulating the hitherto illicit small-scale traffic in land: '. . . evasions had become less frequent, transfers by surrender more common. The attitude of the manorial administration showed signs of stiffening.'[10] This is all the more true in the period we are concerned with. Not only was the seignorial bias against alienation obsolescent, but in regulating rather than

---

[6] These later medieval rentals are often documents of inferior quality; they had less permanent value, as tenements changed hands quickly, and were often poorly written.

[7] PRO SC 6/758/5, mm. 11-24 *passim* (farmer's accounts, 1423-4, 1457-77).

[8] PRO SC 2/153/73, m. 13, 9 June 1433.

[9] PRO SC 2/208/53, m. 3d, April 1425 (John Cubbell's licence to marry his daughter).

[10] *Cart.Nat.*, p. liii.

prohibiting alienation the lord found a valuable source of income open to him at a time when his other revenues were at best static, at worst diminishing. The lord made money every time a villein tenement changed hands: the outgoing tenant paid him a heriot,[11] the incoming tenant an entry fine. An example from the Woolstone court rolls shows how profitable land transfers among his villeins could be to the lord. In 1332 Walter atte Sherde surrendered a messuage and half-virgate to his son William. He paid a cow worth 10s. 0d. as heriot and William paid an entry fine of £1. Walter then provided himself with land by marrying a rich widow; he paid £5 for licence to do so and for her land.[12] In all, the lord made £6. 10s. on these transactions with no outlay at all. Profits of this order could only be made at times when entry fines were high and, as we shall see, entry fines over the whole of our period seldom reached the levels that obtained in early fourteenth-century Woolstone. Nevertheless it is clear that the lord might have a considerable financial motive in regulating and licensing the peasant land market.

Tenants too came to have a certain incentive to transfer their land openly in the manorial court. Transfers made in court probably had a greater security than those made unofficially and illicitly. When a lease was made between two tenants with the lord's licence some of its terms, such as its duration and any reservations made in favour of the grantor, could be recorded in the court roll and referred to in case of dispute by either party. At Woolstone tenants valued the written word quite highly and were prepared or compelled to pay fines for the privilege of having their leases enrolled. With the growth of copyhold the manorial court became increasingly a body recording land transfers.

The traditional machinery of surrender and admittance, by which customary holdings were transferred and through which the lord had earlier been able to limit transfers or keep a check on the descent of tenements, was easily adapted to the new situation in which he no longer wanted to regulate the transfer of customary land but merely to participate profitably in it. This

---

[11] 'By the middle of the fourteenth century . . . the heriot was regarded as a due paid on any transfer or surrender of customary land' (Page, *Crowland*, p. 115).

[12] PRO SC 2/154/77, m. 3, Hocktide 1332.

is not to say that lords in the fourteenth and fifteenth centuries were successful in demanding that all peasant transactions should go through the proper channels of the manorial court. The fines and heriots which represented his profits could be precisely the reason for his tenants' anxiety to avoid using the machinery of the court. By the nature of the court roll, which records only licensed transfers or illegal transfers successfully detected, we cannot hope to discover how much land changed hands secretly. The fact that there are few presentments in our records for illicit land transactions can be interpreted in either of two contradictory senses: either that there was a great deal of illicit conveyancing, of which only a small part was detected, or that detection was so easy that very little illicit conveyancing escaped the notice of the seignorial administration.

Two factors are relevant here: the nature of the seignorial administration, and the level of entry fines. An absentee landlord, such as were the Despencers, lords of Speenhamland, known to his villagers only through his rent collector, would be unable to keep a close watch on illicit transactions among his tenants, especially if he had put the demesne lands out to farm. In contrast the resident lord of a small manor like South Moreton, or the resident bailiff or reeve strictly accountable to an ecclesiastical bureaucracy like that of St. Swithin's or Edington Priory, would have been closely involved with the life of the village and would have been in a good position to know if A were ploughing acres officially held by B. A third situation was where free tenure meant that there was no seignorial control over inter-peasant transactions (as among the many small freeholders of Eastrop), which are not recorded in the court rolls. In any of these situations it was probably harder to detect short-term leases than sales. The second factor, the level of entry fines, is self-evident. At a time when entry fines were high, the incentive to avoid them by transferring land outside the court would equally be high. When the customary entry fine was only, say, two capons, as it was at Coleshill for some 120 years, a tenant might think the price well paid for the security which enrolment of the transaction would bring. As the evidence of entry fines will show, peasants were prepared to pay very high prices for security of tenure during the later Middle Ages.

Entry fines and the demand for land

The principal elements in all villein land transactions were surrender and admission: the outgoing tenant surrendered the
holding to the lord or his representative and the incoming tenant was admitted to it. This formula emphasized the lord's
superior interest in the land, recorded the end of one tenancy
and the beginning of another, and ensured a double profit to
the lord in the shape of heriot and entry fine. Although, technically speaking, legal theory recognized only grants and
surrenders of land, not sales and purchases, in fact sales and
purchases were common. They employed the legal fiction of
the surrender to use, as in the following transaction: 'Roger
Spencer came and surrendered a messuage and virgate to the
use of [*ad opus*] William Jefferys, and William took it . . .'[13]
These surrenders to use between villeins have generally been
taken to represent only sales, and to be the only legal form
which sales of land could take. It is quite possible, however,
that the same formula may have been employed in inter-peasant
leases for long terms. Moreover, it is equally possible that the
normal formula of surrender and admittance itself conceals
many actual sales and leases. The court rolls considered here
record many instances of a tenant taking up land immediately
after its surrender, with such phrases as 'he came at once' (*statim
venit*) or 'after this he came' (*super hoc venit*) and took the land.
Very frequently surrender and admission are recorded in a
single entry or a single sentence. In many such cases, when A
surrendered his land just when B wanted it, and B was on hand
to take it, and the whole transaction was written down as a
single entry, it seems quite possible that a sale was involved,
although there is no way of determining whether, or how often,
this was the case. If such concealed sales were in fact common,
then the real number of inter-peasant transactions in the court
rolls would be very much higher than a simple calculation of
recorded inter-peasant leases and surrenders to use would lead
us to suppose.

The relaxation of seignorial pressure which preserved a rigid

[13] PRO SC 2/153/73, m. 13, 25 May 1434. For a different interpretation of
surrenders to use of peasant holdings see Cicely Howell in Goody, Thirsk, &
Thompson, pp. 127-30.

tenemental structure would not by itself have led to important social change, although it would almost certainly have stimulated the small-scale land market, had it not been for the drop in population in the fourteenth century. This transformed the peasants' situation and had far-reaching effects on the village economy. More land was available from vacant holdings and from those demesnes, or parts of demesnes, which lords could no longer afford to cultivate themselves. Sons no longer had to wait until their father's death or retirement for their patrimony for there were now empty holdings in the lord's hand or unwanted demesne acres available for rent. Compare the position, for example, of William le Sprot of Woolstone, who had to pay £3. 6s. 8d. as an entry fine to succeed to his father's land in 1308, with the position of Woolstone tenants a century later, who could obtain tenements three times the size of Sprot's for about a fifteenth of the price.[14] Again, compare the position of Richard Carswell of Coleshill, who paid £6. 13s. 4d. for a tenement (and possibly a wife) in 1316, with that of John Basset, who took up exactly the same holding in 1386 and paid no entry fine at all.[15]

J.Z. Titow has made an interesting comparison between 'colonizing' and 'non-colonizing' manors in the thirteenth century. He found that on the former, where plenty of land was available to peasants 'there were very few marriages with widows and apparently next to no cases of widows remarrying more than once. . .' in contrast to the latter, where land was in short supply and marriage with widows was common.[16] Much the same phenomenon is found in our records if we contrast not two kinds of manors but the early part of our period with the later part. Compare the entry fine of £5 that marriage with a wealthy Woolstone widow was felt to be worth in 1332 with the almost complete absence of marriage with widows found there a hundred years later, when there were cheaper and more attractive ways of acquiring land.[17]

The entry fines which the lord demanded from every tenant

[14] PRO SC 6/756/3; see below, p. 128.
[15] PRO SC 6/743/4; SC 2/154/1, m. 12, 24 Mar. 1386.
[16] J.Z. Titow, 'Some Differences between Manors and their Effects on the Condition of the Peasant in the Thirteenth Century', *AgHR*, x (1962), 7.
[17] PRO SC 2/154/77, m. 3, Hocktide 1332; see below, pp. 160-1.

(except, in most cases, a widow) newly taking up a villein tenement are a good, although not infallible, guide to the demand
for, and supply of, customary land. They were much less con-
ventionalized than rents and over a period of time reflect the
best price that the lord could get for a holding.[18] Court-roll
evidence from Brightwalton from 1280 to 1449, Woolstone
from 1308 to 1417, and Coleshill from 1379 to 1496 gives us a
record of entry fines which to some extent indicate the demand
for customary land throughout our period, while examples
from the Mackney, Sotwell Stonor, South Moreton, and Letcombe Regis court rolls provide supplementary information.[19]

There are obvious deficiencies in this evidence. The tenements conveyed are expressed in terms of virgates, and local
variations in the size of the virgate make comparisons between
manors unreliable: these have been avoided. A more serious
problem is whether these fines relate to all the land available to
the peasantry or to only a part of it. The availability of land
from other sources, in particular from assart or the demesne,
would slacken the pressure on the customary land to which in
general these figures relate. It is almost certain, however, that
very little if any colonizing was being carried on at either
Coleshill or Woolstone during the period and it is on the Coleshill and Woolstone figures that heaviest reliance is placed.[20]
For these manors too there are enough ministers' accounts
available to give a clear idea of the amount of land which
tenants could obtain on lease from the demesne. For the other
manors these entry-fine figures can be accepted only with the
reservation that they show only the state of supply and demand
on available tenant land and thus underestimate the demand
for land as a whole.

Reference has already been made to the steep drop in entry
fines at Woolstone between the early fourteenth century and
the early fifteenth century. We can date this decline fairly

[18] Entry fines later became fixed, often at some multiple of a year's rent for a
holding, but the extent to which they fluctuated during the fourteenth and fifteenth
centuries suggests that at this time they were regulated only by the laws of supply
and demand.

[19] Below, Ch. III, section 2, for details of sources.

[20] The only reference to colonizing I have found in the Coleshill accounts is in the
account for 1315-16 (PRO SC 6/743/4). From Woolstone there is no reference to
colonizing.

precisely. The Black Death evidently had as severe short-term effects on entry fines as it did on other aspects of the economy of this manor. By far the majority of fines between 1308 and 1348 were over 13s. 4d. Between 1348 and 1390 only four fines reached this level, two of which were marriage fines and entry fines combined. From the 1390s entry fines rose again, although never to their earlier peak of over £6. The high fines paid around 1400 at Woolstone were for holdings much larger than those granted earlier: composite holdings of up to 1½ virgates granted together. Many of these composite holdings also included a toft of unspecified size which may have greatly increased their value. The concessions that the lord was forced to make in order to fill vacant holdings immediately after the Black Death, the many leases of small amounts of demesne land during the fifteenth century, and the fact that not many tenements remained in the lord's hand for long, all suggest that although the pressure on customary land may have slackened somewhat during this period there were still plenty of tenants at Woolstone who were prepared to take up additions to their holdings if the price was right.

Similarly at Brightwalton entry fines were highest between 1281 and 1349. Immediately after the Black Death, when vacant holdings were probably split up and let piecemeal, fines temporarily dropped, but rose again from 1367. The trend is by no means clear, and the position is probably best expressed by saying that the average fine for a complete holding was 23s. 0d. between 1281 and 1351, and 16s. 0d. between 1351 and 1407. This suggests that pressure on the available land slackened off after the Black Death—an impression confirmed, as we shall see, by the evidence of peasant land transactions.[21]

Coleshill between 1377 and 1496 had virtually a buyer's market in land.[22] Entry fines, with perhaps three exceptions, varied between the nominal render of two capons or 6d. and 10s. 0d. In nineteen individual years there were cases of holdings changing hands without any entry fine at all being paid. In three cases this concession was made because the new tenant was the widow of the former tenant, in two because the

[21] Below, pp. 132-3.
[22] Coleshill court rolls: PRO SC 2/154/1 (1 Richard II-1 Henry IV), SC 2/154/2 (10 Henry V-10 Henry VI), SC 2/154/3 (11-37 Henry VI). See also below, pp. 152-4.

tenement concerned did not include a messuage, and in several because the new tenant undertook to repair the holding. But often the concession was left unexplained, and it may be that in these cases the lord was in no position to demand a fine, or that the incoming tenant was in a strong enough position to refuse payment. This was a new state of affairs. A reeve's account for 1316-17 shows that the level of fines at the beginning of the century may have been very much higher, for it enters £6. 13s. 4d. from the fine of Richard Carswell.[23] The record of land in the lord's hand shows that Coleshill was severely depopulated between 1379 and the mid-fifteenth century and that the fall was particularly steep between 1395 and 1424.[24] The priory was clearly having difficulty at this time in finding tenants and was in no position to exact entry fines from those that were forthcoming. Lack of tenants, possibly accompanied by tenants' resistance to paying, made considerable inroads on the expected income from rent as appears in Table IV, which covers the years down to 1424 for which relevant accounts survive:[25]

Table IV
Amounts of assized rent actually paid at Coleshill, 1338-1424

1338	£16. 14s.
1385	£16. 17s.
1395	£18. 10s.
1404	£17. 13s.
1421	£12. 12s.
1424	£17

In each year the total amount of assized rent due was between £20 and £24.

From 1424 to the end of the century between £17 and £19 was paid of the £23 odd that was due. Shortage of tenants only partly explains the low level of entry fines at Coleshill: part of the explanation is that, especially towards the end of our period, and between 1433 and 1459 in particular, many

[23] PRO SC 6/743/4.
[24] PRO SC 6/743/4-21.
[25] This table is based on PRO SC 6/743/4, 7, 10, 11, 14, 20.

tenants preferred leasing demesne land, especially grazing land, and the piecemeal and short-term leasing of vacant holdings to the acquisition of vacant customary holdings. For these, as the entry fines make clear, supply far outran demand.

It is at South Moreton, where £20 was paid in 1326, that we find the highest entry fine in any of our manors, and the fines paid there throughout the fourteenth century and until 1437 were in general higher than those paid at Coleshill, Woolstone, and Brightwalton. Similarly, Mackney and Sotwell Stonor in the fifteenth and early sixteenth centuries saw very high fines in comparison with those found on the manors already discussed. Does this mean that the manors in this second group did not experience late-medieval depopulation and falling demand for customary land? It seems rather that the explanation lies in the fact that tenants who paid these very high fines were paying for special concessions as well as for land. Thus the South Moreton villagers who paid fines (in essence re-entry fines) of £1 in 1361 did so in order that the lord should release their land from the obligations of villein tenure. Those at Mackney in 1426, 1455, 1458, and 1466, and those at South Moreton in 1387, 1430, and 1437, who often paid fines of several pounds, did so in order to secure the reversion of their holdings to their children. The high fines paid early in the sixteenth century at Sotwell Stonor were paid, as at Woolstone, for large composite holdings. The Letcombe Regis fines, although few in number, bear out the impression that, apart from payments for special conditions of tenure, the level of entry fines was highest during the early part of our period.[26] It would seem that the demand for available customary land was no longer pressing so hard upon its supply.

Customary land was available, its price was falling, the restrictions on its alienation were slackening, and the manorial courts provided the machinery through which holdings could be transferred; such were the necessary conditions for a free market in land, and all were present, or coming into being,

---

[26] South Moreton: PRO SC 2/154/43, m. 2, 16 Nov. 1326; ibid., m. 9, 11 Nov. 1361; SC 2/154/44, m. 3, 21 Oct. 1387; SC 2/154/45, m. 1, 22 July 1420; ibid., m. 2, 19 Mar. 1437. Mackney: PRO SC 2/154/40, m. 1, 25 Nov. 1426; SC 2/154/41, m. 1, 10 Feb. 1455; ibid., m. 1, 13 Oct. 1458; ibid., m. 3, 5 Mar. 1466. Sotwell Stonor: e.g. PRO SC 2/154/64, m. 1, 29 Oct. 1501. Letcombe Regis: PRO SC 2/154/34-6, *temp.* Henry III.

during our period. Ideally, we should like to extract from our evidence at this point statistics of the number of land transactions made in each year, the size of unit transferred, the ratio of inter-peasant transactions to transactions between peasant and lord, and the proportion of sales to leases. But the records at our disposal are of such widely varying quality and coverage that any such overall figures would be largely meaningless. To conflate the evidence of the land market at Coleshill, where we have a run of almost 180 court rolls, with that from the sparse material from Sotwell Stonor or Mackney, for instance, would produce a most misleading result. Even when a good series of court rolls survives, as at Woolstone, we cannot always be sure that there is a roll extant for every court that was held (and if we check the Woolstone court rolls with the section of the relevant manorial accounts dealing with receipts from the court it becomes clear that many court rolls are missing).

There is a more serious objection to giving overall statistics: the level of activity in the peasant land market and its fluctuations were affected not only by national or county-wide influences, but also by intensely local factors. The price of corn, for instance, may have had a long-term effect on the traffic in customary holdings, but a much more immediate and noticeable impact was made by such factors as the decline of a handful of families, the lord's policy towards his demesne, the peasant's ambitions for his children. Even the Black Death, by far the most generally felt influence, had different effects in different villages. This is not to argue that there are no developments common to the peasant land market in all these manors; as we shall see, there were some very important ones. The conclusion is rather that, in this context, overall statistics are less revealing than the sum of studies of individual manors.

The first impression given by a study of late-medieval peasant land transfers is that of the speed with which land changed hands and the scale on which it did so. We are no longer dealing with Maitland's 'brisk traffic . . . in small parcels of land'[27] but a brisk traffic in complete virgates and half-virgates, in which 60 acres could be transferred in a single transaction and a villein holding change hands five times in as many years.

[27] *Select Man. Pleas*, p. 106.

To concentrate in the following pages on these 'land transfers capable of achieving a permanent reshuffle in the social structure of the country-side',[28] is not wilfully to ignore a mass of small-scale dealings of the type that abound in the thirteenth-century rolls. Land transactions involving only a few acres played a decreasingly important part in the conveyancing business of the manorial courts. Possibly such transactions were being carried out without licence; possibly land was now available so cheaply that small-scale acquisitions no longer attracted the peasant. In any case, transactions involving holdings of less than half a virgate, which Postan describes as 'the current and temporary adjustment to changing individual circumstances', 'a permanent phenomenon',[29] are not considered in the following analysis, although they are taken into account in discussing the building up of peasant fortunes.

We have noted the slackening of seignorial restrictions on alienation, but another, even more important, set of restrictions was also crumbling. For centuries the way villein land changed hands had been determined not merely by the seignorial will but also by the local customs relating to inheritance. The late-medieval court rolls show that these customs, which had dominated village life in the thirteenth century and probably long before, were breaking down completely. Chief among the causes of this was the slackening of pressure on land. In a period of land shortage a tenant would be reluctant to relinquish even a part of his holding unless he was incapable of farming it; hence the old, childless, and infirm predominated among thirteenth-century sellers of land.[30] In such a period, too, heirs would cling to the customs which preserved the integrity of their patrimony and which ensured their eventual succession, for there was no other source of land available to them. Such conditions form the background to the rigid inheritance customs of the thirteenth century. But when, in the fourteenth and fifteenth centuries, the supply of customary land increased in relation to the demand for it, the social situation changed too. Sons no longer had to wait impatiently for their patrimony, as land was available from other sources. Younger sons excluded from succession to the family tenement by the rules of primogeniture, or elder sons excluded by the custom of ultimogeniture

[28] *Cart. Nat.*, p. liv.   [29] Ibid.   [30] Ibid., pp. xxxiv-xxxvi.

known as Borough English, could obtain small holdings and
support themselves. Ageing tenants could exchange their large
holdings, which they could no longer work, for smaller ones.

The long-term social consequences of this change were less
rosy than this picture might suggest, as the subsequent accounts
of the peasantry on these manors will show. Its immediate
effect on the land market, with which we are concerned here,
was twofold. Firstly it stimulated the traffic in land and was in
turn increased by that traffic. Changes in tenure were no
longer only occasioned by the death of the tenant; land changed
hands at random, governed only by the laws of supply and
demand. Secondly, the decline of customary inheritance, with
all its disadvantages, brought about a situation which itself had
almost as many. Customary inheritance had been based on
certain human needs which did not change; fathers still wished
their land to descend to their sons and sons wished it too, even
when both were eager to shed the incidental burdens of customary tenure. Heritability may have decayed in the period of
population decline but its advantages came to be felt as soon as
it had done so. Tenants began to consider heritability a privilege worth paying for and lords were not slow in charging them
for it. New devices were evolved to bolster up the principle,
previously embodied in manorial custom, that land 'ought to
descend intact in the blood of the men who had held it of
old'.[31] The most important of these devices were payment for
reversion, leases for lives, and copyholds.

2 LAND TENURE AND TRANSFER

Woolstone

The chalk downland in which the manors of Woolstone,
Brightwalton, and Letcombe Regis lie was prime sheep country
throughout the Middle Ages and in all three villages sheep husbandry was an important part of the economy of both lords and
tenants. There are signs that the whole of this region was
suffering some kind of a decline by the mid-fourteenth century.
The *Nonarum Inquisitiones* of 1342 suggest that many downland
villages were in a poor state. At Lambourn 'six carucates . . .

---

[31] Homans, *Eng. Villagers*, p. 195.

which used to be ploughed and sown now lie almost uncultivated because of the poverty of the parishioners'.[1] At Compton, near Ashbury, the tithes of lambs and fleeces were worth only 10 marks 'for many causes viz. that there are only two folds of sheep in the parish'.[2] At Letcombe Basset 'the greater part of the land . . . is untilled because of the poverty of the men of the village . . . and there used to be many more sheep . . . than there are now'.[3]

At Uffington, the parish in which the village of Woolstone lay, the assessors reported only that the spring corn had failed,[4] but there is reason to think that Woolstone was experiencing less transitory difficulties than this and that it continued to do so. The yearly accounts of the hordarian of St. Swithin's Priory, Winchester, to whom the revenues were assigned, show that total receipts from the manor fell from about £72 in 1330 to £60 in 1331, £36 in 1382, £30 in 1401, and remained throughout the fifteenth century at only about half their early-fourteenth-century level.[5] The Black Death made a considerable impact on manorial revenues: it meant a 75 per cent drop in corn sales, the loss of a large proportion of receipts from tallage, a drop in the income from rent and entry fines, and difficulties in obtaining customary labour. The manor as a financial unit recovered by the 1370s but, as in so many cases, the plague crisis had accentuated tendencies already in operation: the change-over to hired from customary labour quickened, leaseholds increased, entry fines only occasionally reached their early-fourteenth-century peak. In general the impression of decline that the hordarian's figures give is accurate. By 1420 the priory found it more profitable or convenient to become a rentier, and from that date first some of the demesne land, and later all the demesne, stock, and rents were let to a succession of farmers.[6]

According to a custumal drawn up in 1221, Woolstone then

---

[1] *Non. Inq.*, p. 7.   [3] Ibid., p. 4.
[2] Ibid., p. 6.   [4] Ibid., p. 6.

[5] *Compotus Rolls of the Obedientiaries of St. Swithun's Priory, Winchester*, ed. G.W. Kitchin (Hants. Record Soc., 1892), pp. 253-95 *passim*.

[6] E.C. Lodge in *VCH Berks.*, ii. 185-7. The Priory adopted a general policy of farming out its manors at this period (typed transcripts by J.S. Drew of records of Silkstone, farmed from 1396, Chilbolton, farmed by 1446: Institute of Historical Research, University of London).

had a tenant population of fifty-three.[7] Of these the most substantial were ten virgaters, each with almost exactly the same
sized holding of 20 acres of arable and 7 of downland pasture
super montem. There were thirty cottagers with holdings of 10
acres of arable and ½ to 1½ acres of pasture, and ten 'small
cottagers' (*parvi cottarii*) with a curtilage or some fraction of an
acre. Six of the cottagers held one of these smallholdings in
addition to their basic 10 acres. Finally there were three millers.
The custumal portrays a rigidly stratified society. Apart from
the cottagers who held a little extra land, no tenant held more
than one full holding. All but one of the full cottage holdings
were exactly equal in size, and it was carefully noted of the
exception that 'he holds 1 acre of meadow more than anyone
else of the same tenure'. It is possible, of course, that this rigid
and formal picture of the social structure of the village conceals
a totally different reality, in particular that it conceals the existence of sub-tenancies and sub-tenants. However, judging by
the efficiency with which the priory's representatives were able
to detect the illicit lease of even 1 acre of land, and that on a
short lease, during the fourteenth century, it does not seem
likely that many sub-tenancies would have gone unnoticed. As
a gap of more than a hundred years separates this custumal
from the earliest surviving Woolstone account rolls and court
rolls[8] it would not be surprising if not one of the tenant family
names from the earlier document were to reappear in the latter.
In fact, eleven surnames recur: a turnover of 80 per cent. This
isolated figure tells us little but it is interesting that a similar
turnover was common in the fifteenth century over a period of
only about a third of the length.

There is no late-medieval rental which might be compared
with the custumal to show what changes in population and
social structure had meanwhile taken place. A list of tenants
commuting services in 1434 suggests that the landholding population had dropped drastically,[9] as do the tallage figures, but

[7] Records of the Dean and Chapter of Winchester, Custumal of St. Swithin's
Priory, ff. 178-81.
[8] Woolstone court rolls, PRO SC 2/154/77 (1-21 Edward III), SC 2/154/78 (22-38
Edward III), SC 2/154/79 (39-51 Edward III), SC 2/154/80 (1-13 Richard II),
SC 2/154/81 (14-22 Richard II), SC 2/154/82 (14 Henry IV-9 Henry V), SC 2/154/83
(2-28 Henry VIII); account rolls, PRO SC 6/756/3-25, SC 6/757/1-26, SC 6/758/1-26.
[9] PRO SC 6/758/9.

these are very unreliable indications. A better source is the information relating to land transfers recorded in the court rolls and, indirectly, in the reeve's accounts.

The plague hit Woolstone hard. The first post-plague account of 1352 shows thirteen half-virgates in the lord's hand on account of the pestilence, and this was after three years in which most vacant lands might have been taken up by new tenants.[10] Even taking the number of landholders in 1349 to be what it was in 1221—and it was almost certainly much lower—this would mean that almost a quarter of the landholding population had died or emigrated, besides a corresponding, or perhaps higher, proportion of the landless. None of these thirteen heads of households left relatives willing or able to take over their holdings, which were taken over by entirely new tenants later in the year. These new tenants were only willing to take up the land on new and favourable conditions. Ten of the thirteen were split up among two or more tenants 'to hold at farm until anyone shall come to claim the whole tenement' or 'until a tenant shall be found who will perform the due and accustomed services' or some similar stipulation. Such tenancies involved two principal elements: they were leaseholds rather than ordinary villein tenures 'according to the custom of the manor', and they were held for money rent not labour services. In fact, during the next few years several of these broken-up holdings were reassembled by new tenants anxious for extra land. But the special tenurial conditions which the lord had attached to them, introduced as a temporary expedient, became permanent. The qualifying clause 'until anyone shall come to claim the whole tenement' became a formality, and the tenancies were seldom interrupted by the appearance and substitution of another tenant more acceptable to the lord. These tenants became, in fact, privileged leaseholders with considerable effective, if not official, security. Their entry fines were low, and they had the advantage of paying money rent at a time when the lord was still exacting a substantial amount of labour service at Woolstone.[11]

The effective security of these tenants is well illustrated by

[10] PRO SC 6/756/12.
[11] '. . . the taking up of an escheated tenement was apparently the most favourable opportunity of commuting services' (Levett, 'Black Death', p. 86).

the history of some of the holdings newly acquired after the Black Death. Of seven new tenants who took up vacant half-virgates in the early 1350s 'to hold until any other shall come to pay the accustomed rents and services due therefrom', two were still holding the same land, on the same terms, in the 1380s, one until 1377, one until 1364, one until his death in 1368. Only once was the permanence of these tenures challenged. William atte Hulle in 1368 was ordered to prove his right to his land and he quoted the court roll of 1349 which recorded his admission. He was ordered to produce a copy but apparently never did so.[12] When he died in 1377, this land was distinguished from his other holdings by being held 'at a fixed rent' (*ad certum redditum*) and had become a copyhold in fact, if not in name.[13]

These were not the first leaseholds at Woolstone. It is impossible to say how far back leases to villeins began, but the earliest Woolstone minister's account, dated 1308, does not mention them.[14] The first unambiguous case is the record in 1345 of receipts 'from the rent [*firma*] of Thomas son of Juliana Hanekyn and his sister for two cottages . . . for their lives'.[15] As we have seen, the number of leaseholds increased when empty tenements were farmed piecemeal, and by the 1390s the receipts from leases were of sufficient importance to rate a separate paragraph. The majority of these concerned small amounts of land, fractions of vacant tenements, or odd acres of meadow; only in the 1390s came the beginning of leasing whole tenements for a term of years.

Inter-peasant leases, often made illicitly, are harder to trace. None appears in the rolls before 1339. They might be on a minute scale and therefore go undetected by the manorial authorities, although some were made openly in court, a fine for licence to lease being made and the transaction and its terms recorded on the court roll. Some were made without licence and subsequently detected. There was one lease recorded in each of the years 1339, 1385, 1396, 1399, and 1414, three in 1341, and ten in 1346-7. Apart from this peak, which may have been the result of the authorities catching up on leasing, the process was clearly small-scale. These figures include both

---

12 PRO SC 2/154/79, m. 4, Martinmas 1368.
13 PRO SC 2/154/80, m. 1, 26 Sept. 1377.
14 PRO SC 6/756/3.   15 PRO SC 6/756/11.

licensed leases and presentments of leases made without permission. The court rolls do not generally give the terms of leases, but the roll for 1347 is more explicit:

John atte Mulle because he granted and leased to Stephen de Cauntbury 4½ acres to cultivate for five years past and 3 acres to William atte Hulle for one crop and the same to Robert Martyn, without permission, gives the lord 2*s.* 0*d.* as fine to ratify the said agreement.[16]

In the same court the lessees also paid fines to have their leases ratified. These entries do not show the price that the sub-tenants paid for the land, but it can be assumed that the lessors expected to recoup at least the amount that they had paid to the lord in fines for permission to lease.

Such transactions were not only made between customary tenants of the manor: the presentment of Richard atte Mulle in 1339 'because he granted his land to free men and outsiders to cultivate without permission' shows that there was a market for unwanted villein land outside the confines of this limited social group. The majority of the lessees, however, were customary tenants. A case in 1385 suggests a possible motive for such leases: the tenant had left the manor altogether. 'Walter atte Fleote, who holds a cottage and curtilage, does not live on the said holding but has removed his goods and chattels and lives at Longcot, and leased the said cottage without permission.'[17] Many examples of tenants subletting or selling their land as a preliminary to leaving the manor can be found in the Coleshill court rolls, and although there are no other specific references to the process in the Woolstone records it is very probable that some such arrangement lay behind the many cases of tenants being ordered to 'move their dwelling' back on to their own land.

One reason why inter-peasant leasing did not make more headway at Woolstone is that land leased from the lord was more attractive. As we know nothing of the rents charged by peasants among themselves, we cannot say whether the price of demesne land was a deciding factor here. We have seen that after the Black Death the lord was prepared to break up hold-

---

[16] PRO SC 2/154/78, m. 1, Martinmas 1347.
[17] PRO SC 2/154/180, m. 9, Hocktide 1385.

ings and commute services in order to get tenants. It is possible
that tenants saw an advantage in leasing demesne land or parts
of vacant tenements from the lord and that this advantage lay
in the nature of the land itself. The very large number of
presentments of tenants who let the buildings on their holdings
fall into disrepair suggests that they were interested only in that
part of the holding which could be cultivated. As at Coleshill,
peasants may have been anxious for extra pasture rather than
simply for extra arable; there is not enough information about
peasant stock farming in the Woolstone rolls to verify this. It is
quite probable that sheep farming played a part in the peasant
economy at Woolstone and that extra grazing land was only
obtainable from the lord, not from the villagers.[18]

This, too, might account for the very small number of recognizable inter-peasant sales: one in each of the years 1332, 1337,
1348, 1351, 1378, 1390, 1394, and 1397. A tenant wishing to
acquire an entire new holding could do so from the lord as easily
as from his neighbours and possibly pay a lower price for it. The
figures of receipts from leases (*firme*) in the manorial accounts
confirm this impression. The yield of leases of demesne land
rose from 10*s*. 0*d*. in the 1380s to £2 in the 1420s; the number of
leases of vacant holdings rose from three to four in the 1390s, to
six in 1413, to eight or nine in the 1430s. These figures severely
underestimate the real amount of leasehold, as many small
rents from divided tenements were grouped together under the
heading 'yield of various lands leased this year'.

As we have seen, the Black Death was an important turning-
point in that it brought new land on to the market and enabled
tenants to obtain favourable terms from the lord. Quite apart
from this sudden demographic crisis, the population was also
being slowly diminished by a gradual drain of families away
from the village. The figures for such emigrations are not large:
two tenants are recorded as having left the manor in 1372 and
one in each of the years 1308, 1329, 1332, 1340, 1346, 1374,
1376, 1379, 1383, 1385, 1396, 1409, and 1413. Nevertheless, if
we consider that the court rolls record only emigration by tenants, not by the landless, and that many male tenants who left

---

[18] When the court rolls give details of peasant leases or sales the land is generally
said to be leased 'to cultivate', or for a certain number of crops, suggesting that only
arable was involved.

must have taken their families with them, it is clear that quite apart from losses in the plague there were fewer landholders, or potential landholders, in the village at the end of the fourteenth century than there had been at the beginning. By the 1390s this may have created a situation similar to that following the Black Death, though on a less dramatic scale. The land market responded in much the same way, with more land changing hands in the 1390s and early fifteenth century than at any time since the years just after the Black Death. There were special concessions to be gained from the lord at this period too; tenants took up large composite holdings at low entry fines. For instance in 1415 John Conburgh took a messuage and virgate once Stephen Carter's and a toft and half-virgate once Richard Ballard's, paying an entry fine of £1 of which 16*s*. 8*d*. was remitted in return for his repairing the buildings on the holding.[19] In 1417 John Foxton, the smith, took a messuage and half-virgate with a mill, and another half-virgate with a toft; he paid an entry fine of £1. 6*s*. 8*d*. but a tenant had paid £6. 13*s*. 4*d*. for the mill holding alone in 1325.[20]

Composite holdings were, of course, generally built up more gradually than this. Most of the tenements taken on in this period consisted of single virgates or half-virgates. The accumulation of entire holdings in this way might be combined with small leaseholds; an aspiring peasant would obtain land from any source available. William atte Hulle, for instance, in addition to the virgate he inherited from his father, acquired one virgate leased from another tenant, 4 acres similarly leased, 2 acres from the demesne, two cottages with curtilages, and one vacant half-virgate. He was a sheep-owner and the employer of at least three well-paid servants or farm labourers.[21]

The building up of composite holdings such as Atte Hulle's surely must have fundamentally altered the social structure as described in the custumal of 1221. The court rolls make it clear that a similar document drawn up 200 years later would have had to record not the clear-cut classes of virgater, cottager, and

[19] PRO SC 2/154/82, m. 3, Martinmas 1415.

[20] Ibid., m. 5, Martinmas 1417; PRO SC 6/756/4.

[21] PRO SC 2/154/80, m. 1, 26 Sept. 1377 (death of William atte Hulle); SC 2/154/77, m. 1, Martinmas 1346; SC 6/757/13 (1353-4); SC 6/757/14 (1354-5); SC 6/756/11 (1345-6).

'small cottager' but a much more variegated society, with tenements of widely differing size and composition, many leaseholds, and, at the top of the scale, a few outstandingly large
peasant holdings, built up in the mobile conditions of the late
Middle Ages. The histories of the ten outstanding peasant
families at Woolstone in the early fifteenth century illustrate
the working of the land market: three owed their prosperity to
the favourable conditions immediately after the Black Death,
four to the brisk land market of the late 1380s and 1390s, and
three to their acquistion of double holdings in the early years of
the fifteenth century. The prosperity of this small group contrasts strongly with the failing fortunes of other tenants: of
Piron who left the manor a pauper in 1329, of Ballard who as a
pauper surrendered all his land in 1348,[22] of the seven families
which left the manor during the 1370s and 1380s. Indeed, in
many cases it was on the failure of the latter that the prosperity
of the former rested.

Clearly this may have been a period of opportunity—it was
not one of stability. The Woolstone court rolls show that the
customs of family inheritance were in decline, and were given
their death-blow by the plague crisis. The court rolls of the
1320s, 1330s, and 1340s show the system of family inheritance
still firmly established. Each of the tenants whose death is
recorded during these years was succeeded by an heir from his
immediate family: in eleven cases by the widow, in four cases
by a son, and in one case by a tenant not stated to be a relative
but who bore the same name. Moreover, two of the three surrenders to use in the same period were between members of the
same family. After the plague the situation changed dramatically. Widows continued to take over their husbands' holdings
and in a few cases sons or daughters inherited from their
fathers, but by far the majority of land transactions from 1349
onwards were in no way regulated by the traditional customs of
inheritance. The situation can be summed up in the following
figures, with the reservation that, as they do not divide at the
Black Death but between two fifty-year periods, they partly
conceal the effect of the plague. Between 1308 and 1358 there
were 19 land transactions between members of the same family

---

[22] PRO SC 2/154/77, m. 2, Martinmas 1329; SC 2/154/78, m. 2, Martinmas 1348.

and 52 non-family transactions, and between 1358 and 1408 there were 6 family to about 50 non-family transactions (not including leases).

There are signs that Woolstone tenants valued the security of the written word. William Kynne in 1372 produced a copy of the court roll which recorded his acquisition of his holding in 1349, William atte Hulle in 1364 paid 13*s.* 4*d.* to have an agreement he had made with another tenant enrolled, and in 1368 the court was ordering him to produce, and presumably expected him to possess, a written record of his tenure.[23] Lessees of even very small amounts of villein land paid fines to have their leases ratified. Although copyhold is not mentioned by name at Woolstone, it is surely in these written agreements recorded by the manorial court that the germs of copyhold lay.

Brightwalton

A custumal of 1284 divides the Brightwalton tenants into five groups: 'tenants holding freely', virgaters, cottagers (*cottarii*) holding a half-virgate, villeins holding *gavelland* (assarted land held for money rent), and 'the tenants of a tenement once belonging to Richard of Wallingford'.[24] Some of these categories overlapped: two of the villeins held some of their land by free tenure, and nearly all of the assarted, or newly cleared, land was held by virgaters or half-virgaters in addition to their basic holding. Taking these duplications into account we can reckon the recorded tenants as comprising four freeholders (one of whom was the rector), eight virgaters and two groups of heirs each holding a virgate, seventeen half-virgaters or cottagers, eleven tenants holding only assart land, four other cottagers of whom three were women, and five tenants of Richard of Wallingford's divided holding—a total of forty-nine recorded tenants. By the early fifteenth century the number of recorded tenants had dropped to twenty-nine and the social structure was very different. The large middle class of half-virgaters, now described as 'half-yardlanders', which had

---

[23] Kynne: PRO SC 2/154/79, m. 10, Hocktide 1372. Atte Hulle: SC 2/154/79, m. 4, Martinmas 1368.

[24] *Custumals of Battle Abbey, in the Reigns of Edward I and Edward II*, ed. S.R. Scargill-Bird (Camden Soc., new ser., vol. xli; 1887), pp. 58-71.

included about a third of the tenants in the thirteenth century, had almost completely disappeared. The village population was now more polarized, almost evenly divided between eleven tenants with a yardland or more and twelve cottagers, with the middle range of tenants represented only by four half-yardlanders, two of whom had additional holdings.[25]

The plague probably accounted for part of the population drop: twelve deaths are recorded by April 1349 among the more substantial tenants alone. As one might expect, few family names from the late thirteenth century also occur in the rentals of the early fifteenth century; four in fact do so. Evidence of changes in tenancies provided by the court rolls[26] shows that the plague alone cannot account for the change in social structure. More important was the decline of many middling peasant families. Although these can often be traced as landholders through part of the fourteenth century, only three appear in the early fifteenth century and of these only one was clearly thriving. In four cases changes in tenants' names can be explained by the remarriage of widows, but where the tenants were men, as was more often the case, other factors must have accounted for the disappearance of so many families. Some lost land by forfeit or by surrender, some left the manor, others simply do not appear in the court rolls after a certain date, or at all.[27]

It is interesting that many holdings descended within the family by inheritance until some time in the fourteenth century and were then lost. Lost to whom? There seems to have been no shortage of new tenants. In some cases these new tenants were old-established families which appear in the custumal. The Curteys holding in 1430, for instance, included the land of Burgeys and Wynd, two thirteenth-century names. The Yonges in 1426 held land that had once belonged to at least six

---

[25] PRO SC 12/5/23 (Henry VI?).

[26] Brightwalton court rolls: PRO SC 2/153/67 (8-35 Edward I), SC 2/153/68 (1-20 Edward II), SC 2/153/69 (1-49 Edward III), SC 2/153/70 (2-23 Richard II), SC 2/153/71 (16-22 Richard II), SC 2/153/72 (1-10 Henry IV), SC 2/153/73 (2-28 Henry VI; 1, 11 Edward IV), SC 2/153/74 (2 Henry VII), SC 2/153/75 (4 Henry VII), SC 2/153/76 (2-24 Henry VII), SC 2/153/77 (4-20 Henry VIII).

[27] e.g. PRO SC 2/153/69, m. 28, 18 July 1368 (John atte Crouch); SC 2/153/69, m. 4, 6 Nov. 1331 (William de Eversole); SC 2/153/67, m. 10d, 18 Sept. 1348 (Simon Daunger); SC 2/153/70, m. 12, 31 Dec. 1388 (John Jordan); SC 2/153/72, m. 5, 18 Oct. 1403 (William Smokyer).

different families who had been their social equals in 1284.[28]
Many holdings lost in the fourteenth century went to families
whose own names had disappeared by the fifteenth. But by 1426
by far the greater part of the villein land at Brightwalton was
held by new men who had taken up land in the manor in the last
part of the fourteenth century or in the undocumented years
between 1408 and the date of the rental.

The court rolls provide evidence of a pronounced decline in
family inheritance at Brightwalton, as we see in Table V,
where all the villein land transactions in the court rolls are
divided into family and non-family transfers:

Table V
Villein land transfers at Brightwalton, 1280-1409

	Transfers within the family (%)	Transfers outside the family (%)
1280-1300	56	44
1301-1340	37	63
1341-1362	40	60
1363-1382	34	66
1383-1402	13	87
1403-1409	19	81

Pressure on land from the late thirteenth century until the
Black Death was apparently considerable. Entry fines were on
average £1. 6s. 8d. from 1281 to 1344. Tenants were willing to
pay up to £3. 6s. 8d. for holdings and land did not stay in the
lord's hand for long. Heirs were apparently forthcoming when
a tenant died and widows were in demand. The effect of the
Black Death was to reverse this situation. From 1348 to 1407
entry fines were on average 16s. 0d. Ten of the larger tenants
seem to have died in the plague[29]—the total number of deaths
must have been much larger—and, although six of these dead
tenants were survived by capable heirs who inherited their
land, it was from this time that inheritance began gradually to
decline. Some empty holdings may have been broken up in

[28] PRO SC 12/5/23.   [29] PRO SC 2/153/69, m. 1º. 3 Apr. 1349.

order to get tenants, for the court rolls from this date onwards show low entry fines being paid for small parcels of land. The 1380s and 1390s saw a greater change. This was when customary inheritance and transactions within the family declined most steeply. It was just at this period, as we have seen, that many middling peasant families at Brightwalton faded out. Land transactions reached a peak in 1394 and 1395 surpassed only by the many changes of tenancy after the Black Death. Some of these transactions during the peak years represent the acquisition of land by the newcomers who figure so largely in the 1426 rental.[30] These were small acquisitions, but they were the foundation of the much larger holdings such families had in the fifteenth century. The terms of tenure changed too over this period, although the actual chronology of the change is hard to date, and several kinds of tenure existed side by side. There was an increasing tendency to record the exact terms on which a tenant held instead of using the conventional phrase 'according to the custom of the manor'. Four types of tenure are principally represented in the Brightwalton court rolls: leases for terms of years, leases for lives, hereditary tenure, and tenure at the will of the lord.

Examples of leases for years can be found from 1333 onwards, but it appears that such leases were predominantly, although not exclusively, a feature of the 1380s and 1390s. Terms ranged from seven to twelve years, but those of ten years were the most common. Leases for lives are found more frequently: the first occurs in 1301, and leases for one or two lives were common from 1339. Leases for three lives occur twice, in 1380 and 1407. Hereditary tenure, marked by grants to a tenant 'to hold to himself and his heirs', must have been much prized. The phrase occurs in 1302 first, and is found from 1348 onwards. Tenure 'at the will of the lord' (*ad voluntatem domini*), a phrase whose meaning is not entirely clear, may have been less a particular type of tenure than a particular type of procedure.[31] Tenements held at the will of the lord were seemingly ordinary customary tenements, on one interpretation 'their essential features being that the tenant does not possess any instrument recording the transaction, but has, if necessary,

[30] e.g. John Knight, John Wodeward.
[31] Tenure at will is discussed below, Ch. VI, section 1.

to appeal to the records of the court or even to its memory.[32]
The phrase 'at the will of the lord' occurs chiefly in the court
rolls of the 1420s and 1430s at Brightwalton, once connected
with a grant for two lives, once with a grant of hereditary tenure. Were tenements *not* specifically held at will necessarily
copyhold? There is only one specific reference to copyhold but
the rather sparse and comparatively late occurrences of tenure
at will suggest that this may have been so. Occasional leases
between tenants, a category probably much under-represented
in the court rolls, are found in the rolls of the late thirteenth
century and the first half of the fourteenth. Explicit inter-
peasant sales, in the form of surrenders to use, occur in an
isolated couple of cases in the early part of the period. The
fifteenth century provides a sharp contrast in this respect: such
sales became very common then, and in a transaction of 1435
the legal fiction of the surrender was dropped when Thomas
Aylewyn 'purchased' a villein tenement.[33] Two presentments
were made of sales out of court. However, although a good deal
of land may have changed hands illicitly, tenants may have
found that with the demesne at farm and labour services no
longer important the manorial court had ceased to be the instrument of seignorial discipline and simply provided convenient machinery for what had become a free market in land.

Letcombe Regis

Letcombe Regis was one of Berkshire's many manors of ancient
demesne. An extent of 1274 gives the impression of a stratified
society very like thirteenth-century Woolstone.[34] There was a
small upper class of tenants with over one virgate, thirty virgaters, twenty half-virgaters, sixteen or seventeen cottagers or
smallholders. There were nine wicks or dairy farms in the low-
lying meadows of the village: valuable assets for their nine tenants. Sheep and cattle husbandry was clearly important here,
as in most of the neighbouring villages: there was common pasture for 400 sheep and 2 marks' worth for cattle, and the
demesne pasture was assessed at sixteen times the value per
acre of the demesne arable. The next comparable description of

[32] Tawney, *Agr. Problem*, p. 47.
[33] PRO SC 2/153/73, m. 15, 7 June 1435.
[34] PRO SC 12/5/50.

the manor is from a rental of 1454-5.[35] A lay-subsidy return of 1332 suggests that the population turnover meanwhile was almost complete, for only eight surnames survived the half-century from 1274 to that date.[36] By 1454 Letcombe had changed considerably. Instead of a society with a large middle group of virgaters and half-virgaters and much smaller groups of rich peasants and cottagers, there were now two large composite holdings (one of a messuage, mill, 2¾ virgates, and 10 acres of meadow; one of a mill, five cottages, two messuages, a half-virgate, a croft, and 8 acres), two smaller composite holdings, and two holdings of basically one virgate each. It is improbable that these six tenants were the only landholders in the village—it is just possible that they were the only freeholders.[37] In no sense can this rental be used as a guide to population. But it does show how some villagers, as at Woolstone, had been accumulating tenements and building up substantial farms. It would be interesting to know whether the peculiarities of tenure on ancient demesne had done anything to facilitate this process.

South Moreton

Rentals survive for South Moreton only from 1451[38] and the early sixteenth century,[39] but the lay-subsidy assessment of 1332[40] and twenty court rolls between 1322 and 1455[41] give some idea of fourteenth- and fifteenth-century developments. Particularly useful are the lists of recognizances in the court rolls of 1361 and 1396.[42] The 1451 rental names from twenty-four to twenty-six tenants (some names are illegible) of whom eight were virgaters, eight half-virgaters, and from four to six cottagers. There were two larger holdings of 1½ and 2 virgates and one of unspecified size held by the *firmarius*. The size of the

---

[35] PRO SC 12/1/1.

[36] PRO E 179/73/7.

[37] The heading of the rental is partly missing but mentions *liberi tenentes* and it may be that it was drawn up to list only free tenants and their rents.

[38] PRO SC 12/5/52.

[39] PRO SC 12/5/54.

[40] PRO E 179/73/7.

[41] PRO SC 2/154/43-6.

[42] PRO SC 2/154/43, m. 9, 26 Oct. 1361; SC 2/154/44, m. 7, 14 Dec. 1396.

remaining holdings cannot be determined. By the time of the next extant rental, probably early in the sixteenth century, the recorded tenants had apparently decreased to seventeen: five virgaters, three cottagers, five tenants with composite holdings of over one virgate, and four with holdings of unspecified size. Apart from suggesting a slight fall in population and a tendency for composite holdings to be built up during the fifteenth century, this does not tell us very much about social change. The court rolls, however, reveal a little about the twenty-nine villagers who were assessed for tax in 1332 and about the origins of the tenants named in the later rentals. Three of the taxpayers who also appear in the court rolls—Henry Husy, lord of the sub-manor of Huses, and John and William de Yonge, whose descendant was lord of the sub-manor in 1375—were local gentry or yeomen.[43] Three families seem to have disappeared as tenants in the late fourteenth century, and one, although its members appear in the court rolls until 1436, seems not to have been particularly thriving in Moreton: one member left in 1381, one in 1430, one in or before 1436.[44] Only two families, the Brownyngs and the Randolfs, were evidently thriving in the fourteenth century, and of these only the Brownyngs still held land in 1451. A search for the origins of the tenants of 1451 confirms this impression that the late fourteenth century was in some way a difficult time for many South Moreton villagers; only three of the nineteen surnames of 1451 appear in the late-fourteenth-century court rolls. A similar impression of instability is given by the high turnover between the 1451 rental and that of the early sixteenth century: they have only four surnames in common. Clearly the fifteenth century at South Moreton was a time of opportunity for new men. The court rolls show that here, as elsewhere, inheritance was in decline. Of the recorded land transfers, non-family outnumber family transactions by eighteen to four. The decline was by no means complete. The Brownyng family's land, for instance, was kept within the family by a series of inheritances throughout the fourteenth and fifteenth centuries, and it was probably precisely this continuity of tenure that was the basis of their

[43] *VCH Berks.*, iii. 500.

[44] Sanguine: PRO SC 2/154/43, m. 2, 2 Oct. 1383; SC 2/154/45, m. 1, 22 July 1420; SC 2/154/45, m. 2, 24 June 1436.

long-lived prosperity. There were two taxpayers of this name in the lay-subsidy return of 1332. In the rental of 1451 a Richard Brownyng held what had probably been family land for several generations, and three other members of the family were also tenants, two holding a half-virgate and one a cottage. A damaged rental of 1492 suggests that there were then at least three Brownyngs still holding land in South Moreton but an early-sixteenth-century rental records no tenants of that name, and another family had taken on part of their land.[45]

The Randolf family provides a good contrast and illustrates how a peasant family, probably of much the same standing as the Brownyngs, could quite quickly disappear. The Randolfs were acquiring a good deal of land during the fourteenth century, leasing land from other tenants for a heavy fee to the lord (10 marks) in 1340, and buying their land out of villeinage in 1361.[46] In the 1380s the family probably included at least two tenants with holdings of well over a virgate with additional closes and crofts, but by 1451, possibly by 1399, all the Randolf land had passed to other tenants.

Clearly heritability, with an adequate supply of heirs, was desirable. Only after the breakdown of customary inheritance did its advantages come to be felt, and tenants endeavoured either to reinforce it or to find some substitute. At South Moreton the transition from villeinage to other forms of tenure is particularly clearly marked. In 1361 four tenants came into court and paid fines of up to £1 to release their land from villeinage and hold it instead for life (*ad terminum vite*).[47] To release land from villeinage seems not to have been the same thing as commuting the labour services due from it, for one of these transactions ends with the phrase 'and he shall drive the lord's plough every day'—perhaps this was a service holding. The tenant in question owed boon-works, and we know from the court rolls that labour services were far from extinct on the manor at this time. These expensive conversions of tenure were followed in the next year by a thorough inquiry into the tenures of all the tenants.[48] Copyhold seems to have been established

by this time: at least two are said to hold 'by written agreement'
(*per scriptas*). It is possible that this rather unusual term may
indicate free tenure by charter, but its recurrence in another
phrase, 'by written agreement for a term of years' (*per scriptas
ad terminum*), suggests some kind of agreement with the lord
which had been committed to writing. There are further references in the 1380s to written agreements which may have
approximated to copyholds: Roger Brownyng and his wife,
taking up a holding in 1384, agreed to give heriot 'as in the
indentures'. This formula was repeated on three other occasions
in the same court and twice on the creation of long leases in
a court of 1387.[49] Some kind of written convention as to the
amount of heriot due from the holding and when it was to be
paid seems to have been essential in differentiating these tenures from the villeinage in which the land used to be held, for
these transactions laid particular emphasis on it. By the 1430s
copyhold or some version of it was the predominant tenure.
Stipulations about heriot were common. The privilege of paying heriot only on the death of the last tenant named in the
'writing' was a prize for which tenants were willing to pay substantial entry fines. A transaction of 1437 shows how important
agreements about heriot were in these tenures. John Cotwell and
his wife and son took a virgate for their three lives and it was
agreed that the lord should only receive a heriot after the death
of the last of them, 'and the said John gives 10 marks as fine to
have this concession'.[50] It is not easy to understand the significance of such an expensive privilege. Why was Cotwell prepared
to pay such a large sum simply to avoid paying two heriots? It
may be that such a payment exempted a tenant from paying
heriot on subsequent or temporary alienations but as none can
be traced in the rolls this cannot be confirmed. Another possible
explanation lies in the symbolism of the heriot: it represented
the ending, albeit temporary, of the tenant's estate in his land
and its return to the lord. This is precisely what fifteenth-
century copyholders were anxious to avoid. If they could not
secure copyholds of inheritance, they were determined to establish the principle that their estate should not terminate, even

[49] PRO SC 2/154/44, m. 3, 8 Nov. 1384, 21 Oct. 1387.
[50] PRO SC 2/154/45, m. 2, 19 Mar. 1437.

symbolically, until the death of the last member named in the copy.

Legal security, however, did not mean economic security at South Moreton, any more than anywhere else. By 1440 copyholds, of any of the types we have mentioned, were possibly the predominant tenures. In the 1430s five tenants took up copyholds or very long leases but neither they nor their heirs were still in possession of their land by 1501. The sole representative of these five families was the descendant of Richard Tyler, and he was merely a cottager. The important South Moreton tenants—Leyver, Whichley, Cowper—were then new men who had built up their fortunes out of the holdings left empty by fifteenth-century copyholders, whose attempts at security had proved to be empty formulas.

Sotwell Stonor

This manor is only sparsely documented for our period but there are indications that some of the tendencies found elsewhere in the county were also at work in the rich arable country of the Vale of the White Horse. Three rentals show that the number of tenants dropped from thirty-four to seventeen between 1361 and 1425, and probably still further by 1509.[51] The two earlier rentals do not give the size of holdings, but it is clear that in 1509 the village land was very unevenly divided. Five composite holdings were outstanding, each built up out of 2 half-virgates, crofts, closes, and cottages formerly in the possession of five or six peasant families. There were eight small-scale composite holdings as well, comprising only cottages with small amounts of land attached. Between these extremes there were only two tenants of middling status: one with a half-virgate, one with 2 virgates.

The Sotwell Stonor court rolls cover only a small part of our period, from 1366 to 1434, and thus permit no general analysis of the land market there.[52] They show, however, the situation created by the trend away from customary inheritance and towards new tenures. By the fifteenth century, the ancient

[51] PRO SC 11/4 (rentals, 1361 and 1425), SC 11/65 (rental of Sotwell Stonor and Sotwell St. John, 1509).
[52] PRO SC 2/154/61-5.

customs of inheritance were observed only in the case of widows. This is not to say that the rights of other heirs had been completely forgotten or were openly conceded to have lapsed. After Thomas Cowper died, for instance, some time before 1426, the new tenant for his land was admitted to it only when it was found that Thomas had left no blood relations on the manor.[53] But heirs must in the majority of cases have been lacking, or unwilling to take on the family land, for non-family transactions outnumbered family ones by fifteen to three.

Sotwell tenants were following much the same course as those at Mackney, buying reversions and taking up leaseholds for lives. Here too they were prepared to pay large sums for this degree of certainty of tenure; we have comparatively few examples of acquisitions of land at Sotwell, but the majority (seven out of twelve) were made by tenants taking land for three lives. There are two recorded purchases of reversions: in 1422 on the death of Richard Slade his widow resigned her right in his land, whereupon his mother inherited with reversion to another son, daughter-in-law, and grandson, and in 1420 John at Wode took up a large composite holding 'with reversion to his wife and son'.[54] These did not, however, differ in essence from leases for lives. In fact, of course, it is often impossible to distinguish these tenures from copyholds for lives; the history of copyhold must go back much further than specific references to it by name suggest. When a tenant took land in the manorial court it may often have happened that he was given—or more probably sold—a 'copy' of the transaction without the fact being recorded. Tenants at Woolstone and many other manors may have paid special fines 'for enrolling' (*pro inrotulando*) their tenancies, but this is not to say that when we do not come across such fines, or specific references to 'writings' or indentures, copyhold has not yet made its appearance. It is often mentioned incidentally, particularly when a tenant's right was challenged. This is the case at Sotwell: an early-sixteenth-century list of 'the copyholders in Whatcombe and Sotwell'[55] gives the dates of the copies of nine tenants, none of which is before the reign of Henry VII, but there are

[53] PRO SC 2/154/62, m. 5, 9 May 1426.
[54] Ibid., m. 1, 27 Oct. 1422; ibid., m. 7, 19 Oct. 1430.
[55] PRO SC 2/154/64, m. 2.

signs that the tenure was known here much earlier. In 1422 John Bailly, marrying the widow of Thomas Doget, produced a copy in court showing Doget's, and his widow's, right to his holding. In 1433 John Pope, on the death of another tenant, produced a copy by which he had previously been granted the dead man's land, or its reversion.[56]

The exaction of recognition payments served the purpose from the lord's point of view of reviewing the holdings, rents, and tenures of at least the more important of his tenants. They may have been the occasion for changes in rents, but also for the issue or sale of copies. Four lists of recognition payments at Sotwell, dated 1366, 1422, 1425, and 1430, show how the very uneven distribution of land reflected in the early-sixteenth-century rental dated back to the early fifteenth century. All the tenants of 1509 were comparative newcomers with the exception of the Pope family who held between them the biggest composite holdings in the village. Their history is instructive. An earlier generation of Popes had been actively accumulating land by the 1430s: in 1425 John Pope the elder paid recognition for a five-part holding and between them the family then held 6 half-virgates, beside odd acres and crofts. In 1430 there were four Popes with composite holdings in Sotwell Stonor and two of them were jointly farming the adjoining manor of Sotwell St. John for ten years at £26 a year. The Popes sold land to each other, as when in 1433 John Pope the elder, probably as an old man, divided up his holding and sold it off to his two sons. Between the 1430s and 1509 the family's land expanded considerably, but these earlier acquisitions remained as its nucleus. By the sixteenth century, although the most important tenants on the manor, they may not actually have been resident there. A court roll of 1502 shows that Ambrose Pope left the manor that year, while taking up a large holding in the same court.[57]

Mackney

The Mackney court rolls are much fewer than those which survive for the other manors studied, and are confined to the

56 PRO SC 2/154/62, m. 1, 27 Oct. 1422; ibid., m. 7, 17 Mar. 1433.

57 Ibid., m. 4, 15 Mar. 1425; ibid., m. 7, 19 Oct. 1430; ibid., m. 8, 9 Oct. 1433; PRO SC 2/154/64, m. 1, 29 Oct. 1502. See also below pp. 175-6.

latter part of our period.[58] They show, between 1356 and 1472, a ratio of eleven recorded non-family transactions to six within single families. Tenants can be seen endeavouring to keep land within the family by taking leases for two or three lives and paying high prices for reversions. An entry of 1455 shows that tenants were buying and selling reversions among themselves: John Downe in that year paid the large sum of 12 marks 'for licence to grant to William Browne the reversion of a messuage and 2 virgates, a cottage, 2 acres, and a close for the term of his life after the death of the said John Downe'.[59]

It seems as though there may have been some kind of dispute over security of tenure for copyholders at Mackney. When John Letkyn took up a smallholding in 1472 it was stipulated that the lord should have the power to evict him if the rent was withheld or any damage done 'this copy entirely notwithstanding' (*hac copia in aliquo non obstante*).[60] If such a stipulation was the exception rather than the rule, as it seems to have been, then it implies that other Mackney tenants had achieved greater security than those at Woolstone or Coleshill where not only were such forfeitures common, but the lord's right to enforce them apparently unchallenged. This impression is borne out by the fact that early in the fifteenth century Mackney villagers were obtaining tenancies which, although specifically at will, none the less ensured hereditary succession by the phrase 'to hold to himself and his [i.e. his heirs] at the will of the lord'. High entry fines, of £4 to £8, were paid for these holdings, giving no sign that tenure at will diminished their desirability.

Speenhamland

Speenhamland and Eastrop lay in very different geographical and agricultural regions, but had an important factor in common: they were both very close to—were virtually suburbs of—a borough. Considering each in turn may reveal a little about the effect of town on village.

Speenhamland is in the Kennet valley, near Newbury of which it is now part. Newbury, after a period of decline in the

---

[58] PRO SC 2/154/1:9-41 (1356-1472).
[59] PRO SC 2/154/41, m. 1, 10 Feb. 1455.
[60] Ibid., m. 4, 12 Oct. 1426.

fourteenth century, was a thriving town in the fifteenth, regaining its earlier medieval status as an important weaving and trading centre on a main route between London and the west.[61] The economy of the surrounding villages must have been closely linked with that of the borough. The history of Speenhamland tenants suggests that this village, however, did not necessarily follow Newbury's lead towards late-medieval recovery and Tudor prosperity. We have no court rolls for the manor, but a valuable series of rentals.[62] Speenhamland in 1376 was a village of smallholders and burgesses. A rental of that year shows that out of thirty-five tenants, eighteen had burgage holdings of unspecified size, which probably consisted of a house in Newbury itself and land in the fields, and the remainder had crofts. Five subsequent rentals shows that the landholding population dropped to twenty-five between 1376 and 1428 and then remained virtually stagnant until the mid-sixteenth century. In spite of this virtually stable total population, turnover was considerable. Five surnames from 1376 recur in 1428, and the same number from 1428 in 1546. It may be connected with this instability that few holdings had names deriving from their owners' surnames: most were topographical. The ease with which burgages could be transferred made for a great deal of subletting.[63] The legality of such proceedings, though, means that the rentals record sub-leases quite openly and thus present a clearer picture of the tenurial situation than would the rentals of a manor where subletting was forbidden. Sub-tenancies are shown by entries such as 'John Squire for the tenement in which William Smith lives'. The chief tenant of one rental might be the sub-tenant of the next; thus John Squire was leasing land from John Norreys in 1454. Freedom to alienate land also meant freedom to build up composite holdings, and this tendency was clearly at work during the fifteenth century. Here, as before, it is necessary to distinguish between the

---

[61] E.C. Lodge in *VCH Berks.*, ii. 198.

[62] PRO SC 11/68 (1376), SC 12/5/59 (1428), SC 12/5/60 (1453), SC 12/5/61 (1458), SC 12/5/62 (1546), SC 12/5/64 (1564).

[63] 'Sometimes a free power of alienating his tenement is conceded to every burgess . . . in general the power, very commonly assumed, of bequeathing burgage tenements "like chattels" seems to have been ascribed to custom rather than to express grant' (Pollock & Maitland, i. 645).

accumulation of small accretions of land and the formation of much larger units.

By far the richest man in Speenhamland in the late fourteenth century was William Wode. Wode was no peasant: he held land in neighbouring villages and sub-manors elsewhere in the county. Though not armigerous, he probably held in all as much landed property as many knights did. The Speenhamland rental of 1376 is endorsed with a rental of 'certain of the Wode lands and tenements in Newbury, Speenhamland, and Speen and from whom they are held' and this document shows how closely Wode was involved with the local peasant land market. Through subletting he had become the effective landlord of many Speenhamland tenants. In the following list of Wode's holdings names that occur as tenants' names in the Speenhamland rentals are in italics:

A chief tenement in which he lives, with cottages on each side and a garden
A tenement once John Palley's
A parcel of land recently acquired from William Miles
A shop acquired from Katherine *Abberbury*, sublet to John *Smith*
A tenement which John Colnetts held, sublet to John *Smith*
A butcher's stall, sublet to Robert *Bocher*
A tenement called *Campodonne*, sublet to John *Dyer*
A tenement called Deconnes, sublet to John Champs
Tenements called Marchant and Poppardes, sublet to Edward Townesend
A tenement called Leycestor
Various lands and tenements which he acquired from William *Brykenyle*
Land over Bolter's
A croft called Colpepers
A meadow which he acquired from Roger Lovekyn, sublet formerly to John Clerk, later to Thomas Knight
6 acres sublet to John Pole
A meadow
12 acres

With his eight sub-tenants and over twenty acquisitions of land Wode must surely have made his presence felt locally as a land-owner, albeit a small-scale one, as effectively as did the distant Despencers, lords of the manor.

The holding of the Abberbury family in 1428, as far as we can tell from the rent paid for it, was a similar, though smaller, accumulation of land. Katherine Abberbury, the tenant in 1428, was also holding three burgages in Newbury in 1436. By 1453 the holding had been split up between nine different tenants, and it is possible to see from the description then given that it had consisted of four burgages, three meadows, and an unspecified amount of arable. Neither the Wode nor the Abberbury family was represented by a landholder of consequence in Speenhamland in 1450. The third important family there in the fifteenth century, the Benets, seems to have survived there longer. Here again we see a large holding which was not simply that of a thriving peasant, though it included much peasant land. The Benets were Newbury people and one of them at least was a fuller there. They do not appear to have held land in Speenhamland much before 1428, when two members of the family held a large composite holding: the name does not appear in the 1376 rental or in any fourteenth-century tax return for Speenhamland. Two Benets still held land there in 1453, but their holding had diminished by 1458 and the sixteenth-century representatives of the family had only a tenement, 'his mede', and 'his lands in the field'. Again, John Norreys, who had a considerable amount of land during the 1450s, much of which he sublet to other tenants, and whose descendant Sir John Norreys was one of the largest landowners of 1546, was clearly no peasant. There are, in fact, only two Speenhamland families in the fifteenth century, the Squires and the Botelers, which look at all like thriving peasants, and neither appears to have been holding land in the village in the sixteenth century. By that time very few of the fifteenth-century names are to be found in the Speenhamland rentals, their place seemingly having been taken by those of new tenants some of whom, like Richard Herd of London, may have been absentee landowners or outsiders. In general, Speenhamland shows a very different development from that of a purely agrarian manor. It seems to have been less a self-contained community, producing a peasant aristocracy from its own ranks, than essentially a suburb, closely involved with the nearby borough and dominated not by local yeomen but by local gentry and burgesses. These, rather than the peasantry, took advantage of the freer land market which burgage tenure made possible.

Eastrop

Eastrop lay just outside the Wiltshire borough of Highworth and provides another example of a village closely connected with a town economy. Its population, however, differed in some important respects from that of Speenhamland. Although Eastrop and Highworth fields were adjacent and many tenants held land in both, Eastrop was a separate manor with a separate court. Although many of its tenants may have had property or interests in the town they are nowhere described as burgesses. Moreover, Highworth is near the two important sheep-farming regions of the Lambourn Downs and the Wiltshire Downs, 6 miles east of the wool centre of Cricklade. Prosperity in this region depended on the wool market and the important local figures, as we shall see, were butchers and graziers rather than weavers, fullers, or merchants. The impact these people made on the economy of villages like Eastrop was considerable.

Internal changes in social structure are hard to estimate as we have only one Eastrop rental, for 1473, which gives the names of thirty-eight tenants, twelve customary and twenty-six free.[64] Of the customary tenants, five were smallholders, four had holdings of 2 virgates, two had more substantial holdings, and the size of the remaining holding is not given. The free-holds are not all described and their nominal rents are no clue to their size, but several of them seem to have been smaller than half a virgate, three were probably virgates, one consisted of a messuage, two cottages, and 3 virgates. By far the most important holdings in the village were the undoubtedly free Hungerfordscourt and Mandevilles. Both were held by customary tenants in 1473, although they were far from being villein tenements in origin. Their rents were far higher than those of any other holding[65] and occasional descriptions show that they were substantial properties. Mandevilles was probably in origin the manorial demesne and manor house of the family who held Eastrop manor before it was acquired by Edington Priory. In the early sixteenth century, and very likely in the fifteenth, it consisted of the chief messuage with 3 vir-

---

[64] PRO SC 11/704.

[65] Compare £3. 6s. 8d. for Hungerfordscourt, £2. 10s. for Mandevilles with 18s. 0d. or 19s. 0d. for customary 2-virgate tenements.

gates, 6 acres of meadow, and three enclosed pastures called Courtescloses.[66] Hungerfordscourt, possibly once land of the lords of Hungerford, in 1467 had 7 virgates and extensive grazing rights.[67] There was a third holding of comparable size but of different character and origins. Described in a charter produced in the manorial court in 1426,[68] it was evidently the result of the piecemeal accumulation of land by a small freeholder: twelve different parcels of odd acres, half-virgates, messuages, and crofts collected during his lifetime and thenceforward conveyed by charter and inheritance as one tenement.

Apart from the descriptions of these three larger holdings there is only slight evidence for the accumulation of property. In some cases we can guess that a particular holding may have been acquired for the sake of the market rights attached to it, for in general those which included land in Highworth or a stall in Highworth market were more highly rented than purely agrarian ones.

The lay-subsidy return for Eastrop for 1332 gives the names of twenty-six taxpayers.[69] Fifteen of their surnames also appear in the court rolls of the early fifteenth century which start in 1422,[70] three continue to appear until the 1450s, and three recur in the rental of 1473. The predominance of small freeholds at Eastrop profoundly affected the nature of the land market there. The advantage of freehold to the tenant lay not only in its security of tenure but in the low and fixed reliefs payable on succession. The heir to a freehold could not be outbid, as many customary tenants must have been in times of land shortage, by a neighbour willing to pay a higher entry fine. Reliefs themselves could be avoided and even the poorest freeholder could ensure that his land never escheated to the lord by the device of enfeoffment to use. Thus, John Avenell of Eastrop before his death enfeoffed John Offington and John Parker

---

[66] PRO SC 2/208/55, m. 15, 26 May 1501.

[67] PRO SC 2/208/41, m. 2, 7 May 1467.

[68] PRO SC 2/208/53, m. 5, 15 Oct. 1426.

[69] PRO E 179/196/8.

[70] Eastrop court rolls: PRO SC 2/208/14 (14, 15 Henry VIII), SC 2/208/40 (17–19, 21 Henry VI), SC 2/208/41 (5–9 Edward IV, 49 Henry VI, 11 Edward IV), SC 2/208/42 (5, 6 Henry VIII), SC 2/208/43 (21, 26, 27 Henry VIII), SC 2/208/53 (10 Henry V, 1–17 Henry VI), SC 2/208/54 (20–36 Henry VI), SC 2/208/55 (2, 4, 21 Edward IV, 1–16 Henry VII).

with the tiny holding of 3½ acres. When Avenell died the homage was in vain ordered to produce his heir to do fealty and pay relief for his land. She was already in possession, one of the feoffees having quite legitimately leased it to her for life. She continued in possession undisturbed, with none of the parties having done fealty or paid relief.[71]

Freehold may have removed the incentive found at South Moreton and elsewhere for tenants to look for the security provided by copyhold or leases for lives. The growth of such leases was notably slow at Eastrop at a time when it was making headway elsewhere. The court rolls contain eight cases of a tenant taking up land with his wife and child. Four of these date from the very end of our period and three involved members of the same influential and prolific family, the Cubbells. In two cases exceptionally high entry fines were paid. Copyhold too made slow progress and copies are only mentioned specifically three times; again a Cubbell was involved. Here, as at South Moreton, the origins of copyhold seem to have been connected with written agreements about the amount of heriot due from a tenement and when it was to be paid. The slow development of new tenures did not mean that customary inheritance remained well established. We have only four cases of customary tenants succeeding to family land, and here again three involved members of the Cubbell family. There were three payments for reversion. Although the comparatively low level of entry fines does not suggest that pressure on available customary land was very heavy, the security of tenure and low rents of their free neighbours' land must have been a subject of envy to the Eastrop villeins, many of whom could have bought them up many times over.

The ease with which free land could be alienated by lease or sale meant that many inter-peasant land transactions must have taken place out of court. Subletting was common; the rental of 1473 shows that the Edington administration had permitted eleven free tenants to sublet their holdings. Cases of illegal subletting, and references such as that in 1424 when 'it is ordered to inquire into those who are illegally occupying various parcels of land belonging to John Cubbell's holding'[72]

[71] PRO SC 2/208/53, m. 5, 15 Oct. 1426; ibid., m. 4, 8 Apr. 1426.
[72] e.g. PRO SC 2/208/53, m. 3, 4 Nov. 1424.

suggest that it, too, was probably quite common. The mixture of tenures and the multitude of small leases between tenants could lead to confusion. Several tenants held both free and villein land and although the compiler of the rental was apparently quite capable of distinguishing those who held freely and those who held in villeinage we occasionally find that the court, and perhaps the tenant himself, 'does not know how he holds this land'. Not all the free tenants seem to have held by charter and could show written proof of their rights as Thomas Stone did in 1426 when he came into court and showed the deed by which Ralph de Mandeville had granted his ancestor what amounted to a small estate.[73] Perhaps in view of the lack of written titles and the very small size of many of these freeholds it is surprising that there was not more confusion. The predominance of freehold, besides slowing down the growth of new tenures and reducing turnover among tenants, had an important effect on the social structure of the village; it meant that there was little opportunity for the accumulation, such as we have seen elsewhere, of large composite holdings of customary land. Quite simply, there was not enough of such land available to make this possible. The chief source of land open to the aspiring unfree tenant was the demesne, although he could hope to add to his holding piecemeal by subletting land from his neighbours. Thus it was that the only really large holdings in Eastrop during the late fifteenth century were the two large leasehold farms, Mandevilles and Hungerfordscourt, which had been carved out of the manorial demesne. In general, it seems that the greatest value of all was attached to the possession of grazing land and rights. The really important people in Eastrop were not those with the most land but those with the most sheep, and these, by the end of the fifteenth century, had come to dominate the economy of the village.[74]

Englefield

This manor in the south-eastern woodland part of the county was from the mid-twelfth century until 1585 in the hands of the

[73] Ibid., m. 6, 15 Oct. 1426; and see also the charter similarly produced by Robert Whone in the same court.

[74] See below, pp. 172-3.

locally powerful family of Englefield. A large collection of surviving rentals makes possible a more thorough examination of turnover among tenants than is possible for the other manors.

The fourteenth- and fifteenth-century rentals show a slight increase in tenants between 1331 and 1349, followed by a fall throughout the rest of the period (see Table VI):[75]

Table VI
Number of tenants at Englefield, 1331-1496

1331	69
1348-9	71
1349	67
1402	53-55
1441	48
1474	29
1496	25

The apparently steepest decline occurred between 1441 and 1474. However, the appearance of a great many new surnames in the rentals on 1348 and 1349 suggests that there may have been a great loss from the plague which was quickly made good and concealed by an influx of new tenants. Comparison of the rentals shows that of forty-seven surnames listed in 1331, twenty-three recurred in 1349, a turnover of 51 per cent in eighteen years. Of the thirty-nine new names which had appeared by 1349 all but three had done so very recently, for they do not appear in the 1348 rental. Turnover between 1349 and 1402 was 79 per cent, between 1402 and 1441 62 per cent, between 1441 and 1474 79 per cent, and between 1474 and 1496 55 per cent. Although there were a few families which were longer-lived (in 1402 there were three tenants whose forebears had held land in 1331, and a descendant of one of these is found in 1496) the general picture is one of considerable instability, particularly after the plague crisis and between 1441 and 1474. In this last period new tenants outnumbered old by three to one, and the active land market which this re-

[75] PRO SC 11/57, mm. 5 (1331), 6 (1348-9), 7 (1349); SC 11/58 (1402); SC 11/59 (1441); SC 12/5/32 (1474); SC 12/5/33 (1496).

flects, together with the overall fall in the number of tenants, provided the opportunity for the accumulation of land by the few. Large composite holdings were probably rare before this time but the 1474 rental has careful marginal notes which record successions to tenancies and these make it clear that a few powerful villagers had engrossed many peasant holdings. In particular, Thomas Tovy had taken over eight tenements.

The high turnover following the Black Death suggests that the plague crisis must have had the same effect on customary inheritance as it had at Woolstone and Brightwalton. The small number of surviving court rolls for Englefield do not allow much in the way of analysis,[76] but villein land transactions were predominantly non-family ones. The tenurial situation was complicated. There was a high proportion of free land: twelve of sixty-nine tenants listed in 1331 were freeholders, and there were still twelve in 1474, by then forming a much higher proportion of the population. Leases for terms of years and for lives are found in the fourteenth century and a court-roll entry probably made late in the reign of Edward III suggests that tenure in villeinage 'according to the custom of the manor' was by then obsolescent: it was ordered that all tenants should show how they held their lands and tenements 'for life, for years, by copy or by charter'.[77] Seven tenants thereupon came into court and showed the copies by which they held their tenements for life; an eighth claimed to hold a half-virgate on lease for seven years 'and showed nothing in writing'. We have unfortunately no further information about the growth of copyhold; by 1526 it was clearly the normal unfree tenure there for in that year it was ordered that 'all customary tenants are to show their copies to the steward and those without copies shall have a day to require them from the steward under pain of forfeiture'.[78]

It does not seem that the security bestowed by copyhold spelled security of any other kind. The history of the eight copyholders mentioned in the Edward III court roll was much the same as that of their South Moreton counterparts. None of their names reappear as those of important tenants in the fifteenth century, and indeed by 1474 nearly all the Englefield

[76] Englefield court rolls: PRO SC 2/154/23-6 (1346-1577).
[77] PRO SC 2/154/23, m. 10, n.d.
[78] PRO SC 2/154/25, 6 Apr. 1526.

holdings were unimportant in comparison with the large composite tenement pieced together by Thomas Tovy, a stranger.

Coleshill

Five rentals of 1348, about 1379, 1394-5, 1424, and 1473, and a survey of 1520, although varying in scope and reliability, give a rough guide to the population of Coleshill during the later Middle Ages and show changes in its social and tenurial structure.[79]

The rental of 1348 is partly illegible and probably incomplete but that of about 1379 is minutely annotated and corrected. Changes of tenure were noted and the new tenant's name written in above the old. It may have been because these alterations had become too extensive that the next rental, of 1394-5, was drawn up, for this 'Examination of rents' incorporates all the corrections and additions made to that of 1379 and was itself later copiously annotated. It is clear that we are concerned here with a seignorial administration capable of keeping a close watch on land transfers, and that these two documents accurately report the contemporary tenurial situation. The recorded manorial population of about 1379 was divided into sixteen tenants holding over one virgate, fifteen virgaters, ten half-virgaters, and ten cottagers. Thus about a third of the unfree tenants were fairly substantial peasants and nearly all had viable holdings. At a first glance Coleshill was a prosperous village community. Another entry in the rental modifies this first impression: fourteen cottages were in the lord's hand 'almost derelict' and three valuable parcels of meadow, generally leased, lacked tenants. The fourteen empty cottages suggest a diminished population, but one in which it was not the ranks of the more important tenants that had been reduced; indeed half the tenants with a basic holding of a half-virgate or more had accumulated small additional parcels of land. Not only smallholdings had been accumulated in this way. Nearly every entry in the rental gives the name of the former tenant and in only four cases are the two family names the same. The Latin of the document poses a problem of interpretation: the former tenants are described in some entries as having once (*quondam*) held the holding, in others as having recently (*nuper*) held it.

[79] PRO SC 11/804 and SC 2/208/60 (1348), SC 11/807 (*c*.1379), SC 12/26/58 (1394-5), SC 11/814 (1424), SC 11/823 (1473), SC 11/838 (1520).

Was this a real distinction? The usage of the court rolls seems to favour interpreting *quondam* as pointing to a more distant past than *nuper*, and if this distinction is valid it can tell us a little about the chronology of the land market. Nearly all the former tenants of half-virgates are described as *nuper*, while those of the larger holdings are predominantly *quondam*. It seems that the large-scale changes of tenancy had taken place earlier than the smaller. Only small parcels of land had been acquired from the demesne. These are limited conclusions when compared with the picture of land transactions provided by the court rolls.[80] But the court rolls for Coleshill survive only from 1377 and their evidence, although vivid and detailed, is only in a very limited sense retrospective. The rental of about 1379 does at least give an indication of what had been happening in the village earlier in the fourteenth century. Clearly there had been an active land market in conditions which had provided the opportunity for sixteen peasant families to build up and maintain holdings of between 25 and nearly 100 acres, and which had also made possible much accumulation of small parcels of land, chiefly by the virgater class.

By 1394, the total number of tenants had fallen very slightly, from fifty-one to forty-four. The number of tenants with more than one virgate remained the same (and was therefore a larger proportion of the whole); the number of virgaters had fallen by three, of half-virgaters by five, of smallholders by one. But this apparent stability needs to be contrasted with two other facts: the large turnover of surnames between the two rentals and the exceptional number of land transfers which took place on this manor during the 1390s. Twenty-nine surnames found in the rental of about 1379 are missing in 1394-5 and fifteen new names have gone some way to replace them. This represents a turnover of 64 per cent in only fifteen years. But although a very large number of land transfers must have taken place during those fifteen years and although, as we shall see, this was a time of decline or extinction for many peasant families, the total number of tenants was not substantially affected. It seems that there was still sufficient demand for land to fill vacant holdings and to prevent their accumulation in the lord's hand.

[80] Above, p. 116 n. 22.

The account rolls confirm this: the lord was losing only a small fraction of his expected rent income at this time through inability to find tenants.

By 1424 the situation had changed drastically. The recorded manorial population had dropped from forty-four to eighteen. Land worth £1. 13*s*. 10*d*. a year was in the lord's hand through lack of tenants and was being leased out piecemeal, and 3¾ virgates (about 80 acres) which had once been tenant land had been permanently taken into the demesne. The demesne was at farm and all the tenants' labour services had been commuted. There had been a great deal of small-scale enclosure: altogether twenty-two closes, generally named after their tenants, are mentioned. Clearly the village changed more dramatically during these twenty-nine years than at any other period covered by our documents.

As well as the demesne arable, farmed since before 1424, the manor house, parsonage, and some valuable grazing land were now also out at farm. The administration seems to have adopted a new attitude towards rents by this time; holdings are no longer described in terms of virgates of fractions of a virgate, and their rents are no longer based on the customary 10*s*. 10*d*. for a virgate with its commuted services which appears as the standard rent in all the previous rentals. Rents were now much more varied, and if we could discover the size of these 1473 tenements we should probably find that they were rented at so much an acre.

The survey of 1520 is divided into two parts. The first, headed 'Free tenants', is concerned with the sub-manor of Lynt (in Inglesham, 3 miles north-west of Coleshill); Lynt tenants are not included in this discussion. There follow, under 'Customary tenants', the names of twenty-three tenants—a slight recovery in population—of whom five or six held more than one virgate, seven or eight were virgaters, five were half-virgaters, and four including the vicar were smallholders. Thus nearly all the tenants were sufficiently provided with land and almost a quarter were fairly substantial landholders. One of the virgaters was also the farmer of the demesne.

One of the most striking features of these rentals, apart from the severe drop in the number of tenants that they show, is the very high turnover of surnames: 64 per cent between 1379 and

1395, 86 per cent between 1395 and 1424, 78 per cent between
1424 and 1473, and over 50 per cent between 1473 and 1520.
Yet in spite of the lack of stability which these figures suggest,
and the drop in tenant population, the social structure of the
village does not appear to have changed very radically. The
upper class of villagers with more than one virgate formed
much the same proportion of the tenants as a whole at the end
of our period as they had at the beginning, and the proportion
of smallholders did not change much either. Although the
average number of land transactions per year did not appreci-
ably rise at Coleshill during this period, there were three clearly
marked peaks in the land market there in 1380-2, 1391-2, and
1427-8.[81] These peaks are not very impressive in terms of the
number of transactions that they represent (eleven in one year
is the highest figure) but they are significantly above the overall
average of between one and two transactions at each court.
Even eleven transactions are more than are found at Woolstone and slightly more than the peak figure at Brightwalton. It
is important here to bear in mind the total size of the village
population, for this gives the figures their real significance.
Coleshill at this time probably consisted of well under fifty
households. Two years in which nineteen changes of tenure
took place would surely have seemed a period of great social
change in such a small community.

How far are these peak years economically significant, and
how far do they merely reflect chance demographic circumstances such as an exceptional number of deaths, or the
coming-of-age of an exceptional number of young men in need
of land? Of the nineteen transactions in 1380-2 five transfers
were occasioned by death, two by tenants leaving the manor,
and six by tenants surrendering their land. Of the thirteen
holdings which thus came on to the market five were immediately taken up and, in all, ten tenants acquired new holdings in
these years. In 1391-2 there were two deaths, two sales, two
surrenders, and two forfeitures. One of the dead tenants was
succeeded by his widow; there were three new acquisitions of
land. In 1427-8 there were three deaths, three forfeitures, and
five surrenders; one tenant left the manor. Four tenants were

81 PRO SC 2/154/1, mm. 3-8 (1380-2), mm. 17-21 (1391-2); SC 2/154/2, mm. 6, 7
(1427-8).

presented for illicitly subletting, one of whom subsequently surrendered his holding. Three of the vacant holdings were immediately reoccupied, one by the widow of the previous tenant with her second husband.

It is clear that a particularly active land market, although indicating a keen demand for land, was not by itself an index of local prosperity, nor did it simply reflect random demographic events. If we take the phenomenon of tenants surrendering all their land or leaving the manor to be an index of some kind of decline, we can see that these years must have been critical ones for Coleshill villagers; nearly half the transfers in 1380-2 and 1390-1 and a quarter of those in 1427-8 were caused in this way. The real meaning of these crisis periods can only be understood in terms of the histories of individual families. Some more general aspects of the land market may however be considered here.

Some evidence has already been produced for the decline of inheritance at Coleshill. The rental of about 1379 showed that only a small proportion of the tenements recorded there had been in the hands of the same family in the previous generation. The high turnover figures already given confirm this impression of the decline of family inheritance. Firmer evidence is provided by the court rolls. Leaving aside inheritance by widows, which we have seen was universally the longest preserved of all inheritance customs, we find only five unequivocal cases of family inheritance. Occasional purchases of reversions among members of the same family are further proof that family inheritance was no longer taken for granted. It is interesting to see that, as at Eastrop, inheritance seemed to be becoming a prerogative of the rich; all the five cases referred to involved the more prosperous families of the village.

The devices which tenants evolved elsewhere to keep their land within the family seem to have been comparatively slow to develop at Coleshill. Copyhold was firmly established by 1551, but none of the copyholds referred to in a rental of that year bears an earlier date than 1528-9.[82] By far the majority of grants of land by the lord were to a tenant and his wife 'to hold for their lives according to the custom of the manor' and from

[82] PRO LR 2/187.

1428 the phrase 'at the will of the lord' was always added. Leases for three lives were rare and grants to a tenant 'and his heirs' were unknown. The absence of these favourable tenures is surprising in view of the fact that the lord was having difficulty in finding tenants throughout this period, particularly in the early 1420s when land in the lord's hand reached a peak of twenty-two tenements plus other lesser properties too numerous to be specified. We have seen how the low entry fines reflect the existence of a buyer's market for tenant land. Perhaps it is here that the explanation lies: entry fines were so low that there was no fear of an heir being outbid for his father's land if he should, in fact, desire to inherit it (the court rolls suggest that he seldom did so desire). Consequently there was no great incentive for tenants to ensure their sons' succession by the devices that evolved elsewhere. Fifteenth-century Coleshill presented many of the characteristics already shown to have been present in the fourteenth century: the disintegration of inheritance customs except in the case of widows, and sudden declines of fortune which were not always to be explained by the advanced age of the tenant and which sometimes presaged his departure from the manor. Again, individual histories bear out the impression given by the land-transaction figures of a crisis in the late 1420s and early 1430s: seven tenants, probably with their families, left Coleshill between 1427 and 1432, while only four such emigrations are recorded for the whole of the rest of the period. There were more cases of subletting during this period, but again we probably only know of the most blatant and large-scale cases, those involving a whole tenement rather than a few acres and, judging by the injunctions to 'live on the holding', those in which the tenant was probably living or farming outside Coleshill as well.

But the outstanding feature of fifteenth-century Coleshill was the rise of a peasant aristocracy which came to nothing. The figures who dominate the records—the Carswells, Kyppyngs, Cubbells, Atte Hulles, and Bakers—seem at first glance to be the founding generation of a prosperous yeomanry. They were building up large holdings, making advantageous marriages, and securing the reversion of their land to their sons. Some were sheep farming on a moderate scale and two at least were prepared to take on the responsibility of leasing the demesne. They were rich enough to employ servants and farm labourers and to entice the lord's employees away from him, and powerful enough to overrun their neighbours' rights of common. Yet of the rich yeoman families of the village in the mid-sixteenth century not one had fifteenth-century antecedents there. Of the names—Champeneys, Pleydell, Perfect, Sklatterford, and Wekes—of the richer copyholders of the 1550s, only Sklatterford appears before the very end of the fifteenth century, and the Sklatterford of 1551 was by no means an important tenant although his predecessor had been the farmer of the demesne. Moreover, the new tenants who moved into the village around the mid-fifteenth century—Bridport, Compton, Ambrose, Bailly, Webbe—do not seem to have been able to consolidate their position any more successfully than the older-established families; none of them appears in the survey of 1520.

Why were the conditions of the fifteenth century, which were apparently initially so favourable to the establishment of a peasant aristocracy, eventually inimical to it? Or, to put the question in another way, what was it in the resources or policies of these families that at first enabled them to build up a strong position and then prevented them from consolidating it? These questions have a wider relevance than to Coleshill alone, and we should now consider some tentative explanations.

3 THE RURAL ECONOMY AND SOCIETY

Family growth and decline

We have seen that in late-medieval Berkshire the fall in population and the leasing of manorial demesnes brought into being a peasant land market gradually freed from the restrictions of customary inheritance. Late-fifteenth- and early-sixteenth-century rentals have shown a small class of tenants able to take advantage of this situation to build up large holdings. The court rolls illustrate the process by which tenants, by holding long leases and copyholds, tried to counteract the decline of inheritance and to ensure the heritability of their land. But the high turnover figures suggest that for many this bid for security was unsuccessful; the decline of many middling peasant families from Woolstone and Coleshill, while not necessarily a sign of individual economic failure, tells us something about the villages concerned and is perhaps a sign that for these families at least they could no longer provide an adequate livelihood. It appears that this was a time of increased social stratification in village society in this region, paralleled in other counties such as Wiltshire and Leicestershire where a thriving yeomanry was able to take advantage of the breakup of manorial demesnes and the freer market in tenant land.[1] Yet one cannot, as has sometimes been done, describe the period as one of general peasant prosperity. Late-medieval conditions that brought prosperity to one peasant family frequently brought decline to another. Of the customary tenants at Brightwalton in 1284, for instance, one family, the Yonges, survived to become prosperous yeomen in the fifteenth century while a dozen others lost all their land or left the manor during the fourteenth. The *Nonarum Inquisitiones* of 1342 testify to the decline and emigration of peasants and to land untilled for lack of tenants in many Berkshire villages. At West Ilsley a third of the arable was untilled and 'the tenants on account of poverty have all departed', at Streatley 'the parishioners of the said village are impoverished so that lands lie uncultivated for lack of tenants'. The greater part of the land at Basildon and Highworth was untilled for similar reasons.[2]

In discussing the differing fortunes of late-medieval peasant families we have first to consider demographic factors. Did some families appear to decline, for instance, simply because they did not produce enough male heirs? A sufficiency of able-bodied males in a peasant family was important not only as a source of sons to carry on the family name, but as labour-power to work the holding. One branch of the Cubbell family at Coleshill and Eastrop managed to retain their land so successfully for so long partly because they were so prolific. On the other hand, an adequate supply of sons did not of itself ensure prosperity and a large family could be a burden on a small holding. When William Kybbull left Eastrop in 1442 with his two sons and four daughters, or when Thomas Curteys left

---

[1] R.H. Hilton in *VCH Leics.*, ii. 185-95; Richenda Scott in *VCH Wilts.*, iv. 40-1.
[2] *Non. Inq.*, pp. 8, 9, 159.

Brightwalton in 1435 with his six children, we may suspect that
these large families, although not necessarily poor, had found
it difficult to support themselves in their native villages.[3]

Our records are not of a quality to permit detailed reconstruction of peasant families, but we can gain some indication
of the availability of male heirs from the terms in which leases
for lives were couched. These extremely seldom specified a
daughter as the third person to inherit; sons overwhelmingly
predominate. Another factor which may have contributed to
the apparent extinction of families through the transfer of holdings to the female line was the custom of inheritance by widows.
Extensive inheritance by widows who later remarried and whose
land then went to their second husbands would have the effect
of permanently removing tenements from one family line to
another. J.Z. Titow has shown how the existence of many marriages between young landless men and older widows well-
provided with land could result in a situation where 'the family
holdings had a way of wandering about, and the notion of a
family holding passing down from father to son, from generation to generation, belongs to the same brand of fiction as that
of the "typical manor" '.[4] Family holdings certainly had a way
of wandering about on the manors we have been considering,
but it does not seem that this was due to a high proportion of
land-transfers made on the remarriage of widows. Such marriages seem to have been rare and, if anything, rarer at the end
of the period than at the beginning. Female tenants as a whole
seem to have formed a small proportion, 16 per cent or less,
of the total recorded tenant population on our manors, as
Table VII demonstrates (the high figure for Englefield in 1349
probably reflects an exceptional situation caused by the death
of many tenants in the plague).

Demographic factors apart, it is possible to isolate certain
common elements in the histories of those families that we know
to have declined. The first of these is the size of the holding.
The half-virgaters seem to have been by far the most vulnerable
group. 'The village smallholders and labourers were . . . the
harvest-sensitive element in rural society . . . it is their mortality that largely accounts both for the height and for the fluc-

---

[3] PRO SC 2/208/54, m. 1, 8 June 1442; SC 2/153/73, m. 14, 12 Jan. 1435.
[4] Titow, *Eng. Rural Soc.*, p. 31.

Table VII

Female tenants on nine manors, 13th to 16th centuries

Manor	Date	Total number of tenants listed	Number of female tenants
Brightwalton	1284	49	6
	1424/6	29	1
Coleshill	1379	51	2
	1395	44	3
	1424	18	0
	1473	22	1
	1520	23	0
Eastrop	1473	38	6
Englefield	1349	67	21
	1402	53-55	2
	1441	48	4
	1474	29	0
	1496	25	0
Letcombe Regis	1274	71	6
	1445	6	1
Sotwell Stonor	1361	34	5
	1425	17	2
South Moreton	1451	24-26	2
	early 16th century	17	0
Speenhamland	1376	35	2
	1428	25	1
	1453	28	2
	1458	24	0
	1546	27	1
Woolstone	1221	53	6

tuations of overall mortality ... In Poland, in China—in fact in all the pre-industrial societies for which evidence is available—the size of the holdings greatly influenced the demographic record, births as well as deaths, of peasant families.'[5] Although we cannot say anything about the death-rate among peasants of this class, the evidence points clearly to a widespread

[5] M.M. Postan and J.Z. Titow, 'Heriots and Prices on Winchester Manors', *EcHR*, 2nd ser., xi (1958-9), 410.

decline in their importance, to which a higher death-rate may well have contributed. At Brightwalton the half-virgaters, who formed a third of the recorded manorial population in the late thirteenth century, were only a sixth of it in the early fifteenth. By far the majority of tenants who disappeared as landholders in the interval came from this class. At Letcombe Regis the large middle group of half-virgaters, a third of the tenant population in the thirteenth century, seems to have disappeared completely by 1445. At South Moreton, where there are no surviving rentals earlier than 1451, the half-virgaters disappeared between that date and the early sixteenth century. At Coleshill their decline is particularly well marked.

The cottagers seem to have been an economically more resilient group, forming much the same proportion of the recorded manorial population at the end of our period as at the beginning. This is not surprising for they were a residuary class, constantly replenished by tenants who for one reason or another were diminishing their holdings or who could only manage smallholdings: widows, younger sons and brothers, ageing or infirm tenants, wage labourers, craftsmen with non-agricultural occupations.

About the landless or near-landless we have practically no information. We can infer though that their ranks must have been swelled by those tenants we know to have surrendered all or most of their land. Many of these may have left the village, many more must have died without the fact being recorded. The lord could claim no heriot from a landless man and the only financial interest he retained in the emigrant was the very small sum which he could exact, with difficulty, as chevage. Many landless people became wage labourers and worked for the lord or for other lords or for their richer neighbours. With the decrease in labour services there must have been considerable demand for local wage labour, and cases of offenders against the Statutes of Labourers show that wage workers might be in a favourable position *vis-à-vis* their employers.[6] At Coleshill the fourteenth-century manorial accounts show large numbers of labourers hired for harvest work and mowing and it is

---

[6] J.A. Thompson, 'Offenders against the Statutes of Labourers', *Wiltshire Archaeological and Natural History Magazine*, xxxiii (1903-4), 384-409.

reasonable to suppose that many of these were local men and women.[7]

References to the employees of customary tenants are fairly common. At Woolstone, for instance, examples come chiefly from the 1370s and 1380s, but as several are concerned with the payment of excessive (i.e. higher than statutory) wages, they may reflect the increased interest the manorial administration was taking in wage regulation after the re-enactment of the Statute of Labourers. The employee (*serviens*) of William atte Fleote is mentioned in 1369 when he broke the lord's pinfold to get back some of his master's stock, and William had another employee who is mentioned in 1381.[8] Other Woolstone employers included John Redewynd, clerk, whose servant left because his wages were unpaid, and John Polhampton, the smith.[9] The most interesting cases concern the employees of William atte Hulle. Three were presented for taking excessive wages in 1374 and 1375. One of them provides a vivid example of upward mobility: John Poltene, employed by William probably as a farm labourer in the 1370s, rose to take over a holding that had belonged to his employer's wife and later to acquire four other holdings as well.[10] At Eastrop, tenants' employees are mentioned in 1428 when Richard Cubbell's servants were accused of taking his sheep from the lord's pinfold, and in 1474 in the will of Nicholas Fortey, but there must have been many in the village, especially on the large leasehold farms.[11] At Coleshill employees are first mentioned in 1377 when John atte Hulle claimed ten years' arrears of wages from his master.[12] An interesting entry occurs in 1392 when William Howhurd(?) was accused by Henry Bailly of taking away Bailly's shepherd to work for him instead; the damage to Bailly

---

[7] e.g. for 49 men and women hired for one day to weed the lord's corn, 18*s.* 1*d.* (PRO SC 6/743/9: reeve's account for 1390-1). These weeders are distinguished from customary tenants who were also paid.

[8] PRO SC 2/154/79, m. 6, Martinmas 1369; SC 2/154/80, m. 5, Martinmas 1381.

[9] PRO SC 2/154/80, m. 15, Hocktide 1389; ibid., m. 16, Martinmas 1389.

[10] PRO SC 2/154/79, m. 15, Hocktide 1374; ibid., m. 18, Hocktide 1375; SC 2/154/81, Martinmas 1392; SC 6/757/2 (1406-7); SC 2/154/80, m. 14, Hocktide 1388; ibid., m. 16, Martinmas 1389.

[11] PRO SC 2/208/43, 8 July 1428; Prerogative Court of Canterbury, 18 Wattys, will proved Feb. 1474.

[12] PRO SC 2/154/1, m. 1, 24 Oct. 1377.

from this loss was reckoned at 40s.0d.[13] That there was competition among tenants for the available labour supply is shown
by the 'excessive' wages which some Woolstone labourers were
able to obtain and by the occasional cases of tenants abducting
their neighbours' workers. Even more striking is the evidence
from Coleshill that there was competition for labour between
the tenants and their lord. In January and October 1398 a very
interesting ordinance was proclaimed in the manorial court:
'All the tenants are ordered not to employ the lord's workers
[*famulos*] any longer on their own work.'[14] The immediate
occasion for this ruling may have been a case in 1398 in which
the lord's shepherd was accused of working for a tenant while
employed by the lord,[15] but it probably also reflects a more
long-standing source of conflict. The exceptionally high wages,
by Berkshire standards, that were being paid at Coleshill during the fourteenth century show that wage-labourers there were
in a good bargaining position.[16] The fact that agricultural
labourers could command high wages must have made unpaid
labour on the demesne, where it remained, all the more irksome. The Coleshill court rolls of the 1370s and 1380s contain
many cases of refusal of labour services, sometimes by a dozen
tenants at a time, and in 1377 'all the tenants who should work
at harvest did not work on account of a great rumour among
various other tenants'.[17] At Woolstone what looks like a concerted refusal to work took place in 1343, when eighteen tenants
neglected to bind the lord's corn and seventeen did their harvest work and threshing badly.[18] The difficulty in exacting
labour services must have swung many lords in favour of
commutation.

The fact that he could get well-paid employment locally made
a great deal of difference to the position of the landless or near-
landless man. A cottager and his family could not live off their
land, but they could supplement their income by working for
others. The half-virgater in a bad year quite probably could not
live off his land either, but the demands of cultivating it may

[13] Ibid., m. 18, 14 May 1392.
[14] Ibid., m. 26, 25 Jan. 1398; ibid., m. 22, 14 Oct. 1398.
[15] PRO SC 2/154/1, m. 26, 25 Jan. 1398.
[16] E.C. Lodge in *VCH Berks.*, ii. 193-6.
[17] PRO SC 2/154/1, m. 1, 24 Oct. 1377.
[18] PRO SC 2/154/77, m. 11, Martinmas 1343.

well have meant that no such respite was open to him. The many actions for debt in the court rolls show that peasants very frequently had to borrow from their richer neighbours and the Coleshill accounts show that tenants very often fell into arrears with the rent. For instance the account rendered there for 1423-4 by the farmer, rent-collector, and hayward (*messor*) shows that arrears of rent amounted to £45. 11*s*. 10½*d*.[19]

Clearly there is no universally valid figure for an adequate provision of land for a peasant family. A smallholder with 15 acres in an area with good land might be better off than one with twice that amount where the soil was poor. Although the evidence is not available in our sources which would permit calculations of peasant budgets, it does seem that the half-virgaters were more vulnerable as a class than their richer or poorer neighbours. One important factor in the security of such smallholders was their rights of common. Such men were, in a way, artificially protected by the open-field system, which provided them with cheap pasture for their stock and arable of roughly equal value to their neighbours'. Their position was thus undermined during our period by two developments which accompanied the rise of the yeomanry: enclosure, and massive trespasses on the common land by peasant sheep-owners.

The common factors in the rise of richer tenants in village society are easier to isolate. They were outlined by R.H. Tawney and have since become commonplaces of medieval agrarian history. The most important—although by no means the only— ways by which peasants improved their position were demesne leasing, accumulation of holdings, enclosure, and specialization.

Demesne leasing and accumulation of holdings

The farmers (*firmarii*) of demesnes in our records were of two types: local men and outsiders. At the beginning of this period of demesne leasing the former probably predominated. That customary tenants were available who were prepared to take on the financial responsibility of the demesne is some indication of local prosperity. A good example of local farmers is the Yonges at Brightwalton, a family which included at least two and

[19] PRO SC 6/743/18.

possibly three farmers in the fifteenth century and whose members were substantial customary tenants as well. Richard Combe, farmer of Woolstone in the 1440s and 1450s, had been a tenant there in the 1420s. Many farmers, though not manorial tenants, were local men in the sense that they came from nearby villages. When they were manorial tenants, farmers were (as we might expect) substantial ones. The Popes at Sotwell, the Cubbells at Eastrop, and the Yonges at Brightwalton were all among the largest landholders in their villages before they leased the demesnes.

In another category were those farmers who established themselves in a village after taking over the demesne, as the Kyppyngs and probably the Sklatterfords did at Coleshill. Some farmers had previously been members of the manorial administration: Kyppyng had been rent collector at Coleshill. In contrast, some farmers were strangers to the village. This is particularly true of those later in our period, and in some cases a local man was succeeded by an outsider. Such a development was found at Sotwell and Coleshill, and parallels the situation found at, for instance, Crawley: 'While the first four farmers were Crawley tenants, the others were apparently from elsewhere. And this was to be typical of the subsequent period. As more and more capital was required to carry on the business of agriculture, outsiders came to have an advantage.'[20] One of the Eastrop farmers, Bally or Viteler, was very likely a local businessman.

Although the farmer is often presented as one of the prototypes of the successful late-medieval peasant, the forerunner of the prosperous yeoman at the home farm of the sixteenth century, few of our Berkshire examples seem to have established any lasting position in their neighbourhoods, and even fewer seem to have had local descendants of any note there under the Tudors. There were, after all, certain disadvantages in the farmer's position. His capital assets were probably not large, while his liabilities might be considerable. At Coleshill, for instance, William Kyppyng took on for twelve years the demesne arable, the dairy herd, and a considerable amount of grazing land. He had to make a profit from 84 acres in bad

---

[20] N.S.B. and E.C. Gras, *The Economic and Social History of an English Village: Crawley, Hampshire, A.D. 909-1928* (Cambridge, Mass., 1930), p. 83.

years as well as good, and was responsible for what might be very expensive repairs. Whether because of his inability to pay his debts, or simply his unwillingness to do so, he fell quite heavily into debt, owing over £10 in 1443. One of his successors owed £15 in 1464.[21] At Woolstone the farmer absconded: in 1440 no farm was paid 'because the farmer has made off [*fugavit*] to Culham with his goods and manorial stock, viz. 87 sheep, 5 cows, 4 oxen, 4 young cattle, 10 quarters of wheat, 14 quarters of barley, and other dead stock'.[22] Even if farmers were capable of raising the £10 to £30 required to cover their rent each year, another factor was permanently working against them: they leased only those parts of the demesne which the lord, with all his superior resources, did not find it profitable or practicable to cultivate himself. At Coleshill, for instance, the lord was gradually almost abandoning arable farming in favour of stock farming during the late fourteenth and fifteenth centuries. He leased the unwanted arable and reserved most of the valuable grazing land. Similarly at Woolstone the priory reserved enough pasture for its sheep—its primary concern—and leased the arable and some of the other stock. Only a study of a great many more farmers' accounts and indentures would allow any conclusion about the profitability of demesne leasing in Berkshire at this period; but the fact that few of the farmers in our records founded enduring fortunes, even on a modest scale, suggests that it might have been a precarious undertaking.

If demesne leasing was not at this period any guarantee of economic success, even less so, it appears, was the accumulation of customary land which so profoundly altered the structure of so many fourteenth- and fifteenth-century villages. Were the yeomen of the sixteenth century the descendants of the richer tenants whom we have seen emerging on several manors and who provide such a contrast to their declining neighbours? Often the absence of later evidence prevents our discovering whether or not there was such a link, but the histories of many Coleshill tenants shows that the prosperity of the late-medieval peasant aristocracy was short-lived. This development seems to have been paralleled at Speenhamland, where the larger tenant

---

[21] PRO SC 6/745/9; SC 6/746/21. [22] PRO SC 6/758/12.

holdings had disappeared or were much diminished by the six-teenth century. At Englefield the chief tenant after 1474 was a comparative newcomer; at South Moreton the early-sixteenth-century rental is dominated by the names of men who had set-tled in the village only in the later part of the fifteenth century. There are some notable exceptions such as the Popes at Sotwell Stonor, and doubtless if there were more villages with plentiful records for the fifteenth and sixteenth centuries many more links could be established. But this seeming lack of continuity between medieval and Tudor yeoman is paralleled in the his-tory of more important Berkshire families: 'Another feature of the county's history has been that very few families of signifi-cance held land in any quantity before the sixteenth century. Almost alone of more modern landlords Eyston of East Hendred and Pusey recall pre-reformation lay estates.'[23]

Enclosure and sheep farming

Did improvements in technique account for differing peasant fortunes? Our sources reveal very little about peasant land use, but they give incidental information about two aspects of this subject, enclosure and peasant sheep farming. Berkshire by the early sixteenth century was a county of small-scale enclosures and little depopulation resulting from enclosure. M. Beresford has summed up the results of the 1517 inquiry as showing that enclosure there was a small-scale affair, with the average enclosure involving only a few acres and resulting in little depopulation and no lost settlements. Tawney found a very similar picture, with lords being responsible for only 42 per cent of the total acreage enclosed and 'much small enclosing by small men'.[24] With two notable exceptions[25] our documents, when they refer to enclosure at all, bear out this impression. Nearly all the fifteenth-century rentals refer to tofts, crofts, and small (presumably enclosed) pastures held in severalty. At

---

[23] F. Hull, *Guide to the Berkshire Record Office* (Reading, 1952), p. xi.

[24] M. Beresford, *The Lost Villages of England* (London, 1954), pp. 339-40; Tawney, *Agr. Problem*, pp. 154-5.

[25] The *Nonarum Inquisitiones* reported that at Hamstead Marshall the earl of Salisbury had imparked and enclosed 300 a. of what had been arable land (*Non. Inq.*, p. 8). At Sotwell Stonor common land had been 'unjustly enclosed' by the prior of Wallingford and Sir William Rede by 1502 (PRO SC 2/154/64, m. 1, 29 Oct. 1502).

Speenhamland, for instance, William Wode's holding in 1376 included cottages, gardens, a parcel of land, two crofts, and two meadows. In 1546, although most of the arable there was still in open fields, many tenants had meadows or plots.[26] Rentals from Sotwell Stonor, South Moreton, and Letcombe Regis all mention crofts and closes. Woolstone's court rolls contain scattered references to peasant enclosures. Although we cannot assume that all such small enclosures were of recent origin, it is significant that at Coleshill their number grew from five in 1379 to twenty-five in 1424. The later rentals, of 1473 and 1520, do not list as many and it may be that by this time they were so common that they were understood as included in every holding. By 1520 nearly every holding had its close, generally of pasture, attached. Small enclosures gave rise to many petty disputes between tenants, mostly concerning trespass. At Woolstone in 1391 it was presented that one tenant had encroached on (*nimis usurpavit*) another's close and broken down a fence there.[27] It was ordered that the fence should be removed and the boundaries fixed between the two parties 'where they anciently used to be' (*ubi antiquitus stabant*) so it may be that a new and illicit enclosure was involved.

The lord's enclosures, being on a larger scale altogether, could cause much more trouble. At Coleshill a long series of fence-breaking offences and ordinances shows that this was a deep-rooted cause of dispute. There were quite large areas of enclosed demesne pastures in the fourteenth century, the largest of which, Fresden, contained at least 66 acres. From 1385 there are references in the accounts to a 'new pasture', 'the lord's enclosure', and 'the great enclosure'.[28] With the fall in the number of tenants more land was taken into demesne and enclosed. The account for 1421 shows fifteen tenements in the lord's hand and put into the enclosure.[29] Other vacant holdings were added to the enclosed pasture in 1424 and in 1425 the lord was prepared to exchange land with his tenants in order to add to his enclosed land. In 1422, Sowthedonne pasture, formerly leased, was granted to the tenants for their

---

26 For references to the rentals in which such enclosures are mentioned see above, pp. 135, 139, 143, 152, 154.

27 PRO SC 2/154/81, m. 2, Hocktide 1391.

28 PRO SC 6/743/7, 12. 29 PRO SC 6/743/14.

common in exchange for the pasture called Oshull.[30] By 1520, 400 acres had been enclosed and kept in hand for the lord's stock, while much other enclosed grazing land was rented out to the farmer.[31] The lord's enclosures evidently were a source of conflict with the tenants. In 1425 it was ordered that no tenant should pasture his animals in the lord's field or allow them to cross it, and five tenants were presented for this offence.[32] The many fence-breaking offences led to a by-law in 1449 that set a fine of 3s. 4d. for hedge breaking.[33] The offences did not stop and the ordinance was repeated. A case of 1428 shows that there could be concerted, or even planned, action by tenants: fourteen were presented together for fence breaking that year.[34]

A basic source of conflict between the lord's economy and that of his tenants, and between tenants themselves, was the development of peasant sheep farming. Berkshire, particularly the downland area, was a wool-producing area in the Middle Ages, and peasant flocks, although their size and numbers are hard to estimate, were important in this part of England. In neighbouring Wiltshire there was 'a considerable number of small sheep farmers . . . on the downs; some were probably to be found on every manor in or near the hills'.[35] Large flocks belonging to villeins were to be found on the estates of the duchy of Lancaster, the Lords Hungerford, and the bishopric of Winchester.[36] Inter-commoning disputes in many downland Berkshire villages show that this grazing land was still well stocked in the fifteenth century, even though, as the *Nonarum Inquisitiones* suggest, there had been a considerable decline in sheep farming by 1342. There is scattered evidence in our records of peasant sheep farming at Brightwalton, Mackney, Sotwell Stonor, and Woolstone, but by far the fullest and most coherent information comes from the two Edington Priory manors, Coleshill and Eastrop.

---

[30] PRO SC 6/743/17.

[31] PRO SC 11/61.

[32] PRO SC 2/154/2, m. 5, 18 Oct. 1425.

[33] PRO SC 2/154/3, m. 10, 25 Apr. 1449.

[34] PRO SC 2/154/82, m. 9, 4 Dec. 1428.

[35] Richenda Scott in *VCH Wilts.*, iv. 29.

[36] R. Payne, 'Agrarian Conditions on the Wiltshire Estates of the Duchy of Lancaster, the Lords Hungerford and the Bishopric of Winchester', *Bulletin of the Institute of Historical Research*, xviii (1940-1), 116-18.

At Coleshill landlord and tenants were both raising sheep in the later Middle Ages. The priory diminished its demesne arable from 349 to 84 acres between 1316 and 1421, when it leased it out and concentrated almost entirely on sheep and dairy farming and horse breeding.[37] It kept a flock of 1,000 to 2,000 sheep throughout most of our period and trebled the number of its cattle between the 1390s and the mid-fifteenth century. It was in the interests of this policy that the large-scale enclosure already noted took place and that the pasture of vacant holdings was taken back into the demesne. Leases of demesne pasture to the tenants indicate the growing importance of stock farming in the peasant economy. In 1316 there were no such leases 'because there is plenty' and no taker could be found.[38] From 1367 to 1406 the tenants were paying a total of between £1 and £8 each year for agistment, herbage, pasture, and hay. The amount dropped sharply between 1406 and 1421 in which year, the accountant noted, much land that had formerly been leased was needed by the lord for his own stock. From 1433 to 1459 there was a sharp rise in the amount of grazing rented out by the lord, who received between £10 and £34 a year from this source. The priory kept no sheep at Coleshill from 1459 to 1465 and so extra grazing came onto the market. Much of it was leased to outsiders, many from neighbouring Eastrop.[39] These outsiders became an important force in the village economy. The manorial accounts from 1433 include stockmen's accounts for sheep and draught stock 'of the lord and outsiders', and these must have increased the pressure on the available grazing to which the high rents for pasture testify. Further evidence comes from the many trespass and overstocking cases in the court rolls, which reveal individual tenant flocks of up to 120 sheep. The stint seems to have varied with the size of the holding. In the sixteenth century it stood at 22 sheep, 2 horses, and 2 oxen per virgate.[40] A series of manorial ordinances forbade overstocking and regulated the renting out

[37] The areas of demesne under crop as recorded in the accounts were 1316, 349a.; 1385, 148 a.; 1390, 188 a.; 1391, 195 a.; 1405, 181 a.; 1421, 84 a. (PRO SC 6/743/4, 7-9, 12, 14.)

[38] PRO SC 6/743/4.

[39] e.g. £2. 13s. 4d. from 30 a. leased to the tenants of the lord of Eastrop henceforward (PRO SC 6/746/14, collector's account, 1460-1).

[40] PRO LR 2/187.

of pasture in what looks like an attempt to maintain some kind of acceptable balance in the village economy and to prevent its domination by outsiders. Thus in 1383, 'any villein tenant letting out pasture for sheep must have, in return for the pasture belonging to a virgate, ½ acre of well-manured arable land' and again, in 1494, 'no tenant shall let out the pasture from his holding to any stranger, but to his neighbours if any of them shall need it'.[41]

The Eastrop records show tenants there raising sheep on a scale which must have dominated the economy of the village. Repeated injunctions to tenants not to exceed their stint or infringe the communal arrangements about pasture were ignored. The stint of free tenants was apparently recorded in their charters: 50 sheep for each virgate, 25 for each half-virgate, 12 for a quarter-virgate. The customary tenant was allowed 50 sheep a virgate, a ram, and three draught animals.[42] These stint figures come from a manorial ordinance of 1466, but its reference to 'the usual custom' points to an established arrangement. The stint at Eastrop was thus over twice that at Coleshill and large tenant flocks, sometimes of 300 or 400 sheep, are frequently recorded.[43] Here too, however, local graziers were usurping the customary tenants' rights of common. William Gynnere of Hampton, Thomas Martyn of Westrop, John Williams of Highworth, Edward Pencote of Inglesham, William Gaye and Thomas Fylton of Sevenhampton, Thomas Robyns of Shrivenham, the farmer of the abbess of Godstow, who pastured large numbers of their sheep on Eastrop commons, although all local men, were outsiders in the sense that they were not customary tenants of the manor and consequently had no rights of common there. Possibly they had bought grazing rights from Eastrop tenants; a manorial ordinance of 1499 forbade this and prescribed severe penalties.[44] Trespass on such a scale and overstocking on a similar scale by Eastrop peasant sheep farmers themselves must have done much to disrupt the agrarian arrangements of the village. Indeed, in a year such as 1499, with nearly 1,000 sheep reported as straying on the lord's

---

[41] PRO SC 2/154/1, m. 10, 29 May 1383; SC 2/154/4, m. 10, 13 Apr. 1494.
[42] PRO SC 2/208/41, m. 3, 17 Oct. 1466.
[43] e.g. PRO SC 2/208/54, m. 2, 8 Apr. 1444.
[44] PRO SC 2/208/55, m. 12, 17 Apr. 1499.

and peasants' barley, it is hard to see how normal agriculture was continued at all.

In villages such as these, it is clear, peasant sheep farming was of great importance. But can we say that it was the day of the small man? There were several small peasant flocks, of less than fifty sheep, at Coleshill and a few at Eastrop as well. But their owners, particularly if they happened to be tenants of small holdings with consequently a small stint, may have found it difficult to compete successfully, especially towards the end of the fifteenth century, with larger-scale sheep farmers. When there was enough pasture available small-scale sheep farming may well have been a paying proposition. But with the lord a sheep farmer himself, and often a cattle farmer as well, with rich graziers from the neighbourhood prepared to pay good prices for hay and grazing land outside the confines of their own villages, pressure on the available pasture became considerable.[45] The Coleshill accounts show that when the lord needed pasture peasant needs might go by the board. In such circumstances villages in sheep country might come to be dominated not by the enclosing landlord of a later period, but by a handful of local men.

The peasant aristocrats

Many of the thriving peasants that we have encountered in the records of these ten manors conform to Mildred Campbell's description of the Tudor yeomen: 'A group of aggressive, ambitious, small capitalists, aware that they had not surplus enough to take great risks', but also 'determined to take advantage of every opportunity, whatever its origin, for increasing their profits'.[46]

Such a man at Coleshill for instance could accumulate 3 or 4 virgates, probably between 60 and 80 acres, for nominal entry

---

[45] Examples of outsiders trespassing are found at Coleshill as at Eastrop. A list of *messor*'s attachments for 1447 gives the names of 7 trespassers from neighbouring villages, while a court roll of the following year lists 11 such offences (PRO SC 2/154/3, m. 8, 5 Aug. 1447; ibid., m. 9, 27 June 1448). At Mackney trespasses with up to 160 sheep and in one case 39 oxen by tenants from Moreton were reported in Edward III's reign (PRO SC 2/154/39).

[46] M.L. Campbell, *The English Yeoman under Elizabeth and the Early Stuarts* (New Haven, 1942), p. 104.

fines. His rent per virgate was seldom more than about 10*s*. 0*d*. Some of his land might have been improved by enclosure, and he could lease additional pasture or arable from the lord. He might have a house and buildings worth from £7 to £10, on which the lord would do the major repairs. He might own a flock of over 100 sheep, and three or four horses, and employ three or four labourers. He might hold office in the manorial administration or hire the mill to which all the manorial tenants owed suit. He could ensure, at a price, that his son inherited his land—and his family might be prolific enough to ensure that when a member of it died no one but another member took over his holding. His relatives might be powerful men in a neighbouring village, sheep-owners on an even larger scale, or manorial officials or farmers of the demesne there. Some of his relatives who had left the district might have prospered in the towns or gone abroad as soldiers; one might be rumoured to be worth 100 marks. This is not a fictional peasant. All these examples are drawn from the history of the Cubbell family at Coleshill and Eastrop. Parallels could be found, and have been quoted, among the Popes at Sotwell, the Yonges at Brightwalton, the Carswells at Coleshill, and the Atte Hulles at Woolstone, and, if we had more court-roll evidence, probably in many other Berkshire villages.

This peasant aristocracy apparently came to nothing, yet in its time its fortunes must have seemed secure. The houses which Edington Priory built for its tenants at Coleshill—investments of up to £10[47]—were built for the kind of men who would soon call themselves yeomen but whom the lord was careful to call his bondmen or villeins (*nativi*). This question of status was important. It was by no accident that when the homage at Coleshill was ordered to compel John Cubbell, 'worth 100 marks', to return from Newbury to his home village, he was described as 'the lord's villein regardant of this manor' (*nativus domini regardans huius manerii*) and that another member of this prosperous family was described as 'the lord's villein by blood'.[48] The incidents of personal servitude—the payment of merchet, chevage, and tallage—were found all over Berkshire in the fifteenth century and long survived the com-

[47] PRO SC 6/744/17, 22.
[48] PRO SC 2/154/4, m. 16, 22 Oct. 1505; SC 2/154/25, m. 1, 6 Apr. 1526.

mutation of labour services. Merchet and chevage, in one form or another, are found on all ten manors considered here, and recognition payments on many of them. At Woolstone the villeins were heavily tallaged. Yet we find notably few cases of villeins trying to free themselves from the bonds of personal unfreedom. Most of these cases come from one manor, Woolstone, and even there tenants seem to have been concerned with specific aspirations for themselves and their children rather than with personal freedom as such.[49] Many South Moreton tenants paid fines in 1361 to release their land from villeinage, possibly to convert it to copyhold, but tenure, rather than status, seems to have been the issue here.

However, an interesting case from Sotwell shows that bondage could still be profitable to a lord and a burden to his tenants. In 1509 Ambrose Pope was a tenant at will of 1½ virgates and some 30 acres. On the dorse of a court roll of 1510 appears the following petition possibly of the same date and perhaps presented in Chancery. It highlights the anomalous position of a man who clearly considered himself, and was considered by his neighbours, a substantial free yeoman, yet who was technically still his lord's bondman.

Lamentablye complenyth and schewyth hym unto your most noble grace your continuell oratour and dayly bedman Ambrose Pope of Satwell within the countie of Berk' that wher' as oon Sir Adryan Foskewe knyght hath at many and dyvers tymes but late hath causyd your poure oratour to comme befor' hym as hys bound man and so hath recevyd of hym iiij li' st'[50] in mony and ware after that the seid Sir Adryan Foskewe manacyd and thretyd your poure bedman yf that he wold ones denye that he was bounde unto hym he wold cast hym in perpetuall prison by reason wherof your pour' oratour for fere of suche enprisonment in no wyse durst not displese hym but hath recompensyd and payd unto hym all suche sommes of mony as he ever requyryd of hym and as yett he never se eny maner of wrytynges of the seid Sir Adryan Foskewe wherof he shuld cleym and schaleng' such boundag' of hym or of hys predycessors never offendyng in ther lyves contrary to your graces lawys that eny man can tell of wherfor yf it wold plese your grace your seid orator hath at all tymes payd at

---

[49] E.C. Lodge in *VCH Berks.*, ii. 187. This comment should be revised in the light of Rosamond Faith, 'The "Great Rumour" of 1377 and Peasant Ideology', in *The English Rising of 1381*, ed. R.H. Hilton (Cambridge, forthcoming).

[50] i.e. £4 sterling.

your graces lon' and at all other paymentes toward the mayntenyng
of your wares and lyke as a trewe and faythfull subgeytt hath in hys
house sufficient harnes to helpe your grace yf ned therto shold requyre
and is at all tymes at your plesur' redy both body and goodes to hys
lyvys end desyryng your most a bundant grace to be mevyd wyth
pety so that the seid Sir Adryan may nott from henseforth trouble nor
wex your pour' orator except he can exibite byfor' your grace sufficient wrytyng auctencyall wherby he may laufully requyr' such
boundag' of your pour' orator or els to recommpense and pay hym
ayen all suche sommes of mony as he hath wrongfully takyn and wyth
holdyn awey from hym and that your grace wold graunnte to your
bedman suche wrytynges under your seale concernyng the premyss'
that he may be no further trobelyd nor wexyd by the seid Sir Adryan
Foskewe nor hys successors but only to be determinyd by your grace
and he shall dayly pray to God for the preservacion of your most
noble grace long to endur' in prospyryte et cetera.[51]

Like many of his contemporaries, Pope had great faith in the
written word. Fortescue hardly needed 'any manner of writing'
to prove his right to tallage his own villeins. But was Pope a villein? His family were certainly customary tenants in the fifteenth century; his ancestors paid recognition fines and
transferred their land by surrender and admittance in the
manorial court. The 1509 rental states clearly that he held at
the will of the lord and a relation in the same rental owed week-
work. But the Popes had also included one copyholder, John
Pope, who produced his copy in court in 1433,[52] and it was possibly on the family's possession of at least one, possibly more
than one, written title to its land that Ambrose Pope based his
claim to personal freedom.

In general, though, the personal implications of villeinage,
where they survived, were irksome rather than onerous, and in
one particular—ease and security of transfer—villein land even
had advantages lacked by freehold. What mattered to a peasant in the fifteenth century was very likely less whether he had
to pay for permission to marry off his daughters or to leave the
manor but, rather, whether he had both economic opportunity
and tenurial security. We have seen that the fifteenth-century
village offered considerable economic opportunity to thriving
peasants and that they were not slow to take advantage of it.

[51] PRO SC 2/154/64, m. 6.
[52] PRO SC 2/154/62, m. 9, 23 Mar. 1433.

The question of security is harder to investigate. Clearly the kind of security that regular customary inheritance bestowed was a thing of the past. But did the new tenures—copyholds and leases for lives or for years—offer any greater security? Certainly the customary tenant who still held his land without benefit of written record might now be in a precarious position, for the custom which had protected his ancestor's tenure had been undermined; in his case the will of the lord was all-important. Forfeitures of holdings for illicit sublettings, non-payment of rent, or unlicensed marriage show that it was not an empty phrase. The question of the legal security of copy-holders depended on the attitude of the king's courts, and is beyond the scope of this study. But on the economic security of the emerging yeoman of the later Middle Ages our records speak clearly: their prosperity; although impressive, was short-lived, and the new men of the Tudor age supplanted them.

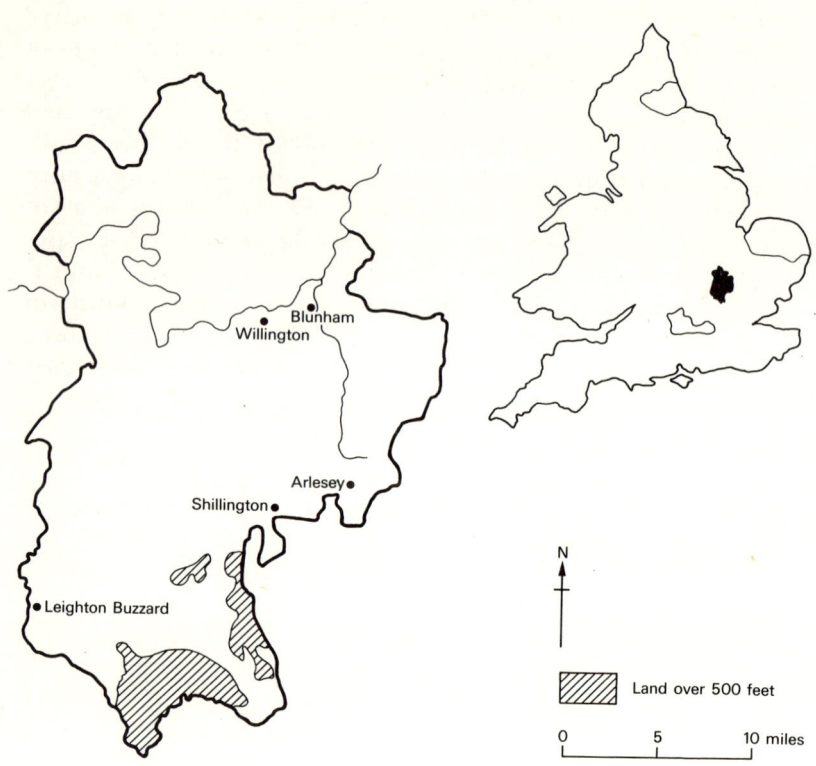

III   BEDFORDSHIRE
showing the places discussed in Chapter IV

IV Bedfordshire: Fifteenth Century*

1 THE COUNTY

Agriculture and estate administration

The most striking feature of the landscape of fifteenth-century Bedfordshire (as of the modern county) must have been the Chiltern Hills which extend into the south of the county and reach a height of 800 feet near Dunstable. Elsewhere the landscape is unremarkable—subdued and undulating, an area of shallow valleys, low ridges, and flat clay vales.

Arable land in the Chilterns had long lain in enclosures, but elsewhere Bedfordshire was a county of late enclosure. In many parishes open-field agriculture persisted into the late eighteenth and early nineteenth centuries. When the commissioners of enclosure investigated the county in 1517 they discovered very few cases of arable which had been enclosed after 1485.[1] What evidence we have suggests that, had they pursued their inquiries further into the past, they would not have stumbled on the sort of wholesale enclosure which other midland counties underwent between about 1420 and 1480. The only example of a complete, deliberate depopulation and enclosure appears to be that of Higham Gobion. While the manorial records of the mid-fifteenth century suggest a still-flourishing community, by 1519 the parish lay enclosed and there was but one parishioner.[2] When Leland travelled through the county in the 1530s or 1540s, he noted some enclosure between Ampthill and Dunstable, but this was probably at the expense of the waste,

---

* This chapter is based on A.C. Jones, 'The Customary Land Market in Bedfordshire in the Fifteenth Century' (Southampton University Ph.D. thesis, 1975). This thesis includes detailed case studies of landholders and landholding families in the places investigated. I am indebted to Professor P.D.A. Harvey, who taught me as an undergraduate and then guided my research, for constant help and encouragement extending over many years.

[1] *The Domesday of Inclosures, 1517-18*, ed. I.S. Leadam (Royal Historical Soc., 2 vols., 1897), ii. 459-75.

[2] Bodl. MSS Beds. Rolls 2, 3; Godber, *Beds.*, p. 139. The lay-subsidy roll of 1524 recorded two men at Higham Gobion (PRO E 179/71/110, m. 4).

save in the Chilterns.[3] Here and there, piecemeal enclosure may have occurred, but the sum total seems negligible. In the main, Bedfordshire was an open-field county. There were, however, various forms of open-field parish: orthodox two-field and three-field arrangements, and more complex systems. The local land market operated within the framework of the open-field system, and, as we shall see, it would be a mistake to imagine that peasants used the market to overthrow communal agriculture by rearranging and enclosing their holdings.

In many Bedfordshire villages, as in other parts of the country, there are signs that the fifteenth century saw a growth in pasture farming. Court rolls provide the main evidence, for many contain references to the overstocking of common pastures, the fixing of stints, and the trespass of animals in arable land. Bedfordshire wills, which have survived in increasing numbers from about 1480, show that many individuals held large flocks of sheep at their death. Flocks of between forty and sixty sheep were, no doubt, more common than larger ones, but none the less represented a valuable asset.[4] Some men farmed sheep on a considerable scale. In 1519 John Crawley of Luton made bequests totalling 178 sheep.[5] In the same year Thomas Hobson of Sutton left a flock in excess of 250 sheep, one equalled in size perhaps by that of John Heywood of Podington in 1516-17.[6] Some landlords had still larger flocks. In 1501 John Middleton sold his interest in Sharpenhoe, at the foot of the Chilterns, along with 600 ewes.[7] In 1513 John Sylam of Bramingham manor in Luton left bequests of 750 sheep.[8] Some thirty years later, when Sir John Gostwick of Willington wrote instructions for his son, he assumed that the manor could support 300-400 ewes.[9] Recent research has suggested that sheep farming was not the pro-

---

[3] L.M. Marshall, *The Rural Population of Bedfordshire, 1671-1921* (BHRS, vol. xvi; 1934), pp. 25-6.

[4] *English Wills, 1498-1526*, ed. A.F. Cirket (BHRS, vol. xxxvii; 1957), pp. 46, 53, 75.

[5] Ibid., p. 46.

[6] Ibid., pp. 77, 80.

[7] *CCR* 1500-9, p. 13.

[8] Godber, *Beds.*, p. 160.

[9] A.G. Dickens, 'Estate and Household Management in Bedfordshire, c.1540', *Gostwicks*, p. 43.

fitable activity it was once thought to have been in the fifteenth century.[10] Perhaps ordinary villagers took advantage of the withdrawal of some landlords from raising sheep to meet local demands themselves. The local land market provided one way in which individuals could obtain land on which to pasture flocks.

Any increase in pasture farming was probably at the expense of the amount of arable under cultivation. The returns to the *Nonarum Inquisitiones* in 1342 suggest that many Bedfordshire villages shed some arable long before the fifteenth century. Of some 111 villages, 49 recorded a contraction of arable as a reason for the low level of their taxation.[11] While the occasion of the tax no doubt produced exaggerated claims by the villagers, the testimony of the *Inquisitiones* is probably too widespread to be disregarded. Unfortunately, the *Inquisitiones* provide the only detailed insight into the abandonment of land in the county. After 1342 the process can be detected only where tenements tumbled into ruin and land reverted to the lords' hands through lack of tenants.

As we have seen, open-field cultivation survived alongside pasture farming. To judge from the bequests in Bedfordshire wills, by the late fifteenth century barley was the principal grain crop grown in all parts of the county. Wheat was another crop grown in most localities and it was probably the main cash crop. Of the county's markets in the sixteenth and seventeenth centuries, those at Bedford, Biggleswade, Luton, and Shefford specialized in corn.[12] In Leland's opinion, Luton was 'a very good market town for barlye'.[13]

By the end of the fourteenth century some landlords had begun to abandon demesne cultivation and to let out their lands and their farm buildings. At Shillington, in the south of the county, Ramsey Abbey continued to exploit a part of the demesne into the 1380s, but by 1406 the entire demesne had been let to the tenants along with the stables, cowsheds, and

[10] T.H. Lloyd, *The Movement of Wool Prices in Medieval England* (Cambridge, 1973), pp. 24-30.

[11] *Non. Inq.*, pp. 11-21; A.H.R. Baker, 'Contracting arable lands in 1341', *Miscellanea* (BHRS, vol. xlix; 1970), 7-18.

[12] A. Everitt in *Agr. Hist. Eng.*, iv. 589.

[13] *The Itinerary of John Leland in or about the years 1535-43*, ed. L.T. Smith (London, 5 vols., 1907-10), v. 7.

barns.[14] At Podington, in the north-west, the Greys of Ruthin had started to lease small parcels of the demesne to their tenants by 1384.[15] At Willington, in central Bedfordshire, the demesne was entirely at farm by 1383.[16] At Leighton Buzzard, in the south-west, the process appears to have been complete by 1407,[17] while at Sutton, a duchy of Lancaster manor in the east of the county, the demesne was at farm by 1394-5.[18] On all these manors, the demesne was let to local tenants, either piecemeal or in standard portions. No doubt this happened on many other manors too. On some by the middle of the fifteenth century the demesne was in the hands of a single lessee or farmer. Thus the impact of leasing on the local land market varied from place to place, though where extra land was available its presence on the market may have depressed both the demand for customary holdings and the level of rents. As the sources are so patchy, for many manors we can only guess that their lords followed the general trend towards leasing. For others, especially those in the hands of the local gentry, the exploitation of a part or the whole of the demesne may have continued well into the fifteenth century. On manors where there were stands of timber, landlords usually retained the woodland in their own hands. Wood was a valuable commodity and cut timber and standing underwood were sold off at a profit.

For the 300-400 manors in the county in the fifteenth century, there are now few series of account rolls. Those sources which have survived allow us to make only very general observations about manorial income. Some Bedfordshire manors do show signs of a falling income during the century and some fared worse than others. At Willington the income of the manor may have fallen by as much as one-quarter between the 1390s and 1458. On the Westminster Abbey manor of Holme and Langford in the east of the county, the farm of the manor, which stood at £13. 6s. 8d. in 1443-4, had declined to £12 in 1448-9 and to £8 in 1473-4, at which level it remained into the sixteenth century.[19] At Sutton there was a like fall in the income of the duchy of Lancaster. The cash received from the

14 PRO SC 6/741/23-5.
15 BRO OR 798, m. ld.
16 BRO R 213/12/120.
17 Below, p. 228.
18 PRO DL 29/2/4.
19 WAM 7566-71.

manor, which totalled £64 in 1397, fell to £55 in 1401, £53 in 1429, and £49 in 1430.[20] In the second half of the century the income of Leighton Buzzard showed a longer-term decline, but it was slight and here the accounts leave the impression that successive lords of the manor exploited the manor to some effect.[21] The Greys of Ruthin are prime examples of lords who maintained and even increased their income by efficient estate management. The clear value of their Bedfordshire property increased from £339 in 1467-8 to nearly £362 in 1498.[22] One of the ways in which this increase was achieved appears to have been the control the Greys exercised over the customary land market on their manors.[23] In general, the fifteenth century probably saw both the smaller and the greater lay landlords increasing in wealth. Despite declining profits, some Bedfordshire manors were clearly very valuable. Willington still brought in over £40 in 1458.[24] The net income from Leighton Buzzard in the second half of the century invariably exceeded £100 a year.[25] The rents and farms which Reynold Bray drew from his manors of Eaton Bray and Houghton Regis at the end of the century amounted to between £128 and £134.[26] The prosperity of the county as a whole is reflected in the lay-subsidy returns of the fourteenth and sixteenth centuries. In 1334 Bedfordshire was one of the richest counties in England in terms of assessed lay wealth per thousand acres. By 1515 the lay wealth of the county had increased, but that of other counties had increased more, for Bedfordshire was then no longer one of the richest.[27]

Villagers and their lords

The wealth of the county remained firmly anchored in the countryside. The principal towns—Bedford, Dunstable,

[20] PRO DL 29/2/5-10.
[21] Jones, 'Beds. Land Market', pp. 143-8.
[22] *Grey Valor*, pp. 26, 29-35.
[23] Below, pp. 198-200.
[24] BL Add. Roll 657.
[25] Jones, 'Beds. Land Market', p. 268.
[26] WAM 9219A, 9219B.
[27] R.S. Schofield, 'The Geographical Distribution of Wealth in England, 1334-1649', *EcHR*, 2nd ser., xviii (1965), 483-510.

Leighton Buzzard, Luton, and Biggleswade—were all small. Only Bedford was a self-governing borough. The lives of most of their inhabitants were intimately bound up with the agriculture of the surrounding area. The villages and hamlets in which the greater part of the population lived were scattered more or less evenly over the county. Unlike other midland counties, Bedfordshire suffered little desertion of settlements in the later Middle Ages, though a number of sites appear to have undergone a contraction in their size after 1300. As deserted and shrunken villages are not a prominent feature in the present-day landscape, little research has been directed at the history of the county's rural settlement. It is clear, however, that practically all the villages which have disappeared or shrunk were poorer and smaller in the fourteenth century than the average village in the county. The evidence of the *Nonarum Inquisitiones* suggests that the process of contraction was well under way by 1342. Apart from Higham Gobion depopulation was probably the result of a combination of factors at work over a considerable period of time. The distribution of depopulated and deserted sites shows a marked concentration on the heavy clays of south-central Bedfordshire. Once the pressure of population on the land had eased, small settlements farming damp, heavy soils were the scene of the greatest shrinkage in population. The recovery in the population level in the wake of the Black Death was slow. Over England as a whole, the population in the 1520s may perhaps have been about the same as in 1377.[28] In Bedfordshire, it appears, recovery lagged behind other areas, for as late as 1563 the population of the county may not have exceeded that in 1377.[29] One result of the fall in population and of its slow recovery was a growth in peasant mobility.[30] On some manors in the county, rent rolls continued to decline in the fifteenth century as villagers sought better opportunities elsewhere. Rural mobility probably had a threefold effect on the land market. In terms of the number of transactions presented in the courts, the market on the rural manors slackened, though the average size of land transfer

---

[28] J. Cornwall, 'English Population in the Early Sixteenth Century', *EcHR*, 2nd ser., xxiii (1970), 44.

[29] J. Cornwall, 'An Elizabethan Census', *Records of Buckinghamshire*, xvi, No. 4 (1959), 264.

[30] Raftis, *Tenure*, pp. 153-82.

increased as many more full tenements came on to the market. For those who remained in their villages, there were considerable opportunities to amass property. Finally, greater mobility may have increased the population of some country towns, such as Leighton Buzzard, and have added to the demand for land in their immediate vicinity.

We have little evidence of the size and character of the villages themselves in the late Middle Ages. In plan many must have resembled villages found all over the midland plain. But the houses of the villagers no doubt varied from place to place in their construction. Probably only the larger houses of the more prosperous resembled types common in the southern half of the country in general. In the north of the county surviving post-medieval houses resemble houses in some of the more backward areas of northern England rather than those in the south. They are simple in style and meanly built, probably deriving from a single-storey house with an open hearth.[31] The houses of the villagers in the fifteenth century were probably equally simple in construction. In this area 'stone cottages sufficiently substantial to survive to the present day were rarely erected before the eighteenth century'.[32] Further south, on more productive soils, houses may have been larger. However, the typical peasant house of the fifteenth century does not appear to have been particularly strong or large, for it was a relatively simple matter to move it lock, stock, and barrel. Some of the changes in house-styles found in different parts of the Midlands did percolate into Bedfordshire. At Barton in 1464 Thomas Gregory was fined 2*d.* for failing to repair his *insethous* which needed attention to the straw, the foundations, and the mud walls.[33] At Podington in 1476 two tenants were fined for not repairing the *stonework* of their houses.[34] The foundations and the *stonework* in these cases were probably the stone plinth on which walls of wattle and daub or of cob were erected.

In the fifteenth century Bedfordshire court rolls contain many references to the dilapidation of messuages. Tenants

[31] N.W. Alcock, 'Timber-framed Buildings in North Bedfordshire', *Bedfordshire Archaeological Journal*, iv (1969), 57-9.

[32] J.A. Shepherd, 'Vernacular Buildings in England and Wales', *Transactions of the Institute of British Geographers*, xl (1966), 22-3.

[33] PRO SC 2/179/70, m. 2.

[34] BRO OR 802, m. 1-1d.

were frequently ordered to repair their buildings, were fined for not doing so, or agreed to build new ones (or repair old ones) when a tenement changed hands. In some cases, no doubt, tenements fell into disrepair because individual tenants were too poor to maintain them. On the whole, the shrinkage in village populations presents a more plausible explanation for most of the dilapidation rather than continuing rural impoverishment. Some tenants with houses in need of repair held two or more tenements and probably had little incentive to maintain all their property in good condition. John Ward of Shillington, although fined in 1428 for neglecting his property, was the most active land dealer of his generation in the manor.[35] For their part, landlords anxious to maintain their rent rolls were prepared to encourage tenants to take on holdings by grants of timber or cash towards the upkeep of the property. At Podington tenants sometimes received timber or underwood with which to repair their houses.[36] In 1413 Richard Tommes received 26*s.* 8*d.* towards the cost of repairs in addition to an allocation of wood.[37] And in 1457 Richard Addereston was excused the entry fine on a tenement he had acquired because it was ruinous; he too received timber.[38] Similar grants were made on the manors of Ramsey Abbey.

For the well-to-do, wills provide some insight into the sorts of possessions found in their homes at the end of the fifteenth century.[39] For the farmers and peasants who formed the greater part of the rural population there is less detail. The lay-subsidy rolls of 1523-5 suggest that in some parts as much as one-half of the rural population were labourers, assessed on wages of £1 a year.[40] Unfortunately the subsidies took no account of customary holdings. Thus an assessment of property or wages does not necessarily do full justice to individual circumstances. The middling peasants, those assessed on goods worth £5, were probably mostly customary tenants, though we usually have little idea of the size of their holdings. In Buckinghamshire, particularly in the north of the county, a relatively large amount of land was held freely in 1522, and much of this was

[35] PRO SC 2/179/59, m. 4; see below, pp. 210-11.
[36] BRO OR 798, mm. 10, 12; OR 799, m. 1.
[37] BRO OR 799, m. 8.
[38] BRO OR 800, m. 16.
[39] Godber, *Beds.*, pp. 165-7.
[40] Ibid., p. 214.

held in quite small parcels by local yeomen and husbandmen.[41] In 1279 in the two northern hundreds of Bedfordshire as much as 46 per cent of the land had been held freely,[42] and it seems likely that landholding in this part in 1522 was similar to that in neighbouring Buckinghamshire. In other parts of the county there may not have been so large a proportion of free land. However, rentals and court rolls of individual manors in the centre and south of the county suggest that in the fifteenth and early sixteenth centuries freeholds could be as numerous as copyholds. Many freeholds were very small, but one man often held several scattered among neighbouring villages. Many tenants held both free and customary land.

In Buckinghamshire in 1523 the gentry and the peers owned between them about 61 per cent of lay-owned land, with the rest in the hands of lesser landowners.[43] There was probably a roughly similar division in Bedfordshire though few villages in Bedfordshire can have had a resident squire. Most lords held more than one manor, and the greater the size of a man's estate the greater was the likelihood that he held land in other counties. By 1500 there were between 300 and 400 manors in the county but only about 125 parishes. Thus there were on average three manors to a parish, and those with a single manor were rare. As the average size of a rural parish was about 2,250 acres, many manors were very small.[44] In the fifteenth century, 70 per cent of the manors in the county were owned by laymen. In 1412 an income tax was levied on owners of lands and rents worth £20 or more a year at the rate of 6s. 8d. for every £20, and the surviving returns provide a fairly comprehensive guide to the more prominent lay landlords at that date.[45] While some (perhaps many) incomes were under-assessed, and the returns excluded many of the parish gentry whose estates were worth less than £20 a year, they do give

---

[41] *The Certificate of Musters for Buckinghamshire in 1522*, ed. A.C. Chibnall (Historical MSS. Commission, Joint Publications No.18; Bucks. Record Soc., vol.xvii; 1973), pp. 17-21.

[42] Kosminsky, *Studies*, p. 90.

[43] J. Cornwall, 'The Early Tudor Gentry', *EcHR*, 2nd ser., xvii (1964-5), 461.

[44] The range was from less than 1,000 a. to over 15,000 a. at Luton, but here there were at least 27 manors.

[45] *Feudal Aids*, vi. 391-8.

some indication of the relative wealth and importance of Bedfordshire landowners.

In 1412, the largest lay estate in Bedfordshire was held by Reynold Grey, lord of Ruthin. In addition to his land in the palatinate of Chester and the marcher lordship of Ruthin he held manors scattered over seven other counties in the Midlands and East Anglia.[46] By the 1460s, with the acquisition of Ampthill, Bedfordshire had become not only the administrative base of the midland estates but also the county in which lay the Greys' favourite country residence.[47] Not every landlord established the same close connections with Bedfordshire as the Greys. Of the total landed wealth encompassed by the income tax, 60 to 65 per cent was in the hands of gentry, knights, and nobility who were not first and foremost Bedfordshire men. Many local men held only one or two manors.

In the fifteenth century, religious houses owned some 30 per cent of the manors in the county. Of this proportion, perhaps 110 manors in all, Bedfordshire houses held half. The rest were shared between twenty other foundations, no one of them, with the exception of the Knights Hospitallers, holding more than four manors. The principal foundations within the county were mostly small in terms of their personnel and modest in terms of their endowment. Apart from cartularies they have left behind them few records. In the fifteenth century, in common with lay lords, the religious houses probably let out most of their demesnes, perhaps retaining some land in the immediate neighbourhood of the foundation. Although several of the Bedfordshire houses held land in other counties, they usually held the core of their lands around their site. Thus Woburn Abbey held a block of land in the west of the county, Bushmead Priory held several manors in and around Eaton Socon in the north-east, and Dunstable Priory held land in the south-west. The estates of the gentry, on the other hand, tended to be scattered more widely throughout the county.

The fifteenth century was a period of flux in the descent of lay estates in Bedfordshire. We can trace the descent of some sixty-seven (out of seventy-eight) of the estates which were listed in the returns of 1412. Of these, 40 per cent (27)

---

[46] *Grey Valor*, pp. 6, 22.   [47] Ibid., p. 46.

remained in the one family throughout the century, 27 per cent (18) passed from one family to another by marriage, 27 per cent (18) passed from one family to another by purchase or some other means, and the remaining 6 per cent (4) had a more chequered descent, passing from one family to another by marriage and then to another family by purchase. When we examine the descent of as many lay estates as possible (199 out of about 240 manors), we find that 38 per cent (76 manors) descended in the male line of the one family, 24 per cent (48 manors) passed out of one family by marriage, while 38 per cent (75 manors) eventually passed from one family to another, unrelated family. As families died out in the male line or died out completely, so newcomers took their place or established families stepped in to enlarge their own estates. When John, Lord Wenlock, died in 1471, his estate in and around Luton was granted to Thomas Rotherham, then bishop of Lincoln. By 1500 the Rotherhams had amassed a large estate in the south of the county.[48] Another man who built up a sizeable estate in Bedfordshire at the end of the century was Sir Reynold Bray, who was granted a part of the lands of the Zouches of Harringworth when they were forfeited in 1485.[49] After the death of Sir John Cornwall, Lord Fanhope, in 1443, Lord Edmund Grey was eventually able to step in and purchase all Cornwall's land in Bedfordshire, including the fine castle at Ampthill.[50]

Among the men who bought land and property in the county in the fifteenth and early sixteenth centuries there were several London merchants. The only London merchant listed as a taxpayer in Bedfordshire in 1412 was Stephen Spelman who held a manor in Maulden.[51] However, Sir Adam Francis, who held Eyworth, was the son of a London mercer,[52] and Sir Henry Brounflete (later Lord Vescy), who succeeded to the Bedfordshire lands of his father, Sir Thomas, owned merchant ships and at one time sought membership in the Grocers Company in London.[53] During the century, London merchants began to

---

[48] Godber, *Beds.*, p. 159.
[49] *CP*, xii, pt. 2, pp. 945-7.
[50] *Grey Valor*, pp. 34-5.
[51] *Feudal Aids*, vi. 397; Thrupp, *Merchant Class*, p. 367.
[52] *Feudal Aids*, vi. 395; Thrupp, *Merchant Class*, pp. 284, 341-2.
[53] *Feudal Aids*, vi. 393; Thrupp, *Merchant Class*, p. 243.

buy land, particularly in the south of the county, well within reach of the city. Alexander Heued (or Hened), citizen and wax-chandler of London, bought land in Luton in the early years of the century.[54] Richard Sutton, draper, held land at Stopsley in Luton when he died in 1430.[55] Richard Drake, merchant of the staple, sold his estate in Shillington in 1502.[56] Richard Fermour, gentleman and grocer, built up an estate in and around Luton in the 1520s.[57] John Morecote, gentleman, bought freeholds in a number of parishes in the 1490s, as well as 58 acres of copyhold land in Sundon and Luton.[58] George Monoux, master of the Drapers Company, and Lord Mayor of London in 1514, was another Londoner who bought both freeholds and copyholds in the county. He was just one of a number of Londoners who invested in copyholds at Leighton Buzzard.[59] The willingness of merchants and gentlemen to hold land in customary tenure is a sure sign of the security of title which accrued to copyhold, and their involvement in the market is one of its more fascinating aspects.

The proximity of London also drew Bedfordshire men there. Thomas Northfeld of Eaton Socon apprenticed his son Walter to Stephen Sampton, bowyer, in 1442.[60] Thomas Chamber, grocer of London, who died in or around 1488, had been born in Blunham.[61] Other men made more of a mark. Thomas Chalton, son of Thomas Chalton of Dunstable, was a member of the Mercers Company, and Lord Mayor of London in 1449.[62] In fact there were several links between merchants at Dunstable and at London: the Fayreys held land in both towns,[63] and the family of William Cantelowe, mercer of London, was related to the Dunstable family of Pycot, prominent

[54] PRO CP 25(i)/6/73, fo. 18; CP 25(i)/6/74, fo. 23. This Alexander seems an interesting character if we may identify him with the Alexander Hened alleged to be a villein of Higham Gobion (PRO C 260/131/21).

[55] *Test. Records in London*, p. 178.

[56] *CCR* 1500-9, p. 259.

[57] BL Egerton MS 1938, fos. 42r-52v.

[58] PRO CP 25(i)/6/83, fo. 24; *CCR* 1485-1500, pp. 321, 368.

[59] Godber, *Beds.*, p. 140; see below, pp. 234-5.

[60] *Calendar of Plea and Memoranda Rolls of the City of London, 1437-1457*, ed. P.E. Jones (Cambridge, 1954), p. 46.

[61] *Test. Records in London*, p. 41.

[62] Godber, *Beds.*, p. 158; Thrupp, *Merchant Class*, p. 330.

[63] Godber, *Beds.*, p. 158.

in the second half of the fifteenth century.[64] Other members of Bedfordshire families who became Lord Mayors of London included William Stocker of Eaton Socon (1484) and William Boteler of Biddenham (1515-16).[65]

Land, of course, was a safe investment, and an additional attraction lay in the effective lordship over men which it bestowed. The Bedfordshire landlords and the London merchants who bought up land in the county probably paid about twenty years' purchase, that is twenty times the annual value of a rent-charge. This was the usual price for land in the fifteenth century (and on into the eighteenth century), though we have little evidence of prices actually paid in Bedfordshire. The significant relationships which the ownership of a manor brought to a landlord lay not so much with poor peasants as with the well-to-do villagers who farmed the demesnes and the parish 'gentry' who acted as bailiffs, stewards, and receivers. In turn it was these men who had the contact with the peasantry. Sir John Gostwick was voicing the opinion of every lord when he wrote to his son in the sixteenth century: 'Ye must have some honest man to have the charge of your husbandry . . . This man if he be an honest man shalbe the key of your husbandry and shall bring you and your wife much quietness . . . In anie wise, take good hede to whome and how you lett your fermes.'[66] It was not easy to unearth honest and effective estate officials, but at the local level it was these men who provided the link between lord and tenant in the fifteenth and early sixteenth centuries, especially when many manors lacked a resident lord. The bailiffs, rent collectors, and farmers became increasingly important and influential within their communities. As local representatives of the lord they fulfilled a vital rôle in the workings of the local land market, for it was through these men that many transfers of customary land took place out of court. Their presence contributed to the flexibility of customary tenure, for holdings could be taken up at any time as long as formal registration was made at the next court.

[64] F.A. Page Turner, 'The Bedfordshire Wills and Administrations proved at Lambeth Palace and in the Archdeaconry of Huntingdon', *BHRS*, ii (1914), 47-8; *CCR* 1485-1500, p. 176; Thrupp, *Merchant Class*, p. 328.

[65] Godber, *Beds.*, p. 140.

[66] A.G. Dickens, 'Estate and Household Management in Bedfordshire, c.1540', *Gostwicks*, pp. 38-44.

These men were also in a position to benefit greatly from the land market. Several amassed large holdings of customary land in various Bedfordshire manors. Higher in the social and administrative scale there were men like Richard Carlile, Bedfordshire receiver to the Greys in 1467-8, who bought a manor in Roxton in 1472,[67] and Christopher Wase, receiver to Alice Chaucer at Leighton Buzzard in the 1460s and 1470s. Wase was mayor of High Wycombe in 1480, and at his death left freehold property in that town, as well as copyhold lands elsewhere in Buckinghamshire.[68] It was the local officials and their overseers who were responsible, directly or indirectly, for the compilation and care of the records which record the market in customary land. It is to these we now turn to examine the land market on a number of rural manors in Bedfordshire.

2 FOUR RURAL MANORS

The customary land market

The market in customary land was regulated by local manorial customs. In fifteenth-century Bedfordshire the customs resembled those found in many different parts of the country. The two principal forms of customary tenure—for a term of years or for life on the one hand, and in perpetuity by inheritance on the other— existed side by side on different manors. The first major signs of the disappearance of villein disabilities, particularly labour services, are found in the 1370s and 1380s. On some manors tenants already held their land by copy of court roll, a development possibly associated with the commutation of services into cash rents. On the manors of Ramsey Abbey copyholds for terms of years began to replace the traditional servile tenures in the 1370s. Thereafter this tenure was gradually converted to copyhold of inheritance.[1] Thus the Cranfield custumal of 1484 stated that the customary tenants held to them, their heirs, and assigns, whereas most entries in the abbey's court book were copyholds for years or for life.[2] At

---

[67] *Grey Valor*, pp. 46-7; *VCH Beds.*, iii. 321.   [68] *Buck. Archdeaconry Cts.*, pp. 137-8.

[1] Raftis, *Tenure*, pp. 65-6.   [2] Ibid., p. 202 n; BRO AD 341.

Willington by 1383 the former tenants in villeinage held their land by copy for life or for terms of years.[3] By the beginning of the fifteenth century customary tenures at Blunham and Podington, manors of the Greys of Ruthin, were copyholds for terms of years or for life.[4] In some places copyholds of inheritance replaced servile tenure: this was so at Arlesey and at Leighton Buzzard.[5] Giving a tenant a copy did not remove legal disabilities, for at law copyhold was no different from villeinage. The customs which grew up around copyhold both expressed the security of a tenant's title and enshrined the disabilities which continued to attach to customary tenure.

Bedfordshire court rolls and custumals show that customary tenants enjoyed freedom of alienation provided their transfers were presented in the manor court. At Cranfield the tenant had the right to alienate either in court, or at any other time into the hands of the steward, bailiff, or headborow (chief pledge), provided the alienation was then presented formally at the next court.[6] The right to alienate outside the court, followed by formal presentation, was important, especially in manors where courts were held only once or twice a year. In this case the tenant made his alienation into the hands of one of the manorial officials or in front of witnesses. The importance of their testimony can be judged from an entry in the Ramsey court book in 1419-20. Adam Yonge sought entry to a half-virgate in Shillington which he claimed Richard Grene had surrendered to him out of court. However, Adam was unable to produce witnesses to the alleged transfer and the land passed to Richard Grene's son.[7] Customary tenants also had the right to sublet a part of their tenements or to lease them outright. On the manors of Ramsey Abbey a tenant could sublet his land for up to three years without formal licence.[8] For longer periods he required a licence for which he paid fine. On other manors the period in which informal subletting was allowed may have been less—two years,[9] or a year and a day.[10]

---

[3] Below, p. 203.
[4] BRO L 26/51; OR 798, m. 3.
[5] Jones, 'Beds. Land Market', pp. 92, 153.
[6] BRO AD 341.
[7] BL Harley MS 445, fo. 106[r].
[8] BRO AD 341; BL Add. Rolls 39774, 34322; BL Harley MS 445, fos. 7[r], 149[v].
[9] As on the estates of St.Albans Abbey (Levett, *Studies*, p. 188).
[10] Kerridge, *Agr. Problems*, p. 50.

When tenants attempted to evade the regulations governing the transfer of land, the steward of the manor court stepped in to seize the land into the lord's hands. A common pretext for the steward's intervention was the attempt to escape the entry fine. Another was the attempt to convey customary land by charter, as if it were free land. The steward also retained land when no heir was forthcoming. A proclamation was made in court for an heir, but if no one established a claim the steward could grant the tenancy to anyone willing to take it.

On the Bedfordshire manors which we shall examine, inheritance was nominally by primogeniture. In practice, a father could divide his land between any or all of his children. In the fifteenth century it was usual for husband and wife to hold their land jointly. A widow enjoyed freebench, a life estate in her husband's land, which was an attraction to those seeking land, a wife, or both. More than once the Ramsey court book recorded the remarriage of a widow in the guise of a man entering her land.[11] When a husband proposed surrendering land which his wife had once held as a widow, the steward would examine the woman secretly in court to ensure that she agreed to the transfer. On other occasions widows and elderly folk made maintenance arrangements a condition of transferring their land to someone younger. At the other end of the age-range, a minor was sometimes placed in wardship, or pledges found for the payment of the rent if a minor was admitted to his land.

It is because these customs and constraints were enforced and obeyed that we have so much detail in court rolls about the land market. The application of the body of custom enables us to distinguish between inheritance arrangements and sales, to trace fluctuations in the levels of rents and entry fines, and aids us in outlining the careers of individuals. This section discusses the land market on four rural manors in Bedfordshire: Blunham, Willington, Shillington, and Arlesey.

Blunham

The parish of Blunham lies in the angle formed by the confluence of the rivers Ouse and Ivel. The village itself lies on the

---

[11] BL Harley MS 445, fo. 130ᵛ; Raftis, *Tenure*, pp. 40, 219-20.

west bank of the Ivel, some 7 miles east of Bedford. The land in
the parish is low-lying, mostly below 100 feet. The soils consist
of alluvium, river gravels, and a loamy boulder clay. These are
more fertile and more easily worked than the heavier clays in
parishes further south.

In the fifteenth century there were three manors in the
ancient parish. One lay to the south, centred on Moggerhanger.
In mid-century the ownership of this manor passed from the
Trumpington family to the Enderbys.[12] A second manor had
passed in 1422 to Elizabeth Braybroke, Baroness St. Amand.
She outlived her husband, William Beauchamp, by some thirty-
four years and died in 1491 when her son, Richard Beauchamp,
inherited.[13] The third manor had passed from the Hastings to
the Greys of Ruthin at the end of the fourteenth century.[14]
Blunham was one part of a considerable estate which the Greys
built up by inheritance and purchase in Bedfordshire.[15] The
Hastings inheritance greatly enhanced the Greys' prosperity.
It raised them from the lesser baronage to the ranks of the
wealthier nobility, although the family had to wait until 1465
for the earldom of Kent.[16] By 1467-8, Earl Edmund's net income was well over £1,100. To this total the Bedfordshire
manors contributed £339, of which Blunham accounted for
nearly £37.[17] The story of the Greys in the later Middle Ages
was one of remarkable success. The heads of the family combined political and financial acumen with simple good fortune:
'. . . all the normal hazards to baronial fortunes were avoided.
Between 1325 and 1490 . . . there were only four heads of the
house, yet there was not a single minority.'[18] The fortunes of
the family were reversed in the 1520s when Earl Richard dissi-
pated much of its wealth.[19]

A mid-sixteenth-century terrier of the Grey's manor in
Blunham shows that it included between a third and two-fifths

[12] *VCH Beds.*, iii. 230.

[13] *CP*, xi. 301-3.

[14] *Grey Valor*, pp. 4-6.

[15] Ibid., pp. 6, 59.

[16] Ibid., pp. 3-4; *The Marcher Lordships of South Wales, 1415-1536: Select Documents*,
ed. T.B. Pugh (University of Wales, Board of Celtic Studies, History and Law Series,
vol.xx; 1963), p. 145 n.

[17] *Grey Valor*, pp. 22-7, 30.

[18] Ibid., p. 3.

[19] Ibid., p. 35 n.

of the land in the parish. The terrier listed about 680 acres of arable land held by the tenants, 225 acres of demesne arable, and 66 acres of the rector's glebe.[20] To this we should add perhaps 100 to 150 acres of meadow and pasture, both tenant and demesne.[21] Thus the size of the manor probably exceeded 1,100 acres. The arable lay divided between three open fields— South, Middle, North—and the tenants' holdings were scattered in strips in fifty-four furlongs.[22] Some demesne arable lay in compact parcels within individual furlongs, some lay in strips.[23] Various freeholds were held of the manor in Blunham and in the surrounding villages: Willington, Girtford, Sandy, Tempsford, and Everton.[24] Many of these were very small: in 1457, eleven people held less than 5 acres each. Some were larger. For example Sir Walter Trumpington, lord of Moggerhanger, held a half-virgate, and John Broughton held a hide and a watermill. These two men, and other freeholders, had land and interests elsewhere—John Gostwick, bailiff of nearby Willington, held a freehold of 1½ roods in his native village.[25]

The Greys' manor has left us sources for a study of landholding at Blunham fuller than those for most Bedfordshire manors. There are court rolls for 1413-51 and 1455-7, the series resuming again in 1513. There are rentals for 1457 and 1498, and several from the sixteenth century. There is the Charter of 1471. The great valor of the Greys' lands for 1467-8 includes Blunham, and there are accounts for 1468-9, 1497-8, and 1502-3.[26] These sources reveal the interest which the Greys took in the management of their estates, but as they all derive from the same manor they do not show the situation in the village as a whole. Nor are they full enough to give a complete picture of the one manor. It is particularly unfortunate that the court rolls break off just as the series of rentals starts. Although we can compare the land market between 1413 and 1457 with that in the sixteenth century, the redistribution of land which

[20] BRO L 26/214.
[21] PRO DL 43/14/3, fos. 64ᵛ-65ʳ; BRO L 26/154, L 26/212.
[22] PRO DL 43/14/3, fo. 64ᵛ.
[23] The size of demesne parcels in the terrier ranged from 1 r. to 30 a.
[24] BRO L 26/154, L 26/212.
[25] BRO L 26/154. John Gostwick was bailiff of Willington in 1457-8 (BL Add. Roll 657). The family had yet to rise to more than local prominence.
[26] *Grey Valor*, p. 30.

took place between 1457 and 1498 cannot be traced in detail.
However, some of its results can be seen in the rental of 1498.

The rental of 1457 listed sixty-five tenants on the manor of
Edmund Grey.[27] The demesne arable, though still identified as
such, was let at farm. There were forty-one tenants of customary land, twenty tenants who held only freeholds, and a further four men who farmed parcels of the demesne but held no
other land in the manor. Several of the customary tenants also
held parcels of freehold land and portions of the demesne. The
distinction between free and customary tenure was important,
for the freeholds were held for very small sums of money. But
in terms of status the type of tenure mattered little. Although the
rental, in common with many documents in the Greys' archive,
appears to have been a realistic one, it did not include every
tenant.[28] We do not know the number and extent of the omissions, but they were probably few. As it stands, the rental of
1457 shows that thirty tenants held the greater part of the
customary land at that date. This consisted of thirty-two holdings: twenty-three half-virgates, six quarterlands, and three
cotlands.[29] The sizes of holdings actually varied more than this
regular distribution suggests, for several people held portions
of the demesne or freeholds. This is shown in Table VIII, which
covers all the customary tenants of the manor (except the
Wymonds and Yerelds as mentioned below) and all the lands
they held in the manor, including demesne and freeholds:

Table VIII
Amounts of land held by customary tenants at Blunham, 1457

Description of holding	Number of tenants
Under 10 a.	16
10-19 a.	12
20-29 a.	4
30-39 a.	2
40-49 a.	3

---

[27] BRO L 26/154.

[28] While the rental did not mention the Samwell family, other sources suggest they
were a local family (BRO L 26/54, m. 12; L 26/212).

[29] A cotland was about the same size as a quarterland, some 7 a.

Table VIII excludes freeholders who did not hold customary land. It also excludes the holdings of the elder and younger John Wymond and the elder and younger John Yereld, for the rental failed to distinguish consistently between father and son; between them the Wymonds held 40 to 50 acres of customary land and demesne, the Yerelds over 60 acres. Some, perhaps many, of the customary tenants must have held land in other manors within the parish or in other villages. However, the rental may well reflect the situation in the village as a whole. The two main groups of customary tenants were the small-holders and those with a middle-sized holding. A smaller number of men had taken advantage of the abandonment of demesne cultivation to build up larger tenements.

In 1471, Earl Edmund 'strongly reaffirmed his seignorial rights over the tenants of Blunham'.[30] The result of this reaffir-mation was the Charter, written 'at the especiall labour, instaunce, and request of our Tenauntes'.[31] The Charter was an attempt to codify the procedures for the alienation of custo-mary land, and is in fact the earliest Bedfordshire custumal of its kind. The tenants were given complete freedom of alienation provided they observed certain conditions. Tenements could be sold or let whole, but when a person wished to alienate a part of his holding it was established that a half-virgate (14 acres) was to lose no more than 8 acres and that a quarterland (7 acres) was to lose no more than 4 acres. The entry fine paid by the incoming tenant was fixed at 6d. an acre,[32] and 20d. for each acre of meadow. A fine was levied on the tenant who sold a house: 'as ofte as any tenaunte alieneth or chaungeth any Mess' or Cotage, he shall paye to us the duble of his rente that is leyde and asigned unto the same Mess' or Cottage for the fyne of the same.'[33] The Charter recognized the free market which had developed amongst the tenants and may well have given it a new impetus. At the same time it attempted to con-trol the excessive fragmentation of holdings.

The rental of 1498 provides an opportunity to assess the changes of the second half of the fifteenth century in the light of

---

[30] *Grey Valor*, p. 29.
[31] BRO L 26/229.
[32] Not 6d. on a tenement as stated in *Grey Valor*, p. 29 n.
[33] This was a fine paid by the seller, not the entry fine.

the earlier rental and of the Charter. It listed seventy-two tenants: thirty-nine customary tenants, twenty-four who held freeholds, and nine who held only portions of the demesne at
farm.[34] Although the number of tenants had risen only slightly
between 1457 and 1498 there had been a rapid turnover in their
ranks. Both rentals contained about fifty different family
names but only nineteen were common to both. The greatest
change had taken place amongst the customary tenants: only
six of the families holding standard tenements in 1457 still held
similar holdings in 1498. However, family stability was probably greater than this figure suggests. Inheritance by daughters
and widows would have carried land, on marriage or remarriage, to different families.

Family changes were associated with a demand for land which
had led to the disintegration of holdings. From the rental of
1498 we can piece together the constituent parts of eight former
half-virgates. Although each had been held by one tenant, the
eight were now divided into forty-four parcels shared amongst
twenty-one tenants. The Charter of 1471 had not been without
effect, for in every case a messuage and a residue of 6 acres
were retained in the hands of one of the tenants. However,
fragmentation had brought about some changes in the size and
structure of holdings. Between 1457 and 1498 there had been
a slight increase in the number of smallholders (twenty, against
sixteen in 1457).[35] In part this was the result of the breakup of
the half-virgates; in part it was the result of reorganizing the
demesne leases. In 1457 the parcels of the demesne let at
farm were held in eight units of 10 acres 1 rood each, three of
20½ acres each, and one of 41 acres. In addition there were
three small parcels: 1 acre, 1½ acres, and 7½ acres. In 1498
there were eight units of 12 acres each, and five of 24 acres
each. There were two small parcels: 1 acre and 1½ acres.
Although the proportion of the demesne arable in the hands of
the customary tenants increased between 1457 and 1498, the
number of customary tenants who shared this land fell by one,
from ten to nine. The reorganization and the change-over in
the lessees brought about a greater concentration of land in the
hands of fewer tenants and probably encouraged the market in

[34] BRO L 26/212.   [35] Those with less than 10 a. of land.

customary holdings. In 1498, the greater part of the customary land was held by about the same number of tenants as in 1457 (twenty-nine as against thirty). Portions of the demesne still accounted for a substantial part of some of the larger holdings. Some tenants had amalgamated holdings while others had added small parcels of arable to their holdings as and when they could.

During the sixteenth century landholdings underwent further changes. The number of tenants fell;[36] individuals amassed larger holdings, probably driving some of the smallholders off the land and into the ranks of the landless labourers. By 1559 seven customary tenants (out of a total of twenty-seven) had holdings in excess of 40 acres. Most of these consisted of customary land and portions of the demesne. Robert Osburne's holding consisted of 2 half-virgates, 1 quarterland, a cotland, 29 acres in small parcels, 9 acres of meadow, and a portion of demesne (25 acres of arable, 2 acres of meadow). In all, his arable holding did not fall far short of 100 acres.[37]

The process of accumulation can be followed in the court rolls of the manor. Between 1413 and 1457 the rolls recorded some 115 changes in tenancy. Of these, twenty-five were transfers of ownership within the family and eighty-five were transfers of ownership outside the family, either by sale or by action of the lord's steward.[38] Analysis of the land market (the eighty-five) shows that one-fifth of the transfers involved just messuages or cottages, perhaps with a croft or garden, while four-fifths involved parcels of land: twenty-five were transfers of half-virgates, twelve of quarterlands, and twenty-three of parcels of 4 acres or less. It seems clear that up to 1457 the land market was running at a low ebb. When land changed hands, it was either in the form of a standard holding, or a small piece of land.

The Charter and the rentals of 1457 and 1498 suggest a growth in land dealing in the second half of the fifteenth century. This suggestion is borne out by the sixteenth-century court rolls.[39]

[36] The mid-16th-century terrier listed 50, excluding the glebe and the land of the old Fraternity (BRO L 26/214).

[37] BRO L 26/156.

[38] The remaining five appear to have been transfers outside the family on death.

[39] There are court rolls for 1413-57 (BRO L 26/51-4) and for 1513-73 (BRO L 26/55-60).

Between 1513 and 1573 some 260 tenancy changes were recorded on the rolls, of which about 190 were transfers outside
the family. Three-quarters of these involved arable but only
just over one-quarter involved land alone. The greater part
consisted of arable plus a messuage or cottage or some other
piece of property. The majority of land transfers, whether with
or without other property, were small in size, usually less than
5 acres.

A comparison of the land market in the first half of the
fifteenth century with the market in the sixteenth century shows
that several changes took place between 1413 and 1573. Transfers of standard holdings declined in number considerably,
from three-fifths of recorded transfers between 1413 and 1457
to just over one-fifth of the total between 1513 and 1573. There
was a corresponding increase in the number of transfers of
small parcels of land. The land market at Blunham in the sixteenth century included more small parcels of land, and it
appears to have been twice the size of the market a hundred
years previously. The decline in transfers of larger land units
and the growth in the number of small transfers were probably
the result of an increased demand for land. It is tempting to see
this in turn as the result of an increase in the village's population.

As we have seen, the Charter of 1471 laid down standard
rates for entry fines. Before the middle of the century, rents
and entry fines charged on alienations of half-virgates and
quarterlands varied markedly. In so far as there was any norm
in the first half of the century, the most frequent rent for a half-
virgate was 2s. 0d. with an entry fine of 20s. 0d. There was no
set pattern in the rents and fines charged on quarterlands,
though the fines on alienation or succession were frequently
lower, sometimes as little as 6d. or 7½d.[40] The rental of 1457
probably represented an attempt to regularize rents, for it
listed rents of the half-virgate and quarterland as 8s. 4d. and
4s. 2d. respectively.[41] These figures remained unaltered in
1498, and appear to have continued throughout the first seventy
years of the sixteenth century. By 1498 individual portions
of customary arable land were rented from the lord at 4d.
an acre.[42] The different levels of rent charged on different

[40] e.g. BRO L 26/51, m. 2; L 26/53, m. 14.

[41] BRO L 26/154.   [42] BRO L 26/212.

half-virgates and quarterlands after 1513 reflect variations in the size of the tenements—an effect of the Charter of 1471 and its concern to maintain the integrity of the tenement. The sixteenth-century court rolls show that the entry fine paid by the incoming tenant was one year's rent on a standard tenement,[43] and, for individual acres of land and meadow, 6*d.* and 20*d.*, the amounts laid down in the Charter.[44] Thus in or about 1457 there was a significant increase in the cash rents of half-virgates and quarterlands and an equally significant decrease in the level of their entry fines. In the second half of the fifteenth century the rents and fines were brought under review and standardized. No doubt Earl Edmund wished to regularize his income.

Willington

Willington, just to the west of Blunham in the valley of the Ouse, was one of the few single-manor parishes in the county. The manor was larger than the Greys' in Blunham, perhaps some 1,600 acres in all. It descended in the Mowbray family. When John Mowbray, second restored duke of Norfolk, died in 1432, the greater part of the Mowbray estates were held in dower by his widow, Katherine Nevill.[45] The next two dukes of Norfolk would have been among the richest of English magnates had not Katherine retained her lands until her death in 1483.[46] In the fifty years after her first husband's death, Katherine survived a further three husbands. When she died she had out-lived all her Mowbray descendants.[47] The dukedom passed to John Howard and with it went Willington, only to be sold to Sir John Gostwick in 1529.[48] Sir John came from a family, long settled in Willington, which provides a good example of self-

[43] Not two years' rent as stated in *Grey Valor*, p. 29 n.

[44] BRO L26/56, m. 7; L 26/57, m. 4; L 26/229.

[45] *CP*, ix. 606; *CCR* 1429-35, pp. 204-5, 208-14.

[46] T.B. Pugh, 'The Magnates, Knights and Gentry', *Fifteenth Century England, 1399-1509: Studies in Politics and Society*, ed. S.B. Chrimes, C.D. Ross, and R.A. Griffiths (Manchester, 1972), p. 124 n.

[47] *CP*, ix. 606-7; K.B. McFarlane, *The Nobility of Later Medieval England* (Oxford, 1973), pp. 154-5.

[48] *VCH Beds.*, iii. 263.

made men prospering in their native village and emerging into the gentry in the sixteenth century.[49]

The bailiffs' accounts of the later fourteenth century show Willington to have been a valuable property. The net income enjoyed by Thomas Mowbray in the 1380s was frequently over £50 a year.[50] The greater part consisted of £22. 13s. 4d. from 34 half-virgates (at 13s. 4d. each), £25. 6s. 8d. from the farm of the demesne to local tenants, and £5. 6s. 8d. from the farm of the watermill.[51] By 1457-8 there were signs that the manorial income had contracted, perhaps by as much as one-quarter. In that year the income from the farm of the demesne was £18, from the mill £3. 13s. 4d., while loss of rent from the customary holdings amounted to £5. 18s. 7d.[52] Manorial administration was not necessarily more inefficient under Katherine Nevill and her husbands than under the dukes of Norfolk, for a declining income was by no means peculiar to Willington. The manor was still a desirable possession in 1458, when Katherine and her third husband, John Beaumont, received a net income from Willington of £40. 15s. 6¼d.

By 1383 changes had occurred among the customary tenants of the manor. Whereas they formerly held their land in villeinage (*nuper tenentes in bondagio*), the half-virgaters now held by copyhold for a term of years or for life.[53] The court rolls of the fifteenth century show that the only consistent traffic in land was that in standard holdings—the quarterland and, more especially, the half-virgate, which consisted of about 10 acres of arable.[54] Between 1394 and 1426 some sixty-two changes in tenancy were recorded on the rolls. Between 1451 and 1481 the number recorded was fifty. Over four-fifths of all these involved a standard tenement. Before 1426 the transfer of ownership outside the family accounted for about 70 per cent of all transfers. By the second half of the fifteenth century nearly 90 per cent of the transfers involved a break in family descent.

Between 1408 and 1423 at least eighteen tenements, mostly half-virgates and quarterlands, passed into the lord's hands,

[49] H.P.R. Finberg, 'The Gostwicks of Willington', *Gostwicks*, pp. 57-75.
[50] BRO R 213/12/120-30.
[51] BRO R 213/12/120.
[52] BL Add. Roll 657.
[53] BRO R 213/12/120.
[54] BRO R 212/12/1-53A (1394-1467); BL Add. Roll 26813 (1467).

and these years probably witnessed a decline in the total number of tenants. Certainly land on which family inheritance had ceased accumulated in the lord's hands. The gap in the court rolls between 1426 and 1451 has removed any chance of tracing the succession to land, but there are one or two indications of the sort of process at work. In 1411 Felicia Prentys entered into full possession of a messuage and a half-virgate on the death of her husband.[55] Five years later she was forced by infirmity to relinquish her holding.[56] In 1417 the lord was able to find a tenant, but, by the autumn, the tenement had reverted once more to his keeping.[57] It remained in his hands until at least 1423.[58] By 1478 Felicia was still remembered in Willington, but only in the name of her former land (*mesuagium vocatum Felicia Prentyse*).[59]

Changes in the manor in the early fifteenth century had an effect on customary rents. In 1382-3 the rent of a half-virgate was 13*s*. 4*d*.[60] It remained at this level until 1426. Between 1451 and 1481 the average rent for a half-virgate was 10*s*. 6*d*., a significant decline, especially in the light of the level of entry fines. Between 1394 and 1426 the highest entry fine levied on the half-virgate was only 1*s*. 4*d*.,[61] and the usual fine was 8*d*. or 1*s*. 0*d*. As far as we can tell, these low rates continued throughout the period 1451-81.[62] Not only did rents fall in the fifteenth century but also no attempt was made to recoup the loss of income by demanding higher entry fines. It seems clear that a declining population forced rents down. The same thing happened on the demesne. To maintain an income from this source, Katherine Nevill was forced to make fresh bargains at a reduced rent.[63] In these circumstances it is not surprising that there was little or no demand for a market in odd parcels of land.

---

[55] BRO R 212/12/13.
[56] BRO R 212/12/20.
[57] BRO R 212/12/22, 23.
[58] BRO R 212/12/33.
[59] BRO R 212/12/59.
[60] BRO R 213/12/120.
[61] In 1395 (BRO R 212/12/3).
[62] We have only three entry fines recorded.
[63] New demesne leases were made in 1449 (BRO R 212/12/37).

Shillington

The abbey of Ramsey held four main manors in Bedfordshire: Cranfield in the west, and Barton, Pegsdon, and Shillington in the south. Barton, a single-manor parish, lies at the foot of the Chiltern escarpment, the village lands extending southwards into the hills. Shillington and Pegsdon lie east and further north of Barton, in the low-lying claylands. Pegsdon was one of a number of hamlets within the large parish of Shillington. It was exploited separately in the early fourteenth century as a corn-growing manor.[64] In the fifteenth century the greater part of the abbey's demesne at Pegsdon was farmed by a lessee, again separately from the parent manor.[65] The Bedfordshire manors of the abbey were among its richest. Until the 1370s, when the abbey began to lease its demesnes, they were exploited directly.[66] Then the manors were granted to the cellarer, rendering cash quotas: £48 from Barton, £60 from Cranfield, £80 from Shillington and Pegsdon together.[67]

The tenurial history of Shillington in the later Middle Ages is complex. The abbey's manor included the village itself and the surrounding hamlets of Hanscombe End, Upton End, and Woodmer End. It also included land in Holwell, Stondon, and Apsley End. Pegsdon, a distinct manor, had its own fields, as did Hanscombe. It is clear from the abbey's court book[68] that the customary land in Pegsdon, Stondon, and the other places was considered appurtenant to the main manor. As far as we can tell, the manor court at Shillington served the abbey's tenants in all the surrounding settlements. Alongside the abbey's manor there developed other manors in the fourteenth and fifteenth centuries, centred on Apsley End and Holwell.[69] In addition, Richard Brygg (or del Brugge), Lancaster King-of-Arms, held lands in Pegsdon worth £5 a year in 1412.[70] Little

[64] PRO SC 6/741/19, m. 5; SC 6/741/11-13.
[65] PRO SC 6/741/22, m. 5.
[66] Raftis, *Ramsey*, p. 240.
[67] Ibid., p. 259.
[68] The court book (BL Harley MS 445) was compiled primarily as a register of entry fines levied on customary holdings. It contains entries for many of the abbey's manors for the years 1398-1456.
[69] *VCH Beds.*, ii. 295-6.
[70] *Feudal Aids*, vi. 396.

more is known of this land after Richard's death, shortly after, save that it passed to his son William Bruges, created Garter King-of-Arms in 1417.[71]

Shillington and Pegsdon continued to be an important source of income to Ramsey Abbey during the fifteenth century, long after the first steps had been taken to abandon demesne cultivation. The survival of a few manorial accounts for the later fourteenth century enables us to reconstruct the way in which the demesne at Shillington was leased. The account roll for 1368-9 recorded fourteen parcels of demesne arable and pasture leased to various tenants of the manor.[72] The arable totalled 66 acres. Between 1368-9 and 1380-1 the amount of arable at farm increased by just 1 acre.[73] A year later, in 1381-2, the acreage at farm had nearly quadrupled to about 218 acres (in forty-six parcels). Most of these parcels (86 per cent) were smaller than 7½ acres in size.[74] By 1405-6 a second policy had taken effect.[75] In the account roll for that year the 218 acres were described as demesne leased 'of old' (*de antiquo*). Another entry recorded the lease of a further 240 acres of new (*de novo*) arable to various tenants. The rent for the new farms was 6*d.* an acre, whereas under the old system rents had varied from 4*d.* to 1*s.* 0*d.* an acre. Thus by 1405-6 a distinction had been made between a casual policy which had developed over some thirty or forty years and the conscious decision to let out most of the remaining demesne. The distinction becomes clear when the descent of parcels of demesne is traced in the court book and in the rental of 1437-8.

The court book shows that the ownership of the parcels of demesne quickly assumed the characteristics of customary tenure. The abbey let out demesne parcels at will, for a term of years, or for life. The tenants could surrender them to one another in the same way that copyholds were transferred. The demesne was described in the court book in two ways. Firstly there were the parcels *de antiquo* described in acres. Secondly there were the parcels *de novo*, described as portions (*sortes*) or

[71] *Test. Records in London*, p. 28; *CP*, xi, appendixes, p. 74 n; H.S. London, *The Life of William Bruges, the first Garter King of Arms* (Harleian Soc., vols. cxi, cxii; 1970), pp. 5, 7.

[72] PRO SC 6/741/21.　　　　[74] PRO SC 6/741/24.
[73] PRO SC 6/741/22, 23.　　　[75] PRO SC 6/741/25.

shares (*loti*).[76] In the rental of 1437-8 the old demesne can be identified either from its description or from the former tenants whose names are listed.[77] Most of the men and women who had formerly held parcels can be identified from the account rolls of the later fourteenth century. The only information in the rental about the new demesne concerns four portions (*sortes*) and three other parcels. Of these seven holdings, all but two were held together with one portion of *burylond* and 1 acre of *newmanlond*. In addition other tenants, who did not hold portions of demesne, held portions of *burylond* and *newmanlond*. The regularity of the entries on the rental describing the tenancies of *burylond* and *newmanlond* suggests that they were the new demesne.[78] In 1437-8 thirteen tenants rented fourteen portions of *burylond*. Two held, in addition, 1½ virgates of customary land, five held virgates, and two held half-virgates. One tenant held 18 acres, another 8 acres, a third held 1 acre. At Shillington as at Blunham several tenants were able to take advantage of the leasing of the demesne to add considerably to their holdings. The land let out before 1382 gave the tenants the chance to add to their holdings in a piecemeal way. By 1406 the final abandonment of demesne cultivation had been achieved by dividing the remaining land into standard portions.

If the account rolls show how the tenants of the manor were able to benefit from the leasing of the demesne, the court book, supplemented by the court rolls and the rental of 1437-8, shows how tenants built up their holdings and disposed of their land. Between 1398 and 1458 the court book recorded some 244 transfers of land at Shillington. Of these 56 arose from family inheritance and the remainder resulted from the traffic in land and redistribution by the lord. Three-quarters of the latter (146 out of 188) involved arable; the distribution of parcels by size is shown in Table IX, where the figures may be compared with those from Barton and Cranfield. At Barton, there were 141 transfers between 1397 and 1457. Of these, 40 represented some form of inheritance arrangement. Most of the others involved some land. At Cranfield, the total number of transfers

[76] BL Harley MS 445, fo. 100ʳ⁻ᵛ.

[77] PRO SC 11/43.

[78] Names such as *burylond* and *newmanlond* were commonly given to demesne at farm (Kerridge, *Agr. Problems*, p. 87).

Table IX

Transfers of customary and demesne arable at Shillington, Barton, and Cranfield, 1397-1458

Description of holding	Shillington		Barton		Cranfield	
	Number of transfers	Percentage	Number of transfers	Percentage	Number of transfers	Percentage
Under 5 a.	27	18	6	7	26	24
5-9 a.	12	8	1	1	5	5
10-14 a.	5	3	2	2	7	7
15-19 a.	3	2	—	—	—	—
Over 19 a.	1	—	—	—	2	2
Quarterland	—	—	—	—	7	7
Quarterland-½ virgate	—	—	—	—	1	—
½ virgate	29	20	19	21	39	37
½ virgate-1 virgate	3	2	—	—	14	13
1 virgate	44	30	58	64	3	3
1-1½ virgates	1	—	—	—	2	2
1½ virgates	4	3	4	4	—	—
1½-2 virgates	3	2	—	—	—	—
2 virgates	6	4	1	1	—	—
Over 2 virgates	8	6	—	—	—	—
Total	146	98	91	100	106	100

was 178. Of these, 127 resulted from traffic in land or the intervention of the lord.

On these three manors the virgate and half-virgate remained
the basis of landholding and they made up the greater part of
the tenements to change hands. The transfer of a standard
holding was usually associated with the transfer of a messuage,
a croft, the odd plot of land (*placea*), and meadow. In a Ramsey
Abbey cartulary the size of the virgate is said to have been
12 acres at Shillington, 24 acres at Barton, and 48 acres at
Cranfield.[79] A variation in the size of the virgate is reflected in
the transfers in the court book. At Shillington the commonest
unit of tenure and the commonest tenement to change hands
was the virgate. At Cranfield it was the half-virgate, and at
Barton the virgate. We may imagine a situation in which the
tenants at Shillington could transfer most effectively a 'small'
virgate. At Barton, a 'middle-sized' virgate marked the effective
upper limit to most transfers, while at Cranfield, a 'large' virgate encouraged traffic in the half-virgate. It is probably significant that it was only at Cranfield, where there was a 'large'
virgate, that there were also quarterlands. Here a quarterland
was a holding of viable size.

The small number of land transfers of a few acres at Barton
was the result of a peculiarity in the division of land in that
manor. There were there a great many crofts and closes which
were mostly very small.[80] These were transferred from one tenant to another in the same way as the standard holdings. In the
court book the acreage of the crofts and closes was rarely given
and they have not been included in Table IX, but it seems
probable that the turnover in these supplemented the turnover
in small parcels of land in the open fields. On all three manors
the traffic in land included demesne as well as customary land.
As the former accounted for many of the transfers of small parcels, the importance of the standard tenements in the turnover
of customary land was even greater than Table IX might
suggest.

The survival of both court book and rental for Shillington
suggests at first sight that we can obtain a fairly full insight into
the distribution of land amongst the manorial tenants between

[79] *Cart. Mon. Ram.*, iii. 211-13.   [80] Ibid., i. 477-86.

1400 and 1460. The rental of 1437-8 freezes at one point the activity recorded in the register. A comparison of the two sources shows that neither is comprehensive. The rental recorded fifty-two family names (seventy tenants in all). An index of families and individuals for the fifteenth century shows that there were many people named in the court records who did not appear in the rental. This is not surprising, for not all inhabitants of the manor would have held land and not every person mentioned in the court rolls was necessarily an inhabitant. However, there were at least nineteen families which we might expect to find among the tenants in 1437-8 but which were not in fact recorded on the rental. Several of these had been resident in the manor for many generations. At least thirteen of these families had members who are known from the court book to have held land in or around 1437. It appears that the rental was not a comprehensive list: several names were overlooked, names often long-established in the manor.

The court book appears to be a full record of land transfers. All but five of the fifty-two family names in the rental occur in the court book. Of these five, three are known from the rental alone.[81] Thus for most tenants recorded in 1437-8 there are entries in the court book, and as has been shown, the book recorded several tenants who held land but who were not included in the rental. While we may approach the court book with some confidence, the amount of information on any one tenant is limited. The survival of the court rolls has been too sporadic to provide much additional detail. We cannot usually be sure of the date of a person's first entry to land, and the date of a person's death often has to be inferred from incidental detail in the court book.

From the biographies of tenants built up from all the sources we can see that few individuals participated in more than three or four transactions. John Ward was the most active land dealer of his day. Between 1406 and 1450 he was involved in thirteen transfers, taking on land and shedding it.[82] At its largest, in 1426, his holding included 4 virgates and 12 acres accumulated in odd parcels. In amassing his land he paid over

[81] The other two were the rector and John Wenlock, later Lord Wenlock.
[82] Jones, 'Beds. Land Market', p. 265.

£5 in entry fines. He does not seem to have been averse to a bargain: in 1409, 1413, and 1426 we see him surrendering tenements only to take on others. If John Ward stands out from his fellow tenants in his use of the land market, he was by no means the only tenant to hold land for forty years or more. Thomas Bradefan held his land from 1398 (or earlier) until his death in 1438-9.[83] Philip Multon's tenancy lasted at least forty-four years, between 1414 and 1458.[84] John atte Brook held land in Shillington for half a century.[85] In fact the main impression left by the court book is one of stability. Before 1460 the land market ran at a low level. The small number of transfers of land, especially of small parcels, suggests that there was little demand for land. The speculation in land which occurred at Arlesey and at Leighton Buzzard at the end of the century was not a feature of the market in southern Bedfordshire before about 1450. During the fifteenth century a number of tenants left the manor. Their tenements fell vacant and passed to those who stayed behind or to newcomers.[86] Some tenants took advantage of this movement and of the availability of the former demesne to amass holdings in excess of 50 acres.[87] The majority of Shillington tenants in the first half of the century appear to have remained 'middling men', holding a virgate, and perhaps an extra half-virgate or virgate and some demesne.

As the court book was essentially a record of the entry fines paid to the abbey, rents were not of immediate interest to its compilers and were not often recorded. While we have information about entry fines, particularly for half-virgates and virgates, at Barton, Cranfield, and at Shillington, we have little for rents, apart from what we learn in the Cranfield and Shillington rentals.[88] On all three manors the entry fines for standard tenements varied considerably and at random throughout the first half of the fifteenth century. At Cranfield the average fine on a half-virgate was 4s. 8d. and it was about the same at

[83] BL Harley MS 445, fos. 3ʳ, 178ʳ.

[84] Ibid., fos. 92ʳ, 256ᵛ.

[85] Ibid., fos. 16ʳ, 229ᵛ.

[86] Raftis, *Tenure*, pp. 153-82.

[87] In addition, several men must have held land elsewhere. Walter Swyft, tenant at Shillington in 1454, held land in Brill and Oakley, Bucks. (BL Harley MS 445, fo. 249ᵛ; Bodl. MS DD Barrett A 2, Brill and Oakley, No. 12).

[88] PRO SC 11/42, 43.

Barton. At both Barton and Shillington the average fine on a virgate was about 9s. 0d. In each case deviations from these averages were so great that they are scarcely meaningful except as measures with which to judge the occasional large fine. However, standard fines of 3s. 4d., 6s. 8d., or 13s. 4d. were often levied on tenements in all three manors. Where we have details of rent it is clear that there was no correlation between rent and entry fine. The fine was considerably less than a year's rent, though it showed no fixed relation to it. Like fines, rents varied greatly on standard tenements in the same manor although the rent on any one holding remained stable through-out the first half of the fifteenth century. Entry fines for a par-ticular holding sometimes changed. At Shillington and Barton, where it is possible to trace the fortunes of rents and fines on a number of tenements, it seems that there was no general move-ment in the level of entry fines: some rose, some fell, some remained stable. On occasions the abbey excused a part or the whole of a fine. Between 1400 and 1460 the demand for land (or lack of it) was such that the abbey was unable to use the entry fine as a convenient method of extracting income from its Bedfordshire manors. Like rents, the entry fines charged on the transfer of holdings appear to have been fixed by considerations of custom and the state of the tenement.

The men and women who appear in the court book were either the descendants of the abbey's tenants in villeinage or those who in the fifteenth century took up tenancies on custom-ary land.[89] Amongst the former the disabilities of bondage all but disappeared in the fifteenth century. However, down to about 1400 the abbey continued to extract from its customary tenants payments and services which bore the hallmark of ser-vility. The court rolls of Barton and Shillington contain numer-ous references to labour services withheld or poorly performed and to payments such as *leyrwite*.[90] One way in which the abbey asserted its rights over its customary tenants (and, of course, continued to do so for many years) was in regulating the trans-

---

[89] This section was first published in 1976: A. Jones, 'A Dispute between the Abbey of Ramsey and its Tenants', *EHR*, xci (1976), 341-3. It is reproduced here by kind permission of the publisher and editors.

[90] PRO SC 2/179/34, m. 2d (1350, Shillington); SC 2/179/36, m. 11 (1358-9, Shillington); SC 2/179/36, m. 12d (1358-9, Barton).

fer of land. Transfers of customary land had to be registered in the manor court. While customary tenants could lease land to one another for short terms without the lord's licence, leases by customary tenants to freemen appear to have required this.[91] And, of course, a customary tenant was not supposed to acquire land by charter without his lord's licence, or any land outside his lord's domain. Between about 1360 and 1407 Ramsey Abbey and some of its customary tenants in Shillington and Barton were involved in a dispute over their right to purchase land outside the abbey's manor.

At some time between 1358 and 1366 William de Otteford, then the king's escheator in Bedfordshire, seized lands in Shillington totalling 40 acres. The pretext for the seizure was that the abbot of Ramsey had appropriated land which various bond tenants had held. The appropriation was without royal licence and thus contravened the Statute of Mortmain. The land in question consisted of 15 acres described as acquired from John Whitefelawe through two of the abbot's bondmen, Thomas atte Welle and Robert Whildfole, and twelve parcels amounting to 25 acres acquired through twelve different bond tenants.[92] In 1367 custody of the 15 acres was granted to Matthew de Assheton, parson of Shillington.[93] The other 25 acres appear to have remained in the hands of the escheator until 1373, when Thomas Fauconer was granted the keepership of all 40 acres.[94] This grant threatened the position of Assheton, but the situation was resolved in 1380 when it was agreed that Fauconer should retain the rent from the 15 acres (7s. 6d. a year) during his life, while Assheton remained the keeper.[95] Further orders for the custody of the 40 acres were taken in 1407, 1408, 1444, 1448, and 1475.[96]

In either 1402 or 1403 the escheator was involved again. This time, William Bosoun seized two parcels of land in Silsoe

---

[91] Instances of tenants amerced for unlicensed leasing occur at Barton, 1369 (BL Add. Roll 39473) and at Shillington, 1358-9 (PRO SC 2/179/36, m. 12).

[92] *CFR* 1356-68, p. 354; *CPR* 1370-4, pp. 374, 386.

[93] *CFR* 1356-68, p. 354; *Calendar of Entries in the Papal Registers relating to Great Britain and Ireland: Petitions to the Pope, 1342-1419*, ed. W.H. Bliss (London, 1896), p. 186.

[94] *CPR* 1370-4, pp. 374, 386.

[95] *CCR* 1377-81, p. 412.

[96] *CFR* 1405-13, p. 68; *CPR* 1408-13, p. 42; *CPR* 1441-6, p. 319; *CFR* 1445-52, pp. 109-10; *CPR* 1461-7, p. 331; *CPR* 1467-76, p. 507.

which the abbot of Ramsey had acquired without the king's licence through two of his bondmen, Robert and William atte Fenne. This land consisted of a messuage and 6 acres, and a further acre.[97] Silsoe is a village 3 miles north of Barton, where the Atte Fennes were the abbey's tenants.[98] In 1406 the keepership of this land was committed to William Sare of Barton.[99] Further orders for its custody followed in 1418 (to Simon Sare), 1423, and 1444.[100]

From the bare details of the two seizures we can attempt to piece together the circumstances which lay behind them. The abbot of Ramsey took into his hands certain parcels of land from his bond tenants on the grounds that they, being villeins, had acquired them outside the abbey's fee without licence. By some means, possibly through the tenants, the confiscation came to the notice of the king's escheator who seized the land, claiming that the action of the abbot broke the Statute of Mortmain. From the second incident it appears that there was collaboration between the tenants and the Crown. The William Sare to whom the custody of the land in Silsoe was granted was in fact a bond tenant of the abbot.[101] One of Sare's sureties was a certain John atte Fenne of London.[102] This man may have been related to the Atte Fennes of Barton from whom the abbot confiscated the land in the first place. Thus when the abbot stepped in the Atte Fennes (who would have known of the events at Shillington in the previous half-century) took advantage of their connections to deprive the abbot of the land. Custody was granted to a local man and so they may well have regained their tenure under William Sare. Whatever the outcome for the Atte Fennes and the tenants of Shillington, the events which led to the escheator's intervention appear to represent a local struggle between the abbot and his unfree

[97] *CFR* 1405-13, p. 27.

[98] PRO SC 2/179/36, m. 8d; SC 2/179/43, m. 1; SC 2/179/56, m. 4.

[99] *CFR* 1405-13, p. 27.

[100] *CFR* 1413-22, p. 231; *CFR* 1422-30, p. 46; *CFR* 1437-45, p. 297.

[101] He is described as a villein in the court roll of 1405 when he paid a fine of 6*d.* to send his son Simon to school (PRO SC 2/179/50, m. 4d). This Simon was the man given custody of the land in 1418 (*CFR* 1413-22, p. 231). He features in several grants of land at Dunstable in the 15th century (*A Descriptive Catalogue of Ancient Deeds in the Public Record Office* (London, 6 vols., 1890-1915), i. 401, 436, 449, 537).

[102] *CFR* 1405-13, p. 68.

tenants. The abbot wished to preserve his seignorial privileges; the tenants were seeking opportunities to enlarge their holdings free from this control. Their reaction was an ingenious attempt to undermine the abbey's rights, and one in which they appear to have achieved the tacit support of the Crown. The struggle provides a vivid illustration of the decay of villein disabilities and the growing power of customary tenants to protect their own interests. The mobility of rural society in the later fourteenth century brought to the peasantry connections and influence in places which had been denied to their ancestors.

Arlesey

The village of Arlesey lies in the south-east of Bedfordshire, 5 miles east of Shillington. The land in the parish is level and low-lying, below 200 feet; the soil, a heavy chalky clay. There were three manors within the parish. One had been a part of the original endowment of Waltham Abbey. After the Conquest the abbey was temporarily shorn of much of its lands, but regained them, and the Arlesey Bury manor remained in its hands until the Dissolution. In the fourteenth century the second manor passed to the De la Pole family. William de la Pole's son, John, married Joan Cobham in 1362. Their daughter, another Joan, Baroness Cobham, held the manor of Etonbury until her death in 1434.[103] Her daughter by her second marriage,[104] a third Joan, married Sir Thomas Brooks. Their granddaughter, Elizabeth, married Robert Tanfield, and these two were in possession of the manor in 1480.[105] The rental of William Tanfield, drawn up in 1519, shows that his income from rents in Etonbury was about £12. 15s. a year.[106] A third, small manor belonged to Llanthony Priory.[107]

The surviving records of both main manors are largely court records. Most of those for the Etonbury manor date from the sixteenth century, and our knowledge of the two manors in the fifteenth century is limited, for we know very little of the

---

103 *VCH Beds.*, ii. 262; *CP*, iii. 345.
104 To Sir Reynold Braybroke; Joan was married five times (*CP*, iii. 346).
105 BRO AD 337.
106 BRO IN 167.
107 Llanthony Secunda, near Gloucester.

income which the lords of the manors received, or of the agricultural organization of the village. On the Arlesey Bury manor most of the demesne appears to have been let to a single farmer from the beginning of the fifteenth century. Now and again the abbot let odd parcels to other tenants.[108] The court register[109] of the abbey's manor partly compensates for the lack of either rentals or a custumal, and it enables us to reconstruct the descent of many customary tenements. From it there emerges a reasonably clear picture of the way in which a few families began to amass copyholds during the fifteenth century. One of them, the Hemmings, eventually ended as owners of the manor. Like the Gostwicks of Willington they provide an example of a local family emerging from obscurity into the ranks of the gentry in the sixteenth century.

Between 1377 and 1536 some 747 transfers of land and other property were recorded in the court register of the Arlesey Bury manor. The range of entries suggests that the register was intended to be a comprehensive account of the customary tenures, which were tenures of inheritance, described as held by the rod (*per virgam*), with entry fines apparently fixed at the will of the lord. Omissions may have resulted from oversight or laxity on the part of the compilers, and, of course, from any successful evasion of the manorial regulations governing the transfer of customary land. However, the register itself testifies to the interest which the abbey retained in the traffic in land and the descent of tenements. For various reasons the steward of the manor court or his deputy sometimes intervened to seize land. In so doing he acted as a redistributive agent, producing the same effect as the straightforward surrender for transfer between tenants. In studying the land market, it is convenient to combine these two ways in which land and other property changed hands, and an analysis on this basis of the types of transfer is given in Table X. Just under two-thirds of the total number of transfers concerned land. Of these, two-thirds (328 out of 481) included arable and two-fifths consisted of arable only. Thus the majority of sales included other sorts of land and property: meadow, crofts, messuages, cottages, gardens.

---

[108] In 1426 the abbot let 10 a. to John Lely for 9 years 'ex assensu Johannis Knotte firmarii domini' (BRO IN 59, m. 6d).

[109] BRO IN 58-62.

Table X

*Transfers of customary land and other property on Arlesey Bury manor,
1377-1536*

	Number of transfers	Percentage
Within the family during lifetime	71	10
Within the family on death	161	21
Outside the family during lifetime	481	64
Outside the family on death	34	5
Total	747	100

The market in arable land was mostly small-scale. About three-quarters of the total number of parcels transferred were smaller than 10 acres and half were smaller than 2½ acres. While these small parcels predominated, the half-virgates and the virgate continued to be recognizable units of tenure throughout the fifteenth century. Where land was transferred together with a messuage or cottage there was a greater likelihood of the parcel of land being larger.[110]

An outstanding feature of the land market of Arlesey was the extent to which certain tenements and parcels of land changed hands without becoming a permanent part of any one person's holding. In Arlesey Bury there was a distinct pool of land and property which habitually reappeared on the land market. This was land on which family inheritance had disappeared as families died out or moved away, and it stands in contrast to the holdings which continued to descend from father to son among the established families. An example will show what often happened. In 1401 the abbot granted a vacant holding to Richard Deye; in 1447 Richard surrendered this to John Deye. John died by 1457, in which year his widow was granted tenure of the holding until their son came of age. By 1472 the tenement had

---

[110] 35 per cent of transfers involving a messuage or cottage and land were 10 a. or more, mostly in the range 11-15 a. The half-virgate contained about 14 a. of arable.

fallen vacant again and was granted to John Smith. In the following year he forfeited the land for withholding his rent. The tenement was then granted to Thomas Hammond. William Hammond, Thomas's son, succeeded to his father's land in 1500. After William's death in or before 1511, his widow surrendered the holding to John Hemming. In 1521 John transferred it to Richard Page. When the land finally passes from view it had passed from family to family without ever having been incorporated fully into a family holding. Throughout its wanderings it kept its separate identity.[111]

This example, together with many others at Arlesey, can be studied particularly clearly because the tenement in question had a distinctive name. At each change in ownership the name of the tenement was recorded in the register. Many tenements were named after families or individuals who had been associated with them at some time. Most of these can be traced in the court register or in the fourteenth-century lay-subsidy rolls.[112] Sometimes the process can be studied as it happened. For example, one half-virgate came to be known as Warens or Mekys. In 1444 it had passed out of the family of Thomas Waryn and between 1460 and 1500 it descended in the Mekys family. Between 1500 and 1518 the holding passed through a further three families, yet it retained by its names its associations with the former tenants.[113] It is clear from the register that the tenement-names referred to those holdings and parcels of land on which family succession had for some reason broken down. It was this land which formed a large part of the customary land market in the fifteenth century. From the court register we can trace for varying lengths of time the changing ownership of seventy-nine named tenements (under forty-seven tenement-names) and seventeen unnamed tenements. They were of all sizes, from a single rood to a full virgate. Some were parts of holdings which had split in two or three. At least 70 per cent of all transfers in the register, whether within the family or

---

[111] Jones, 'Beds. Land Market', p. 94.

[112] *Two Bedfordshire Subsidy Lists, 1309 and 1332*, ed. S.H.A. Hervey (Suffolk Green Books, vol. xviii; 1925), pp. 5-6, 154-5.

[113] BRO IN 60, mm. 2d, 9; IN 62, mm. 1, 4, 6, 10, 12.

outside it, consisted of a part or the whole of one of these ninety-six holdings.

Once a tenement had come on to the land market it was unusual for it to descend in one family. When family ownership disappeared the idea of inheritance faded too. A man might have held a tenement for thirty or forty years but he rarely passed it on to his heirs. Some tenements passed through as many as eight or nine families in the course of a hundred years. There was no discernible rhythm to the intervals at which land was transferred. Periods of thirty years or more in the hands of one tenant were followed by a rapid succession of changes. Most holdings changed hands at least once every twenty years; half changed hands twice as often. As there was little demand for land in the fifteenth century, the supply of land to the market was self-perpetuating while the number of tenants did not grow. The availability of land on which family inheritance had ceased had important consequences for the tenants of the Arlesey Bury manor. It made possible the growth of larger holdings in the fifteenth century. Prosperous tenants could take advantage of the availability of land to increase the scale of their activities. The absence of any specific family ties and claims to the land was one of the attractions of customary tenure as against freehold. The situation at Arlesey was by no means unique. The recurrent transfer of land can be traced on other manors in Bedfordshire. Its symptoms are to be seen in the growth of larger holdings, and in the seemingly haphazard way in which family holdings fluctuated in size throughout the fifteenth century. Not all the land held by one man now passed to his heir.

Between 1377 and about 1480 (after which date the small number of entries in the court register precludes analysis of their trend) the land market at Arlesey was remarkable for its stability. Over a hundred years, there were on average three or four transfers a year. The trend in land dealing shows no dramatic growth or decline down to 1480. Turning to the structure of the market, the years 1377-1400 witnessed a growth in land dealing in small parcels (of less than 5 acres), from 60 per cent of the market to between 75 and 80 per cent. Thereafter a gradual decline set in. Between 1420 and 1460 there was a period of stability in which the proportion of transactions in small parcels fluctuated between 50 and 60 per cent of the total number. The traffic in small parcels then grew in importance between 1470 and 1490, but afterwards appears to have stabilized again at around 60 per cent of the market. From these minor fluctuations we can see that the scale of the market as a whole was probably linked to the scale of the market in small parcels. The level of overall activity tended to follow long-term fluctuations in the latter.

Like the Ramsey court book, the Arlesey register was primarily a record of the entry fines levied on customary tenements. Rents lay outside its scope and were recorded infrequently. However, this limited information is enough to establish that there was no fixed ratio between the entry fine and the annual rent. Neither was there a ratio between the size of fine and the size of tenement. In this respect, the position at Arlesey was similar to that on the Ramsey Abbey manors. Fines levied on parcels as small as an acre and as large as a half-virgate varied considerably and apparently at random. However, the fifteenth century saw a rise in the general level of entry fines. For the fifty-three tenements for which we have a succession of entries there was definite increase in the level of fine on thirty-seven (70 per cent). On seven the level of fine remained stable, while on nine the entry fines fluctuated. The increase in entry fines is particularly noticeable from about 1470. Before that, where we have details of both rents and fines the annual rent was usually greater than the fine. After 1470 the entry fine almost always exceeded the rent. Rents appear to have remained stable throughout the fifteenth century, so the rise in the level of entry fines was real and not relative. Between 1400 and 1530 the average entry fine on a half-virgate trebled, from 6s. 8d. to 20s. 0d., with the significant increase occurring in the later fifteenth century. Presumably the increase in fines came at the instigation of the abbey's officials. With rents stable and protected by custom, the manipulation of the entry fine was the only way in which manorial income could conveniently be maintained or increased. Such awareness of the value of the entry fine in this period is found on other estates.[114]

On the Arlesey Bury manor the fifteenth century was a

---

[114] Bean, *Percy Estates*, pp. 60, 64.

period of flux among the tenants. Families died out or moved away. New ones took their place. Few families living in the manor in or before 1400 still lived there in the early sixteenth century. Among those to survive the century were some which prospered and built up sizeable holdings. Together with a few newcomers, they came to dominate the tenure of customary land. In all these respects, Arlesey must have resembled many other midland manors. But it would be wrong to exaggerate the extent of the mobility which developed. Very few of the new-comers to the manor, whether they settled there or simply invested in land, came from places further than 5 or 6 miles away. Stotfold, Henlow, Hitchin, Meppershall, Shillington, and Cadwell, the places of origin of most of the immigrants, were all close by. The intermarriage of tenants helped to bind the community together where mobility threatened to under-mine it. The links between families which marriage produced were many and complex. Despite the number of recurrent transfers which took place, marriage and inheritance remained of some importance in the redistribution of land at Arlesey. Between 1377 and 1536, 30 per cent of the transfers in the register represented movements within the family. In examining the involvement of individuals in the land market inter-family transfers, particularly inheritance, were often as important as transfers on the open market in their effect on the size of an individual's holding. It was the inherited tenement which provided many with the basis for the development of their property.

The court register contains information about several hun-dred people. For many of them there is just one entry, but for the main group of families resident in the manor we have a fair amount of detail, enough to distinguish successive generations and to provide skeleton biographies of their more important members. The long time-span of the register allows us to study many of these from their first appearance to their death. As the register is a manorial and not a village record, it does not necessarily provide a full picture of a person's activities in Arlesey. We are at the disadvantage of never knowing when it does deal with all a person's interests. Despite these drawbacks, the register probably provides a representative sample of people's involvement in the land market. Between 1377 and

1536 there were sixty-five tenants who dealt in land on five occasions or more, though only thirteen were involved in ten transfers or more. Most of the sixty-five fell into two general categories: twenty-four (38 per cent) were enterers, that is they took on land, and thirty-six (55 per cent) were enterers and surrenderers, that is they both took on land and shed it. The preponderance of the latter to some extent reflects the length and scope of the register: here may be seen the rise and decline of the total holding with the advancing age of the tenant. However, it is interesting to note that we know the dates of death of eighteen out of the twenty-four enterers. As the average time between the first and last transfer of these eighteen was thirty-one years, it would be wrong to imagine that death interrupted the cycle of growth and decline. Some who were active in the land market had holdings that grew and then declined. For others, they reached a peak at or just before death.[115]

Despite the evidence we can assemble for many families and individuals, it would be wrong to conclude that demand for land at Arlesey was very great in the fifteenth century. Three things point to a lack of demand: the recurrent transfer of land, the number of large parcels of land which changed hands, and the small part played by widows in the redistribution of land. Much of the land market, whether small parcels or whole tenements, was supplied from a pool of land on which family succession had ceased. Holdings then passed from family to family in haphazard fashion as individuals sought temporarily to satisfy their desire for a larger holding. Although sales of small parcels of land were numerically more important than sales of larger portions and of whole tenements, few individuals appear to have been confined solely to the small-scale market to extend their holdings. As land was cheap and relatively plentiful, many tenants could take on larger parcels as and when they became available. Thus the development of holdings at Arlesey shows a rather uneven progression—small purchases and sales were intermixed with the acquisition and dispersal of one or more larger parcels of land. In fact one or two transfers of large parcels of land had a much greater effect on the size of a man's

---

[115] Detailed discussion of prominent Arlesey families may be found in Jones, 'Beds. Land Market', pp. 102-23.

holding than the cumulative effect of a number of small-scale transfers. It is noticeable too that the occasions on which tenants engaged in the land market were often spread out over twenty, thirty, or forty years. Few tenants at Arlesey accumulated land or sold it at all rapidly. Those who did were the small number of prosperous and ambitious men who came to dominate the traffic in land at the start of the sixteenth century. In general, widows were not important as a source of land to landless or ambitious men in fifteenth-century Arlesey. This is a sure sign that land was plentiful and that there was little competition for it.[116] In the course of the century some new families established themselves in the manor and took advantage of this situation. In all these respects Arlesey and other rural manors in Bedfordshire were like many others in the Midlands. The situation at Arlesey was in contrast, however, to that at Leighton Buzzard, a small country market town some 18 miles to the west. Here the market in customary land was much larger and the turnover in land more rapid. The principal manor at Leighton Buzzard (which also included the town) was one of the largest manors in the county. Its splendid series of court rolls of the second half of the fifteenth century enables us to study the market there in considerable detail.

3 LEIGHTON BUZZARD

Parish, manors, and town

Leighton Buzzard lies to the north of the Chilterns in the extreme south-west of Bedfordshire. The old parish contained some 8,900 acres set in the angle where the river Ouzel turns northwards to flow into the river Ouse. The river marked the southern and western bounds, and it formed a part of the county boundary with Buckinghamshire. The land in the parish, which reaches its highest point of between 450 and 500 feet in the north, slopes southwards and westwards to the river valley at 275-300 feet. The trend of the slope is broken, firstly by the valley of the Clipstone brook which flows into the Ouzel just to

---

[116] R.J. Faith, 'Peasant Families and Inheritance Customs in Medieval England', *AgHR*, xiv (1966), p. 91.

the south of Leighton Buzzard, and secondly by the hill on which Billington lies. The Ouzel valley narrows northwards as it cuts through the gap between Linslade and Leighton Buzzard and then broadens again west of Heath and Reach. Like so much of Bedfordshire, the soil is largely heavy clay and soil drainage tends to be imperfect. Alluvium covers much of the valley floor.

As well as the town of Leighton Buzzard the parish included a number of small villages: to the north, Heath and Reach; to the east, Eggington, Clipstone, and Stanbridge; and to the south, Billington. In the late Middle Ages, Heath and Reach, Eggington, and Clipstone were separate settlements. Although they were paired for convenience of manorial administration, contemporaries usually distinguished between Heath and Reach or between Eggington and Clipstone when referring to the location of land or buildings.

By 1500 there were several manors within the parish. The principal manor, at that date in the hands of the dean and canons of St. George's Chapel, Windsor, overshadowed the others in size and value. This manor included the town and much of the land in the parish, though the village of Stanbridge lay outside it. An ancient-demesne manor, between 1164 and 1414 it had been part of the English endowment of Fontevrault Abbey. Towards the end of the twelfth century the abbey established a cell at Leighton Buzzard and a part of the property, known as Grovebury, was set aside as its demesne. During the protracted wars with France in the fourteenth century the lands of the alien priories were often in the king's hands. Fontevrault's attempts to retain its lordship seem to have been successful, but Leighton Buzzard was in the hands of a lay keeper from 1338 and long before the end of the century the abbey's interest in the manor was purely financial. In 1414, when the property of the alien priories was finally confiscated, the manor was granted to Sir John Philip,[1] who for the past year had been its keeper for the Crown.[2] He died in 1415 and his child-wife, Alice Chaucer, granddaughter of the poet,[3] eventually married William de la Pole, earl of Suffolk. In 1444

[1] *CPR* 1413-16, pp. 67, 131, 229.
[2] *CCR* 1413-19, pp. 234-5.
[3] According to *CP*, xii, pt. 1, p. 448, she was born about 1404.

William and Alice granted the reversion of the manor and of other lands to Eton College, Henry VI's new foundation.[4] Two years later they granted the college possession of these lands at a yearly rent of £220.[5] The college enjoyed the revenues of Leighton Buzzard for some years, but soon after he came to the throne Edward IV challenged Alice's right to alienate her land.[6] By 1464 Alice, dowager duchess of Suffolk following William's death in 1450, appears to have regained possession of Leighton Buzzard.[7] She was to regain full title in the manor in place of a debt of 2,800 marks owed her by the king.[8] On her death in 1475 Alice was succeeded by her son, John de la Pole. In 1480 he and his wife alienated the manor to the dean and canons of St. George's Chapel, Windsor.[9] There may well have been more to the arrangement than meets the eye. In 1506 John's son, Edmund de la Pole, petitioned Henry VII: '. . . as to the town of Leighton Buzzard, which King Edward enforced the said ducis fader to release to the colleage of Windsor, the said duc besecheth humbly the kinges highness to bee good lord to him therin, and that he maye be restored therunto.'[10] Nothing came of this plea, for the manor remained the property of the dean and canons for over 300 years. On the surface, the vicissitudes of ownership in the fifteenth century were in sharp contrast to the continuity in ownership before 1414 and after 1480: the intervening years were a short interlude between long periods of ecclesiastical lordship. However, the interruptions to the authority of Fontevrault and the system of leasing the manor which the canons inherited probably combined to free Leighton Buzzard from the paternalism which many towns suffered at the hands of church landlords.

Fontevrault Abbey had received grants of land and rent in a number of neighbouring villages. These followed the same descent as Leighton Buzzard and for purposes of account were

[4] *Rotuli Parliamentorum* (Record Commission, 6 vols., [1783]), v. 77-8.

[5] Wind. XV.25.57.

[6] *Rotuli Parliamentorum*, v. 470, 524. His real motive was his desire to despoil Eton College, the foundation of his rival, Henry VI.

[7] Manorial courts were held in her name in 1464 (BRO KK 622, m. 1).

[8] *CPR* 1467-76, p. 362.

[9] *CPR* 1476-85, pp. 172, 219.

[10] *Letters and Papers Illustrative of the Reigns of Richard III and Henry VII*, ed. J. Gairdner (Rolls Series, 2 vols., 1861-3), i. 281.

considered appurtenant to the larger manor. This additional property lay in Bow Brickhill, Simpson, Caldecotte, Stewkley, Radnage, and Northall, all in Buckinghamshire; and in Studham, south of Whipsnade, in Bedfordshire.[11] The other manors in and around Leighton Buzzard in 1500 were smaller than the one which passed to the canons of Windsor. Our knowledge of them is often very limited so, inevitably, our attention turns to the main manor for which many more sources have survived. The Leighton Buzzard court rolls come from this manor.[12] In addition there are twenty-six bailiff's account rolls for the years between 1457 and 1511; they are most complete for the 1490s.[13] Eleven receiver's accounts have survived, appended to the bailiff's accounts, all but three dating from between 1466 and 1477. These two sorts of account show clearly the income which Alice Chaucer and the canons drew from the manor and they provide much incidental detail about the manor and town. The accounts are realistic documents designed to show, to the auditor's satisfaction, the state of the manorial finances at the close of the accounting year (Michaelmas). Unfortunately there are no surviving rentals of the later fifteenth century to complement the extant account and court rolls. The rentals of the first half of the century are not particularly illuminating. Those for Eggington and Clipstone and for Heath and Reach probably date from the middle of the century,[14] while that for Leighton Buzzard and Billington is dated 1407.[15] Some grants and leases supplement the main sources.

The topography of the manor which passed to the canons of Windsor is elusive. While there are many records which show the composition of individual holdings and which provide incidental detail, there are none which give a view of the manor as a whole, or even of the demesne, in the Middle Ages. The arable lay in large open fields. Leighton Buzzard, Heath, Reach, Eggington, Clipstone, Stanbridge, and Billington each had its own fields, though how many is not clear. It appears

---

[11] C. Jamison in *VCH Bucks.*, ii. 90-1; *VCH Bucks.*, iii. 345, 421; iv. 291-2, 460; *VCH Beds.*, iii. 429.

[12] BRO KK 622, 623 (1464-83, 1485-1508).

[13] Wind. XV.61.37, XV.61.39, XV.61.41-67. They are listed in J.N. Dalton, *The Manuscripts of St. George's Chapel, Windsor Castle* (Windsor, 1957), pp. 126-9.

[14] Wind. XV.53.76; XV.53.90.

[15] Wind. XV.61.33.

that those of Heath and Reach were grouped in one system and those of Eggington and Clipstone in another, so the manor contained the whole or parts of five distinct field systems. By Bedfordshire standards Leighton Buzzard had an exceptional amount of meadow. Much of this was in the valley of the Ouzel, especially to the south where the valley was at its widest. Several streams which drained into the Ouzel from the east doubtless had meadow along their banks. A lot of the meadow was demesne and probably lay severally. The tenants' meadow may have been re-allotted annually. Certainly, greater care was taken over its division than was accorded the arable. The description of the latter in the several hundred land transfers of the fifteenth century shows that its measurement was a matter of estimation and customary usage. Meadow, on the other hand, was measured more accurately, with a rod. Compared with the arable it was scarce. Thus each acre was more valuable in terms of rent, and meadow was divided into much smaller parcels. Fallow appears to have provided most of the common land. There were pasture closes in various parts of the manor but most appear to have been part of the demesne. The crofts and tofts in and around the various settlements provided an additional source of pasture to the tenants. There were stands of woodland in the manor, principally in Heath and Reach. Throughout the fifteenth century the sale of timber and underwood brought in a valuable income.[16] A woodward (*custos bosci*) was employed at a yearly rate of 13*s.* 4*d.*

Land, of course, remained the source of most tenants' wealth, whether directly through farming or indirectly through trading in agricultural produce. By the mid-fifteenth century, farming at Leighton Buzzard meant mixed farming in which animals—sheep, cattle, pigs—were important. It is not clear how far this was a new development, for the sources before 1450 are too few to show us. Many by-laws were made to regulate the pasturing of animals by the tenants; they form indirect yet insistent evidence for the importance of livestock to the inhabitants. Most expressed the concern of the community to regulate access of tenants to pasture in order to conserve a

---

[16] e.g. between 1501 and 1504 30 a. of underwood were sold for £20 (Wind. XV.61.63).

limited resource. There were four ways in which this was done. The first and most common was the by-law which forbade commoning in certain furlongs for certain periods of the year. Out of a total of ninety-four by-laws of this kind issued between 1464 and 1508, fully half were directed against sheep. Most of the rest were directed more generally against flocks and herds together. The second involved attempts at communal grazing under a common herder. The third way was to fix a pasture stint. This was applied throughout the manor at the rate of five sheep for each acre a tenant held. The fourth method concerned pigs: a number of by-laws were passed which insisted that pigs turned loose to root should be ringed. This discouraged destructive rooting. Pigs were pastured in common too. These forms of action were almost certainly made necessary by the growing pressure of animals on the common land. Unfortunately we have no direct evidence of the size of tenants' flocks and herds, though some may have run flocks of 100 sheep or more.[17]

Some portions of the manorial demesne and its appurtenances were let at farm as early as 1342,[18] but it was not until the end of the fourteenth century that the greater part of the demesne was leased. No one individual farmed the manor. The arable, meadow, and pasture were let in parcels to the tenants. From the start, leases of ten years or more were common.[19] Throughout the fifteenth century the successive owners of the manor retained in their hands the manor courts and the woodland. The mills, the market and fair, the warren, and the demesne at Grovebury were all let separately at first.[20] By 1456 the last two were farmed together, at that date by William Anable, a member of a Dunstable family long settled in the area.[21] Ten years later they were let to John, Lord Wenlock;[22] following his death at the battle of Tewkesbury in 1471, they

---

[17] Stints were usually defined as 100 sheep per 20 a., perhaps implying that individuals ran flocks of this size.

[18] PRO SC 6/741/4.

[19] e.g. BRO KK 725, fo. 3ʳ (10-year lease, 1398).

[20] Wind. XV.61.35 (1439-40).

[21] Wind. XV.61.37.

[22] Wind. XV.61.41. Wenlock's career is described by J.S. Roskell, 'John Lord Wenlock of Someries', *Publications of the Bedfordshire Historical Record Soc.*, vol. xxxviii (1958), 12-48.

were farmed to Thomas Fowkes and Richard Smith.[23] In 1480 the dean and canons granted a life-lease of Grovebury to Cecily, duchess of York, mother of Edward IV.[24] In 1505 Grovebury was let for a term of thirty years to Thomas Hobbes,[25] Thomas Rowthale,[26] and Richard Rowthale.[27] William Hancock farmed the mills for thirty years between 1455-6 and 1485-6.[28] Richard Hancock, probably William's son, was the miller in 1492.[29] The stallage and tolls of the market and fair were usually farmed to the bailiff. Local gentry and others were quick to seize the chance to farm parts of the manor. In particular Grovebury, with its meadow and pasture in the Ouzel valley, was an attractive proposition. In the first half of the sixteenth century other parcels of meadow and pasture were taken on lease by various local gentry.[30]

Between 1457, when the main series of accounts starts, and 1511, when it breaks off, there were only three bailiffs. Richard Southwode, a local man from Billington, held the position until 1475.[31] He was followed by William a Lee, who was bailiff until the end of the century—he received a life-grant of the office from John de la Pole and was retained by the canons at the same yearly fee, £6. 13s. 4d.[32] He may possibly have been a member of the Alley family of High Wycombe.[33] Richard Rowthale was bailiff in the first decade of the sixteenth century. Each bailiff was accountable to the receiver, until 1480 an important intermediary in the flow of cash from the manor to its owner. Christopher Wase was receiver to Alice Chaucer,

[23] Wind. XV.61.46. Fowkes was a local man who ended up in Bedford gaol in 1480 (*CPR* 1467-76, p. 80; *CPR* 1476-85, p. 212).

[24] Wind. XV.25.63.

[25] A canon of Windsor, he became dean in 1507 (*Fasti Wyndesoriensis: The Deans and Canons of Windsor*, ed. S.L. Ollard (Windsor, 1950), pp. 38-9).

[26] Prebendary of Leighton Buzzard; secretary to Henry VII; bishop of Durham, 1509 (*Dictionary of National Biography*, under Ruthall).

[27] Probably a relation of Thomas. He was bailiff of the manor at the beginning of the 16th century (Wind. XV.61.64-7).

[28] Wind. XV.61.37-51.

[29] BRO KK 623, m. 21. He was not necessarily the farmer.

[30] Wind. XV.25.75; XV.25.91.

[31] BRO KK 622, m. 12d; Wind. XV.61.39-48. He died in 1475 (BRO KK 622, m. 48).

[32] Wind. XV.61.49.

[33] *The First Ledger Book of High Wycombe*, ed. R. W. Greaves (Bucks. Record Soc., vol. xi; 1956), pp. 49, 52-3.

and it is his accounts that survive. Wase was a man of some standing in his home town of High Wycombe. He was mayor in 1480.[34] Richard Fowler was receiver before Wase. He was also steward of the manor between 1473 and 1476.[35] Sir William Stonor, a relation of Fowler and a friend of Alice Chaucer, was steward between 1478 and 1482.[36] But not all the officials were men from outside the manor. Hugh Billingdon served as steward in 1466. Then the senior member of a long-established local family, he was a man of some substance.[37] However, from the 1480s the canons of Windsor acted as manorial stewards and receivers, one man effectively combining the two posts. The manor for which these men were responsible was both large and valuable. Throughout the fifteenth century the gross receipts of the manor and its appurtenances regularly exceeded £140. Between 1489 and 1511 the net income which the bailiff handed over fluctuated between £102 and £118.[38] By the standards of the day, the accounts reveal to us a competent financial administration. The gift of the manor to the canons of Windsor was clearly a generous one and it appears all the more surprising in the light of the declining fortunes of the De la Poles in the later fifteenth century. But, as we have seen, more may have lain behind the gift than meets the eye.[39]

The most important settlement in the principal manor was the town of Leighton Buzzard. It grew on the east side of the river Ouzel at a point where the valley narrows between two low ridges. The present-day town retains something of the medieval street-plan. The junction of the roads from Linslade (to the west), Billington (to the south), and Heath and Reach (to the north) marks the centre of the town. The town build-

[34] L. J. Ashford, *The History of the Borough of High Wycombe, from its Origins to 1880* (London, 1960), p. 48.

[35] Wind. XV.61.41, XV.61.47-8. Fowler's biography is summarized by Somerville, *Lancaster*, i. 391. With Alice Chaucer and John Broughton, Fowler was a founder of the Fraternity of Leighton Buzzard (*CPR 1467-76*, p. 417).

[36] BRO KK 622, mm. 50-4; Wind. XV.60.54; Somerville, *Lancaster*, i. 391; *Stonor Letters and Papers, 1290-1483*, ed. C. L. Kingsford (Camden 3rd Series, vols. xxix, xxx; 1919), i, p. xxiii; ii. 140).

[37] Described as 'gentleman' in *CPR* 1429-36, pp. 75, 81, and PRO C 1/21/1. He was coroner of the liberty of Grovebury in the 1450s (*Bedfordshire Coroners' Rolls*, ed. R. F. Hunnisett (BHRS, vol. xli; 1961), p. xliv).

[38] Calculated from Wind. XV.61.53-67.

[39] This paragraph summarizes Jones, 'Beds. Land Market', pp. 136-48, where the accounts are analysed in some detail.

ings, houses, cottages, and crofts spread out along these streets, the plots running back at right angles to them. At the end of these tenements were the fields and closes. The main clusters of farms and cottages lay in the 'ends'—*Leckende, Lovetende, Northende*—at the further end of the main streets. Nearer the centre were other houses and buildings. The town had a court house,[40] a prison, at least one forge, shops, and a permanent or semi-permanent market shambles.[41] The market extended westwards from the cross in the town centre along what is now Bridge Street towards the bridge over the Ouzel.[42] In the sixteenth century Leighton Buzzard had a specialist cattle market.[43]

The lay-subsidy roll for 1524-5 provides an indication of the town's population in the late Middle Ages, but we can make only a rough estimate from it.[44] The roll lists 131 people in the town, and it may have had a total population of between 550 and 650 with perhaps a further 250-300 in the villages of the parish, excluding Stanbridge.[45] The aggregate taxable wealth of the Leighton Buzzard inhabitants was assessed at £16. 19s. 4d.[46] Of these, sixty-three were assessed on wages of £1 a year and a further twenty-seven on goods worth £2 a year. These two groups made up the labouring class, though among those assessed at £2 were probably some small landholders and craftsmen who hired themselves out as part-time workmen. Twenty-eight people were assessed on goods valued at between £3 and £10. They constituted a lower middle class of farmers and tradesmen. Above them was an élite of some thirteen men whose assessments ranged from 20 marks (£13. 6s. 8d.) to £40. These wealthier people owned half the aggregate assessed wealth. At their head was William Taillour, local merchant and land speculator, assessed on goods worth £40.[47] Others

[40] BRO KK 623, m. 55; Wind. XV.61.48.
[41] Wind. XV.61.39, XV.61.43, XV.61.49; BRO KK 622, mm. 32d, 47d; KK 623, m. 46.
[42] Godber, *Beds.*, p. 161.
[43] A. Everitt in *Agr. Hist. Eng.*, iv. 590.
[44] The roll for 1523-4 is defective. Without this it is difficult to be at all accurate (J. Cornwall, 'English Country Towns in the 1520s', *EcHR*, 2nd ser., xv (1962-3), 54-69).
[45] Following Cornwall in *EcHR*, 2nd ser., xv (1962-3), 59-60.
[46] PRO E 179/71/114, mm. 2-4.
[47] Jones, 'Beds. Land Market', pp. 180-2.

were members of long-established local families; a few were newcomers to the town.[48]

The subsidy assessment of 1524-5 can act only as a rough guide to the distribution of wealth among the population as a whole and to the wealth of individuals. Men were assessed on their most important source of income, and at Leighton Buzzard this was in almost every case considered to be goods. Income from land was the feature that distinguished gentlemen from yeomen: 'practically all gentlemen were landowners, many yeomen were not. When the yeoman was a freeholder his estate did not amount to more than £5 or £6 a year. The £10 freeholder would have been a gentleman.'[49] At Leighton Buzzard, where so much land was copyhold, the subsidy assessment underestimates the importance of land to the community and to the individual. For all his local prominence, William Taillour was not exceptionally wealthy by the standards of many early Tudor provincial merchants and yeomen. By 1508, he had amassed well over 100 acres of land in the main manor, but he was essentially a tenant rather than a landowner and this probably explains why he is never apparently called gentleman.

Six miles to the east of Leighton Buzzard lay Dunstable, another Bedfordshire market town. It is unfortunate that the subsidy assessment for neither 1523-4 nor 1524-5 has survived in full, so denying us a comparison between the two towns. Dunstable was no larger than Leighton Buzzard, yet its assessment was higher.[50] The number of wealthy men whose assessment on goods ranges upwards from 20 marks was greater. The wealthiest Dunstable man of whom there is a record—Ambrose Bradman—was assessed on goods worth twice those of William Taillour at Leighton Buzzard.[51]

The court rolls and other sources[52] provide glimpses of the trades and traders of the town. There were any number of

---

[48] Ibid., p. 150.

[49] Cornwall in *EcHR*, 2nd ser., xvii (1964-5), 464-5.

[50] £30. 6s. 3d. in 1523 compared with Leighton Buzzard's £16. 19s. 4d. in 1524 (PRO E 179/71/109, m. 3; E 179/71/114, m. 7).

[51] Bradman's goods were assessed at £80 on both occasions (PRO E 179/71/109, m. 7; E 179/71/114, m. 7).

[52] Leighton Buzzard was a peculiar in the diocese of Lincoln. Wills were proved locally and few survive.

brewers, ale-sellers, and bakers, and those who brewed and baked probably combined these activities with others. There were tanners and glovers.[53] These men, like the butchers, no doubt relied on the town's cattle market for their raw materials. Some may have had their own flocks and herds. There were dyers, tailors, and hosiers too.[54] In fact, Leighton Buzzard seems to have been a local centre for the leather trade, for cloth-making, and for cloth-working.[55] The local mercers and chapmen—like Thomas Smalhard,[56] John Esgoer,[57] and William Taillour[58]—traded in a variety of goods, both in Leighton Buzzard and in the surrounding countryside. In the fifteenth century Leighton Buzzard men traded at Aylesbury, 10 miles to the south-west, and, no doubt, elsewhere.[59] But the majority of inhabitants were engaged in humbler activities, principally agriculture and those crafts and trades which it fostered. Many were labourers and servants employed full-time by the wealthier few. In many aspects Leighton Buzzard resembled other country towns.

Although Leighton Buzzard had no burgage tenure, it appears to have had some claim to borough status. It paid the burghal tenth in 1472-3, but in the 1490s it contributed to the rural fifteenth.[60] Most of the land held by tenants of the manor, whether in the town or in the fields, was customary land—or copyhold. Tenure by copy is first mentioned in the manor records in 1413;[61] as far as we can tell, all customary tenure in the manor by the late fifteenth century was 'inheritance by copy of court roll, finable at the lord's will'.[62] Originally

---

[53] Tanners: BRO KK 623, mm. 8, 29, 37; *CPR* 1467-76, p. 499. Glovers: BRO KK 622, mm. 46d, 57; KK 623, m. 52d.

[54] Tailors: PRO C 1/59/53; *CPR* 1452-61, p. 649. Dyers: Wind. XV.25.55; Godber, *Beds.*, p. 118. Hosier: *CCR* 1402-5, p. 321.

[55] Foreigners from Holland and Brabant settled in Leighton Buzzard in the 15th century. They were very probably cloth-workers (*CPR* 1429-36, pp. 559, 565, 568).

[56] Jones, 'Beds. Land Market', p. 193.

[57] Described as 'mercer' in BRO KK 148.

[58] Jones, 'Beds. Land Market', pp. 180-2.

[59] E. M. Elvey, 'Aylesbury in the Fifteenth Century: a Bailiff's Notebook', *Records of Buckinghamshire*, xvii, No. 5 (1965), 324-5. A Leighton Buzzard glover died in 1499 when he fell into a deep pit on the road to Aylesbury (J. R. Green, *Town Life in the Fifteenth Century* (London, 2 vols., 1894), ii. 31-2).

[60] Wind. XV.61.46, XV.61.55-6.

[61] BRO KK 725, fo. 7ᵛ.

[62] To quote a 17th-century rental (BRO KK 774).

Leighton Buzzard had been an ancient-demesne manor. Tenants in ancient demesne were in a peculiar position at law, and there was considerable difficulty in saying whether they were freeholders or not.[63] In the fifteenth century a tenant who conveyed ancient-demesne land by enfeoffment was considered a freeholder. But it is clear that tenure at Leighton Buzzard remained customary tenure. While the court records yield several examples of attempts to convey customary land by charter,[64] the court officials seem to have been anxious to prevent attempts to convert customary tenure to freehold. Although there came to be little social difference between the two sorts of tenure, the legal distinction between customary land and free was maintained. Customary tenure was a greater source of profit to the lord, particularly in his right to entry fine and heriot. However, any vestiges of servility which attached to customary tenure disappeared during the fifteenth century. The rentals of the early fifteenth century reveal that the basis of landholding had been the virgate and half-virgate. Neither term occurs in the court rolls of the second half of the century. The size of the land market and the disappearance of villeinage rendered the ancient divisions largely meaningless.

During the fifteenth century, Londoners began to invest in copyholds in the manor, chiefly in the town. While we cannot be sure if their interests extended further, presumably some of them traded in the town. Tenant status may have been useful in trade. Richard Hale, citizen and grocer of London, bought land in Leighton Buzzard in the 1460s.[65] He settled this on his daughter, Margaret, wife of John Harryson, citizen and tailor of London.[66] They in turn sold it to John Chester, a merchant of the staple.[67] In 1491, a year after acquiring it, John gave the land to the dean and canons of St. George's Chapel.[68] William Bodley, a London grocer, bought a messuage and close in the town in 1502.[69] A year later he was plaintiff in a plea of debt for

[63] A. W. B. Simpson, *An Introduction to the History of the Land Law* (London, 1960), pp. 155-6.

[64] BRO KK 725, fos. 7ᵛ, 10ᵛ, 11ᵛ, 13ᵛ.

[65] Wind. XV.25.59; BRO KK 622, m. 16.

[66] Probably on his death, about 1489 (BRO KK 623, m. 10; Wind. XV.25.64).

[67] BRO KK 623, m. 11d.

[68] Ibid., m. 17.

[69] Ibid., m. 51d.

22*s.* 0*d.* brought against Richard Freeman: merchants may have been a convenient source of loans to townsfolk.[70] Robert Amadas and Nicholas Worley, London goldsmiths, bought a messuage in Leighton Buzzard in 1505.[71] John Saunders, draper and merchant of the staple, was another London merchant who invested in the manor.[72] In 1508, George Monoux, another draper, bought a messuage and 40 acres of land in Leighton Buzzard. He built up an estate elsewhere in the county and, in 1514, was Lord Mayor of London.[73] Leighton Buzzard was certainly well placed for trade. Watling Street ran close by; Dunstable was only 6 miles away; London just 30 miles further on.

The lay-subsidy roll for 1523-4 lists seventy-six names under Billington, Heath, Reach, and Eggington and Clipstone. Of these, forty-four were assessed on goods and wages worth £2 or less a year; twenty-seven were assessed on goods valued at between £3 and £10 a year; and five men's assessments ranged between 20 marks and £22. Only in Reach, where Thomas Taillour (no known relation to William) and Richard Allen were both assessed on goods worth 20 marks, were there two men whose goods were valued at more than £10.[74] In Heath, John Grisell, gentleman, owned goods whose assessed value (£20) accounted for more than half of the total for the village.[75] William Billingdon in Billington and Thomas Doget in Eggington and Clipstone were by far the wealthiest men in their villages.[76] In the villages, the middle class, those men assessed on goods worth between £3 and £10, formed a greater proportion of the total population than in the town.[77] The labouring class was proportionately smaller.[78] Most of the men in the villages lived by agriculture; the landless tended to congregate in the town.

---

[70] Ibid., m. 55.
[71] Ibid., m. 62d; *CCR* 1500-9, pp. 216-17; *CPR* 1485-94, p. 136.
[72] BRO KK 623, mm. 9d, 42.
[73] Ibid., m. 72d; Godber, *Beds.*, p. 140.
[74] PRO E 179/71/109, m. 9.
[75] Ibid., m. 10.
[76] Ibid., mm. 2-6.
[77] 35 per cent as against 23 per cent.
[78] 58 per cent as against 69 per cent.

The land market in the principal manor

As Leighton Buzzard never became a chartered borough, the manorial courts acted as the main administrative agency in the community. Several courts were held a year. By 1485 a definite pattern had emerged. Five courts met each year—in February, May, August, and October, with one in either April or July.[79] In the second half of the fifteenth century the record of the view of frankpledge followed a set form as follows:[80]

1. Essoins: one tenant's surety for the non-attendance of another.

2. Presentments by the constables, tithingmen, and ale-tasters of Leighton Buzzard, Heath and Reach, Eggington and Clipstone, and Billington.

3. Miscellaneous business: private litigation, elections to manorial offices, by-laws.

4. The names of the jurors.

5. The record of the *Parva curia*: the register of changes in tenancies.

6. Names of the affeerors, the two tenants whose duty it was to assess the amercements levied on offenders.

7. The income of the court.

The August court, which had no view of frankpledge, recorded business for Leighton Buzzard alone, except when by-laws were registered by the other townships. The record of this court usually contained little more than a note of essoins and the names of the jurors and defaulters.

The most impressive series of entries on the rolls comes under the heading *Parva curia*. In this section were recorded changes by both inheritance and surrender. Between 1464 and

[79] Six courts met in 1498 when an extra court was held in June (BRO KK 623, mm. 34d-39).

[80] Leighton Buzzard was unusual in having four views a year. The August court was not a view. The extra views were probably needed for effective administration, given the size of the manor.

1508 over 900 changes were registered. When land changed hands the court-roll entry commonly included the names of the interested parties; the amount and the kind of land; details of any appurtenances such as dwellings, gardens, crofts; the sub-division and location of the land (more especially for small acreages); and the entry fines. From this mass of detail it is a relatively straightforward matter to compile an index of the people involved in land transfers and to distinguish between inheritance and transfers outside the family. Of 907 transfers registered between 1464 and 1508, 604 (67 per cent) were made outside the family during the tenant's lifetime; these consti-tuted the land market proper. Of the rest, 221 (24 per cent) represented family inheritance arrangements, 69 (8 per cent) were unspecified entries to land, usually grants from the lord of property which had come into his hands, and 13 (1 per cent) were extra-family transfers made on the death of a tenant.

Most of the transfers in the land market included arable (424 out of 604). Of these 424, over 80 per cent (352) were smaller than 10 acres and nearly 63 per cent (265) were smaller than 3 acres. Some 288 of the 424 transfers of arable (68 per cent) involved no other sort of land or property, and all but three of these were smaller than 10 acres. Thus the land market at Leighton Buzzard between 1464 and 1508 was chiefly one in small parcels of land. Most tenants were content, or were con-strained, to increase their holdings in the manor by the piece-meal addition of odd acres and half-acres.

Arable was not always sold by itself. Quite often it was sold together with a messuage or cottage and other pieces of land—crofts, gardens, parcels of meadow and pasture. Of 136 trans-fers of arable and other property (out of the total of 424 transfers which included arable), 102 (75 per cent) included a messuage or cottage. Half of these dwellings lay in the town; the rest were distributed more or less evenly between the surrounding villages (excluding Stanbridge). Half of the transfers of land and property (69 out of 136) consisted of parcels larger than 10 acres. As a general rule, the larger the amount of land to change hands, the greater was the likelihood that the transfer included other property. There were also examples of messu-ages and cottages changing hands with no land attached other than a garden or croft. Most of these were in the town (66 out of 85 cases). The turnover in residential property in the later fifteenth century was not great. A natural increase in population may have accounted for a part of the demand. It appears that newcomers and rentiers accounted for a part. A scrutiny of the court rolls suggests that some thirty or forty new men bought residential property in the manor between 1464 and 1508, most of this in the town. Not all of these men settled in Leighton Buzzard. We have already seen how Londoners were beginning to buy up property in the manor. Other men probably acquired messuages for use for business purposes or to sublet: William Taillour bought up six messuages and five cottages between 1497 and 1508.[81] Some tenants bought residential property and open, unbuilt sites adjoining their own buildings, probably to extend their homesteads.

The survival of the court rolls for six years at the end of the fourteenth century[82] provides an opportunity to compare the land market at that date with the market in the second half of the fifteenth century. The comparison can only be tentative for the earlier sample is so much smaller. Between 1393 and 1398 the court rolls recorded 128 transfers, of which 89 were outside the family and 33 were within. Three-quarters of the transfers which made up the land market (the 89) included arable land, and most (50 out of 64) were smaller than 3 acres. There was little dealing in larger amounts of arable, and practically none in dwellings.

From a comparison of the years 1393-8 and 1464-1508 three aspects of the land market stand out. Firstly, when measured in the number of transfers a year passing through the courts, the market was running at about the same level in both periods. Secondly, the land market at the end of the fourteenth century was almost entirely small-scale and characterized by the transfer of land only. Small transfers still dominated the land market at the later date but not to the same extent. Thirdly, a market in larger parcels of land and in residential property had developed by the 1460s. Between 1464 and 1508 transfers of 10 acres or more ran at a level of between 15 and 20 per cent of the market as a whole. It is tempting to see the land market of 1393-8 as being in its last days as an exclusively small-scale affair.

[81] Jones, 'Beds. Land Market', p. 276.   [82] BRO KK 619.

Between 1464 and 1508 there was a gradual contraction in the level of the land market at Leighton Buzzard. The decline was not continuous but probably marked a real decline in activity. Throughout the second half of the fifteenth century the market in small parcels of land (less than 5 acres) remained fairly constant as a proportion of the total volume of transfers, never falling below 65 per cent. In the 1480s it amounted to 80 per cent of the market. The market in larger parcels, having grown in the first half of the century, did not develop significantly after 1460. Any rise or fall in the level of the market as a whole was a response to the fluctuating demand for small parcels of land.

As the court rolls of Leighton Buzzard did not record names of tenements the phenomenon of recurrent transfers is much less noticeable here than at Arlesey. Nevertheless, many examples of the recurrent transfer of land can be traced in the court rolls. For most we have no more than two recorded changes in ownership. This simply reflects the limited time-span of the rolls. A number of holdings changed hands three times or more, enough to suggest that the phenomenon at Leighton Buzzard was similar to that at Arlesey. The interval between transfers varied haphazardly, and the vast majority represented a clear break in family ownership.

Despite the similarities, there were important differences between Arlesey and Leighton Buzzard. At Arlesey, where we can trace the descent and partition of many holdings in the fourteenth and fifteenth centuries, the demand for land was met largely from those parcels on which family inheritance had ceased. Individuals were not constantly selling parcels of land from their own family holdings. At Leighton Buzzard there appears to have been a greater continuity in landholding, a greater demand for land, and a greater tendency for holdings, once abandoned by a family, to fragment rather than to retain their unity and identity (as exemplified at Arlesey in the tene-ment names). It seems that fewer families died out or moved away from the principal manor during the fourteenth and fif-teenth centuries, and that fewer holdings were left vacant. Where they were, they did not retain a separate identity but split into several parcels. The result was a greater tendency for the market at Leighton Buzzard to be supplied with land from a family holding rather than from a distinct pool of property. Whereas recurrent transfers accounted for about 70 per cent of the land market at Arlesey, at Leighton Buzzard their share was smaller, probably about 20 per cent. This, together with the disappearance of the virgate, suggests that the integrity of the tenement was abandoned in the face of the demand for land. On the rural manors, where the demand for land was not so great, the virgate and half-virgate survived.

In a manor as large as Leighton Buzzard, the patchwork of holdings was intricate to the point of confusion. When land changed hands, terriers were frequently and necessarily included in the record of the transfer copied on the court roll. The information in the terriers can be used to investigate the scatter of land and the extent to which people tried to rearrange their holdings to overcome this. Unfortunately we do not possess sufficient detail to reconstruct the layout of the fields and furlongs in the late Middle Ages. The terriers in the court rolls were limited in their scope. They usually named the township in which the land in question lay and the furlongs in which it lay divided. Some recorded the owners of adjoining land. Most described small parcels of land: of 139 terriers discussed below, only twenty (14 per cent) described parcels larger than 5 acres.

The fields of the manor were arranged in the classic midland pattern. They lay open, divided into numerous furlongs by balks, headlands, and tracks. A tenant held his land in strips scattered over several or many furlongs. A strip consisted of one or more selions, the basic division of the furlong, and could measure anything from ½ rood to 2 acres or more. Sometime in the first half of the fourteenth century a tenement in Eggington and Clipstone was divided, on the steward's order, between a number of tenants.[83] The record of this division provides our earliest opportunity to study the scatter and size of one person's strips. John Gilbert held about 21 acres of arable made up of some forty-five strips in twenty-one furlongs. Eleven strips measured 1 rood, thirty measured ½ acre, three measured 1 acre, and one measured 1½ acres. There were ten furlongs in which John had held more than one strip.[84] Later

[83] BRO KK 624, m. 4.

[84] Two ½-acre strips were not located; for a third, a furlong-name is illegible.

examples show the same kind of scatter. In 1464 William Straunge surrendered to John Morell junior a holding of 34½ acres in the fields of Leighton Buzzard. The strips lay in some forty furlongs. There were ten in which William had more than one strip, but only in one did his land exceed 1 acre.[85]

There are three ways in which the terriers can be used to examine the effect of the land market on the structure of a person's holding. Firstly, the location of the strips which made up a transfer can be studied to show how far they were grouped or dispersed. Secondly, we can examine the activities of various individuals to see whether they attempted to group strips together. Thirdly, there are several examples in the court rolls of specific consolidations of land and property.

Where we have the evidence of the terriers, transfers of land larger than ½ acre can be divided into three. Firstly, there were seventy-one in which all strips lay in different furlongs; secondly, there were forty-six in which the strips lay in the same furlong; and thirdly, there were twenty-two in which some of the strips lay in the same furlong. The first category consisted in the main of small parcels of arable, such as 1 acre divided between two furlongs, 2 acres divided between four furlongs. The second category included examples ranging in size from 3 roods to 12 acres.[86] Thirty-one measured 2 acres or less. Of these, fifteen were not in effect single strips but a holding composed of two or more separate strips within the one furlong. Of the examples which measured more than 2 acres, ten lay similarly divided in the furlong; thus there were few examples of the transfer of holdings made up of contiguous strips. The third category consisted mostly of larger pieces of arable, save for a group of transfers of 1½ acres. These were divided in two: a ½-acre strip in one furlong, two ½-acre strips in another.

It appears that tenants made little attempt to consolidate their farms by a conscious attempt to overcome the scatter of strips. This impression may be tested by examining the activities of individual tenants, particularly those who added two or more small parcels of arable to their farms. Where the locations of their purchases are known, we can hope to pick out attempts to group strips in close proximity. In this way we can

[85] BRO KK 622, m. 1-1d; Godber, *Beds.*, p. 162.
[86] BRO KK 622, m. 63d (a 12-a. parcel called Waterfurlong).

study twenty-five tenants in the period 1464-1508. Most, if not all, of these men held more land than the two or three small parcels which interest us here. The larger their holdings, the greater would have been the dispersal of their strips over many furlongs. With this in mind, the importance of the grouping that did take place among the twenty-five was slight and the acreage involved was small. Most strips which people acquired in small transfers were distributed over different furlongs. In fact, many tenants held land in different field systems within the manor.[87]

A few examples have come to light of tenants buying land or property adjoining their own where it is clear that the purchase of the holding was a deliberate act of consolidation. Where a tenant held strips either side of one held by another, there were obvious advantages in acquiring the middle one.[88] Other examples, where the purchaser held land on one side of his new acquisition, may have represented consolidations where a single strip was involved.[89] Where just one strip out of several transferred lay next to the purchaser's land, it may have been little more than coincidence. In the town, a move to enlarge homesteads may have resulted in amalgamations of property.[90]

On the surface, it appears that there was little deliberate consolidation of arable at Leighton Buzzard in the fifteenth century. Some people took the chance to piece together a few strips here and there. Where a great deal of land changed hands, it was inevitable that some grouping of strips would occur, but the land market failed to alter radically the appearance of the open fields. However, while it continually affected the pattern of land ownership, individuals could mitigate some of the effects of extreme fragmentation by recourse to subletting.

At Leighton Buzzard, pleas entered on the court rolls show that tenants did not always directly exploit all the land they held. Throughout the second half of the fifteenth century there were occasions when tenants claimed arrears of rent from their neighbours for land they had sublet to them. In 1468, for example, William Dudle claimed 1s. 4d. from William Trun-

---

[87] Detailed evidence is in Jones, 'Beds. Land Market', pp. 196-7, 271-2.
[88] e.g. BRO KK 622, mm. 29d, 44.
[89] e.g. BRO KK 623, m. 41d.
[90] e.g. BRO KK 622, mm. 2d, 3d, 26, 31, 35d.

chevylle for three pightels and a rood of meadow which Trunchevylle rented from him. One of the pightels lay next to
Trunchevylle's messuage, while another lay between two of his
crofts. The rood of meadow lay next to some of his meadow.[91]
Three years later William Trunchevylle owed rent to Isabel
Ponde for a croft. She also let land to Henry Grisell.[92] In 1507
William Doget claimed rent from four people for parcels of
land of 3 acres, 2 ½ acres, and 1 acre.[93] A year later he claimed
rent from two further sub-tenants.[94] In the first example it is
clear that William Trunchevylle rented this land to simplify his
farming; in the second, Isabel Ponde was a widow and so probably incapable of working all her land;[95] in the third, William
Doget was one of a long-established and relatively prosperous
Eggington family. No doubt he tilled land himself, but he was a
rentier too.[96]

The examples of subletting in the court rolls are, of course,
only those which ended in litigation. As such they do no more
than show that subletting occurred. The full amount may have
been substantial. The examples given above probably typify
the sorts of situation which arose over and again, at Leighton
Buzzard and elsewhere. A man rented land adjacent to some of
his own in order to cut down the time spent in travelling
between furlongs and to give him more scope; another let off
some of his more distant strips to simplify his own holding; the
old and the infirm let land for cash. Wealthier men and merchants who bought up copyholds probably rented out the whole
or a part of their lands. In these ways the fragmentation of holdings was modified. There was not, however, a 'well-defined
movement . . . for the gradual modification or dissolution of the
open field system'.[97] At Leighton Buzzard open-field farming
persisted into the nineteenth century. There is little or no
evidence that the land market in the fifteenth century resulted
in the substitution of a few large blocks for many scattered

[91] Ibid., m. 11.
[92] Ibid., m. 23.
[93] BRO KK 623, m. 69.
[94] Ibid., m. 70d.
[95] Her husband had died in 1469 (BRO KK 622, m. 17).
[96] Jones, 'Beds. Land Market', p. 183.
[97] As believed by Tawney, *Agr. Problem*, pp. 165-6.

strips. Open-field farming was not necessarily as inconvenient and as cumbersome as it appears at first sight.[98]

The tenants and the demand for land

The transfers registered on the court rolls provide a lot of information about the entry fines paid by the incoming tenants. Rents, however, were rarely recorded but our information is enough to show that there was no fixed ratio by the size of holding. Throughout the fifteenth century, entry fines charged on holdings of a similar size varied considerably and apparently at random. It appears that fines were fixed arbitrarily 'at the will of the lord' or by agreement between steward and tenant. Neither the general level of rents nor that of fines seems to have grown during the fifteenth century. Rents remained fixed, protected by custom. As we have no standard from which to work (such as the general level of fine for a virgate or half-virgate), it is difficult to judge movements in the levels of entry fine. A rough and ready guide can be obtained by comparing the levels in the 1390s, the 1460s, and at the end of the century. The comparison is valid for parcels of land alone. Where land was transferred with a messuage and other property, we have no means of deciding the weight to attach to each component in the size of the fine. The usual entry fines charged on small parcels of arable are shown in Table XI.

The figures in Table XI suggest a general stability over the fifteenth century. On larger parcels of land, with or without appurtenances, there was considerable variation in the level of fine but levels appear generally to have been relatively low. Entry fines were seldom over 20s. 0d.; where they were, they were nearly all for large transfers (20 acres or more) which included other property. But large transfers frequently bore a lower fine. The general stability in the level of entry fines at Leighton Buzzard is shown by the fines levied on the recurrent transfers. From these we can see if fines on one holding rose or fell between 1464 and 1508. Of 61 examples, 23 showed a rise in fine (often by very little: ten rose by 8d. or less), 22 remained stable, and 16 showed a decrease. On a number of occasions

[98] J. D. Chambers and G. E. Mingay, *The Agricultural Revolution, 1750-1880* (2nd edn., London, 1970), pp. 48-50.

Table XI
Entry fines at Leighton Buzzard, 1393-1508

Description of holding	1393-8	1464-9	1490-1508
½ a.	4*d.*-6*d.*	4*d.*	4*d.*-6*d.*
1 a.	8*d.*-10*d.*	4*d.*-6*d.*	6*d.*-8*d.*
1½ a.	1*s.* 0*d.*	1*s.* 0*d.*	9*d.*
2 a.	1*s.* 0*d.*	1*s.* 0*d.*	1*s.* 0*d.*-1*s.* 4*d.*
2½ a.	—	1*s.* 0*d.*-1*s.* 8*d.*	1*s.* 0*d.*-1*s.* 8*d.*
3 a.	2*s.* 0*d.*	2*s.* 0*d.*	1*s.* 3*d.*

the fine charged on one holding rose and then fell, sometimes to its former level, sometimes lower.

Here we have considered only the impersonal, statistical aspects of the land market and its effects. However, the wealth of detail in the court rolls and other sources enables us to study the activities of many individuals,[99] and some remarks will not be out of place. It is unfortunate that the short time-span of the fifteenth-century court rolls cuts off our view of the activities of a number of tenants. We do not know what men were doing before 1464 and after 1508. To take a particularly frustrating example, we can study William Taillour amassing one of the largest copyhold farms in the manor. We know that he was the richest man in the town in 1524 and that he did not die until 1537 or 1538. Yet after 1508 we all but lose track of him.[100] For only a few tenants can we hope to trace the whole or the greater part of their activities. For most we have only a partial record, and then only a record for one manor. As the principal manor was a large one it is likely that a number of tenants did not hold land elsewhere, but we do not know who these men were or whether they were in a majority. For these reasons, even more so than at Arlesey, the court rolls can only show particular sorts of activity. However, the court rolls are far more detailed than the registers for Arlesey and Shillington. For many tenants at Leighton Buzzard we possess the raw materials for biographies,

[99] Jones, 'Beds. Land Market', pp. 171-94.
[100] Ibid., pp. 180-2.

and these give some indication of the people who played a prominent part in the life of the community.

Besides the locals, there were several, perhaps many, tenants of the manor whose main interests lay elsewhere. There were also families for which it is difficult to judge where their main interests lay. As we have seen, London merchants were one sort of tenant. Another was the county gentleman who had land nearby and who bought up a copyhold or two. John Broughton, esquire, who owned the main manor in nearby Toddington as well as much land elsewhere, held land from Alice Chaucer in Grovebury in 1457.[101] In 1466 he tried to avoid paying an entry fine on four selions of copyhold land acquired from William atte Hall.[102] Richard Decons, who inherited a small manor in Leighton Buzzard at the end of the fifteenth century, bought three messuages in 1501 and 6 acres of land in 1503.[103] He also held land in Marston Moretaine and Flitton (both in Bedfordshire), and in Clifton Reynes (Buckinghamshire).[104] On the same social level as Decons was Richard Cutte, brother of Sir John Cutte, the receiver-general of the duchy of Lancaster in the 1490s.[105] Richard married a daughter of John Billingdon of Leighton Buzzard. He made his will at Leighton Buzzard in January 1505, leaving £20 apiece to his two sons.[106] Shortly before this, in 1504, he had bought 20 acres of copyhold in the manor.[107] Lower down the social scale were families like the Kegills of Edlesborough (Buckinghamshire), the Turneys of Slapton (Buckinghamshire), the Wigges of Mentmore (Buckinghamshire), and the Pedders of Totternhoe (Bedfordshire), all of whom had held copyholds in the manor at some time in the later fifteenth century. Then there were other families holding larger tenements in the manor, who held land in neighbouring villages and for whom it is difficult to decide where their main holdings lay. For example, Robert Ryot alias Newman held land in Leighton Buzzard and in Winslow (Buckinghamshire), while the Stan-

---

[101] BRO KK 771.
[102] BRO KK 622, m. 7.
[103] *VCH Beds.*, iii. 407; BRO KK 623, mm. 47d, 66.
[104] *VCH Beds.*, iii. 309, 328; *VCH Bucks.*, iv. 318.
[105] Somerville, *Lancaster*, i. 401.
[106] *Buck. Archdeaconry Cts.*, pp. 197-9.
[107] BRO KK 623, m. 60.

bridge family, to take a more complicated example, had several branches holding land in a number of villages, as well as in Stanbridge and Leighton Buzzard. Another Stanbridge family, the Boynons, also held land in the manor and elsewhere. The Gurney family, a branch of which settled in Eggington and Clipstone in the later fifteenth century, was a third family which held land in various villages. No doubt several other families had a similar scatter of interests.[108]

Within Leighton Buzzard itself we can distinguish about 100 tenants who dominated the turnover of land in the manor between 1464 and 1508. Among them were several individuals and families who stood out from their fellows by the scale of their activities. From the great amount of detail recorded on the court rolls we can draw together several general conclusions about holdings (the way in which they grew and diminished, the effects of inheritance and speculation, the emergence of large holdings, the location of a man's land), and about the people involved in the market (the different social groupings, the men from outside the manor, the influence of widows).[109]

At Leighton Buzzard in the later fifteenth century there were two principal sorts of cycle in the development of a copyhold tenement. On the one hand there were those built up piecemeal over a number of years, and although we rarely see the complete cycle we may include those holdings which were sold off in the same way as representative of the same pattern. Some acquired holdings were very small. John Hogge, for example, accumulated 10½ acres in twelve transfers between 1471 and 1486, while Richard Wayn acquired 7 acres in nine transfers between 1483 and 1506.[110] Others were larger, although we can observe a ceiling of roughly 60 acres. The holdings which fell in this first category were mostly those belonging to local men. Often a part of the land acquired or sold off included an inherited portion, but it is striking how often we have little or no detail about a person's original holding. A person's purchases in one year were his sales in another.[111] On the other

108 Sources for the history of these families are listed in Jones, 'Beds. Land Market', pp. 172-3.

109 Detailed case studies are ibid., pp. 174-94, 273-9.

110 Ibid., pp. 190, 277, 279.

111 As in the 12th and 13th centuries on the estates of Peterborough Abbey (King, *Peterborough*, p. 169).

hand, there were holdings which were accumulated rapidly, or in a few large transfers. These were usually the holdings acquired by the wealthier members of the community or by outsiders. It does not seem an exaggeration to call some of their activities speculation. This can be seen clearly in the case of William Taillour, in some of the holdings gained by marriage with widows, and probably where men acquired large holdings and subsequently sold them intact. Tenements accumulated in these ways were often very large, over 100 acres. It is striking to see at Leighton Buzzard, as at Arlesey, that these considerable copyhold estates emerged at the end of the fifteenth and at the beginning of the sixteenth centuries.

With local families, whether from the gentry or from the main body of tenants, inheritance continued to play an important but by no means an overwhelming part in the redistribution of land. As far as we can tell, holdings were not often passed on intact from parent to child. As we have seen, the statistical evidence for a market in small parcels of land is impressive. When seen through individual examples, this market takes on a new significance. Gradual, piecemeal accumulation and dispersal was the typical story. A man might inherit a large holding, but he reverted to buying up small amounts of land. Another might pass on land to a son or sell off a large portion, but again he reverted to the piecemeal disposal of his remaining acres.

Whereas Leighton Buzzard was a large manor with several settlements, in practice most tenants held at least half their land in one township, though at some time in their lives many held land in two or more. Of eighty-six tenants for whom we have evidence of five or more land transfers, most (70 per cent) held at least four-fifths of their land in one township, and a third of them appear to have held all their land in one only. However, at some period half held arable in two or more townships within the manor. Usually a tenant's holding in a second township was very small, and it is clear that most had home farms from which to extend their activities. Still, the fact that men were prepared to own small plots of land scattered over two or more field systems suggests that distance was no great drawback to the acquisitive. John Hogge's 10½ acres were spread over four field systems.[112]

[112] Jones, 'Beds. Land Market', p. 277.

During the later fifteenth century, it appears that the group of between 90 and 100 tenants which effectively dominated the turnover in land at Leighton Buzzard increased its hold on the market. This can be seen in part in the growth of large holdings and the concentration of land in fewer hands. It can also be seen in the source and direction of land transfers; between 1464 and 1508, 54 per cent of the people from whom the active land dealers gained land were other active land dealers. In the same period, 61 per cent of the people to whom active land dealers transferred land were other active land dealers. At the same time this group also dominated the government of the manor. It was these men who were elected constable, tithingman, and ale-taster, and who served most frequently on manorial juries. Two-thirds of their number held, for varying lengths of time, at least one of the three main offices. Where land was so important to the community it was inevitable that there should have been a close link between landholding on the one hand and authority and responsibility on the other. It is possible that the bare record of the manorial court roll hides from view the kind of oligarchy that often developed in country towns in the Middle Ages.[113] But the market in copyholds was noteworthy for the different sorts of people it attracted. Aldermanic merchants rubbed shoulders with prominent local families and the peasantry in the competition for land. While it is interesting to see outsiders taking advantage of the free market which had developed, the locals formed the backbone of the market. Leighton Buzzard yields several examples of families anciently settled in the manor whose members were, at the end of the fifteenth century, prospering into the ranks of the yeomen and gentry.

One convenient way in which a man could obtain land for the first time was by marrying a widow. In the later Middle Ages widows were an attraction to the landless or to the ambitious at all levels of society. In rural society, in a period when inheritance customs generally lost much of their strength, widows' rights remained strong. Where a widow had a life-estate in land, or held it in her own right, she was susceptible to remarriage, especially where the demand for land was maintained. At Leighton Buzzard widows often played an

---

[113] Cornwall in *EcHR* 2nd ser., xv (1962-3), 54-69.

important part in the land market. For example, between 1477 and 1486 Agnes Skylful surrendered parcels measuring 2½ acres of land and 4 roods of meadow, 6 acres of land, and a further 2½ acres;[114] and Margery Lockley sold three parcels of arable totalling 9 acres in 1487.[115] However, many widows were considerable landholders and so were a prize to a new husband. Other widows, perhaps older women, did not remarry but sold their late husband's land. Alice Southwode, widow of the former bailiff, transferred 90 acres to John Billingdon in 1490.[116] He had already acquired 27½ acres from two other widows.[117] Isabel Godynche sold 60 acres of land to Richard Assheby in 1503.[118] Assheby was probably one of a family of local freeholders. In 1501 and 1502 he had begun to acquire copyholds in the manor,[119] and it looks as if his large purchase from Isabel was the work of a man who stepped in at the strategic moment. Occasionally we have an insight into the arrangements which lay behind the sale of land by a widow. In 1501 Isabel Capron surrendered to John Tommys a messuage and close, 11 perches of meadow, 48 acres of land, and another close, all in Billington. Isabel retained a tenement and close in which she lived. John agreed to maintain at his own expense three cows and three sheep belonging to Isabel and to deliver to her the issue of an acre of wheat, an acre of barley, and an acre of beans. He further agreed to pay her 3s. 4d. a year for the rest of her life and to pay to her or her executors £5. 10s. for the land.[120] The same conditions remained in force when Tommys sold the land in 1502.[121] Arrangements of a different sort were made by Juliana Grisell in 1506. She transferred to her executors 35 acres of land for them to sell, the proceeds to be spent for the good of the souls of her late husband and herself.[122] In 1507 the executors sold 12½ acres of this land to William Hicches and 10 acres to William Taillour, and in the following year an acre of meadow and a close to Richard Aleyn.[123] At Arlesey, where the demand for land was not nearly so strong as at Leighton Buzzard, widows featured far less prominently in the transfer of land in the fifteenth century.

[114] BRO KK 622, mm. 45, 66; KK 623, m. 4.
[115] BRO KK 623, mm. 6d, 7.
[116] Ibid., m. 12d.
[117] BRO KK 622, mm. 5d, 16d.
[118] BRO KK 623, m. 55d.

[119] Ibid., mm. 48d, 51d.
[120] Ibid., m. 47.
[121] Ibid., m. 52.
[122] Ibid., m. 66d.
[123] Ibid., mm. 70, 71d.

· The Bedfordshire court rolls of the fifteenth century contain plenty of evidence that ambition and investment were the driving forces behind many land transactions. While the lot of the peasantry in general improved, one development in rural society which has attracted much attention is the growth of a group of wealthy peasants. The ownership of land conferred status at all levels of society, not least in the village. In the fifteenth century the customary land market was invaded by men of superior social status to the peasant. This invasion dated largely from the last two or three decades of the century. Although the copyholder may always have had less security at law than the freeholder, merchants and gentry were probably at an advantage in acquiring copyhold land; their security and interests were protected in some measure by their social status. They approached the steward of the manor as an equal or near-equal. Thus, attracted by the ease with which it could be bought and sold, merchants and gentry invested and speculated in copyhold land. They were joined in this by the wealthier members of the peasantry, the emergent yeomen, who also bought and sold with an eye to the profit to be made. The existence of a yeoman class within the ranks of the peasantry was no new development; what was new was the increased size of this group. By the end of the fifteenth century it had come to dominate the turnover of land at both Arlesey and Leighton Buzzard.

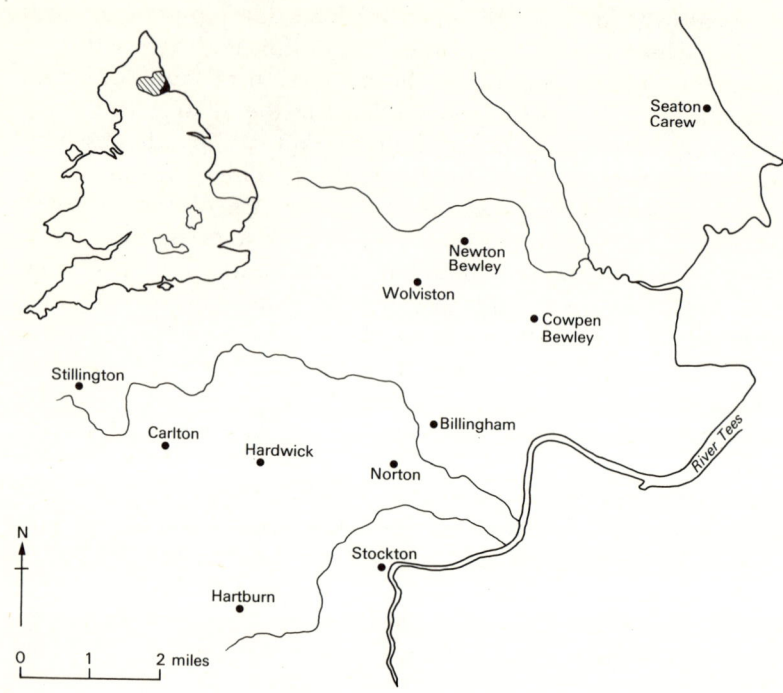

IV SOUTH-EAST DURHAM
showing the places discussed in Chapter V

V South-east Durham:
Late Fourteenth and Fifteenth Centuries*

1 THE VILLAGES AND THEIR RECORDS

The area and its early history

Billingham, Carlton, Cowpen Bewley, Hardwick, Hartburn, Newton Bewley, Norton, Seaton Carew, Stillington, Stockton, and Wolviston are all situated within an area of about 60 square miles in the south-east of the county of Durham. All lie within the ward of Stockton, one of the four administrative divisions of the county, and all are of great interest to the historian in having a large number of surviving medieval records. The bishop of Durham, Durham Cathedral Priory, and Merton College, Oxford, were the principal manorial lords of the area; much of the land there was held by one or other of them. Since the soil, relief, and climate are almost identical in all eleven villages, an examination of their records should show the general effect of differing lordship on a comparatively small society in the later Middle Ages. This study is confined almost exclusively to the century and a half following the Black Death and material outside this period has been used only to illuminate the social history of the area between 1350 and 1500.

Much reliance has been placed on court rolls and many of the so-called new approaches to the use of court rolls, which consist largely of using simple statistical techniques, have been adopted here. The debt owed, therefore, to historians such as J.A. Raftis[1] and W.O. Ault[2] has been considerable. It has to

* T. Lomas, 'Land and People in South-east Durham in the Later Middle Ages' (Council for National Academic Awards Ph.D. thesis, 1976). The entire area is now in the county of Cleveland. Aspects of the subject discussed in the thesis but omitted here include topography, field systems, and local administration. I am indebted to Dr A.J. Pollard of Teesside Polytechnic and Professor R.B. Dobson of the University of York for their valuable assistance.

[1] As in Raftis, *Tenure* and *Warboys*, and, of his other works 'The Concentration of Responsibility in Five Villages', *Medieval Studies*, xxviii (1966), 92-118; 'Changes in an English Village after the Black Death', ibid., xxix (1967), 158-77; 'Social Structures in Five East Midland Villages: a Study of Possibilities in the Use of Court Roll Data', *EcHR*, 2nd ser., xviii (1965), 83-100.

[2] As in Ault, *Open-field Farming*, and of his other works 'Village By-laws by

be acknowledged that there has been some criticism of the use of statistical methods in medieval social history. Nevertheless most of this criticism is directed at the production of general conclusions from inadequate material and is inapplicable here precisely because so much source material survives.

Most of south-east Durham is low-lying. After the departure of the Romans the area became part of the kingdom of Bernicia. During the Middle Ages Durham was the greatest liberty in private hands in England; within it the bishop virtually replaced the king as the head of local administration. The origins of this palatinate are obscure. Most historians have stressed the importance of the church and especially of the cult of St. Cuthbert. Cuthbert, a seventh-century prior and bishop of Lindisfarne, was venerated widely within a few years of his death in 687. By the time of the Norman Conquest the inhabitants of the area were known as *haliwercfolc*, men holding land under the church of St. Cuthbert.[3] Jean Scammell has pointed out, however, that the history of the liberty really started afresh with the Conquest. The bishop of Durham was thereafter so powerful that he had 'no difficulty in dominating or merely surviving any attempt . . . at shire administration, especially since the bishop owned the essential requirement of government and survival, Durham Castle, the only secure refuge between Tyne and Tees'.[4]

The bishop's dominance as principal landlord within the palatinate was soon challenged in certain areas. In 1083 the second Norman bishop of Durham, William of St. Calais, replaced the secular canons at Durham Cathedral by Benedictine monks who had recently resettled the old foundations of Benedict Biscop at Jarrow and Monkwearmouth.[5] By the end of the first decade of the twelfth century the cathedral priory had been given a share of the endowments of the see. The gradual extension of the territory belonging to the priory has already

---

Common Consent', *Speculum*, xxix (1954), 378-94; 'By-laws of Gleaning and the Problems of Harvest', *EcHR*, 2nd ser., xiv (1961-2), 210-17.

[3] E. Craster, 'The Patrimony of St. Cuthbert', *EHR*, lxix (1954), 199.

[4] J. Scammell, 'The Origins and Limitations of the Liberty of Durham', *EHR*, lxxxi (1966), 453.

[5] F. Barlow, *Durham Jurisdictional Peculiars* (London, 1950), p. xviii.

been well covered by other historians but it should be remarked that the monks used a series of forged charters in disputes over the extent of the monastic estate and, in particular, their rights over churches. Many of their claims were acknowledged in an agreement of 1229.[6]

The south-east of the county was divided largely between the bishop and the prior. During the later Middle Ages Carlton, Hartburn, Hardwick, Norton, and Stockton were included in the bishop's estate while Billingham, Cowpen Bewley, Newton Bewley, and Wolviston belonged to the cathedral priory. Billingham was probably the first place in the area to be settled; in fact E. Craster believed that it came into the see's possession before any other lands between Tyne and Tees.[7] Simeon, a monk at Jarrow around the end of the eleventh century, referred to Billingham being in the possession of Ecgred, bishop from 830 to 845.[8] Although Simeon then related how Billingham was ʻseized some thirty years later by Aelle, king of the Northumbrians, it appears to have been recovered for St. Cuthbert's community on his death.[9] The Vikings then ravaged the area and Billingham came into the possession of one Scula[10] but William the Conqueror restored it not to the bishop but specifically to the cathedral priory.[11] This grant probably included the vills of Cowpen Bewley and Newton Bewley. There is no earlier reference to these two places but they were confirmed as belonging to the priory during the reign of Henry II.[12] In fact, Newton Bewley may not have been in existence for long. Tenants there were immune from paying a render called gillycorn, a privilege generally allowed only to tenants of land known to have been assarted from the waste after 1200.[13] The same grant by the Conqueror may also have included some of Wolviston, but not all as it occurs among the places released to Bishop William of St. Calais by Robert, earl of Northumberland, in the late eleventh century.[14] Other land in Wolviston was gradually acquired by the priory.

---

[6] Ibid., pp. 4-40.

[7] Craster in *EHR*, lxix (1954), 186.

[8] *Symeonis Monachi Omnia*, ed. T. Arnold (Rolls Series, 2 vols., 1882-5), i. 108.

[9] Ibid., i. 55.   [10] Ibid., i. 208.

[11] *Historiae Dunelmensis Scriptores Tres*, ed. J. Raine (Surtees Soc., vol. ix; 1839), Appendix, p. xx.

[12] Ibid., Appendix, p. lviii.   [13] *VCH Durh.*, iii. 199.   [14] Ibid.

Of the villages in south-east Durham which were in the episcopal estate in the later Middle Ages, Norton was probably the first to fall into the hands of the bishop. The Liber Vitae of Durham, a register of the see's benefactors, contains a charter granting the bishop Norton with its appurtenances; the donor was Ulfcytel son of Osulf.[15] The date is uncertain, but by the first half of the eleventh century Norton church was clearly distinct from Billingham and the grant may have been considerably earlier than this.[16] Ulfcytel's charter may also have included Stockton and Hartburn as henceforward these places appear to have been part of the bishop's possessions. Probably during the late twelfth century Stockton was divided into the borough and vill. T. Sowler has suggested that the borough was created then by Bishop Hugh Pudsey[17] and it is unlikely that it existed earlier for there is no reference to it in the Boldon Book of 1183. Carlton does not appear to have been included in Ulfcytel's grant but it seems likely that it came into the bishop's possession at an early date because Bishop Ealdhun gave the vill as dowry with his daughter to the son of the earl of Northumberland in the late tenth century;[18] by the twelfth century it had been restored to the bishop's estate.

Stillington and Seaton Carew belonged to Merton College, Oxford. Unfortunately little is known about their early history. About 1200 Robert of Amundeville granted to Ralph of Hamsterley 2 bovates of land at Stillington which had been the property of Robert son of Huchtred.[19] About 1247 what was described as the whole manor was granted to Walter of Merton by Ralph Amundeville.[20] John of Hamsterley also released at least a part of his holding to the college in 1290.[21] Seaton Carew is first mentioned between 1146 and 1151 when Robert de Brus held 230 acres of demesne there as part of Hartness.[22]

[15] *Liber Vitae Ecclesiae Dunelmensis*, ed. J. Stevenson (Surtees Soc., vol. xiii; 1841), p.57.

[16] Craster in *EHR*, lxix (1954), 193.

[17] T. Sowler, *A History of the Town and Borough of Stockton-on-Tees* (Stockton, 1968), p. 17.

[18] *VCH Durh.*, iii. 317.

[19] Ibid.

[20] *The Early Rolls of Merton College, Oxford*, ed. J.R.L. Highfield (Oxford Historical Soc., new ser., vol. xxiii; 1964), p. 17.

[21] *VCH Durh.*, iii. 318.

[22] Ibid.

This land, however, never appears to have been part of the Merton estate. The college held only a small area acquired in 1268 when Bishop Stichill of Durham granted 8 bovates to the college.[23] Other lands in the village in the fourteenth and fifteenth centuries were in the possession of the Lumley, Langton, and Hayton families[24] but no medieval records survive for these properties.

Population

By the later Middle Ages these vills seem to have been quite populous. The records of 1350-1500 for the episcopal and priory vills in south-east Durham provide more than 3,000 different names and this can represent only a small proportion of the total number of inhabitants because it would be unrealistic to suppose that they are all referred to in the surviving documents. Women, in particular, are notably absent. On the episcopal lands only 22 per cent of names listed are female and the figure on the priory's lands is only 36 per cent.

Table XII is an attempt to estimate the population of south-east Durham in the later Middle Ages although the figures can only be highly speculative. Medieval demographers have long deplored the fact that population estimates can be little more than ingenious conjecture.[25] Moreover, Durham probably presents more problems than most English shires because it is not mentioned in such documents as Domesday Book, the Hundred Rolls, the lay-subsidy assessments, or the poll-tax returns. The county is fortunate though in that villein lists are sometimes attached to the court records of the priory. These name all members of each family with the exception of the mother, even if they lived outside the village; this is particularly useful in attempts to estimate a household multiplier. The villein lists for south-east Durham show that the average number of children per family in each list never fell below 2.25 and

---

[23] *Early Rolls of Merton College*, p. 43.

[24] *VCH Durh.*, iii. 368-9.

[25] J. Cornwall, 'English Population in the Early Sixteenth Century', *EcHR*, 2nd ser., xxiii (1970), 44; J.T. Rosenthal, 'Medieval Longevity and the Secular Peerage, 1350-1500', *Population Studies*, xxvii (1973), 287.

Table XII

Population in south-east County Durham, 1350-1801

	Estimated average population, 1350-1500	Population in 1801
Norton	715	965
Billingham	570	335
Wolviston	452	411
Stockton	363	4,009
Cowpen Bewley	328	128
Carlton	210	99
Hartburn	159	104
Newton Bewley	155	88
Total	2,952	6,139

never exceeded 2.92. They also demonstrate that the majority of medieval families did have children.

The figures in Table XII should be taken as the minimum likely population of these villages in the later Middle Ages. They are based on the assumptions that all the adult males in the village are mentioned in the surviving documents,[26] that there were as many adult women as men,[27] that 70 per cent of the population married,[28] that each family produced an average of 2.25 children,[29] and that there were no illegitimate births.[30] The records for the episcopal vills cover a total of 110 years between 1350 and 1500 and the priory's records 135 years between the same dates; it is assumed that the former cover three and a half generations and the latter four and a half. Compared with the medieval figures are those of the 1801 census. When it is borne in mind that the medieval populations are almost certainly underestimates the comparison is

[26] This is, of course, unlikely. Many of the poorer villagers may never have been mentioned in the documents.

[27] This is probably a fairly safe assumption (E.A. Wrigley, *Population and History* (London, 1969), p. 16).

[28] This almost certainly errs on the low side (ibid., p. 90).

[29] This is the lowest multiplier obtained from the villein lists.

[30] Although there would have been some illegitimate births, the ecclesiastical authorities of south-east Durham in the later Middle Ages were fairly strict over this matter.

remarkable. Norton and Stockton had undergone some indus-
trialization during the eighteenth century, but the other
villages appear to have had larger populations in the later
Middle Ages than at the beginning of the nineteenth century.
Although there may have been boundary changes, the eight vills
are contiguous and thus the overall area covered is less likely to
have altered. The total population is therefore of significance.
If Stockton is omitted, the total population of the seven other
places in the later Middle Ages (average minimum) and in
1801 was 2,589 and 2,130 respectively. Although the figures
must be treated with extreme caution, it does seem as if the
area's rural population in the late Middle Ages was higher than
it was on the eve of the industrial expansion of Teesside in the
nineteenth century.[31]

Before 1350 it may well have been higher still. The Black
Death had probably affected the area severely. There are
preserved among the records of Durham Cathedral Priory
three surveys of tenants who died during the period of the
Black Death.[32] They show that forty-six tenants in all died at
Billingham, thirteen at Newton Bewley, and twelve out of the
free tenants at Wolviston. In a rental of 1347, eighty-four
tenants are listed under Billingham, twenty-two under Newton
Bewley, and sixty-six under Wolviston (of which twenty-nine
were free tenants);[33] to these one must add the fifteen bondage
tenants at Billingham who held exclusively for labour services.
Clearly the mortality rates of the south-east Durham tenants
were high, ranging from 41 per cent of all tenants at Wolviston
to 46 per cent at Billingham and 59 per cent at Newton Bewley.

These tenants were not the whole population but the
documents do provide some further information. The list of
Billingham tenants has against the names of thirty-four of the
victims the names of the successors to their holdings. Until
the Black Death most lands were descending within the family,
but seventeen of these thirty-four appear to have been unrelated to the previous tenant. It follows that the families of the
tenants were affected as much by the pestilence as the tenants

---

[31] The 1563 household census suggests that population was fairly high in south-east
Durham.

[32] DCD Loc. iv, 141, 146, 147.

[33] DCD BR, 1347-8.

themselves. The court rolls for the episcopal lands also demonstrate that the 1350s were a time of upheaval. At Norton, in particular, there were a great many grants of licence to marry in 1350, and on all the episcopal manors in south-east Durham the number of land transactions rose to a very high level. Between 1350 and 1355 there was an average of 5.4 transfers per manor per year, a figure never approached again during the next century and a half. Even though many died of the plague, however, this did not mean that the plague affected all the south-east Durham villages to the same extent. Studies of various estates have shown that there could be considerable variation within a very small area.

The plagues, however, did not end with the Black Death, and several historians have shown that the subsequent outbreaks of the plague must have had a severe effect on the population in the later Middle Ages;[34] the population was given little chance to recover and may have continued to decline throughout the later Middle Ages. There is little doubt that the south-east Durham population was reduced considerably by the Black Death but, as elsewhere, things seem outwardly to have soon returned to normal. The manorial structure was hardly altered and, although much land was passing outside the family, vacant tenements were still being filled. The usual complement of three halmote courts continued to be held each year on the priory's manors and there was no speeding up of the leasing of the manorial demesnes. The Durham evidence seems to support the view that much of the population was surplus to the economy by the mid-fourteenth century and that the plague of 1348-9 was more purgative than calamitous in its economic effects.[35] By the last quarter of the century, however, the situation was different. Vacant tenements could not be filled, demesne leasing became widespread, buildings became derelict, and seignorial attempts to enforce repairs failed. It appears, therefore, that south-east Durham

---

[34] S.L. Thrupp, 'The Problem of Replacement Rates in Late Medieval English Population', *EcHR*, 2nd ser., xviii (1965), 104; Hatcher, *Cornwall*, p. 129; C. Creighton, *A History of Epidemics in Britain* (Cambridge, 2 vols., 1891-4), i. 207-25; M.M. Postan, 'Some Economic Evidence of Declining Population in the Later Middle Ages', *EcHR*, 2nd ser., ii (1949-50), 230.

[35] A.R. Bridbury, 'The Black Death', *EcHR*, 2nd ser., xxvi (1973), 591.

experienced a demographic crisis only towards the end of the century. The later pestilences following the Black Death may have been the principal cause—the north was certainly badly affected in 1379 and 1391. The population shortage almost certainly continued into the fifteenth century. Unfilled and derelict tenements continued into the first two decades of that century after which their numbers began to decline slowly. However, land still seems to have been freely available and few appear to have deemed it necessary to keep land within the family. Both bishop and prior found it difficult to collect rents in full, the prior was forced to abandon entry fines, and both landlords reduced servile payments and amercements. If there had been any population pressure, the lords would surely have been able to dictate different conditions. The plagues of 1413, 1438-9, and 1479 may well have provided a check on population growth.[36]

Although historians have proposed various patterns of population change in the late Middle Ages[37] it is generally agreed that the population had begun to rise before the end of the fifteenth century. The evidence from south-east Durham also appears to confirm this: references to vacant tenements cease and the proportion of land passing within the family increased. This is not to suggest a population explosion—the lord still seems to have been in a weak bargaining position and there was plenty of available land. It has been shown above that the rural population of the area was probably at least as high in the later Middle Ages as it was in the early nineteenth century and in the fifteenth century it was almost certainly less than it had been in the early fourteenth.

The medieval records

The principal sources for the medieval history of south-east Durham are located in the Public Record Office, the muniment room of Merton College, and the Prior's Kitchen in Durham. These house respectively the main archives of the

---

36 J.M.W. Bean, 'Plague, Population and Economic Decline in England in the Later Middle Ages', *EcHR*, 2nd ser., xv (1962-3), p. 430, suggests that 15th-century plague was largely an urban phenomenon, but some plagues certainly affected much of the countryside as well.

37 Chambers, op. cit., p. 14; Postan in *EcHR*, 2nd ser., ii (1949-50), 245.

bishopric of Durham, Merton College, and Durham Cathedral Priory.

Until 1868 all of the bishops' records were kept in Durham but they were not well looked after. A writer in the last century mentioned valuable records that 'have been used to stop up holes to keep rats and mice out of the Muniment rooms, to light fires and even to make bonfires on public rejoicings'.[38] As a result, the vast majority of the documents were transferred to the Public Record Office in Chancery Lane.[39] The bishops' estate records, however, were passed on to the Ecclesiastical Commissioners in 1876, and in 1956 were returned to Durham, leaving in the Public Record Office in principle only the administrative records of the palatinate.[40] The principal episcopal records used for this study are the court and account rolls. The court rolls for the bishop's manors are in book form and each volume usually covers a single episcopacy. They are arranged by manors and are referred to as halmote court books. Between 1350 and 1500, eight of these court books survive but they are not complete.[41] For example, the long episcopacy of Thomas Hatfield (1345-81) is only covered until his seventeenth year and no halmote court records survive for his successor, John Fordham (1382-8). Unfortunately there are few surviving financial records for the bishopric before the fifteenth century. Account rolls for several officers have survived but the most useful are the collector's accounts. The collector for each of the four wards of Chester, Darlington, Easington, and Stockton accounted separately to the bishop. Twenty-three collector's accounts survive for Stockton Ward for the period before 1500 but only one is earlier than 1400.[42] There are also eighteen coroner's accounts (1413-80),[43] seventeen bailiff's accounts (1413-98),[44] and twenty-eight accounts of the receiver-general (the earliest being 1416-17).[45] Amongst other miscel-

---

[38] W.A.L. Seaman, 'The Tools of Local History', *Durham County Local History Soc. Bulletin*, x (1969), p. 31.

[39] *Sixteenth Report of the Deputy Keeper of the Public Records* (London, 1854), pp. 44-93.

[40] *Guide to the Contents of the Public Record Office* (London, 3 vols., 1963-8), i. 177.

[41] PRO DUR 3/12-19.

[42] DBR CC 188857, 188799, 188825, 190246, 188827, 188828, 188829, 188830, 188800, 188801, 188831-4, 188802, 188836-9, 188804, 188806, 188807.

[43] DBR CC 188879-97.

[44] DBR CC 188859, 188862, 189813, 188866-73, 188815, 188939, 190244.

[45] DBR CC 188714, 189754-5, 190258, 189756-63, 189765-9, 189771, 189681, 189698.

laneous episcopal records are two valors (1463-4, 1478-9),[46] a sergeant's account for 1348-9,[47] and an account of the surveyor of the works of Stockton for 1412-13.[48] Unfortunately, no extents survive for the bishop's lands and only two medieval surveys: Boldon Book, compiled as early as 1183, and Hatfield's Survey of about 1382 which contains a full list of tenants with the quantity of land they held along with an enumeration of the services belonging to each manor.[49]

Compared with the extant records of the episcopal and priory estates, the Merton College muniments come a poor third, and among them far more documents have survived for Stillington than for Seaton Carew. In fact, for the period from 1350 to 1500 there are only two court rolls[50] and the main sources for these two places are the account rolls and indentures. For accounting purposes the two manors were included with the Northumberland properties of Embleton and Ponteland and fifty-six accounts relevant to this study have survived.[51] The indentures are even more valuable, being lists of tenants with the value of the arrears which they owed at a particular date. Sixty-five of these indentures have survived; most fall in the period from 1380 to 1410 and there are none later than 1438.[52] Amongst the other extant Merton documents are four accounts of collectors' expenses, six repairs accounts, and two rentals for Stillington.[53]

The priory records have long been regarded as of national importance. Sir Maurice Powicke once declared that 'no diocese in England is so rich in historical material, peculiar to itself' and Hubert Hall wrote in 1925 that there was 'no other monastic collection that can equal them in economic as well as

---

[46] DBR CC 189817, 189676.   [47] DBR CC 190265.   [48] DBR CC 188926.

[49] *Boldon Buke*, pp. 11-15, 51-3; *VCH Durh.*, iii. 330-1, 337; *Hatfield's Survey*, pp. 164-80.

[50] MM 6184, 6184c.

[51] MM 5966, 6019-21, 6023, 6035, 6037, 6038, 6046, 6049, 6051, 6052, 6055, 6058, 6062, 6069, 6080, 6083, 6088, 6091, 6098, 6102, 6107, 6111, 6115, 6119, 6137, 6139, 6140, 6144-6, 6148, 6150, 6153-6, 6158, 6159, 6161, 6164-6, 6170, 6172, 6173, 6177-80, 6182.

[52] MM 6022, 6044, 6047, 6049-51, 6055, 6062, 6066, 6078, 6086, 6092, 6101, 6104, 6116, 6121, 6132, 6133, 6142, 6143, 6155, 6160, 6163, 6166, 6167, 6168, 6172, 6178, 6179.

[53] MM 6096, 6166, 6173, 6179; MM 6167, 6168, 6172, 6173, 6179; MM 6188b, 6188c.

in archaeological and ecclesiological importance'.[54] Fortune has favoured the priory documents. Firstly, the custodians have generally been conscientious men; secondly, the documents have always been kept in places which have probably been dry; and thirdly, there was no breach of continuity at the Dissolution. Overnight the last prior became the first dean and the last major obedientiaries became the first canons.[55]

The priory's court records are of three types. There are the halmote court books which are concerned solely with land transactions and the halmote court rolls which dealt generally with the unfree tenantry. The contents of both were derived from the same manorial courts, called halmotes as on the episcopal estates. Thirdly, there are the court records of the free tenants, whose court was held separately in Durham. The halmote court books are remarkably complete and three books survive which cover the whole period from 1400 to 1529;[56] the land transfers which they record were dealt with thrice yearly at the courts. Each halmote court roll consists of several membranes of either parchment or paper stitched together in Exchequer fashion and each covers all the priory's manors within the county. The series is not complete, however, and although no decade between 1350 and 1500 is completely unrepresented the fourteenth century is much better served than the fifteenth.[57] The court records of the free tenants are by no means as useful as the halmote court records, often being no more than a list of suitors with amercements against their names for non-attendance.[58]

[54] J. Conway Davies, 'The Muniments of the Dean and Chapter of Durham', *Durham University Journal*, xliv (1951-2), p. 87.

[55] Ibid, p. 88.

[56] DCD HCB 1-3.

[57] DCD HCR, autumn 1364, spring 1365, autumn 1365 to spring 1392, autumn 1393 to spring 1399, summer 1400 to spring 1401, autumn 1404, spring 1405, autumn 1407, spring 1409, autumn 1409 to spring 1412, summer 1413 to spring 1414, summer 1420 to spring 1421, summer 1423, summer 1427 to spring 1429, summer 1430, autumn 1430, autumn 1431, summer 1432 to summer 1438, summer 1439, autumn 1449, spring 1450, spring 1460 to autumn 1460, summer 1465 to spring 1466, autumn 1466, spring 1467, summer 1472 to spring 1479, summer 1482 to spring 1483, summer 1487, autumn 1489 to spring 1493, summer 1494 to summer 1495, summer 1497 to spring 1498, summer 1499 to spring 1501.

[58] DCD Loc. iv, 26, 27, 29, 31, 34, 40, 41, 46, 66-8, 70, 71, 73, 75, 76, 82, 83, 85, 91, 95, 98, 104, 107, 109, 118, 123, 128, 131, 134, 140, 154, 193-5, 198, 200, 204, 206, 208-10, 212, 234, 237.

The mainstay of the financial records is the bursar's annual account rolls which are among 'the longest non-governmental accounts ever produced in England'.[59] Some 120 of them have survived for the period between 1350 and 1500 giving an almost unbroken series,[60] but the manorial accounts are much less numerous. The prior had his own manorial demesnes which are referred to in the documents as Billingham, Bellasis, and Bewley but there are few accounts for these. No post-plague manorial accounts have survived for the first two and there are only a few extant accounts for Bewley in the 1370s and for 1405-8.[61] Other bursar's records have proved valuable, especially the rentals for 1332-3, 1347-8, 1382-3, 1396-7, 1411-12, and 1495-6.[62] There are also the gillycorn rentals; gillycorn was a rent payable to the almoner at the rate of a thrave of twenty-four sheaves for every tenement. In practice the rent was often commuted in the fourteenth century but in some places sheaves were paid as late as 1456.[63]

A good series of charters has survived for the priory's estates in south-east Durham furnishing much information on the development of free tenures. Over 400 have been used in this study. Like the episcopal lands, however, the priory's lands have few surviving medieval surveys. One survey of the priory's estates was the Melsanby Feodary, compiled between 1233 and 1244; the original record has not survived, but we have a rental of freehold estates which was based on it and which was compiled about 1430.[64] It appears that successive rentals or feodaries were compiled from time to time and it is almost certain that the original included bond as well as free

[59] R.B. Dobson, *Durham Priory 1400-1450* (Cambridge, 1973), p. 260.

[60] DCD BA, 1349-50 to 1363-4, 1365-6 to 1368-9, 1370-1, 1371-2 to 1381-2, 1383-4, 1384-5, 1386-7, 1388-9 to 1391-2, 1394-5 to 1397-8, 1399-1400 to 1402-3, 1404-5, 1406-7 to 1412-13, 1414-15 to 1416-17, 1418-19 to 1429-30, 1431-2 to 1443-4, 1445-6, 1446-7, 1449-50, 1453-4, 1454-5, 1456-7 to 1458-9, 1462-3, 1464-5 to 1476-7, 1478-9, 1479-80, 1481-2 to 1488-9, 1492-3 to 1499-1500.

[61] DCD MA Bewley, 1369-70, 1372-3, 1374-5, 1375-6, 1405-8; Billingham, 1335, 1337-8, 1338-9, 1343-4; DCD Misc. Ch. 73 (Bellasis, 1305-6).

[62] DCD BR, 1332-3, 1347-8, 1382-3, 1396-7, 1411-12, 1432-3 (summary only), 1495-6.

[63] C.M. Fraser, 'Gilly-corn and the Customary of the Convent of Durham', *Archaeologia Aeliana*, 4th ser., xxxiii (1955), 35-60 *passim*.

[64] *Feodarium Prioratus Dunelmensis*, ed. W. Greenwell (Surtees Soc., lviii; 1872).

tenants. There are also several lists of villeins and a list of free tenants who died in the Black Death.[65]

The surviving medieval records of south-east Durham are certainly impressive and compare favourably with those of any similar area. It is only the number of surveys and taxation lists that is disappointing. W. Longstaffe, after studying the priory's court rolls, commented that 'it is hardly a figure of speech to say we have in them village life photographed'.[66] This is an exaggeration. For instance, on the lands of both the priory and the bishop only the customary tenants were bound to attend the halmote court; but the Durham court rolls do not appear to be too deficient compared with many for other similar estates, for manorial courts were often confined to the unfree sections of the population. In general the records from the area are mostly at least as detailed as their counterparts elsewhere.

Nor is there any evidence that they are less trustworthy. Bishop and prior seem to have had efficient administrative systems. In theory, the bishop's administrative system was not greatly different from that of the king. Until the mid-fifteenth century the steward was the most important administrative official in Durham,[67] being responsible for all land business such as the farming of the boroughs, leasing out demesnes and mines, and holding the manorial courts. The importance of the steward declined in the early fifteenth century after Bishop Langley made the receiver-general his principal officer in the palatinate.[68] The sheriff and the four coroners generally operated at a more local level. The former was responsible for prisoners, presiding over the county court, controlling inquisitions, taking the profits of jurisdiction, confiscating goods and lands, and taking charge of waifs. Coroners collected free rents and inquired into burglaries and kidnapping. Below these officers were the local officials such as the reeve, collector, ale-taster, and constable.

---

[65] DCD Loc. iv, 141, 146, 147.

[66] *Halmota Prioratus Dunelmensis, AD 1296-AD 1384*, ed. W.H. Longstaffe and J. Booth (Surtees Soc., vol. lxxxii; 1889), p.ix.

[67] G.T. Lapsley, *The County Palatinate of Durham* (New York, 1900).

[68] R.L. Storey, *Thomas Langley and the Bishopric of Durham, 1406-37* (London, 1961), p.80.

The administrative system at Durham Priory was rather different. The bursar was the chief financial officer. There were seven other obedientiaries with specialized offices—the hostiller, almoner, chaplain, sacrist, commoner, feretrar, and terrar—but even when considered together their revenues were less than a third of those controlled by the bursar.[69] As far as the priory's tenants was concerned the lay steward was the next most important officer. The halmote courts were usually presided over by bursar, terrar, and steward, and leasings were generally the duty of the terrar. At the village level we find the reeve, collector, ale-taster, and constable just as on the bishop's manors.

Although Jean Scammell argues that the palatine administration was not very efficient[70] this does not seem to have been the case in the local estate-administration of either the bishop or the priory. The halmote courts were held regularly thrice yearly throughout the later Middle Ages and appear to have dealt with their business no less efficiently than elsewhere. The whole range of local officials continued to be appointed throughout the period and they seem to have been active in their duties: there are in all 10,123 presentments recorded in the surviving court rolls of the nine episcopal and priory manors in the later Middle Ages. Moreover, despite the close scrutiny to which local officials were subject, there appear to have been few prosecutions for dishonesty or inefficiency. Similarly there is no evidence of inefficiency in the financial records; on both episcopal and priory lands great care seems to have been taken to ensure that all local revenues and expenses were accounted for. R.L. Storey has shown that Bishops Hatfield (1345-81), Skirlaw (1388-1405), and Langley (1406-37) showed considerable interest in the administration of the palatinate.[71] Likewise studies of the Merton estates have shown that the college maintained a close watch on its possessions.[72]

[69] Lomas, 'Durham Cath. Priory', *passim.*

[70] Scammell in *EHR*, lxxxi (1966), 470-1.

[71] Storey, op.cit., p.70.

[72] R.H. Hilton, 'Kibworth Harcourt: a Merton College Manor in the Thirteenth and Fourteenth Centuries', *Studies in Leicestershire Agrarian History*, ed. W.G. Hoskins (Leicester, 1949), pp. 17-40; Harvey, *Oxon. Village*, pp. 87-90.

2 TENURE, STATUS, AND MOBILITY

Tenure and its obligations

Hatfield's Survey mentions five types of unfree and three types of free tenure on the episcopal lands in about 1382. The former were cotland, farmland, maleland, exchequer land, and bondland and the latter were drengage tenure, military land, and burgage tenure. Boldon Book in 1183 lists cotland in twenty-three of the episcopal vills and Hatfield's Survey in twenty-seven. In the south-east of the palatinate there was cotland at Norton, Stockton, and Hartburn. In Boldon Book Norton is stated to have twelve cottagers holding tofts and crofts and 13 acres between them in the fields, for which they rendered 16*s.* 0*d.* The cottagers also had to help with hay-making and with the stacking of the corn and hay. There were only three cottagers at Stockton when Boldon Book was compiled and at Hartburn there were two who shared 24 acres. The holdings of the south-east Durham cottagers must have varied considerably in size but this accords with what has been found on estates elsewhere in England.[1] Between Boldon Book and Hatfield's Survey the basic structure of the cottage tenements in south-east Durham hardly appears to have changed. In 1382 two cottagers were listed as living in Stockton and three in Hartburn, while at Norton there were eleven tenants with full cottage tenements and two more who shared one between them. It is uncertain if labour services were actually exacted here in the later Middle Ages; it is probable that they were not even though the works are still listed. In 1382 Robert Dycon owed for his cottage at Stockton three harvest boons and he also had to carry hens and eggs for the lord anywhere within the county. At Norton and Hartburn labour dues seem to have been rather more severe; in those vills a cottager owed thirteen days' work, but as they were valued at only ½*d.* each they probably did not involve a whole day's labour.[2]

Boldon Book records a class of tenant known as lessees or farmers (*firmarii*) in ten of the episcopal vills in the county.

---

[1] Bennett, *Eng. Manor*, p. 36; Kosminsky, *Studies*, p. 36.
[2] Cf. Bennett, *Eng. Manor*, 104.

Norton had twenty farmers in the twelfth century holding 40 bovates of land between them. A rent of ½ mark was due for every 2 bovates besides labour services. These comprised ploughing and harrowing ½ acre of arable land, finding two men to cart hay and corn, and four boon-works which were owed at harvest with all the household except the housewife. Stockton had six farmers holding 9 bovates of land and they owed the same works as their counterparts at Norton. At Carlton, farmland is the only type of tenure recorded in Boldon Book; twenty-three tenants held 46 bovates of it and they also performed labour services similar to the farmers at Norton while also owing two hens and twenty eggs for their tenure. The amount of farmland seems to have declined during the later Middle Ages. The entry for Norton in Hatfield's Survey concludes with the statement that 8 of the 40 bovates mentioned in Boldon Book had since become free land and by then the number of farmers at Stockton had shrunk to two.

Farmland appears to have been very similar to maleland. Maleland was not common in the twelfth century and the only reference to it in Boldon Book relates to the north-east of the county.[3] By the time of Hatfield's Survey, maleland was unfree tenure although many people referred to as malmen appear to have had fairly large holdings. Norton had twenty-four of them in 1382, each holding 24 acres. Certain labour services were owed for maleland: ploughing and harrowing at the rate of ½ acre for every 2 bovates, finding two men to spend two days helping with the corn and hay harvest, doing four harvest boons with every member of the household except the housewife, repairing the mill, and cleaning out the mill-race. Malmen also owed carriage service including taking wine across the Tees and carting timber for the repair of Stockton manor house. By the fifteenth century this last duty appears to have been replaced by a render called *woodlades*, valued at 38*s*. 9*d*.[4] When labour services were commuted is not certain although in 1411 all tenants of maleland in Stockton and Norton had commuted their special mowing works. Malmen had effectively ceased to be a distinctive class after the Black Death although sixteen are

[3] G.T. Lapsley in *VCH Durh.*, i. 281.
[4] DBR CC 188859 (1413-14).

still recorded as living in Norton in 1440-1[5] and references to maleland continue to appear throughout the later Middle Ages.

Exchequer land also appears to have been very like maleland; an entry in the halmote court roll for 1468 refers to a lease of 2 bovates of maleland 'otherwise called exchequer land' (*terra scaccarii*).[6] No mention is made of exchequer land in Boldon Book although it is distinguished from maleland in Hatfield's Survey. Labour services for this land were either light or non-existent but various other rents were owed. For example in 1382 William Shepherd and Robert Slowbek of Stockton held a messuage and 2 bovates of exchequer land which had previously been bondland; for it they paid a rent of 16*s.* 8*d.* and various renders such as *scatpenys, averpenys,* and *wodelades,* two hens at Christmas, and ten eggs at Easter. In all six tenants held exchequer land at Stockton in 1382, twelve at Hartburn, sixteen at Norton, ten at Carlton, and three at Hardwick.

The most common of the unfree tenures were the bondlands. These are almost certainly the lands that are entered in Boldon Book as held by the villeins. In south-east Durham the villein holding was then generally assessed at 2 bovates; Norton had thirty villein holdings in 1183, Hartburn twelve and a half, Stockton eleven and a half, but there were none at Carlton. The labour services attached to these bondlands were fairly heavy. Three days' week-work had to be performed throughout the year except at Easter and Whitsun and during the thirteen days of Christmas. Four harvest boon-works, which involved reaping with all the household except for the housewife, were also demanded, as well as reaping 3 roods of oats and ploughing and harrowing 3 roods of oats stubble. Every villein plough team had also to plough and harrow 2 acres and for that week they were quit of week-work; they received an allowance of food for this as well as on the great boon days. Besides these labour services, various renders were also due, including *scotpenys* (2*s.* 6*d.*), *averpenys* (1*s.* 4*d.*), *wodelades* (2*s.* 1*d.*),[7] a half scot-chalder of oats, and two hens at Easter. By the time of Hat-

[5] DBR CC 188825.

[6] *VCH Durh.*, iii. 183.

[7] N. Neilson in 'Customary Rents', *Oxford Studies in Social and Legal History*, vol. xi (Oxford, 1910), argues that *scat* was a general term for tributary rent (p. 28), *wodelade* a due in place of carting loads of wood (pp. 53, 63), and *averpenny* a due in lieu of carting outside the manor (p. 64).

field's Survey, Stockton had eleven tenants with bondland (each of them had 2 bovates), Hartburn had thirteen, Norton twenty-seven, and Carlton nineteen. The number of bondlands fluctuated slightly in the later Middle Ages; in 1440-1 the numbers at Stockton, Norton, and Carlton were ten, thirty, and eighteen respectively.[8] The works due in 1382 were almost identical to those described in Boldon Book, although the tenants of Stockton paid an extra due called *castelman* in the later Middle Ages. This was probably paid in lieu of guarding the bishop's castle at Stockton and it never amounted to very much—in 1382 it was only valued at 12*d*. for the whole manor. One render which disappears in the later Middle Ages is cornage. Boldon Book states how the village of Norton had been excused cornage 'for lack of pasture' and it is likely that it was paid for the right to pasture cattle; it was a common rent in the four northern counties.[9] A few dues were owed by the whole vill and not by any particular group of tenants or type of tenure; one of these on the episcopal lands was the milch cow. At both Stockton and Hartburn the vill as a whole was responsible for providing the bishop with a milch cow or the monetary equivalent (6*s*. 0*d*.); the vill of Norton was responsible for two cows.

By the later Middle Ages drengage was a form of free tenure. Its origins and development, however, have been the subject of much confusion and speculation.[10] A few drengage holdings are mentioned in Boldon Book, including one at Sheraton and one at Butterwick (some 6 miles north and north-west of Wolviston), but the tenure was far more common by the time of Hatfield's Survey. There the nearby vill of Preston was said to be held by drengage tenure although in the collector's accounts of the fifteenth century the whole of the village was leased at free farm.[11] All drengage rents were collected by the coroner who was described in 1413-14 as the collector of all

[8] DBR CC 188825.

[9] G.T. Lapsley saw cornage as a seignorial due probably for pasture rights but N. Neilson argued that it was a form of geld levied in the north on the number of animals held instead of land (Neilson, op. cit., pp. 120-2).

[10] F.W. Maitland, 'Northumbrian Tenures', *EHR*, v (1890), 625-32; J.E.A. Jolliffe, 'Northumbrian Institutions', *EHR*, xli (1926), 1-42.

[11] In Boldon Book Preston was held by villeins and thus the land was probably bondland. It is interesting that drengage tenure was being created here more than a century after the Norman Conquest.

free rents.[12] However, labour services were owed. Sir Roger Fulthorpe had a drengage tenement at Norton in 1382 for which he owed thirty-two days' work in the year and four boon-works at harvest time. All members of the household with the exception of the housewife had to help with these harvest boons. Sir Roger also had to find four carts to do a day's work (or two for two days) in the lord's corn. At Carlton, however, the duty of the drengs amounted to no more than accompanying the bishop on his great hunt. But in the later Middle Ages drengage was not widespread on the episcopal estates of south-east Durham, being confined to Preston, Norton, and—a small amount—Carlton.

Free land in general was plentiful throughout the bishop's estates although the amount varied considerably from place to place. Most of this free land was held by military service. Large free tenements were not common in south-east Durham; no tenants on the episcopal lands there held more than 4 bovates of free land. If labour services were owed they were invariably light. For example John Laycan, who held two messuages and 2 bovates of free land in Hartburn, had only to ensure that the watermill at Norton was kept clean.[13] Other rents, too, as we shall see, were low compared with those for unfree lands.

The only other type of tenure on the episcopal lands was burgage tenure. In the south-east of the county this existed only in Stockton. By 1382-3 the borough of Stockton appears to have been of some importance. Its tenants were then described as those 'within the borough' (*infra burgum*) and those 'outside the borough' (*extra burgum*); thirty-eight persons were in the first category and forty-five in the second. The tenants 'within the borough' were almost certainly those who had burgage tenements there, doing suit at the borough court and being quit of all tolls in the liberty of Durham except in the wapentake of Sadberge. Rents on the burgage plots were not uniform, which suggests that they were not all of the same size; thus John Ydonneson paid 6*d*. rent for his plot whereas John of Laton, who shared a plot with another person, paid 8*d*. It is just possible that the rents varied because they were fixed by individual negotiation with the lord. No mention is made anywhere

[12] DBR CC 188879.   [13] *Hatfield's Survey*, p. 170.

of labour service or other obligations owed by the burgesses but this does not prove that they did not exist; the privileges of burgesses might be strictly limited especially if they had been granted no charter to confirm their rights. At Stockton the burgesses had been refused a charter, which would have given them the privileges enjoyed at Newcastle upon Tyne.[14] The forty-five tenants 'outside the borough' were outsiders, most of them coming from adjoining villages such as Hartlepool, Yarm, and Sedgefield. It is easy to assume that these people were absentee landlords who sublet their tenements but there is in fact no evidence of subletting. Indeed, if this was so we should be at a loss to know who these sub-tenants were. They were certainly not men from the neighbouring episcopal or priory vills. Neither does it seem likely that the tenants 'within the borough' were sub-tenants of those 'outside the borough'. A second possibility is that these outsiders were merely holding on to the burgage plots for speculative purposes and to take advantage of any privileges. A third possibility is that the tenants 'outside the borough' may never have had tenements there at all but because they were able to enjoy the rights and privileges of the borough of Stockton they came to be regarded as its burgesses. This would not have been unique; H.P.R. Finberg has shown that a similar situation existed in Devonshire.[15]

Most of the types of tenure which existed on the episcopal lands also existed on the priory's estates. In the south-east of the county, however, there are no references to malmen (although there are a few to maleland), farmland, exchequer land, or burgage tenure. Cotland was undoubtedly the poorest of the priory's tenures. The number of cottage holdings varied but it is unlikely that their number was ever large. If anything, the holdings of the priory cottages were slightly larger than those on the episcopal lands; most had 6 acres of land. Nearly all labour services from cotlands had been commuted by the later Middle Ages but some were owed at Billingham and Cowpen Bewley. In 1386-7 the harvest works of the Cowpen Bewley cottagers were valued at £2. 2s. 10d., but because of the

decay of some of the cotlands the services were worth only
£1. 9s. 8d. in 1419-20.[16] Threshing works, valued at £1. 7s. 6d.
in 1386-7,[17] were also due from the Cowpen Bewley cotlands.
Labour services due from the Billingham cottagers seem rather
more severe; in 1394-5 their general works were valued at
£2. 16s. (4s. 0d. per cottage) while harvest works, supposed to
last for ten days, were worth £1. 8s. (2s. 0d. per cottage).[18]

The basic unit of unfree tenure on the priory's lands was the
bondland or hosbondland. By the later Middle Ages the two
were synonymous, although there may have been different
tenant obligations in earlier times. In 1332-3 the bondland
tenants owed labour services whereas the hosbondland appears
only to have paid rents.[19] The acreage of the tenements varied
from village to village but, as on the episcopal lands, 30 acres
was the most common. In fact this seems to have been the normal definition of bondage tenements throughout the north-east
of England. Throughout the later Middle Ages there never
appear to have been more than sixteen bondage tenements at
Billingham and the same number at Cowpen Bewley. Labour
services and rents were fairly heavy. In 1375-6 the Billingham
bondland tenants owed harvest works on the manorial demesne
of Bellasis valued at £12[20] and general works at Billingham
worth 3s. 0d. per holding.[21] Likewise the bondland tenants at
Cowpen Bewley owed harvest works on the Bewley demesne
valued at £8 and other works there worth £1. 17s. 6d.[22] Some
other light services were also due along with several renders. As
on the episcopal lands cornage was exacted, Billingham rendering a total of 13s. 4d., Wolviston 12s. 10d., and Cowpen
Bewley 13s. 4d.[23] All the south-east Durham priory vills except
Newton Bewley owed a due called *averpenys*. Unlike the episcopal estates, however, only the bondland tenants were liable; the
rate according to the 1396-7 rental was 10d. per holding.[24] Less

[16] DCD BA, 1386-7, 1419-20.
[17] DCD BA, 1386-7.
[18] DCD BA, 1394-5.
[19] DCD BR, 1332-3.
[20] DCD BA, 1375-6.
[21] DCD BA, 1381-2.
[22] DCD BR, 1382-3.
[23] Ibid.
[24] DCD BR, 1396-7; the following description of the rents due from the priory
manors is drawn primarily from this same rental.

common on the priory's estates was a payment called *messing-penys*.[25] Only eight of the priory's vills paid it but these included Cowpen Bewley and Billingham which were each liable for 12*d*. The render called *wodeladepenys* was levied only on bond-age tenants who paid 1*s*. 3*d*. for each holding. *Ladhors* and *cartsilver* seem to have been peculiar to Billingham and Cowpen Bewley; probably they represented some form of carrying ser-vice and again only bondage tenants had to pay. In 1396 the rate was 5*s*. 0*d*. for each tenant at Cowpen Bewley but only 3*s*. 4*d*. at Billingham. Amongst other renders were *colthaver*, a rent of two bushels of oats from each bondage tenement in Bill-ingham and Cowpen Bewley; *ladesilver* worth 16*s*. 8*d*. and owed only by the Cowpen Bewley bondage tenements; *avermalt*, a rent of 3 quarters 4 bushels of corn paid by each of the bond-land tenants at Billingham and Cowpen Bewley in 1396; and a render at Cowpen Bewley called *rentgese* or *halfpenygese* which was worth 5*s*. 6*d*. This last due does not appear to have been collected after 1407. Gillycorn has already been mentioned. It was levied on some free tenements besides bondage holdings.[26] Tenants of land known to have been assarted from the waste after 1200 were specifically acquitted from payment; the whole of Newton Bewley was immune. Payment was in corn at the rate of a thrave of twenty-four sheaves for every tenement or ploughland. In theory most of the villages belonging to Durham Cathedral Priory were liable for gillycorn but in practice only villages in certain parishes paid; Billingham was one of these.

Because the priory had no boroughs in south-east Durham the only free tenements on its lands there were held by drengage or military tenure. Most were in Wolviston where there were fourteen drengage holdings. As on the episcopal lands, most of the free tenements on the priory's estates were not large; many did not differ from the customary holdings although some were between 50 and 150 acres. Labour services on these free hold-ings were light or non-existent, although certain renders were

[25] *Messingpennys* does not appear to have been levied on the episcopal estates; on the estates of St. Paul's Cathedral, London, 14 loaves of bread were paid *ad mescingam* (*The Domesday of St. Paul's of the Year 1222*, ed. W.H. Hale (Camden Soc., old ser., vol. lxix; 1858), p. 43).

[26] C.M. Fraser, 'Gilly-corn and the Customary of the Convent of Durham', *Archaeologia Aeliana*, 4th ser., xxxiii (1955), 37.

paid. Free tenants paid homage to the prior, swore fealty, and paid a relief. They also owed suit of the free court, although in practice suitors were allowed to absent themselves on payment of 6*d*. Suit at the local mill was rigidly enforced; the free gave a thirteenth of their grain just as the unfree did. The fact that many of the free tenements paid rates similar to customary tenements of the same size suggests that they had been former customary holdings which had been given the normal rights of freehold. After 1290 there appears to have been some contraction in the amount of freehold arable in south-east Durham; by 1500 Wolviston had lost some 500 acres of freehold and Billingham 300 acres although the records do not tell us what happened to this land. Cowpen Bewley had no freehold at all by the end of the fifteenth century. In 1332 William son of Richard de Fery paid 6*s*. 8*d*. rent for 100 acres of free land in Cowpen Bewley, but fifty years later only 5 acres of free land are recorded for the whole village.[27]

Because so few records survive it is almost impossible to reconstruct the tenurial system at Stillington and Seaton Carew. Nevertheless, a rental compiled for Stillington in 1445 demonstrates that the hosbondland was the basic unit of unfree tenure[28] but defined as 24 acres, unlike those on the episcopal and priory lands. The 1445 rental also shows that Stillington had little free land and in another of 1500-1 most of this manor's land was described as either townland or *maynland*.[29] The latter was almost certainly the demesne land which had been split up and divided among the villagers, while the former was probably hosbondland, for the hosbondland and townland are never mentioned together. The value of townland was considerably less than demesne land; in 1399 a bovate of townland was worth 16*s*. 0*d*. as against 24*s*. 0*d*. for a bovate of demesne land.[30]

The differences between the types of tenure on the various estates do not appear to have been great. On all three estates the hosbondland or bondland was the basic unit of unfree tenure. Both priory and episcopal vills contained cotland and

[27] DCD BR, 1332-3, 1382-3.
[28] MM 6188b.
[29] MM 6182.
[30] MM 6047.

maleland and many renders owed on the one estate were also owed on the other. There were some differences. Exchequer land and farmland were not found on the priory's land in south-east Durham—neither were certain renders such as *scot-oats*. However, there was often as great a difference between vills on the same estate.

Because medieval land measurements are so unreliable, it is impossible to calculate accurately in what proportions the land was divided between the various tenures in south-east Durham. The medieval acre could be very different from the statute acre of today. The measured acre was only one of three different meanings of the word. It could also be a strip-shaped piece of land of almost any size so that there could be variations even within the same vill. Again, it could be a fiscal unit, a relic of ancient tax assessment.[31] The uniformity of the bondage and cottage holdings in south-east Durham makes it almost certain that they were measured in these fiscal acres which may have borne little relation to acres on the ground.

Although accurate ratios cannot be given, it can be assumed however, that the proportion of free tenures was small and getting even smaller in the later Middle Ages. Compared with some estates elsewhere the proportion of free land in south-east Durham was always low.[32] Particularly remarkable, however, was its concentration. Most of the free holdings on the priory's lands were in Wolviston; neither Newton Bewley nor Cowpen Bewley had any free land in the fifteenth century. Likewise on the episcopal lands the nearby vills of Preston and Grindon consisted totally of free holdings in the later Middle Ages whereas Stockton and Norton had little free land. However, south-east Durham was by no means the only part of medieval England where there were large differences between the tenure in vills over a small geographical area.

An initial glance at the labour services owed by the south-east Durham villagers in the later fourteenth century suggests that they were heavy. Tenants of cotland seem to have performed an average of one day's work per week (or paid the monetary equivalent) and the tenants of bondland about three days.

[31] Maitland, *Domesday*, p. 475.
[32] e.g. Kosminsky, *Studies*, pp. 12-14, 99-103; Hilton, *Medieval Society*, pp. 129-31.

Most of the works were connected with the harvest, ploughing, and harrowing, although carrying services to Durham and washing and shearing sheep in the area known as Le Holme were also important.[33] Compared with other estates elsewhere, however, the south-east Durham tenants were not saddled with excessive labour rents. Not all labour services would have been exacted in the later Middle Ages. E.M. Halcrow has pointed out that many were remitted on the priory lands even when the demesnes were being directly exploited.[34] Hired seasonal and permanent labourers had long been used extensively on the south-east Durham manors.[35] Seasonal work was performed largely by hired labourers in the thirteenth century. Thus before the Black Death many of the manorial tasks were not performed by tenants as part of their labour services. When the three priory demesnes in the south-east of the county were finally leased—Billingham in 1359, Bellasis in 1373, and Bewley in 1409[36]—labour services were mostly commuted. The bishop retained some land in demesne at Stockton throughout the fifteenth century but there is no evidence that tenants performed week-work on it.

Free land, freedom, and villeinage

In the early Middle Ages there must have been a close connection between tenure and legal status in Durham as elsewhere, but this had broken down by the early fourteenth century.[37] Was there still any correlation at all between tenure and personal status in south-east Durham in the later Middle Ages? The exact importance of legal status in medieval times is not entirely clear. Edward Miller remarks that on the bishopric of Ely estates in the thirteenth century 'the surveyors were relatively incurious about personal status so far as classifying the peasantry was concerned'.[38] However, R.H. Hilton writes of the later Middle Ages that 'the classification of tenure and status in manorial documentation as between free and villein

---

[33] Le Holme lies to the south-east of Cowpen Bewley.
[34] Halcrow, 'Durh. Cath. Priory', p. 96.
[35] e.g. in 1305-6 Bewley had 5 carters and 22 ploughmen (DCD MA, 1305-6).
[36] DCD BA, 1359-60, 1373-4, 1409-10.
[37] Cf. Miller, *Ely*, p. 142.
[38] Ibid., p. 129.

was still important . . . The demand for freedom was a weighty slogan in 1381.'[39] Certainly it would be wrong to suggest that legal status was of no importance in late-medieval England. It is likely that the free enjoyed a considerable advantage socially as well as in their own self-esteem but the records have little to say on this. All we can consider here is the possible connection between legal status and the material position of the villagers. The majority of the south-east Durham tenants held by unfree tenure but by the mid-fourteenth century most of them were held to be personally free. We can learn most about the effects of tenurial and legal status in the area by looking at two much smaller groups: those at the top of the tenurial scale, who held by free tenures, and those at the bottom of the legal scale, the personally unfree villeins.

Leaving aside the burgesses of Stockton—their position, as we have seen, was a peculiar one—the number of tenants holding by free tenures in south-east Durham was small. In 1414 Stockton had less than twenty, Wolviston twelve, and Billingham three, while there were none at all at Cowpen Bewley or Newton Bewley.[40] One might suppose that because the units of freehold land in the area were generally small those who held them were not important people. However, many of the freeholders of south-east Durham also had holdings elsewhere; nor of course were freemen restricted to free land. Among the tenants listed in the coroner's account roll for the episcopal lands in 1460-1 one finds such names as Fulthorpe, Seton, Claxton, and Blaykeston.[41] These families were of the armigerous class. Sir William Fulthorpe held a messuage and 30 acres of the bishop at Norton whilst a William Fulthorpe, who may or may not have been the same person, held a messuage and 15 acres of the priory at Wolviston in 1414.[42] Roger Fulthorpe, who was presumably of the same family, held land both in Norton and in Hardwick in the later fourteenth and early fifteenth centuries. Moreover, his possessions extended far beyond south-east Durham for a surviving inquisition post mortem shows that he also had lands in Westmorland.[43] On

[39] Hilton, *Eng. Peasantry*, p. 24.
[40] DBR CC 188879; DCD Loc. iv, 143.
[41] DBR CC 188884.
[42] DCD BR, 1414-15.
[43] *Calendar of Inquisitions Post Mortem*, xiv. 146.

another occasion he is recorded as a steward holding the manorial court at Stillington.[44] Another member of the same family, Alan Fulthorpe, held the village of Grindon at farm. The Fulthorpes had been long prominent in Durham. Sir Roger had been a judge of common pleas and the Chief Justice of the palatinate under Bishop Hatfield. He was later attainted for treason but his son was granted his possessions. These included the manor of Tunstall, near Sunderland, and, in south-east Durham, the manors of Thorpe Thewles and Hurworth and lands in Hartlepool, Thorpe Bulmer, Norton, Wolviston, Burn Toft, and Whitton, as well as at Frosterley in Weardale and at Layton and Thirkleby in Yorkshire.[45]

Charters show that several of the free tenants on the priory's lands were merchants. John of Billingham, who with his wife was a grantor of lands in Wolviston in 1344, was described as a merchant from Hartlepool, and John Mappas, who held land at Wolviston in 1490, was the son and heir of a merchant from Newcastle upon Tyne.[46] Other freemen had varied professions. Alan Whitehead, who is listed in the 1413-14 rental, is shown in an earlier charter to have been the vicar of Tynemouth in Northumberland, and John Simson, who appears in the Melsanby Feodary, is described as a goldsmith from Newcastle upon Tyne.[47] The Steres were free tenants on the priory's estate but they also served the bishop as bailiffs at Bishop Middleham.[48] Few of the free tenants of south-east Durham belonged to the peasantry; most seem to have been well-to-do men who had land and positions both within the region and beyond it and who must have taken these holdings simply in order to sublet them at a profit. Many of the people described in the court rolls as servants (*servientes*) were employees of the free tenants.

There is some reason to suppose that these free tenants tried to close their ranks so as to exclude those of unfree status from taking over freehold land. On the episcopal lands the coroners' accounts regularly list the same names over many decades; it

[44] MM 6080.

[45] R. Surtees, *The History and Antiquities of the County Palatinate of Durham* (London, 4 vols., 1816-40), iii. 76.

[46] DCD 1.10 Spec. 35, 60.

[47] DCD 1.10 Spec. 41 (1370); *Feodarium*, p. 29.

[48] *Hatfield's Survey*, p. 236.

suggests that the land market in freehold was fairly inactive. There is a fair amount of evidence that freehold seldom came on to the open market. John son of William was a villein at Norton in 1354 who had acquired a free tenement on the same manor; thereupon the order was given in the halmote court that the reeve must seize the tenement.[49] A similar case occurred in 1420-1: William Barne had taken 1 bovate of free land in Preston near Stockton but when it was realized that he was a villein it was taken from him, and although he was prepared to pay a rent of 10*s.* 0*d.* it was preferred to let it out to others for only 6*s.* 8*d.* rather than return it to him.[50] All this is a far cry from some parts of England where the acquisition of pieces of free land by villein tenants was already a normal part of rural landholding by the late thirteenth century. It seems that even in the early fifteenth century there was some reluctance to allow free land on the episcopal estates to fall into the hands of the unfree.

We find a similar situation on the priory's estates. In the 1347-8 rental the only free land recorded appears to have been in the hands of free tenants.[51] After the Black Death, however, a certain amount of free land does seem to have passed to the unfree. The 1382-3 rental lists eleven tenants of free land of whom three appear to have been villeins.[52] Probably the shortage of tenants after the plague gave a few unfree tenants the chance to take over free land but most of the free land still remained in the hands of those of free status. In 1396-7 nine of the twelve tenants holding free land were personally free and in 1411-12 nine out of eleven.[53] The Melsanby Feodary enables us to trace the descent of thirty-two freehold properties in Billingham and Wolviston over 200 years and demonstrates that much free land remained in the possession of the particular free families for many generations. For example, in the time of Prior Melsanby (1233-44), Robert son of Robert Rikelott was given all the lands which his father had held of the priory at Billingham except for 1 acre.[54] The land seems then to have

[49] PRO DUR 3/12 (spring 1354).
[50] DBR CC 188881.
[51] DCD BR, 1347-8.
[52] DCD BR, 1382-3.
[53] DCD BR, 1396-7, 1411-12.
[54] DCD 1.9 Spec. 35.

descended within the same family until at least 1414.[55] By 1430 it had passed into the hands of one Robert Jackson; nevertheless, it had certainly been in the possession of a single family for almost 200 years. Many similar examples can be cited and even where one finds land passing outside the family there are sometimes clear reasons for this. Thus, the Melsanby Feodary shows why the Offington family lost control of their possessions in Wolviston: there was a failure of male heirs and Walter of Offington divided the land between his four sisters.[56]

Thus in personal as well as tenurial status the freeholders formed the top layer of the manorial tenants of south-east Durham. Below them came the mass of the tenantry, those who held unfree land but were personally free. At the bottom of the scale came another smaller group, those who were themselves unfree, the villeins (*nativi*). Not only was their status low in law but villeinage seems to have been despised by other villagers. Thus, it was ordained at Newton Bewley in 1365 that no one should call another a villein (*rusticus*) here on pain of ½ mark's amercement.[57] The by-law was repeated at Wolviston in 1378 when an amercement of 20*s*. 0*d*. was threatened.[58] Down to the mid-fifteenth century the prior regularly had lists of villeins compiled. This was done by sworn inquests and the villeins were catalogued by families. They never formed more than a small proportion of the population and their numbers declined in the course of the fifteenth century. In 1386 on the priory's manors in the area there were fifty-five villeins belonging to fourteen families.[59] In 1407 there were still fourteen families but the total number of villeins had risen to sixty-four; by 1460 there were only thirty-two from eight families in all and by this time villeins had entirely disappeared from all other parts of the priory's estate.[60] On the episcopal lands there are no corresponding lists, but since there is not a single reference to villeinage in the fifteenth-century court rolls we may assume

[55] DCD Loc. iv, 143.

[56] *Feodarium*, p. 36.

[57] DCD HCR, autumn 1365. Walsingham applied the word *rusticus* to the rebels of 1381 (*Thomae Walsingham Historia Anglicana*, ed. H.T. Riley (Rolls Series, 2 vols., 1863-4), ii. 18).

[58] DCD HCR, summer 1378.

[59] DCD HCR, spring 1386.

[60] DCD HCR, autumn 1407, spring 1460; Lomas, 'Durham Cath. Priory', p. 64.

that there too there were few if any tenants who were personally unfree.

Exactly what happened to the villeins is uncertain, although there were several ways by which they might have gained freedom. Manumissions by the lord were rare although John son of Richard Gibson was declared free after an inquiry at Wolviston in 1407. No one was allowed to be a cleric and unfree, so a villein was automatically freed if he took holy orders. This happened to John May, another tenant of the prior, who entered holy orders in 1440 and finished his life as an Augustinian canon at Hexham.[61] Freedom might also be obtained by flight[62] or by marriage. If Glanvill is to be believed all children of mixed marriages were unfree;[63] but this does not appear to have been the case in practice. Later legal writers such as Bracton and Fleta declared that the child took the status of his father and this seems to have been the case in south-east Durham in the later Middle Ages. The fines for merchet suggest that such mixed marriages were quite common. Thus at Norton in 1353 Johanna Sandy married John of Elstane who was personally free[64] and in 1407 Alice the daughter of John of Monkton of Billingham was said to be living as the wife of a free tenant of the manor.[65] The decline in population caused by the Black Death probably increased the likelihood of mixed marriages. Finally the dying-out of families must have helped the decline in the number of villeins in the later Middle Ages for by this date no one could be recruited to the ranks of the personally unfree and no new villein families appeared on the priory's lands in the fifteenth century.[66]

What is perhaps surprising is that villeins were not necessarily tenants of the smallest holdings of unfree land, nor were they insignificant in the village community. If one compares the list of villeins in 1407 with the 1411-12 rental, it becomes

---

[61] Lomas, 'Durham Cath. Priory', p. 62.

[62] e.g. Raftis, *Ramsey*, p. 136.

[63] P.R. Hyams, 'The Proof of Villein Status in the Common Law', *EHR*, lxxxix (1974), 732.

[64] PRO DUR 3/12 (autumn 1353).

[65] DCD HCR, autumn 1407.

[66] This was also the policy on other estates in the later Middle Ages, e.g. *The Caption of Seisin of the Duchy of Cornwall*, ed. P. Hull (Devon and Cornwall Record Soc., new ser., vol. xvii; 1971), p. xliii.

apparent that many of the villeins had substantial holdings.[67] John May of Billingham, Richard Gibson of Newton Bewley, and John of Monkton of Cowpen Bewley were villeins who held the standard bondage tenement. In addition many of the villeins were village office-holders. For example John son of Roger, a villein of Cowpen Bewley, also served at least once as a reeve, once as a collector, and was a juror at least fifty-nine times and a pledge eight times; we know too that he had a maid-servant. There are several other similar examples. They demonstrate that being at the bottom of the legal scale was not tantamount to living at the lowest economic or even social level.

It is very often assumed that all medieval people were either on one side of the legal fence or the other. If one was free there was freedom of movement, freedom to alienate property, and less rent to pay per acre. If one was unfree there were labour services, court amercements, entry fines, tallages, multure, merchet, leyrwite, heriot, and inability to move from the manor.[68] In south-east Durham, however, the position was less clear-cut. It seems as if the unfree tenants on the priory's estate had to swear not to leave the manor. Thus in 1374 Robert son of Eustace Fristerlyng of Hesleden, a villein, came into court and in the presence of officials and villagers swore that he was subject to the jurisdiction of the prior and convent of Durham and would not leave their land.[69] In practice, however, things were rather different.[70] There is in fact little evidence to suggest that the unfree were being forcibly kept in their native villages. Certainly villeins were occasionally ordered to return to their lands—as Fairjon was ordered back to Wolviston in 1367[71]—but neither the bishop nor the prior appears to have issued more than a handful of these injunctions. Certainly too chevage payments for permission to live away from the manor, common on many estates in the later Middle Ages, were rare in Durham. Villeins were living in other villages and by no means all of them were doing so illicitly; for example, Robert Gent

[67] DCD BR, 1407-8, 1411-12.
[68] Hilton, *Decline*, p. 24.
[69] DCD HCR, autumn 1374.
[70] Raftis, *Tenure*, p. 136.
[71] DCD HCR, spring 1367.

and his sons were described in 1353 as villeins from Carlton who were living at nearby Whitton.[72] Likewise in 1377 Thomas Richardson, the son of Gilbert of Billingham, one of the prior's villeins, was living at Melsonby near Richmond, some 20 miles away.[73] No orders were given for these villeins to return home. Where they went—the extent and pattern of migration from these villages—is to be considered later. For the present we may simply conclude that the bishop and the prior would have found it difficult to prevent either their free or their unfree tenants from going exactly where they pleased in the later Middle Ages and that in fact there is no evidence that they seriously tried to do so.

Most historians have little doubt today that the alienation of land by the unfree was a reality at least by the later Middle Ages. In fact, it seems as if the status of the tenant was unimportant; the status of the land was what decided whether or how it could be alienated.[74] In south-east Durham even this seems to have hardly mattered by the later Middle Ages; the tenants of all types of unfree land seem to have been free to dispose of it largely as they pleased. In theory, all chattels should have reverted to the lord on the death of an unfree person and on the priory's lands by-laws insisted on this. In practice, however, things may have been very different. This was certainly the case on many estates throughout the country.

As we have seen, lands held by unfree tenure paid heavier rents than free lands. For example at Stillington Thomas Henman paid 7*d.* a year for a free messuage, 23 acres of arable, and a little meadow, whereas John Sergeantson paid 4*s.* 0*d.* for a cottage and 2 acres.[75] But apart from this, those who were personally unfree also had to make other payments. Thus John del Raw of Cowpen Bewley in 1364 had to pay 6*s.* 8*d.* to be allowed to send his son to school.[76] What is significant, however, is that there is no evidence that the lord was refusing to allow unfree persons to enter the church or to go to school; if he had the

---

[72] PRO DUR 3/12 (spring, 1353).

[73] DCD HCR, spring 1377.

[74] Cf. *Cart. Nat.*, pp. xli-xlviii; Levett, *Studies*, p. 223.

[75] MM 6188b. This was common elsewhere (e.g. Hilton, *Eng. Peasantry*, p. 227; *Caption of Seisin*, p. xxvii).

[76] DCD HCR, autumn 1364.

available money, the unfree person was probably able to do most of the things which his free counterparts could do.

Nor were those tenants who were personally free necessarily immune from servile incidents if they held by unfree tenures. In some parts of the country the free were completely excused dues such as merchet and heriot[77] but this was not the case in south-east Durham. For example, Robert son of Robert Rikelott at Billingham was personally free but he owed both heriot and merchet.[78] All the same, the free were less heavily burdened: many freemen holding by unfree tenures were completely excused merchet whereas those personally unfree paid fairly large sums. In fact, the general level of merchet was high in the fourteenth century, and the fine was often in excess of 5s. 0d.[79] The burden, however, lessened. Although merchet was exacted throughout the fifteenth century, it was demanded from fewer of the tenants and the amount paid was reduced; after 1411 no one paid more than 12d. Other dues—heriot, aids, and gillycorn—were levied more consistently on the unfree although the free were not completely immune.

We have seen that the villeins might serve as village officials, but this duty was not theirs alone; those who were free might also be called on to serve.[80] In 1393 at Newton Bewley Robert Shakelok was both collector and a constable.[81] Thomas Williamson was a freeman at Wolviston but he also served as a collector, constable, and juror and in the same village in 1385 two of the eight tenants elected to ordain and regulate the affairs of the village were free.[82] In 1382 seven of the personally free were even summoned before the halmote court because they had not maintained the village pound (*hirsilleum*).[83] However, the free tenants were specifically excused some tasks; at Billingham in 1367 £2 amercement was levied 'on all tenants except for the free because they had not cleared the watercourse at le Northgait'.[84] In general, though, there was no clear

---

[77] e.g. Douglas, 'East Anglia', p. 72.

[78] DCD 1.9 Spec. 35.

[79] In Staffs. the Audleys generally exacted 1s. 0d. and the Bassetts of Pattingham 4s. 0d. for merchet (Hilton, *Eng. Peasantry*, p. 236).

[80] Bennett, *Eng. Manor*, p. 169.

[81] DCD HCR, autumn 1393.   [82] DCD HCR, autumn 1385.

[83] DCD HCR, autumn 1382.   [84] DCD HCR, summer 1367.

distinction between those of free and unfree status in obligations of this sort.

One very real difference at least on the priory's estates concerned suit of court. The prior's freemen had to attend the free court which met in Durham every three weeks. These free courts met more frequently than the halmote courts but in practice there was much more laxity. No tenant was expected to attend every session. A list of tenants owing suit at the priory's free court at Durham in 1372 shows that some owed suit five times a year and the other tenants three times.[85] In any case suitors were allowed to absent themselves from these courts unless required to answer a plea or show their charters. Many rolls are nothing more than a list of tenants who fined for permission to be absent or were amerced for not appearing; the amount was always 6*d.* Thus on one occasion in 1424, twenty of the forty-six suitors paid fines for permission to stay away and the rest simply failed to appear. At the same time the Durham free court was not a purely formal institution; in 1400 all the free brewers of Wolviston were ordered to be attached to appear at the next free court for ale offences.[86] Entry to free land and inquisitions post mortem were also dealt with. Most of the court's business, however, consisted of private pleas. Despite this there were many similarities between the free courts at Durham and the halmote courts for the villeins. Both courts declined in importance in the fifteenth century; in fact it is likely that they had ceased to play an important part in the lives of most villagers long before 1500. No records of the priory's free court survive after 1427, and although it continued in formal existence its income after 1460 was always fixed at 6*s.* 0*d.*;[87] this rather suggests that no one even bothered to attend. But besides this obligation to the free court, those freemen who held by unfree tenures were sometimes bound to attend the halmote courts. Sir Robert Claxton was reminded in the halmote court in 1460 that he had to mend the watercourses.[88] Freemen amerced in the halmote court included William Chapman of Wolviston in the later fourteenth century

---

[85] DCD Loc. iv, 194.
[86] DCD HCR, autumn 1400.
[87] This is the total sum for the whole palatinate.
[88] DCD HCR, summer 1460.

who was amerced on five occasions and Thomas Williamson of Cowpen Bewley who was amerced no less than seventeen times in the later fourteenth and early fifteenth centuries. Freemen often acted as pledges to the unfree. The same Thomas Williamson, a free tenant, is shown in the records to have been a pledge on sixteen occasions; in only four instances was he pledge to another freeman.

Legal status does not appear to have been fundamentally important in later medieval south-east Durham. Villeins seem to have lived much the same lives as those who were personally free. Any difference was likely to be one of degree rather than of kind; in practice there was a greater gulf between those who held by free and by unfree tenures than between those of free and unfree status. There may have been a social advantage in being free but it is difficult to believe that the advantage was a strong one. In the course of the fourteenth and fifteenth centuries the Durham courts seem to have been decreasingly concerned with legal status and there was certainly no lack of local contact between free and unfree. Nor can one detect a clear economic distinction. Obviously some of the large free-holding families such as the Claxtons and Steres lived more comfortably than many unfree cottagers but there were rich and poor among the free and unfree alike. All in all, legal status counted for very little certainly in 1500 and probably already in 1350. In fact the period seems to have witnessed little change in this respect; the courts declined in importance, dues such as heriot and merchet were reduced, and labour services declined, but there were no apparent cataclysmic changes. Old distinctions fell into disuse gradually; they were not removed through a conscious policy of the bishop or prior.

Mobility

We have already seen that not only the freemen but also the unfree villeins could in practice move away from south-east Durham if they wished. Those leaving can be divided into those moving permanently and those who left only for a time. The priory's villein lists are useful in that they mention all members of families living outside the village. They suggest that sons and daughters were leaving their native villages infre-

quently. In 1395 the only villein family whose children lived in
a different place from their parents was the Jonson family of
Cowpen Bewley: four of the sons and one of the daughters were
living in the neighbouring village of Billingham.[89] Similarly in
1407 only Robert Saunderson who held lands in Whitby, some
30 miles away, had moved far from his native village.[90] By the
1460s, however, rather more villeins were living away from
home including Robert Gibson at Seaton Carew, his brother at
Greatham, John Saunderson at Norton, William Richardson
at Carlton, Robert Richardson at Hart, and John Gibson at
Bradbury.[91] None of these villeins had moved more than 10
miles away. The records certainly give no indication of any
veritable tide away from south-east Durham in the later Middle
Ages.

The records may be deceptive either through clerical inefficiency or because no attempt was made to record those who
had moved a long way and who were thus difficult to trace. The
freemen of the city of York in the later Middle Ages included a
number with the surnames Bewley, Wolviston, and (less
significantly, for there were other places in the region with the
same names) Norton and Stockton.[92] But other records do not
suggest that there was much migration from south-east
Durham. We do not find, for instance, that many were leaving
their villages to marry elsewhere: most marriages involved
local people. Where the villein husband was an outsider, his
place of origin was usually recorded in the court rolls, from
which we can tell that the majority of marriages involved part-
ners from the same village. Moreover, when the husband did
come from a different place this was always within the county
and nearly always in its south-east quarter. On the other hand,
interestingly, we find no particular tendency to select a partner
from a village of the same lordship.

The impression therefore is that villagers tended not to leave
their native villages and that this was probably from choice
rather than compulsion. Nor should it be supposed that the

[89] DCD HCR, autumn 1395.

[90] DCD HCR, autumn 1407.

[91] DCD HCR, spring 1460.

[92] *Register of the Freemen of the City of York*, ed. F. Collins (Surtees Soc., vols. xcvi, cii;
1897-1900), i. 94, 157, 189.

south-east Durham villages were self-contained enclaves. Their inhabitants came into frequent contact with those from elsewhere. Many travelled often in the service of the manorial lord; on the priory's lands carrying services to Durham continued into the later Middle Ages. Some villagers travelled outside the palatinate and, equally, visitors from other places came to south-east Durham. For example, in 1456-7 John Henrison of Billingham went to York to buy fish and John Kellow of Tollerton, near Boroughbridge, was paid 3s. 4d. for carrying 260 stockfish from York to Billingham.[93] Likewise in 1400-1 John of Bellasis travelled to Westmorland on the prior's business;[94] the longer journeys tended to involve the richer rather than the poorer villagers. Probably most villagers did not journey outside their county.

The court rolls also point to considerable contact between neighbouring villages. Many of the reported trespasses in the fields were by people from adjoining villages. At Carlton in the later Middle Ages 11 per cent of presentments for trespass involved outsiders although in the other villages the proportion was less than 5 per cent. The vast majority of these outsiders came from other villages in south-east Durham, Gateshead and Thirsk being the most distant places of origin mentioned.

3 LAND AND ITS TRANSFER

The record of land transfer

Surviving records dealing with land in Durham in the later Middle Ages are good, particularly those relating to the priory's lands. For these, besides several surviving rentals, there is an almost complete record of customary-land transfers for the period 1364-1500. The halmote court functioned as a land registry, and since there survives an almost complete set of court rolls from 1364 to 1400 we have a nearly complete set of land transactions. After 1400 the court books compensate for the fewer surviving court rolls. These books contain nothing but admissions to and surrenders of land and the three books provide almost complete coverage from 1400 to 1528. The

---

[93] DCD BA, 1456-7.   [94] DCD BA, 1400-1.

records for the episcopal villages are not as extensive. Nevertheless, the bishop's halmote court books contain 10,075
entries dealing with land transfers there during a total of 110
years between 1350 and 1500.

However, if the records give a complete record of dealings in
customary land, then the amount of land which a person is
recorded as acquiring should be balanced exactly by the
amount that returned from him into the lord's hands either on
his death or by earlier surrender. This in fact is very seldom the
case even on the well-documented priory lands. Of the 1,136
persons involved in land transfers in the four priory villages in
the later Middle 'Ages only 425 are recorded as both acquiring
and relinquishing land. Moreover in only a few of these 425
cases do the admissions and surrenders balance. There are
several possible explanations of this.

Firstly, there is the problem of surnames. Evidence even
from the more progressive south of England in the fifteenth
century suggests that there was still some inconsistency and
confusion over the use and inheritance of surnames. Surnames
in Durham are certainly confusing. The least reliable appear to
have been those ending in -son. Names such as Robinson,
Saunderson, and Jackson appear regularly in the court rolls
but in the early part of our period they are not used as inherited
surnames and simply tell us the names of a man's father (or,
sometimes, mother). Thus John the son of William Emmotson
is referred to as John Wilkinson in 1407.[1] By the early fifteenth
century, however, names of this sort were starting to be
hereditary. At Billingham in the late fourteenth and early fifteenth centuries one finds a father and a son described as
William Thomson the elder and the younger; if the surname
had not become hereditary, William Thomson the younger
would have been known as William Williamson or Wilkinson.
Where a parent's name is used as a surname it is sometimes
possible to reconstruct families and to trace inheritance of land
even though the surname is not inherited, especially if the
parent's Christian name was relatively uncommon.

This is harder with the other types of surname. There are
those connected with occupations. Examples from the area are

---

[1] DCD HCB i, autumn 1407.

Baxter, Clerk, Dycon, Feryman, Fisher, Gardener, Shepherd, and Warenner. Occasionally these described the trade followed. In 1421 we find that the farmer of Newton Mill was Robert Milner.[2] Often, however, one finds Milners and Smiths who were unconnected with these trades and whose surnames were thus hereditary. And of course even where men had the same surname as their trade, one must not assume that these surnames were not hereditary; occupations were sometimes handed down within the family. Then there were surnames derived from actual place-names, such as Richmond, Arsom, and Wearmouth. By the later Middle Ages the majority of such names were clearly hereditary but there were exceptions. For example, Robert of Carlton on the episcopal lands was the father of Richard Hartburn.[3] Another group of surnames derived from local topography, such as Del Toune, Grene, and Attwood, and some of these may still not have been hereditary by the fifteenth century. The same is true of the many surnames found in the area which refer to the physical attributes of a person, such as Fairjon, Hardlad, Litilfair, and Sparrow.

Finally there is a particular problem over women's surnames as usage seems to have been even less consistent than for men. A woman did not necessarily take the surname of her husband, especially if he was the second husband. Thus Isabella del Holme was the wife of Henry son of Alan (Billingham, 1371), Alice of Derwent was the wife of Robert Hogge (Billingham, 1374), Agnes del Toune was the wife of John Taillour (Newton Bewley, 1380), and Agnes of Bellasis was the widow of Adam of Marton (Newton Bewley, 1389).[4] Nevertheless, most wives on both the episcopal and priory estates in the later Middle Ages seem to have been known by the same surnames as their husbands.

It seems, therefore, that surnames in this area were not necessarily inherited or acquired by marriage in the later Middle Ages but did tend to become more stable in the fifteenth century. However, a problem really arises only when one is attempting to compare surnames over several genera-

---

[2] DCD HCB i, spring 1421.
[3] PRO DUR 3/14 (spring 1408).
[4] DCD HCR, summer 1371, summer 1374, spring 1380, autumn 1389.

tions. Most men probably had only one surname during their
lifetime; someone described as John Davidson alias Richardson is the only obvious example of a man with two different
surnames.[5]

Difficulties of identification caused by changing surnames
may then be one reason why the number of admissions and
surrenders of land for an individual seldom tally. A second
possible explanation is subletting. Studies of other areas have
shown that subletting was widespread by the later Middle
Ages.[6] A lease might extend beyond the lessor's lifetime, and if
it was the custom to name the occupier rather than the tenant
of land there would be some confusion in the record.[7] There
are, however, few references in south-east Durham to permission being sought to sublet. From the four priory vills we have
no more than a dozen instances, and although there are sixty-
nine cases on the episcopal lands most concerned widows leasing their late husbands' tenements for a few years because they
were unable to manage the holdings themselves. Certainly the
lord's permission was needed to sublet. For example, when
Robert Hardgill took over the oven in Billingham in 1393, he
still needed permission to sublet it for a single year.[8] There
may, of course, have been a great deal of illicit subletting which
was undetected. The few cases which were discovered were
severely dealt with; thus in 1379 William del Raw and his wife
had two cottages confiscated because they sublet them without
permission.[9] Nevertheless the threat of confiscation may well
have been outweighed by the likelihood of escaping detection:
illicit subletting was certainly common elsewhere.[10] Other
evidence suggests that the authorities could be rather lax over
subletting. The granting of permission to sublet was often but
not always followed by an entry in the court records of the
actual transfer. When in 1374 Alice of Derwent took possession
of her late husband's cottage at Billingham for the rest of her
life she immediately got permission to sublet it, but there is no

---

[5] DCD HCB ii, spring 1447.

[6] e.g. Hatcher, *Cornwall*, p. 139; J.A. Brent, 'Alciston Manor in the Later Middle
Ages', *Sussex Archaeological Collections*, xcvi (1968), 100; Hilton, *Eng. Peasantry*, p. 48.

[7] As at Kibworth Harcourt, Leics. (Howell, *Land, Family and Inheritance*, p. 251).

[8] DCD HCR, summer 1373.

[9] DCD HCR, summer 1379.

[10] Above, p. 24.

record of her actually transferring it until 1388 when it passed to Alice Walker.[11] Similar examples could be quoted. The likelihood is that the transfer of the property to the lessee was simply not recorded. All this, however, hardly proves that illicit subletting was common. The examples cited concern small pieces of land; where larger amounts were involved more care was taken to record the transfers and probably a closer watch was kept.

A third possibility is that there was a considerable amount of private buying and selling which occurred without reference to the court; F.R.H. Du Boulay has shown that on the estates of Canterbury archbishopric in the later Middle Ages there was a tendency for transfers of an acre or less not to be recorded in the court rolls.[12] Occasionally one finds similar instances in south-east Durham. John Ketilman of Wolviston took a cottage and 7 acres in 1387 but what he surrendered in 1399 was a cottage and only 6 acres;[13] it is possible that at some time between the two dates John Ketilman surrendered an acre which was not noted in the court rolls. There is no evidence, though, that such transactions were deliberately omitted; instead one finds a remarkable degree of accuracy over small transfers and units of even a few roods were regularly recorded. Discrepancies are more likely due either to clerical slips or to the imprecision of medieval land description; if the acres recorded were customary ones minor differences of this sort could occur very easily, and if they were fiscal acres the way the holding was described might well have been a matter of indifference.

Finally it is possible that a certain type of land transfer was omitted deliberately from the records. J.A. Raftis noted on the estates of Ramsey Abbey that inheritance by primogeniture was seldom recorded in the court rolls; usually the court was concerned only when a customary tenement was conveyed outside the family.[14] In south-east Durham, however, every type of transaction including transfers from father to son seems to have been recorded in the halmote records.

[11] DCD HCR, summer 1374, summer 1388.
[12] Du Boulay, *Canterbury*, p. 151.
[13] DCD HCR, autumn 1387, spring 1399.
[14] Raftis, *Tenure*, pp. 48-9.

The family and its land

It was arguably a principle of peasant property in medieval England that family land belonged to the whole family: every member had a claim to support from it. The royal courts and the common law ruled that the villein could neither convey nor bequeath his land. Nevertheless, although inheritance customs varied from place to place, the fundamental right of even the villein family to inherit seems never to have been questioned at the level of customary law.[15] Studies of many medieval estates have shown the principle firmly maintained that a holding should descend from generation to generation in a family line. G.C. Homans noted that 'even in the fifteenth century . . . there was a strong sentiment against alienation'[16] and one even finds instances of the lord forcing a tenant to inherit family land. There seems little doubt that throughout the country inheritance within the family was the norm until at least the Black Death.[17]

Among the few extant records of south-east Durham before 1350 are two rentals for the priory's lands; one is dated 1332-3 and the other 1347-8.[18] Seventeen holdings in Cowpen Bewley appear in both rentals; of these five were still held by the same person in 1347-8 as in 1332-3, while certainly five, and probably four others as well, had been transferred to a member of the same family. Thus, of the twelve holdings which changed owners between 1332-3 and 1347-8, at least five, perhaps nine were transferred from one member of a family to another. At nearby Billingham fourteen out of forty-two holdings changed hands between the two dates; of these six descended within the family. At Newton Bewley only four out of twenty-one holdings were in the hands of the same tenant in 1347-8 as in 1332-3, but of the other seventeen only three had passed outside the family. Finally at Wolviston sixty-one holdings were mentioned in both rentals; of these, thirty-six were still held by the same

---

[15] Ibid.

[16] Homans, *Eng. Villagers*, p. 109.

[17] D. Roden, 'Inheritance Customs and Succession to Lands in the Chiltern Hills in the Thirteenth and Early Fourteenth Centuries', *JBS*, vii (1967), 3-4; Levett, *Studies*, p. 223; R.J. Faith, 'Peasant Families and Inheritance Customs in Medieval England', *AgHR*, xiv (1966), 88.

[18] DCD BR, 1332-3, 1347-8.

person at the later date, and of the twenty-five which changed hands sixteen had passed to a member of the same family. This demonstrates a strong desire to keep land in the family; of holdings in the four villages which had a change of tenant between 1332-3 and 1347-8 about two-thirds passed simply from one member of a family to another.

By the end of the fourteenth century, the situation seems to have changed dramatically almost everywhere and family transactions became only a small minority of all transfers.[19] Table XIII analyses land transfers in the four priory vills between 1364 and 1500. Renewals of leases, which account for many entries in the records, are not included. It can be seen that the results from all four vills are remarkably consistent. At Wolviston only 10 per cent of all land transfers involved land passing from one member of a family to another; at Billingham, Cowpen Bewley, and Newton Bewley the figures were 12, 16, and 19 per cent respectively. Of course, the actual proportion of land passing within the family may have been slightly higher because some of the unspecified transfers may have been within the family and the caprices of medieval surnames may also have disguised a few family transfers. Nevertheless, it is unlikely that these were numerous enough to affect the general conclusion. It seems that most of the land transfers in the priory's halmote courts involved alienation from one family to another.

Rosamond Faith shows that the 1380s and 1390s witnessed the steepest decline in customary inheritance and family transfers at Brightwalton.[20] On the priory's lands in south-east Durham, however, the Black Death seems to have had a more immediate effect on inheritance patterns. As we have seen, some two-thirds of all land transfers between 1332 and 1347 were within the family. Of the sixty land transfers in the five years 1365-9, where both the incoming and the outgoing tenant were named, only ten (17 per cent) were family transfers. Similarly, during the periods 1375-9, 1380-4, and 1385-9 the percentages were respectively 20, 28, and 15. The figures then sank even lower. Between 1385-9 and 1470-4, there was no five-year period in which more than 15 per cent of land

---

[19] Above, pp. 129-30, 132, 221, 237.
[20] Above, Ch. III, section 2.

Table XIII
Transfers of properties in Durham Cathedral Priory halmote courts,
1364-1500

	Billingham		Cowpen Bewley		Newton Bewley		Wolviston	
	No.	%	No.	%	No.	%	No.	%
Within the family during lifetime	39	6	28	8	14	9	22	5
Within the family on death	36	6	26	8	16	10	22	5
Outside the family during lifetime	471	74	229	69	88	57	329	78
Outside the family on death	36	6	36	11	15	10	26	6
Uncertain	55	9	11	4	21	14	24	6
Total	637	100	330	100	154	100	423	100

transfers involved land passing within the family; the figure
was usually below 10 per cent, and indeed in 1445-9 there were
none at all out of forty-eight recorded transfers. Towards the
end of the fifteenth century, however, the proportion of family
transfers appears to have increased: in 1470-4 and 1475-9, the
percentages were 37 and 27 respectively. The practice of keeping land in the family which was once more to become common
in the sixteenth and later centuries seems to have begun to
revive in the last quarter of the fifteenth century, after having
been in abeyance for a hundred years.

The records of the bishop's vills are less complete, but they
are full enough to give further evidence of general trends; this
is set out in Table XIV. At first glance there appears to be
great variation between the villages. At Norton more than a
third of all transfers were definitely within the family whereas

Table XIV
Transfers of properties in the bishop of Durham's halmote courts, 1350-1499

	Carlton		Hartburn		Norton		Stockton	
	No.	%	No.	%	No.	%	No.	%
Within the family during lifetime	6	6	15	14	83	20	28	13
Within the family on death	7	6	22	21	55	14	23	10
Outside the family during lifetime	43	41	54	50	202	49	163	73
Outside the family on death	6	6	1	1	7	2	1	0
Uncertain	43	41	15	14	62	15	9	4
Total	105	100	107	100	409	100	224	100

at Carlton the proportion was only about one-eighth. However the difference is partly explained by the large number of entries for Carlton where the previous owner of the land is unspecified. At Hartburn and Norton, where in each case the proportion of such entries is about 15 per cent, the proportion of family transfers was the same, 34 or 35 per cent. At Stockton 23 per cent of land transfers were within the family, and although this might seem relatively low a possible explanation lies in the structure of the vill. Much of it had been demesne and many of the entries were of short leases of such things as the ferry-boat and parts of the demesne; such properties were seldom passed within the family. Nevertheless, the proportion of land passing within the family was significantly higher on the episcopal lands of south-east Durham than on the priory's lands, even though on both estates most transfers between 1350 and 1500 involved land which passed outside the family.

The higher proportion of family transactions on the episcopal lands becomes more marked when we examine the chronological patterns. Although only fourteen out of ninety-seven transfers between 1350 and 1354 were definitely within the family, the name of the outgoing tenant is recorded for only twenty-six transactions in all; accordingly, family transactions formed over 50 per cent of all those between 1350 and 1354, where both old and new owners are known. The proportion then remained between 30 and 40 per cent during each five-year period until the end of the fourteenth century, decreasing in the first half of the fifteenth century as on the priory's lands. Also as on the priory's lands the proportion of family transfers seems to have increased before the close of the fifteenth century: between 1465-9 and 1495-9 never less than 30 per cent (usually nearer to 50 per cent) of all recorded transfers were within the family. Thus, although the episcopal lands tended to have a higher proportion of family transfers, the chronological pattern on both estates was similar. On both, the Black Death probably affected the inheritance pattern severely, but the lowest percentage did not occur until the end of the fourteenth century. Thereafter family transfers were few until the last part of the fifteenth century when there seems to have been a renewed interest in keeping land in the family.

It should be noted that this applies only to customary land; for free land there seems to have been a different pattern. Free tenants seem to have been more concerned to keep land within the family. We have seen how the Melsanby Feodary enables us to trace the descent of many of the free holdings over two centuries.[21] In the few instances where a holding passed to a different family, the cause appears to have been the extinction of the male line. For example Thomas Gretham of Wolviston must have died without surviving male heirs because the estate passed to Cecilia Gretham who was the widow either of Thomas or of his male heir. She was herself a daughter of Thomas Chapman and the inheritance then passed to the Chapman family. The next owner of the holding was Agnes, wife of Richard Dyghton, a daughter of William Chapman.[22]

The rules governing the inheritance of customary holdings

21 Above, pp. 265, 281-2.
22 *Feodarium*, p. 30.

varied from one place to another in medieval England.[23] However, one of the most widespread and most deeply entrenched of all inheritance customs was inheritance by widows; usually the widow had a right to some of the land although the amount varied and most held it only conditionally.[24] It has been shown that on the estates of Durham Cathedral Priory as a whole the rights of widows were acknowledged even before 1350 and that after the widow it was normal for the children to succeed to the holding.[25] On both the bishop's and the priory's lands in south-east Durham holdings were inherited by a single son slightly more often than by a widow. There are ninety-one cases of land passing to the eldest son in the episcopal villages compared with seventy-nine where the widow received all her late husband's estate; in the four priory vills the totals are seventy-four and seventy-one respectively. Where a widow did succeed to her late husband's lands she received the whole inheritance, although normally she had to pay an entry fine. Sometimes the widow chose to alienate the land, usually to a son who undertook to look after her for the rest of her life. There are slightly more instances of widows alienating land to a child on the bishop's lands than on the priory's but on neither estate is the number large. Nor did an inheritance always pass from widow to child, and sometimes it was divided. When William Northird of Norton died in 1417 his widow, Alice, chose to retain a messuage, a bondland, and a cottage but she immediately surrendered another messuage, a bovate of land, another cottage, and 3 roods of meadow to someone outside the family.[26] Many widows must have found it difficult to look after the whole of their late husband's holdings and it is perhaps to be expected that in most cases where licence was given to sublet a tenement on the episcopal lands the tenant was a widow.

The inability of widows to manage their late husbands' estates probably explains why so much land passed directly from father to son; a wife may have already surrendered her

[23] G.C. Homans, 'Partible Inheritance of Villagers' Holdings', *EcHR*, 1st ser., viii (1937), 55; Hatcher, *Cornwall*, p. 64; Faith in *AgHR*, xiv (1966), 77-95.

[24] Above, pp. 129, 139-40, 156; Howell, *Land, Family and Inheritance*, p. 259; Page, *Crowland*, p. 108; Jones, 'Beds. Land Market', p. 59.

[25] Lomas, 'Durham Cath. Priory', p. 25.

[26] PRO DUR 3/14 (autumn 1411).

right to a husband's land by the time of his death and in many other instances the husband must have outlived the wife. Although the cases of a widow or a single son succeeding to land formed the bulk of family transfers, other relatives did occasionally succeed to holdings. Land was sometimes inherited by daughters or by relatives of the same generation; on the episcopal lands there are eight recorded cases of land passing between brothers, two cases of a transfer from a brother to a sister, one from a sister to a brother, and one from a wife to a brother-in-law. Although there are no definite cases of land passing between brothers in the priory's villages, there are nineteen transfers between people with the same surnames, some of whom were probably brothers. Women could, of course, hold land in their own right and on both estates there are several cases of wives giving land to their husbands. Partible inheritance was rare but there are a few instances on the episcopal lands. For example, in 1410 at Hartburn, one of Thomas Barne's sons, John Barne, succeeded to a cottage and bovate of land and another, Robert Barne, to a messuage and 2 bovates. At the same time a third son, Adam Barne, was also acquiring land, although not from his father.[27] Such examples remind us again that the tenants of south-east Durham had freedom to alienate land provided their transfers were recorded in the halmote court. In practice, however, primogeniture was the norm. It should perhaps be noted that the existence of a stepfather did not diminish the rights of children of a first marriage. At Carlton, Alice had been the wife of Thomas Fowler and on his death she had inherited two messuages and 4 bovates of land before marrying William Umfrayson. When the land appeared in the court rolls, however, it was John son of Thomas Fowler who had succeeded to it.[28]

Demesne leasing and the land market

Unfortunately there is little documentary evidence of the land market in south-east Durham before the Black Death. The many surviving charters of the early thirteenth century suggest that there was an active market in small parcels of free land,

[27] PRO DUR 3/14 (summer 1410).
[28] PRO DUR 3/13 (spring 1391).

but the only relevant sources for customary land are the two priory rentals for 1332-3 and 1347-8.[29] A comparison of the two rentals provides no evidence of a market in customary land before 1350. There is little sign of engrossment or fragmentation. The standard holding at Newton Bewley in 1332-3 and 1347-8 was the bondland of 30 acres and the only other holding was the cottage of 6 acres. In 1332-3 two people each held two bondlands which had been divided in two by 1347-8 but otherwise there was little change between the two dates. There is certainly no evidence of the brisk traffic in small parcels of land which A.E. Levett detected on the St. Albans Abbey estates.[30] At Cowpen Bewley seven out of seventeen traceable holdings changed hands between 1332-3 and 1347-8 but none seems to have been enlarged or divided. Probably the fact that most bondlands were held exclusively for labour services would help to prevent the breakup of holdings. In Billingham forty-two separate pieces of land appear in both rentals; of these twenty-eight were still held by the same person in 1347-8 as in 1332-3, six had passed within the family, and only eight had passed to others; again there is no evidence of the fragmentation of holdings and the only important difference between the two rentals is the leasing of some odd acres of demesne by 1347-8. Only at Wolviston is there any evidence of engrossment, perhaps reflecting the fact that it contained a far higher proportion of free tenants and free land than the other vills. The overall conclusion is that the market in customary land in south-east Durham was slack and that there had been little engrossment before the Black Death. The standard tenement, undivided and unaugmented, still predominated there.

The extra land which became available after 1350 came from two main sources. One was the holdings that fell vacant, whether by death or migration. The other was the manorial demesnes. Studies of various estates have shown that direct exploitation of the demesnes was replaced by leasing during the fourteenth and fifteenth centuries.[31] The priory's demesnes in

---

[29] DCD BR, 1332-3, 1347-8.

[30] A.E. Levett, 'The Courts and Court Rolls of St. Albans Abbey', *TRHS*, 4th ser., vii (1924), 67; cf. *Select Man. Pleas*, p. 105.

[31] Above, p. 109; B.F. Harvey, 'The Leasing of the Abbot of Westminster's Demesnes in the Later Middle Ages', *EcHR*, 2nd ser., xxii (1969), 19; Page, *Crowland*, p. 114; Dewindt, *Holywell*, p. 60.

south-east Durham were let out gradually. Leases were originally for a single year, although they were often renewable, and at first tenants were taking up no more than an acre at a time. The leases often stipulated that the lessee had to give back the holding in the same condition as he received it, but the court rolls for the four priory vills show that such stipulations were not always heeded.[32] But it was not long before annual leases of small pieces of the priory's demesnes were replaced by leases of an entire manorial demesne either to a single farmer or to a group of associates. The priory had demesnes at Billingham, Bewley, and Bellasis in the south-east of the county but the only indication of size is at Billingham where a survey shows that there were about 200 acres of demesne arable.[33] The amounts paid in rent suggest that at Bewley the demesne was rather smaller and at Bellasis smaller still. The episcopal demesne in south-east Durham was concentrated in fairly large blocks around Stockton, with some also in Preston, Hartburn, and Norton. The chronology of leasing there cannot be established accurately because when the collector's accounts begin in 1396-7 most of the demesne land had already been leased.

The earliest of the priory's rentals to record the piecemeal leasing of small amounts of demesne land in the area is that of 1347-8; no person held more than 10 acres. Billingham was probably the first of the south-east manors to have its demesne leased outright: part was leased in 1357 when £4. 13*s*. 9*d*. rent was paid in two instalments and the process was complete by 1365-6 when the prior received £16. 13*s*. 6*d*. as rent for the entire demesne.[34] It seems never to have passed into the hands of a single farmer but rather to have been divided into parcels based on a unit of 5 acres 1 rood of arable and 1½ roods of meadow. In 1382-3 none of the lessees held more than 21 acres of arable and 1½ acres of meadow; in that year twenty tenants of Billingham shared the demesne.[35] Although the autumn

[32] This was the case elsewhere; e.g. F.R.H. Du Boulay, 'Who were Farming the English Demesnes at the End of the Middle Ages?', *EcHR*, 2nd ser., xvii (1964-5), 447.

[33] DCD 2.9 Spec. 16 (undated).

[34] DCD BA, 1357-8, 1365-6.

[35] DCD BR, 1382-3.

court roll for 1364 records that Robert Hardgill took over the *manerium* of Billingham for which he was still paying rent in the 1382 rental, he cannot have been holding the whole demesne; it is more likely that the *manerium* included no more than the manor house and its surrounds.[36] Bellasis demesne was leased finally in 1373, although a few acres had been leased before this. The court roll for autumn 1373 contains a very detailed entry recording the lease of the whole demesne, except one small piece, to a William Jackson of Cowpen Bewley; the lease was for fifteen years and the rent was £6. 13s. 4d., but this also included stock.[37] From 1373 until 1500 this rent never changed and the demesne was always either held by a single farmer or shared between two. Bewley was the last of the priory's demesnes to be leased in the south-east of the county and one of the last on the whole of the priory's estates. It was not finally leased until 1409 though there had been partial leases earlier—in 1368-9, for instance, of a portion that brought in £3. 6s. 8d. rent.[38] Like Bellasis, the demesne was leased as a whole, to either one or two farmers.

Most studies of villagers' lands in the later Middle Ages have revealed an active land market, although the date when it became brisk seems to have varied.[39] South-east Durham, however, does not seem to have had a particularly active land market at any time during the later Middle Ages. There were usually between one and three transfers a year in each of the vills; accordingly, the number of transactions dealt with in any one court seldom exceeded one per vill. If anything, slightly more land changed hands on the priory's estate than on the bishop's—an average of 2.7 transactions a year in each vill compared with 1.9 in the episcopal vills; but on neither estate could the land market be called brisk.

One or two trends can be discerned. In the episcopal vills the land market was exceptionally active in the five years following the Black Death but it was much slacker between about 1360

---

[36] DCD HCR, autumn 1364.

[37] DCD HCR, autumn 1373. Bellasis was the tenth of the priory's demesnes to be leased.

[38] DCD BA, 1368-9, 1409-10.

[39] Above, pp. 26-8; R.H. Hilton in *VCH Leics.*, ii. 186; Page, *Crowland*, p. 126; Davenport, *Norf. Manor*, p. 79; Dewindt, *Holywell*, p. 108.

and 1390. The later fourteenth century also saw fewer transfers on the priory's lands; from about three transactions a year in each vill in the 1360s and 1370s, the average fell to below two about the turn of the century. After the beginning of the fifteenth century the number of transactions seems to have increased so that by 1410 the average for each vill was over three on both estates. The number then declined again until the end of the fifteenth century:[40] there were only one or two transfers a year in each vill except in 1485-95 when on the priory's estate there were slightly more.

It is likely that the Black Death was as disruptive on the priory's estate as it had been on the bishop's. Of the tenants listed in the 1347-8 rental few seem active in the land market after 1364. As we have seen, it is likely that the mortality rate was high.[41] As elsewhere, however, things seem to have returned to normal within a short time.[42] On neither episcopal nor priory estates are there any references to land in the lord's hands because of a shortage of tenants until more than twenty-five years after the Black Death. It was only in the last quarter of the fourteenth century that changes appeared; the number of transfers declined and land was passing instead into the hands of the lord. Thus in 1389 there were sixteen vacant tenements in Billingham, Wolviston, and Cowpen Bewley whereas only three transfers to new tenants occurred there during the year.[43] It seems that in the later fourteenth century the south-east Durham villagers were refusing to take up vacant tenements. Sometimes the holding remained vacant for several years. A typical example is Beatrice Tewe's tenement at Billingham which was in the lord's hands by the autumn of 1386 and was still vacant in the autumn of 1397.[44]

Although the episcopal court rolls are missing for the period 1362-88, certain evidence seems to confirm that a similar thing was happening on the bishop's estate. The rolls for succeeding years contain many entries like that referring to William del

[40] For further details see T. Lomas, 'Land and People in South-east Durham in the Later Middle Ages' (Council for National Academic Awards Ph.D. thesis, 1976), pp. 107-68 *passim*.

[41] Above, pp. 259-60.

[42] e.g. Levett, 'Black Death', pp. 76-82; Harvey, *Oxon. Village*, p. 137; Hatcher, *Cornwall*, p. 122.

[43] DCD HCR, spring to autumn 1389.

[44] DCD HCR, autumn 1386, autumn 1397.

Raw, the collector of Stockton in 1400: he was ordered to answer for a share of a tenement and bovate of land because the previous tenant, John Eme, had died and they had been in the lord's hands for the last twelve years.[45] In the 1390s and the early fifteenth century the bursar's account rolls from the priory had attached schedules dealing with waste and decay. The five surviving rolls between 1396-7 and 1402-3 show that the number of waste tenements at Cowpen Bewley varied from four to five in any one year, at Billingham from nine to thirteen, and at Wolviston from four to eight; the rents lost from the waste tenements were respectively £2. 6s., £12. 15s. 0¼d., and £12. 9s. 9d.[46]

The bursar's accounts also show that the lord did not always receive the rent due to him from occupied tenements; this applied even to those held by the richer tenants such as William Jackson, who was allowed £1. 6s. 8d. reduction on the farm of the manor of Bellasis.[47] The bursar's account roll for 1395-6 records that the tenants of Billingham were allowed a total of £22. 7s. 7d. because they were unable to pay their farm.[48] The rents for leased parcels of demesne lands were not always paid in full. In 1384-5 demesne tenants had left £15. 2s. 8½d. unpaid at Billingham and £11. 0s. 8d. at Cowpen Bewley.[49] The situation was probably similar on the episcopal lands; even as late as 1440-1 allowances to the collector included 2s. 7½d. from Pundersland because it was not occupied, 6s. 3d. for the farm of three cottages because they were waste, and £6. 6s. 4¾d. from various other unoccupied lands. At the same time £4 was remitted from the usual £20 farm of Hardwick.[50]

The lord had also to make other concessions. During the fifteenth century the prior often gave gifts to incoming tenants. For example, the tenant who took over 14 acres of arable, 3 roods of meadow, and a salting at Cowpen Bewley in 1439 received 1s. 8d. as a gift from the lord and was excused various dues of salt left unpaid by the previous tenant.[51] At Wolviston

---

[45] PRO DUR 3/13 (summer 1400).
[46] DCD BA, 1405-6.
[47] DCD BA, 1377-8.
[48] DCD BA, 1395-6.
[49] DCD BA, 1384-5.
[50] DBR CC 188825.
[51] DCD HCB ii, autumn 1439.

in the following year John Taillour was given 12*d*. by the prior
to repair the three cottages that he had taken over with 6 acres
of land.[52] For most of the fourteenth century it was nearly
always the tenant who had to repair buildings and land, but in
the fifteenth century the lord often took over this responsibility.

One way in which the episcopal lands differed from the
priory's was in the payment of entry fines (*gresuma*). Before the
Black Death it was normal for an entry fine to be exacted from
the incoming tenant of a customary holding. On some estates,
though not everywhere, these entry fines were abandoned in
the later Middle Ages.[53] On the priory's lands some 70 per cent
of all land transfers before about 1375 involved an entry fine.
However, this figure fell sharply over the next forty years and
by 1420 entry fines had ceased to be exacted on the priory's
lands. It was in this same period, between 1380 and 1420, that
the lord was unable to exact rents in full. On the episcopal
lands, however, the situation was different. There the number
of entry fines was increasing in the decade following the Black
Death but had begun to fall by the 1380s. Between 1390 and
1410 we find the same trend as on the priory's lands: a steep
decline in the proportion of entry fines to total transfers compared with the 1350s and 1360s. However, the similarity
between the two estates ceased around 1410 for there then
began a sudden revival of entry fines on the episcopal lands.
Between 1410 and 1415 an entry fine was paid on forty out of
forty-one transfers; from about 1455 to 1475 between 60 and 70
per cent of all transfers there involved a fine, and although
there were slight variations this proportion was largely maintained to the end of the century.

At Blunham the entry fine on a standard tenement came
to be equivalent to a year's rent.[54] On the priory's lands in
south-east Durham, however, there seems to have been no
consistent amount. Three bondage holdings at Newton Bewley
transferred in 1379 were each held for 30*s*. 0*d*. rent; the entry
fines, however, were 20*s*. 0*d*., 26*s*. 8*d*., and 40*s*. 0*d*.[55] The
gresuma on a messuage and 30 acres of arable at Cowpen

---

[52] DCD HCB ii, autumn 1440.
[53] Above, pp. 114-18.
[54] Above, p. 202.
[55] DCD HCR, summer 1379.

Bewley in 1370 was only 6s. 8d.[56] Entry fines appear to have been a little more fixed on the episcopal estates and most standard tenements there paid an entry fine of 3s. 4d. in the fifteenth century. Overall, however, on the estates of south-east Durham there seems to have been no fixed entry fine even on a particular holding. When Robert Kent inherited a messuage and two bondlands from his father in 1458 the entry fine was 2s. 0d., but when they passed to his own son in 1474 it amounted to 6s. 8d.[57]

Even when exacted, entry fines were not always paid in full. On the priory's lands in particular, large reductions were allowed. Between 1370 and 1374 in the four priory vills entry fines were exacted on fifty-four recorded transfers, but seven of the fines were reduced by a quarter to a half, two by a half to three-quarters and ten by over three-quarters. No such reductions occurred on the episcopal lands but the fines there were often small, sometimes as low as 6d. It seems most unlikely that the priory and the bishop could at any time during the later Middle Ages manipulate entry fines to help compensate for loss of revenue from other sources; the economic tide must have been running very strongly against the landlords.

The most obvious explanation is that there was a surfeit of land in the later Middle Ages. The high mortality in the Black Death and the breakup of the demesne land suggest that there was plenty of land for the remaining villagers. This would inevitably place the lord in a weak position and he had to take holdings into his own hands because he could find no tenants to occupy them. The lord had even to make concessions, by way of gifts and reduced entry fines, in order to get tenants for the better quality land.

It is rather perplexing, however, to find that the amount of land involved in each transfer followed different patterns on the two estates. Transfers of odd acres of land never appear to have been a feature of the episcopal villages in south-east Durham. Transfers of 10 acres or more always accounted for over 60 per cent of all recorded land transactions there, averaged over a five-year period; in fact, the proportion was usually over 80 per cent. In contrast in the priory's vills there were many more

[56] DCD HCR, spring 1370.
[57] PRO DUR 3/16 (spring 1458, summer 1474).

small-scale transfers until about 1430. On the episcopal lands, the majority of transfers involved customary holdings of one or two bovates and this pattern hardly changed during the later Middle Ages. On the priory's lands, however, many transfers involved more than the standard customary holding. Thus between 1460 and 1464 in the four priory vills there were forty-five transfers of land, of which thirty-five involved more than the customary holding of 30 acres. It appears, therefore, that on the bishop's lands the majority of holdings which came on to the market were standard customary holdings throughout the later Middle Ages, but on the priory's lands small-scale transfers dominated the market during the later fourteenth century while the fifteenth century saw larger units transferred.

The individual and his land

Most studies of individual estates have shown that land was being concentrated in the hands of fewer tenants during the later Middle Ages.[58] Because we have no rentals for the episcopal lands, it is difficult to say whether this was taking place on this estate. Hatfield's Survey shows that some multiple holdings existed in 1382 but there is no sign of large peasant landowners. Nevertheless the court records suggest that certain tenants were systematically enlarging their holdings; thus Robert Wilkinson, a cooper at Norton, took a share of a cottage in 1391, a bondage tenement in 1397, the village oven in 1406, the forge in 1416, a messuage and a bovate of land in 1417, the herbage of the Grangefield in 1423, and a cottage in 1438.[59] It is typical, however, that none of his transactions was on a large scale; in fact few people took on more than a couple of standard customary holdings. Many of those involved in the land market were merely taking odd acres of demesne land. No person in the episcopal villages of south-east Durham took part in more than six recorded transactions involving arable land.

There is much more evidence for the priory's lands and a

[58] e.g. Dewindt, *Holywell*, p. 160; Davenport, *Norf. Manor*, Chapter v; Hatcher, *Cornwall*, pp. 225-35.

[59] PRO DUR 3/13 (summer 1391, summer 1397), 14 (summer 1406, autumn 1416, spring 1417, summer 1423), 15 (autumn 1438).

definite trend can be discerned. A comparison of rentals shows that land held by 176 tenants in 1382-3 was held by only 115 in 1495-6.[60] It is obvious that some wealthy tenants had appeared in the villages by the later fifteenth century. In 1382-3 at Cowpen Bewley the highest rent was paid by John del Raw, who owed £1. 13s. 1d. for his lands; by 1495-6 seven tenants there paid over £2. 10s., two of them over £4. 10s., and the general level of rents was substantially higher (Table XV).

The way these wealthy landowners acquired land can be traced in the halmote court books. A case where we see expansion continuing over more than one generation is that of William White of Cowpen Bewley, who in 1495-6 was paying £4. 15s. 5½d. rent for his lands. In 1480 he had inherited from his father, John White, a messuage and bondland, a cottage and 6 acres, another cottage and 6 acres, 6 acres above Colflat, 5 acres above Dorflat, a salting, a share of the meadowland called Levyker, a messuage and 14 acres of arable, an acre of meadow above the Northrow and a dovecote, and a parcel of *ferryland* in Billinghamfield with 3½ acres.[61] Two years later he took over a further messuage, 20 acres of arable, ½ acre of meadow, and a third share of an orchard.[62] It was a similar story in the other priory vills in south-east Durham where the difference between the rent of those who paid the most and the

Table XV

Rents paid at Cowpen Bewley, 1382-3 and 1495-6

Amount of annual rent	Number of tenants	
	1382-3	1495-6
Under 1s. 0d.	2	—
1s. 0d.-5s. 0d.	14	7
5s. 1d.-10s. 0d.	6	4
10s. 1d.-20s. 0d.	3	1
20s. 1d.-£2. 10s.	1	4
Over £2. 10s.	—	7

[60] DCD BR, 1382-3, 1495-6.

[61] DCD HCB ii, spring 1480. *Ferryland* may have been originally part of the lease of the ferry which crossed the Tees.

[62] DCD HCB ii, summer 1482.

average rent of all the tenants was much greater in 1495-6 than it had been in 1382-3.

On many estates in the later Middle Ages there was a quick turnover of land and this certainly seems to have been the case in south-east Durham. In the mid-fourteenth century most customary holdings on the priory's lands were held for a period of a single life; the only exceptions were the holdings of the villeins, held at the will of the lord, and the mills and forges which were always leased for short terms. It was only after 1380 that short leases of other properties appeared in south-east Durham. This, it will be recalled, was the time when the lord was having difficulty filling vacant tenements. Lands held at the will of the lord were never more than a small minority of the total after the Black Death and they had disappeared completely by the end of the fourteenth century. Life leases also gave way to short-term leases. Already by 1400-4 more than half of all land transfers were taken up on leases of nine years or less and by 1430 leases for the life of the tenant had been completely replaced by leases mostly for three or six years—leases for more than twelve years had virtually disappeared after the first quarter of the fifteenth century. Table XVI shows that the vast majority of the priory's leases were for terms of three years or multiples of three years. The only exceptions were some single-year leases of, among other properties, the mills, ferries, and ovens. A few ten-year leases also appeared at the very end of the fifteenth century.

There seems to have been the same trend on the episcopal lands. By the end of the fourteenth century the number of leases for specified periods was increasing and most were for short terms. Certainly by the end of the first quarter of the fifteenth century short leases were predominant. Thus of fifty-seven recorded transfers of land in the episcopal villages of south-east Durham between 1420 and 1424, thirteen were for a single year, eighteen for three years, six for six years, three for nine years, and one for fifteen years; the length of tenure for the other sixteen transfers was unspecified. Here, as on the priory's estate, leases of ten years or less seem to have been the norm.

What is less certain is why these short leases appear. They originated at a time when both bishop and priory were having to make concessions to get tenants for vacant holdings; thus

Table XVI

Length of tenures on the Durham Cathedral Priory manors, 1365-1499

	1-3 years (%)	4-6 years (%)	7-9 years (%)	10-12 years (%)	more than 12 years (%)	for lessee's life (%)	at lord's will (%)	Total number of recorded cases
1370-9	2					88	10	133
1380-9	6	13	2			72	6	71
1390-9	4	3	10	1		66	1	88
1400-9	16	17	19	9	16	22	1	98
1410-19	13	36	25	9	16	5		141
1420-9	32	42	15	8	12	2		143
1430-9	40	40	12	7	1			180
1440-9	40	50	7	2	1			132
1450-9	45	48	4	3	1			151
1460-9	47	42	7	3	1			199
1470-9	37	49	11	3				126
1480-9	56	36	6	1	1			170
1490-9	51	26	16	5	2			150

there is no instance when either lord was able to raise rents in the fifteenth century. With the economic tide running so strongly against the lord, it would indeed be surprising if he was the instigator of the change; certainly he might have bene-fited by being able to regulate rents and the detailed working of the land market, but as it seems to have been the tenants rather than the lord who were dictating conditions it is unlikely that this was what lay behind it. On the other hand it is difficult to see why the tenants would want leases for short terms. If the villagers had been interested in building up and safeguarding holdings, they would surely have wanted long leases. One possibility is that the tenants might have avoided paying entry fines by taking short leases; but although on the priory's lands the abandonment of entry fines coincided with the introduction of short leases this was not the case on the neighbouring episco-pal lands. Another possibility is that intensive cultivation to secure the highest possible yield would result in exhaustion within a few years; but this too is an unlikely explanation as in fact the south-east Durham villagers were retaining their land for longer periods, on average, after the introduction of short leases than they had before. Where a reference is made to admission and surrender to a particular piece of land it is pos-sible to calculate how long tenants held their lands. Over the period as a whole, tenants in each vill (except Carlton) held lands for an average of ten to fifteen years, the length of time being slightly longer on the episcopal estates than on the priory's. But in five of the eight vills tenants appear to have kept their holdings longer in the later period, after short leases had been introduced, than in the earlier period when life leases were the norm. Short leases, therefore, did not necessarily mean that tenants could not build up holdings and retain them for several years. Most tenants were given the option of renew-ing the lease on expiry and some did so. The court records reveal clearly that it was those who accumulated large holdings who renewed their leases; those with odd acres or cottages rarely did so. There appears to have been a direct link between the size of a tenement and the number of times a lease was renewed.

It has already been shown that the number of family trans-fers increased towards the end of the century. Many of these involved large amounts of land and several of those listed with large holdings in the later fifteenth century had the same surname. For example two of the wealthiest tenants at Cowpen Bewley in 1495-6 were Robert and William Clifton; at the same time the widow of Richard Clifton was listed as the lessee of the former manorial demesne at Bewley. The highest assessed tenant at Cowpen Bewley in 1495 was Robert Sheraton but another Sheraton, Thomas, also paid a high rent.[63] The same pattern can be detected in the other villages: by the later fifteenth century, some tenants could be distinguished from their fellows not only by the amount of land they held but also by the length of time they held it. It was the tenants who held large amounts of land who were renewing their leases and it was some of these who were passing down the land within the family.

In some places elsewhere, outsiders and newcomers seem to have played an active part in the land market in the later Middle Ages.[64] However, the majority of tenants in south-east Durham were not outsiders. They were villagers who appear in the court rolls as holding official positions or accused of petty misdemeanours. Thus of the 103 tenants involved in land transfers at Carlton during the period, 76 (74 per cent) were villagers who were mentioned at least once in the court rolls for a matter that did not concern land. At Cowpen Bewley the proportion was 72 per cent, at Stockton 71 per cent, at Norton and Wolviston 66 per cent, at Billingham 65 per cent, at Hartburn 64 per cent, and at Newton Bewley 56 per cent. The actual proportions of local inhabitants among the tenants were almost certainly much higher; many villagers must have held land without being mentioned in other connections in the court rolls. It is probably safe to assume that the majority of tenants in south-east Durham villages were inhabitants of those villages. But if there were few outsiders there were some newcomers. It is possible to find examples of large landholders who had not lived in their village for long. By no means all of the larger landowners were from old-established families. Some had arrived recently and made good almost immediately whereas others had come from families which had long been resident in the village and which had gradually extended their lands. There

[63] DCD BR, 1495-6.
[64] Above, pp. 189-92; Du Boulay, *Canterbury*, pp. 148-9.

was considerable variety; sometimes a wealthy tenant had inherited most of his land whilst sometimes his land had accumulated through his own endeavours.

John Hatcher has shown that the tenantry in late-medieval
Cornwall usually sought to acquire their leaseholds in the same
vill so that they held compact units.[65] This also seems to have
been the case in Durham. The names of the tenants holding in
the priory's vills in 1396 seldom appear in the records of neighbouring vills, whether on the same or a different estate.[66]
A hundred years later, only two of the ten wealthiest tenants in
the 1495-6 rental appear to have held land outside the vill
where they had the bulk of their holdings.[67] The tenants may,
of course, have held further afield but this is unlikely. A villager
who wished to extend his lands outside his own vill would
surely look to adjoining vills especially if there were vacant
tenements there. One can only conclude that most south-east
Durham landholders in the later Middle Ages did not seek land
outside their own vills. Nor do wealthy and influential outsiders appear to have taken an active part in the land market.
At the end of the Middle Ages the villages of south-east Durham
were self-contained communities, each an independent social
and tenurial unit.

In view of this it is not surprising that the major landholders
were much involved in the affairs of their own vills. Office-
holding was concentrated in the hands of a relatively small proportion of families; for example, it was confined to 12 per cent
of the Billingham villagers. The chief office-holders usually
came from amongst those who held large tenements.[68] Thus
the reeve usually came from among the two or three wealthiest
families in his vill and on both the priory's and the bishop's
estates in south-east Durham the office was never held by
anyone holding less than the standard bondage holding of
30 acres. The same is true of most other village offices. The four
or five jurors elected thrice yearly in each vill nearly always
came from among the better-off families; few cottagers held

[65] Hatcher, *Cornwall*, p. 230.
[66] DCD BR, 1396-7.
[67] DCD BR, 1495-6.
[68] This was usual elsewhere (e.g. Dewindt, *Holywell*, p. 224; N. Denholm-Young, *Seignorial Administration in England* (London, 1937), pp. 39-40).

this office. Thus on the priory's estate in 1382 all five jurors at Billingham held at least the standard tenement and four of the five jurors at Cowpen Bewley also had large holdings.[69] The only exception to this pattern was the office of ale-taster, a position usually filled by men holding little or no land.[70] Of the two tasters at Billingham in 1396, for instance, one held 1¼ acres of arable and the other held no land at all. The wealthier tenants did not serve in these positions of responsibility merely on isolated occasions. Many served in several offices, sometimes simultaneously. Robert Hardgill, one of the wealthiest tenants in Billingham, served between 1374 and 1400 as collector, constable, reeve, and juror, frequently holding two or three offices at the same time. Many served in office for many consecutive years and were actively involved in village affairs. John Saunderson, reeve of Billingham between 1365 and 1377, acted as a pledge to his fellow villagers on at least thirty-five occasions.

Some of the earlier generations of wealthy tenants came to nothing. The Hardgills, who were the largest tenants in Billingham in the later fourteenth century, had disappeared from there by 1411-12, and the Fawkes family, who were amongst the wealthiest in Cowpen Bewley after the Black Death, were not mentioned after 1396; seldom did the wealthy families of the period immediately after the Black Death become the rich families of the later fifteenth century. However, some of the landed families of the later fifteenth century do seem to have prospered in later centuries: the Barnes, Bellasis, Chapman, Culy, Davison, Jekill, Sheraton, and Thorpe families had all established themselves by the later fifteenth century and continued to prosper in the sixteenth. Of course, not everyone who held land prospered in the fifteenth century. But for many people there were new opportunities. There was plenty of available land which meant that tenants were no longer so concerned to pass it on within the family. Children could now seek better quality land. It was an age when the lord was having to offer incentives in order to persuade tenants to take on land; the only alternative was to have more land in his own hands.

---

[69] DCD HCR, spring to autumn 1382; BR, 1382-3.
[70] This contrasts with some other estates (e.g. Page, *Crowland*, p. 72; Dewindt, *Holywell*, p. 221).

4 THE LOCAL ECONOMY

The tenants' income

Land was of paramount importance to the medieval peasant. The halmote court records show clearly that the business of these courts was concerned predominantly with land and its exploitation: with tenures, with misdemeanours committed on the land, and with by-laws regulating its use. One of the foremost problems for the medieval peasant arose from the choice between corn and livestock for the land that was available. The court rolls show that straying animals were always a big problem in south-east Durham and that pigs and sheep were a particular nuisance;[1] a great many of the by-laws were concerned with the control of livestock either by regulating stints or by stipulating exactly how land was to be used. Even so the vast number of amercements shows that livestock created problems that were never adequately solved in south-east Durham. This was only one aspect of the measures needed to preserve the arable and protect the corn harvest. Because a tenant could always get land elsewhere there must have semed little need to tend and care for it, and in the later Middle Ages many of the by-laws and amercements concerned the preparation and condition of the arable. The Durham tenants were regularly amerced for not manuring their land as well as for not keeping their holdings in a good state of repair. Overall, the number of agrarian presentments increased during the fifteenth century; on the episcopal lands they almost doubled. As might be expected it was particularly the better-off tenants who were presented for agrarian offences; for example, of the fourteen individuals presented more than ten times for agrarian offences at Stockton between 1350 and 1500 every one held at least the standard customary tenement. Since most of the agrarian offences involved corn or livestock it was obvious that the wealthier villagers were more likely to be involved. It was, incidentally, these same villagers who were the most often amerced for other misdemeanours such as neglect of duties,

---

[1] This was a common state of affairs; see e.g. Ault, *Open-field Farming, passim*; W.O. Ault, 'The Village Church and the Village Community in Medieval England', *Speculum*, xlv (1970), 203.

failure to maintain tenements, or defaulting on debt. But the halmote courts did not particularly exploit the tenants; of the 3,155 individuals named in the records of the bishop's and priory's lands, 208 suffered more than ten amercements and only 60 more than twenty. Each of the bishop's tenants was amerced on average only 4.1 times, and each of the priory's tenants 3.0 times.

The debate concerning the wealth of the medieval peasant has been a long and protracted one; some historians see the peasantry as fairly wealthy, others see it as living not far from starvation level.[2] The discrepancy reflects the general difficulty in ascertaining the standard of living in later medieval England, a difficulty which arises, for the rural economy, from the shortcomings of the written records. Few of the activities many engaged in to supplement the unreliable income from agriculture are ever mentioned in the documents. Nor do they tell us much about the peasant's expenditure; even those payments to the manorial lord that are recorded in account rolls could well be amounts due rather than amounts actually paid, for a series of indentures for the Merton College villages shows that arrears of rent could be considerable. As for the amounts the villagers spent on food, drink, and clothing, the documents are completely silent. Any conclusions about the economic standing of the south-east Durham villagers can be no more than tentative.

However, the corn harvest must have been the basis of most villagers' income.[3] The soils of south-east Durham are low-lying and fertile and accordingly ideal for corn. Until 1343 Bewley supplied more wheat to the priory than any other demesne on the estate, even though it was one of the more distant manors from Durham.[4] After 1470 the vills in south-east Durham were usually the only ones on the priory estates where the tithes were not leased out to local farmers.[5] The amount of

[2] See e.g. Kosminsky, *Studies*, pp. 230-6; Bennett, *Eng. Manor*, p. 89; Howell, *Land, Family and Inheritance*, pp. 147-90; M.M. Postan, 'Investment in Medieval Agriculture', *Journal of Economic History*, xxvii (1967), 585; J.Z. Titow, *Eng. Rural Soc.*, p. 96.

[3] W.G. Hoskins, 'Harvest Fluctuations and English Economic History', *AgHR*, xii (1964), 29.

[4] Halcrow, 'Durh. Cath. Priory', p. 50.

[5] DCD BA, 1470-1500.

each type of corn collected as tithe was recorded in the bursar's account rolls along with the price per quarter. These figures are useful because a large tithe must have meant a good harvest and a small tithe a poor one. The price of corn was invariably high when the tithe was small, confirming that corn was generally scarce when the tithes were small.[6] If the lord did not exact the tithe in corn he exacted a money payment instead which was duly recorded.[7] When the tithe was small, however, no compensatory payment was listed.[8] It is unlikely that the prior allowed the villagers to avoid tithe payments in years of good harvest.[9]

No one type of corn appears to have been dominant in the area. At Billingham barley seems normally to have been the principal crop although large amounts of wheat often figured in the tithes. In the neighbouring vill of Cowpen Bewley wheat seems to have been the main crop and there is little reference to barley production. Barley was almost certainly the main crop at Newton Bewley although peas, beans, and oats were produced in fairly large quantities. Wolviston was producing more wheat than barley until the 1450s, but barley was probably more important in the second half of the century.

Prices each year were, however, always the same in all four priory vills. Wheat varied from 4s. 0d. to 13s. 4d. per quarter and barley from 3s. 0d. to 8s. 0d., but oats averaged only 2s. 0d. and peas were worth only slightly more. Rye usually fetched more than barley but less than wheat. Crops did not succeed or fail to the same degree.[10] A dry summer, for instance, would suit barley more than others. This is reflected in south-east

---

[6] e.g. DCD BA, 1482-3.

[7] e.g. DCD BA, 1381-2.

[8] e.g. DCD BA, 1402-3.

[9] It should be pointed out, however, that corn yields in the later Middle Ages were low almost everywhere. See e.g. R.V. Lennard, 'Statistics of Corn Yields in Medieval England: Some Critical Questions', *Economic History*, iii (1934-7), 181-92; B.H. Slicher van Bath, *Yield Ratios 810-1820* (Landbouwhogeschool, Afdeling Agrarische Geschiedenis, Bijdragen No. 10, Wageningen, 1963), *passim*; B.F. Brandon, 'Cereal Yields on the Sussex Estates of Battle Abbey during the Later Middle Ages', *EcHR*, 2nd ser., xxv (1972), 403-20; J.Z. Titow, *Winchester Yields* (Cambridge, 1972), pp. 43-120; D.L. Farmer, 'Grain Yields on the Winchester Manors in the Later Middle Ages', *EcHR*, 2nd ser., xxx (1977), 555-66.

[10] D.L. Farmer, 'Some Grain Price Movements in Thirteenth-century England', *EcHR*, 2nd ser., x (1957-8), 219.

Durham as the prices of the different grains never remained proportional to each other in the later Middle Ages. Harvest fluctuations have been studied for the later Middle Ages[11] and 1351, 1369, 1438, and 1482 have been seen as particularly bad years. The first two cannot be checked, but the other two were years of very high corn prices on the priory's lands. In fact 1438 appears to have been a year of dearth everywhere and it has been seen as the worst harvest year between 1316 and 1527.[12] If corn prices do reflect the success or failure of harvests, it seems the harvest failed also in 1401, 1409, 1410, 1432, 1437, and 1501. Bad harvests in south-east Durham usually coincide with those which Thorold Rogers identified in England as a whole, though with some variations, as in 1408, 1415, and 1416, when the area did not suffer the poor harvests recorded elsewhere. If there were bad harvests, however, there were also years when the harvests were good and plentiful. Rogers identified particularly good harvests in 1377, 1378, 1388, 1392-4, 1404-5, 1426, 1440, 1442, 1444, 1454, and 1463. Of these, 1388, 1394, 1404, 1426, and 1454 were certainly good years in south-east Durham; for the others no information survives. Corn prices in south-east Durham were below average in 1406-7, 1414, 1418, 1426, 1431, 1434-6, 1446, 1456-8, 1462, 1466, 1472-5, 1479, 1483, 1485, 1493-5, and 1498-9. Rogers estimated that almost one-third of harvests were bad ones in the later Middle Ages and that only about 10 per cent could be called good. In south-east Durham two harvests in every five produced below-average corn prices and large tithes and one in five produced prices far in excess of the average. Although one must treat these figures with caution, they point to rapid fluctuations in the economic position of the late-medieval south-east Durham villager.

While some villagers may have been living very close to the poverty line, others were clearly producing a large surplus in many years in this period. After the leasing of the manorial demesnes the priory adopted the practice of buying corn from tenants. A by-law was issued on the priory's lands in 1371, ordering that no corn was to be sold without the terrar's permission; and subsequent ordinances enjoined that the prior

[11] W.G. Hoskins in *AgHR*, xii (1964), 28-46.

[12] J.E.T. Rogers, *Six Centuries of Work and Wages* (London, 1884), p. 216.

was to have first refusal of the surplus corn of the tenants.[13] The bursar's account rolls record the amount of corn bought by the priory from individual tenants and often the amounts were considerable, especially in the second half of the fifteenth century. At Billingham never less than 100 quarters of barley were bought in any one year between 1455 and 1480 and the amount was usually nearer 200 quarters. In 1467-8 it totalled 213 quarters 7 bushels.[14] Large quantities of wheat were also bought at Billingham, often more than 40 quarters in a year, and similar amounts of wheat were also bought from the tenants of Cowpen Bewley. Even from the small village of Newton Bewley large amounts of corn were sold to the priory: from 1456 to 1480 there was only one year when less than 100 quarters of barley was sold.

Many individuals in these vills sold large amounts of corn consistently over many years. Of the Wolviston tenants who sold corn to the priory, 30 per cent sold it for ten years or more. In fact, comparing the 1495-6 rental with the names of those villagers who sold their excess corn to the lord, one finds that few tenants did not sell corn. Thus all nine of those who had more than a smallholding at Newton Bewley sold large amounts of corn to the priory. Even those with small tenements were sometimes able to sell surplus corn. In 1495 the rent of Robert Kirkham was just 4s. 9d. but he sold corn to the priory every year from 1494 to at least 1500; in 1498-9 he was paid £2. 7s. 3d. from this source.[15] Even those with high rents were sometimes able to pay for them with the corn sales to the lord. For example, the 1495-6 rental gives William Hert's rent as £5. 18s. 7d. but his sales of wheat and barley amounted to £6. 4s. in 1499-1500.[16] Many sold corn of more than one sort. All but 15 per cent of Billingham tenants who sold wheat to the priory also sold barley. Although the sales fluctuated, presumably with the harvests, it is clear that many priory villagers in the later fifteenth century were able to produce enough corn for their own family, pay corn dues such as tithe and multure, keep sufficient seed corn for the following year, and still have corn left over to sell to the priory.

[13] DCD HCR, spring 1371.
[14] DCD BA, 1467-8.
[15] DCD BA, 1498-9.
[16] DCD BA, 1499-1500.

In addition to corn, most tenants must have also owned animals. The enforcement of stints suggests that animals were plentiful in the vills and the proportion of persons amerced for offences with livestock on the episcopal estates ranged from 55 per cent of individuals amerced in the halmote courts at Norton to 68 per cent at Carlton. Unfortunately we do not know how many animals each of these people owned. Records of land transfers sometimes mention livestock; thus at Cowpen Bewley in 1370 Adam Dawson transferred two cows and a horse to his son, along with a messuage and 30 acres.[17] These, however, are minimum figures. The value of these animals to their owner cannot be assessed accurately, nor can the extent of losses from murrain. These certainly affected the south-east Durham stock. The stock keeper of the priory's principal sheep-rearing area at Le Holme accounted in 1351 for the loss through disease of 671 out of a total of 1,747 sheep, though by 1383 the number of sheep there had risen to 5,534.[18] Certainly some tenants further supplemented their income by selling livestock; thus Gilbert Fawkes of Billingham sold the priory a white horse in 1358-9 for £3. 6s. 8d. and another horse twelve years later for £2. 13s. 4d.[19]

There were other ways the villagers might supplement their income.[20] Many of the Cowpen Bewley bondage holders also held saltings and sold salt;[21] thus in 1478-9, 73 quarters were sold to the priory at 4s. 0d. per quarter.[22] In the century following the Black Death it was the wealthier villagers who were normally entrusted with collecting and delivering tithes, work for which they would be paid about £1. 10s. This was no easy task. In 1371-2 at Billingham, John Miryman spent twelve days collecting tithes with his cart but he was also assisted by three others who each worked for three weeks.[23] In the later

---

[17] DCD HCR, spring 1370.

[18] Halcrow, 'Durh. Cath. Priory', p. 76.

[19] DCD BA, 1358-9.

[20] Studies of other areas show that many tenants supplemented their income in a great variety of ways (e.g. Hatcher, *Cornwall*, pp. 222-5; H.C. Darby, *The Medieval Fenland* (Cambridge, 1940), p. 23).

[21] A salting is a salt-water marsh. There had been a salt industry in Cowpen Bewley since at least Roman times.

[22] DCD BA, 1478-9.

[23] DCD BA, 1371-2.

fifteenth century this task passed to professional carters although villagers would occasionally supplement their income by carting outside the area, especially to Durham. Others worked for the lord as builders. The priory appears to have hired men to repair not only manorial buildings, mill, and church, but also the buildings of tenants which had not been maintained. Although some of these were professional craftsmen such as Thomas Laycan, a carpenter employed in 1380-1 at 2s. 0d. per week,[24] most seem to have been part-timers.[25] They included men like William Wodrofe, one of the largest landholders at Wolviston in the later fifteenth century, who, if the records are to be believed, was paid for thirty-eight different repair jobs.[26] Much of the skilled work in repairs was done by outsiders, but more of the less skilled tasks were done by villagers, such as the three people from Stockton who earned £10. 13s. 4d. in 1412-13 by ferrying stores across the river Tees.[27] In fact, over half the men recorded as carrying out repairs for the priory can be identified as tenants who held at least a standard customary tenement. Ale was normally brewed by women, but it was often the wives of the better-off tenants who were the brewers. On the episcopal lands, thirty-five of the fifty-five brewers were wives of men who held offices in the vills; on the priory estates seventy of the 114 recorded brewers were either men who held offices or their wives.[28]

It was the more wealthy tenants who leased the village ovens and in the later fourteenth century it was usually they who held the mills, but in the fifteenth century most of the millers seem not to have been local people. Both the bishop and prior had ferries across the Tees. The priory shared its ferry at Billingham with the landowner on the Yorkshire side so that the lessee of the ferry in the later Middle Ages could take only a half share in the business. The first recorded lease was in 1422 when Adam Lawson, a tenant, took it for nine years for a rent of £2. Throughout the rest of the fifteenth century the lease was

[24] DCD BA, 1380-1.

[25] Wages could be quite considerable (E.H. Phelps Brown and S.V. Hopkins, 'Seven Centuries of Building Wages and Prices', *Economica*, xxii (1955), 202).

[26] This, of course, is based on the assumption that there was only one William Wodrofe. It is also possible that he subcontracted the work.

[27] DBR CC 188926.

[28] This accords with Raftis, *Warboys*, p. 237.

always taken by one of the priory's better-off tenants.[29] Whether the ferry brought in much revenue is uncertain; there was little settlement on the other side of the river and there was the bishop's ferry at nearby Stockton besides a bridge 4 miles away at Yarm. The bishop's ferry does not seem to have been profitable. In 1407 John Osborne of Stockton leased it for eight years at £4 rent, yet in 1438 John Stanlawman paid only £2. 6s. 8d. for a year's lease.[30] In the later fifteenth century the boat was often in the lord's hands for considerable lengths of time. As with the priory's ferry, however, it was nearly always the wealthier villagers who were the lessees.

The tenants' expenditure

The largest single item of expenditure for most tenants will have been the annual rent, and for those who by the late fifteenth century had built up very large holdings this might be a considerable amount. Most rents remained fixed; on both the bishop's and the priory's estate less than 10 per cent of all land transfers between 1350 and 1500 involved a change of rent. Only very rarely before 1400 and never in the fifteenth century was this change an increase. However, this stability is really an illusion since it seems as if many tenants were failing to pay their rents in full. The escalating debts of the accounting officials suggest that the number may have been large.[31] This applied even to the wealthier tenants. In 1377-8 William Jackson was excused £1. 6s. 8d. of the farm of Bellasis manor; and in 1386-7 Robert Hardgill, John Lucklyn, and William Raynald, who were all wealthy Billingham tenants, were allowed £1. 11s. 4d. off their rents.[32] Arrears often built up for the leased demesne lands. For example, in 1384-5 £11. 0s. 8d. was owed by the demesne tenants of Cowpen Bewley.[33] A few villagers seem to have been building up long-standing debts. At Stillington in 1400 eleven villagers had been in debt for more than two

[29] DCD HCB i, summer 1422.

[30] PRO DUR 3/13 (spring 1397), 15 (summer 1438).

[31] Although the arrears in medieval accounts can be misleading (A.J. Pollard, 'Estate Management in the Later Middle Ages: the Talbots and Whitchurch, 1383-1525', *EcHR*, 2nd ser., xxv (1972), 564-5).

[32] DCD BA, 1377-8, 1386-7.

[33] DCD BA, 1384-5.

years and one even owed his rent for 1385; many of these tenants owed substantial amounts, such as William Knollat who owed 3*s*. 8*d*. for 1395 and £1. 12*s*. for 1396, 1397, 1399, and 1400.[34] It should be added, however, that many of these debts were later repaid. Besides the rents, villagers owed their lord other dues, some of them still considerable.[35] Tenants at Billingham in the fifteenth century were liable to thirteen different regular dues. There were also other occasional payments such as the entry fine, merchet, heriot, and mortuary due. Villagers also had to pay for amercements for their various misdemeanours though these can hardly have been financially crippling; in the last quarter of the fifteenth century the total revenue which was exacted in the halmote courts from the five principal episcopal vills rarely exceeded £1.

Villagers had many other expenses besides payments to the lord; there was multure to be paid to the miller and a rent to the baker for the common oven. It also seems that many villagers had their own servants;[36] obviously this would apply largely to the wealthier tenantry. Four-fifths of all identifiable employees on the priory's lands worked for families who held at least the standard customary tenement. Some of the larger tenants had more than one employee; John Alanson of Newton Bewley had at least two maid-servants and John Pottow of Wolviston had one maid-servant and one man.[37]

The ordinary villager of south-east Durham probably devoted little of his income to luxuries. Several lists of *principalia* have survived for the priory's estates. These goods which a tenant left behind when he died were often very scanty. For example, in 1379 the listed possessions of Thomas son of Gilbert of Cowpen Bewley amounted only to 1½ quarters of wheat, a sleeveless tunic, and one brass bowl (*olla enea*).[38] Even the houses of the larger tenants, however, contained only the barest and roughest of furniture; even beds were seldom mentioned. The only items that were widely owned were basic farming implements: ploughs, carts, harrows, scythes, sickles,

---

[34] MM 6047.
[35] Above, pp. 268-75.
[36] This might apply especially to the old (Hilton, *Eng. Peasantry*, p. 50).
[37] DCD HCR, summer 1382, autumn 1385, autumn 1390.
[38] DCD HCR, spring 1379.

spades, forks, hoes, mattocks, seed-lips, and flails.[39] Nor does the medieval villager in south-east Durham appear to have spent very much on the repair of his house; the records show that many were allowed to fall into disrepair and, as we have seen, the lord frequently helped financially with the repair of buildings.

Deficient though they are, the south-east Durham records do show that in the later Middle Ages there were opportunities to supplement from other sources an income based on agriculture. For some of the villagers at least the times must have seemed prosperous. The records of south-east Durham can be seen as supporting the conclusion of A.R. Bridbury that this was a period of tremendous advance 'for its achievements in enlarging the range and enriching the quality of the freedom enjoyed by those who neither rule kingdoms nor control provinces'.[40] Not that all could have lived like this; there is every likelihood that some of the south-east Durham villagers were living perilously close to the poverty line. Nevertheless, the records show that some landholders seized the opportunity for wealth at this time. Some at least would have recognized Thorold Rogers's description of the fifteenth century as 'a golden age of the English husbandman, the artisan and the labourer'.[41]

South-east Durham in this period, then, does not appear very different from other parts of England. Field systems, agrarian practices, tenants, could all be paralleled in most parts of the country. As we have seen, only a minority of tenants held by non-customary free tenure. Labour services of about three days per week in the mid-fourteenth century were not exceptional; neither was their date of commutation. As elsewhere there was a breakdown of the connection between tenure and legal status in the later Middle Ages. As on estates in the south and midlands, there was a land market in south-east Durham in the later Middle Ages. Land passed outside the

[39] R.K. Field, 'Worcestershire Peasant Buildings, Household Goods and Farming Equipment in the Later Middle Ages', *Medieval Archaeology*, ix (1965), 122-5, 137-45, shows that this was the case elsewhere.

[40] A.R. Bridbury, *Economic Growth: England in the Later Middle Ages* (London, 1962), p. 108.

[41] J.E.T. Rogers, *A History of Agriculture and Prices in England* (London, 7 vols., 1866-1902), iv. 23.

family and there was plenty of spare land as the demesnes were farmed out and the high mortality of the times created vacant tenements. As elsewhere there was a tendency for families to build up large holdings. The village hierarchy was not peculiar to this area, nor was the fact that the village officials were usually drawn from the wealthier unfree tenants. The ordinary south-east Durham villager seems to have suffered the same trials and tribulations as his counterparts elsewhere; fears of murrain or a failed harvest must have haunted many late-medieval villagers.

This does not mean that rural society was uniform throughout late-medieval England. Some of the Durham renders such as cornage were rare outside the northern counties; subletting seems to have been less frequent than in many other places; the predominance of local villagers in the fifteenth-century land market and the short length of time that many persons spent in office were certainly not the pattern everywhere in the country. There were even differences between the villages within the area; we have seen how entry fines were retained on the bishop's lands but not on the priory's. But on the whole it seems that the lives of these villagers sufficiently resembled not only those elsewhere in the county but also those in many other parts of the country to rule out any sharp local or regional peculiarities.

The most depressing fact to emerge from this study is that the medieval records are so deficient. The south-east Durham material yields an impressive amount of information but it still leaves too many unanswered questions. Simple social questions like how much parental concern there was for children or what friends the average villager had cannot be answered. There is no information on how hard the medieval peasant really had to work or how he occupied his leisure time. Was there a communal spirit? How much respect was shown to landlords? What was the villagers' attitude generally to life? The medieval documents provide no clues to these problems. To others they supply inconclusive answers. The records of the bishop and priory touch on mortality rates, marriage patterns, population figures, and the amount of mobility, but far more evidence is needed to draw conclusions that are anything but tentative.

VI   Conclusion

1 FORMS OF TENURE

An important book by C.M. Gray on the origin of the legal protection offered to copyholders was published in 1963. In it he looked critically at the conclusions of A. Savine and I.S. Leadam, who had argued that copyholders could successfully bring cases concerning their holdings to the Court of Chancery before (probably well before) 1467 and to the Court of Common Pleas by 1482. Gray showed that the evidence for these dates can be differently interpreted and argued that both were too early. Instead it was only in Henry VII's reign that these cases could be brought to Chancery with any hope of success and not until the 1550s that the common-law courts began to take cognizance of cases over copyhold.[1]

This revised chronology at once leads us to ask why the royal courts were so slow in bringing these copyhold cases within their scope.[2] The last three chapters help to provide an answer. We have seen how John Broughton, esquire, the manorial lord of Toddington (Bedfordshire) held some copyhold land at Leighton Buzzard in 1466; R.H. Hilton has shown that copyhold tenants at Cheltenham included John Throckmorton, esquire, in 1430 and William Grevile, lawyer and judge, later in the fifteenth century.[3] But on the whole it was clearly still unusual for lands to be held in copyhold by members of the gentry, or even by the moderately well-to-do; the speculative market in copyhold land was in its infancy, though we have seen it operating in or beside small towns at Speenhamland and

---

[1] Gray. *Copyhold*, pp. 16-34, 54-68. The contrary arguments of Kerridge, *Agr. Problems*, pp. 65-93, have failed to win acceptance among legal historians (*The Reports of Sir John Spelman*, ed. J.H. Baker (Selden Soc., vols. xciii, xciv; 1977-8), ii. 184-7).

[2] Raftis, *Tenure*, p. 204 n, interestingly puts the opposite question: given that the copyhold cases brought before the royal courts in the 16th century were often the same sorts of grievance as came before manorial courts, why had the manorial court become inadequate to uphold customary law?

[3] Above, p. 246 (cf. the cases mentioned on pp. 189-90, 192, where the late dates may well be significant); Hilton, *Eng. Peasantry*, p. 69.

Leighton Buzzard.[4] Nearly all copyholders were local tenants whose estates were not only small but transitory; again, it was of a later generation of more firmly established families that it could be said, in 1584, that the copyholders of Hertfordshire were 'the most substantialest men of the country'.[5] Hardly any fifteenth-century copyholders could muster the influence and resources that would be needed to persuade the royal courts to break with precedent and hear their grievances—and therewith diminish the rights and powers of their manorial lords. In any case the growing formality and regular routine of late-medieval manorial courts will have given customary tenants increasing security without recourse to the further protection of the royal courts.

But if Gray's work raised this new problem it at once solved a much larger one posed by the chronology of Savine and Leadam: how was it, if the royal courts and lawyers were already taking an interest in them, that customary tenures had escaped their tendency to define and to standardize and were still at the end of the fifteenth century in such an extraordinary muddle? For muddle is what it was. We have seen this clearly in Berkshire and Bedfordshire and it appears too in studies of other areas in the late Middle Ages.[6] It is not just that there were great differences between one place and another in the forms and conditions of tenures; there was not even any particular consistency in terminology. But this is no more than we would expect, given that the tenures developed locally and that the significance of the words describing them would be called in question only in the manorial court. It follows that we should be careful not to suppose that particular words—tenure by copy, at will, in bondage, and so on—had any sort of technical meaning or connotation outside the manor where they were used; there was no need for them to, for as long as they clearly established that these tenures were customary the local interpretation was all that mattered. Nor, of course, should we fall into the related error of carrying back into late-fourteenth- and fifteenth-century customary tenures the rules that the common law later came to devise for copyhold. They simply did not

---

[4] Above, pp. 145, 234.
[5] J.E. Neale, *The Elizabeth House of Commons* (London, 1949), p. 96.
[6] e.g. Harvey, *Westminster*, pp. 268-93; Hilton, *Leics. Estates*, pp. 94-105, 121-30.

apply. To the seventeenth-century lawyer copyhold could be extinguished but could never be created or reactivated; there could be no such thing as changing a property into copyhold from some other form of tenure. Yet we find for instance that at Harmondsworth (Middlesex) in 1390 customary land had been converted to freehold, then brought back into customary tenure again.[7]

With all this local diversity it is hardly surprising that it is difficult to see any pattern in the way local tenures developed over this period. Certainly there was regional variation—we have seen this already. By 1300 the rapidly changing structure of local holdings in Norfolk was producing a diversity of tenures that was far from developing generally in the more conservative fourteenth-century Berkshire and Bedfordshire, while in Durham we are in a different world again, an area where there were scarcely more than minimal changes in tenures between 1350 and 1500. We may reasonably suppose that what happened in Norfolk happened elsewhere in East Anglia too; that what we find in Berkshire and Bedfordshire was common to much of midland and central southern England; and that the manors of three estates in south-east Durham epitomize far wider areas of north-east England. But the extent and significance of such regional variations remain to be discovered.

It would be simpler to identify these variations if we could easily classify the various types of local tenure that we find. But this is harder than might appear. One straightforward distinction that could be made is between contractual and customary tenure—a very basic distinction corresponding to the thirteenth century's separation of free tenure from tenure in villeinage. This distinction was familiar to people at the time; it underlies the late-fourteenth century order to the tenants of Englefield that they should show whether they held 'for life, for years, by copy or by charter' as well as the simple division at Kibworth Harcourt (Leicestershire) between tenants who held in bondage and those who held at will.[8] It is not surprising that

---

[7] G. Jacob, *A New Law-dictionary* (London, 1729), under Copyhold (cf. E. Coke, *The Compleate Copy-holder* (London, 1641), pp. 52-3); J.S. Beckerman, 'Customary Law', pp. 134-5, 367-9 (from PRO SC 2/191/15, m. 7).

[8] Above, p. 151; Cicely Howell in Goody, Thirsk, & Thompson, pp. 132-3.

historians have adopted this classification.[9] In theory it was a very clear-cut one. In the last resort the courts—the royal courts of common law—would have been able to decide to which category any particular holding belonged. But in practice, in everyday local life, the distinction may well have been hard to draw. We have seen how on some holdings on the 1292 Martham survey the distinction between socage and villein tenure was forgotten; how at South Moreton in the late fourteenth century the court rolls fail to show whether particular tenures were customary, with copies, or contractual, with charters; how at Shillington in the late fourteenth and fifteenth centuries leases of parcels of demesne land soon took on aspects of customary tenure, apparently without formal or conscious change; how in fifteenth-century Eastrop it could be recorded that the manorial court, perhaps even the tenant, 'does not know how he holds this land'.[10] We might expect this sort of confusion to arise. By the fifteenth century it seems to have made no difference to the peasant's social status whether his lands were held by contractual or customary tenure[11]—indeed, many held properties both ways. Nor were the free tenures necessarily more favourable economically; on the Durham Cathedral Priory estates the renders due from certain free holdings were so like those of similar customary tenements that they had probably been converted from unfree tenures without alteration of the obligations.[12]

The complexities of local tenures did not start with the Black Death of 1348-9. Certainly we may say that a fairly simple structure of free tenures, villein and cottage holdings was typical of the thirteenth- and early-fourteenth-century manor. But we do not have to look far to find more elaborate arrangements, even outside East Anglia or other areas where rapid division of holdings had complicated the picture. Indeed, the twelfth- and thirteenth-century lawyers and common-law courts, in defining villein unfreedom and its attendant disabilities, may certainly have helped to standardize and simplify local forms of

---

[9] Thus Hilton, *Decline*, pp. 44-51, and Harvey, *Westminster*, pp. 244-93. On the Westminster Abbey estate this logical and straightforward classification clearly works well—but this was a carefully administered estate and if it works less well elsewhere this is not necessarily for want of Westminster's superb archives.

[10] Above, pp. 71, 137-8, 206 (cf. Davenport, *Norf. Manor*, p. 57), 149.

[11] Thus above, pp. 197, 234.

[12] Above, p. 276.

tenure, but they also introduced further complications; their distinction between villeinage by birth and villeinage by tenure pointed the way to a possible fourfold division between free or unfree land held by free or unfree tenants.[13] Thus on the Peterborough Abbey estates in the late thirteenth century any free lands acquired by a villein tenant would be seized by the abbey and granted back to him to hold at the lord's will; this was quite distinct from the customary tenure by which he held his basic holding in the manor.[14] Again, a survey of Sandal (Yorkshire) in 1309 divides tenants into free tenants, villeins (*nativi*), and customary tenants (*custumarii*); only the villeins paid the servile dues of merchet and leyrwite.[15] There was a similar division at Cadland (Hampshire).[16] In Cornwall and parts of Devon there had developed before the fourteenth century a form of leasing known as conventionary tenure, tenure *per conventionem*, which came to be available to both free and unfree tenants.[17]

But if the Black Death did not begin the process of diversifying local tenures it certainly speeded it up. Some changes were a direct and immediate result of the loss of tenants in the plague. In some places manorial lords tried to attract new tenants by offering lighter rents and other improved conditions of tenure; a neat example is on Eynsham Abbey's manor of Woodeaton (Oxfordshire) where, according to a survey of 1366, 'In the time of the mortality of men, the plague which was in the year 1349, there scarcely remained two tenants in the said manor, and they would have left if Brother Nicholas de Upton, then abbot, had not come to a new agreement with them and other surviving tenants'.[18] Here it was simply a question of altering the obligations of villein tenure. Elsewhere completely new tenures were introduced specifically as a stopgap measure. We have seen how villein tenements at Woolstone in the 1350s were divided between lessees who were to hold 'until a tenant

[13] Hyams, *King, Lords, and Peasants*, pp. 107-19.

[14] King, *Peterborough*, pp. 99-102; cf. Davenport, *Norf. Manor*, p. 70.

[15] PRO DL 43/11/17 (I am grateful to Mr D. Bruynseels and Ms M. Stinson for this information).

[16] D.G. Watts, 'Peasant Discontent on the Manors of Titchfield Abbey, 1245-1405', *Proceedings of the Hampshire Field Club and Archaeological Society*, xxxix (1983), pp. 126-7.

[17] Hatcher, *Cornwall*, pp. 52-3, 71-3.

[18] *Eynsham Cart.*, ii. 19.

shall be found who will perform the due and accustomed services'.[19] These would-be temporary tenures can be paralleled elsewhere. They are found at this time on the Westminster Abbey estate and Barbara Harvey has shown that its policy towards its local tenants in the generation after the Black Death assumed that eventually pre-plague conditions would return; it was only after about 1390 that a greater realism prevailed.[20]

In the longer term the usual way of achieving greater flexibility was by leasing, letting out holdings for fixed periods of years or of lives. This could be common-law leasehold, contractual tenure that might be confirmed by a written agreement. Or it could be within the framework of customary tenure, administered wholly through the manorial court. We can detect a gradual growth in leasing in the half-century before the Black Death and a much faster growth in the half-century after.[21] At first it was often small portions of demesne that were leased out to local tenants,[22] but we increasingly find other holdings being leased as well. At Woolstone leasing had begun by 1345; the stopgap tenures introduced in the 1350s took the form of leases; and in the 1390s entire tenements started to be leased for terms of years. At Englefield by the late fourteenth century hereditary customary tenure had been replaced apparently by customary tenure with a fixed term, of years or of lives. In south-east Durham customary tenure for a single life only was prevalent in the mid-fourteenth century, but over the next century came to be replaced by leases for ever shorter terms of years.[23] These developments were typical, but we have seen that they were not universal; on the estates of Westminster Abbey and the bishopric of Worcester leases gave way to hereditary tenures in the early fifteenth century and there must have been many places like Mackney or Arlesey where throughout the fifteenth century

[19] Above, p. 124.
[20] *VCH Oxon.*, vi. 214 (Islip, a Westminster Abbey manor); Harvey, *Westminster*, pp. 244-5, 247, 268-9. Durham Cathedral Priory provides other examples (Halcrow in *EcHR*, 2nd ser., vii (1954-5), 348-9. Woolstone was a manor of Winchester Cathedral Priory, and it may be significant that these estates all belonged to old Benedictine houses.
[21] e.g. Miller, *Ely*, p. 110; Dyer, *Lords and Peasants*, p. 120; Harvey, *Westminster*, pp. 236, 248-56.
[22] Above, pp. 26.
[23] Above, pp. 125, 151, 311.

all tenures were hereditary.[24] The form and development of local tenures seem to have varied a great deal from one place to another and the easiest—and probably the most revealing— way to classify them is simply by their length: hereditary, or limited to one or more lives or to a term of years, or (as we shall see) held at the lord's will.

All the same some general trends can be seen. The spread of leases, of limited tenures, was a move towards greater flexibility. It was also part of a move towards closer definition of tenures, towards stipulating actual conditions and obligations instead of leaving them to be determined, as occasion arose, as declared local custom in the manorial court. This has already been noticed at Brightwalton, and in fact the entries on manorial court rolls of admissions to holdings usually become more and more detailed, more and more specific, as time goes on.[25] We have seen other instances of the same trend in the precise definition of entry fines at Blunham and (a much more usual development) of heriots of South Moreton and Eastrop.[26] Other developments have been more often discussed: the rapid and almost total disappearance of week-work as a form of rent, the more gradual but steady decline of boon-work obligations, the decline of the various incidents and disabilities of servile tenure. All these are commonplace, though we still have much to learn of their detailed chronology and of their variations between different regions and different estates. Closely related is the decline in the number of tenants whom manorial lords claimed to be villeins by blood.[27] Even in the conservative Durham, where the cathedral priory was still compiling lists of its villeins, there were few of them in the mid-fourteenth century, and a hundred years later hardly any at all.[28] At the other end of England, in Cornwall, villeins are last heard of in 1406.[29] In the manors we have looked at in Berkshire and Bedfordshire

---

[24] Harvey, *Westminster*, pp. 276-8; Dyer, *Lords and Peasants*, pp. 292-4; above pp. 142, 216.

[25] Above, p. 133. The gradual elaboration of formulas of admission can be followed on the court rolls of the Cambridgeshire manors of Crowland Abbey, 1290-1430, printed in Page, *Crowland*, pp. 331-448.

[26] Above, pp. 198, 138, 148; cf. Dyer, *Lords and Peasants*, pp. 285-6.

[27] Thus Hilton, *Eng. Peasantry*, pp. 24-5; Harvey, *Westminster*, pp. 275-6; Dyer, *Lords and Peasants*, pp. 269-75 (cf. p. 242).

[28] Above, p. 282.

[29] Hatcher, *Cornwall*, pp. 61-2.

the question of personal villeinage seems practically never to have arisen. When manorial lords in the sixteenth century claimed that their tenants were villeins by blood we see either isolated pockets of continuing archaic custom or else deliberate attempts to resurrect a legal concept that was in practice long dead.[30] All these trends form the general background to two further developments in tenures: the spread of one old form, tenure at will, and the emergence of one new one, copyhold.

Tenure at will was known to Bracton, and although it was not common before the late fourteenth century there is no difficulty in finding instances of it much earlier. On the bishopric of Ely estates in 1251 some tenements were held 'from year to year at the will of the lord'.[31] The phrase seems to have meant what it said: tenure could be ended or renegotiated whenever the landlord wished. C.M. Gray has pointed out that this was effectively the position of free men who held villein lands,[32] and it is interesting that, as we have already seen, in the late thirteenth century the abbot of Peterborough applied it to the reverse situation, to free lands acquired by his villeins which he had taken into his own hands and granted back to them again. In the second half of the fourteenth century tenure at will seems to have spread. Thus on the estates of Westminster Abbey and the bishopric of Worcester—to take two recent studies—we find it being used along with leasing as a tenure that offered the flexibility that lords were seeking in the generation or so after the Black Death, but by the early fifteenth century it had declined sharply in favour of more stable, more closely defined, arrangements—a change that can be paralleled by its disappearance from Durham Cathedral Priory's lands at about the same time.[33] In some places, however, what was called simply tenure at will continued throughout the fifteenth century; thus in 1472 the tenants of Tilsworth (Bedfordshire) were divided between those who held freely and those who held at will.[34] There may well have been a regional difference; we do

[30] Hilton, *Decline*, pp. 49-50, gives interesting examples; Kerridge, *Agr. Problems*, pp. 90-2.
[31] Miller, *Ely*, pp. 109-10, 136 n.
[32] Gray, *Copyhold*, p. 6.
[33] Harvey, *Westminster*, pp. 246-8, 276-7; Dyer, *Lords and Peasants*, pp. 292-4; above, p. 311.
[34] Godber, *Beds.*, p. 139.

not find simple tenure at will on any of our Berkshire or Bedfordshire manors, whereas in late-fourteenth- and fifteenth-
century Leicestershire it seems to have been quite common.[35]

However, this may reflect a verbal rather than a tenurial
difference, for it is not always easy to distinguish simple tenure
at will, without further qualification, from what we do find on
several of our Berkshire manors and commonly elsewhere too,
that is the addition of the phrase 'at the will of the lord' to the
description of tenures that are very much more closely and
elaborately defined.[36] This too can be found well before the
mid-fourteenth century. On the Gloucester Abbey estates in
the 1260s some tenants who owed heriot, merchet, and other
characteristically villein obligations were said to hold 'at the
will of the lord for life by fixed service'.[37] On the published
court rolls of Crowland Abbey's three Cambridgeshire manors,
starting in 1290, we find the phrase occurring in successive formulas for admission to nearly all customary holdings.[38] Its
occasional omission there may be a slip or a change in style by
clerk or steward;[39] it is unlikely to reflect any tenurial distinction. By the late fourteenth century the usage was not uncommon—it occurs for instance on St. Albans Abbey's manorial
court rolls[40]—and in the fifteenth century we find it applied to
tenures variously defined and of varying lengths. We have seen
it occurring in tenants' admissions for terms of lives at Coleshill
and Brightwalton and for indefinite, hereditary tenure at
Brightwalton and Mackney.[41] In Leicestershire it was certainly
used for grants for specified terms or by customary tenure as
well as for simple tenure at will.[42] The general purport of the
phrase was of course to underline the precariousness of the
tenure, to show that the tenant had no rights at common law,[43]

---

[35] Hilton, *Leics. Estates*, pp. 95-6, 122-3, 127; Cicely Howell in Goody, Thirsk, &
Thompson, pp. 132-3.

[36] Harvey, *Westminster*, p. 246, gives a very clear account of this distinction.

[37] Hilton, *Eng. Peasantry*, p. 145.

[38] Thus, as instances of successive formulas, Page, *Crowland*, pp. 332 (1290), 355
(1326), 393 (1355: applied to tenure for life, not indefinite), 421 (1394).

[39] Ibid., pp. 333, 346-7.

[40] Levett, *Studies*, p. 153.

[41] Above, Ch. III, section 2.

[42] Hilton, *Leics. Estates*, p. 127; Cicely Howell in Goody, Thirsk, & Thompson, p.
134.

[43] Gray, *Copyhold*, p. 9.

but it would be wrong to see its use—or its absence—as having particular legal meaning. It seems to have been no more than a common form that might or might not be included. In some places a distinction was made between simple customary tenure, which was specifically 'at the will of the lord', and tenure by copy, which was seen as giving greater security; this was the case on the estates of Ramsey Abbey, and we have seen that it may also have been so at Brightwalton.[44] But in some places too, tenure by copy was itself described as being at will; at Cuxham (Oxfordshire) we find in 1488 a tenant who held specifically by copy of court roll at the will of the lord, but the same combination is implied by earlier references there to the customary tenants in general as holding by copy (in 1398) and at will (as in 1458).[45]

We can trace the beginning of copyhold, tenure by copy of court roll, back to the early fourteenth century. But until the Court of Chancery started to take a regular interest in it at the very end of the fifteenth century it would again be wrong to see a tenant's possession of a copy of the court-roll entry of his admission as having any technical significance, or indeed to suppose that there was such a thing as copyhold in the sense of a distinctive tenure except occasionally in a purely local context. In a few places a distinction seems to have been drawn between the more privileged of the customary tenants who were given copies and the less privileged who were not; thus we have seen that at Willington the half-virgaters held by copy.[46] But more often, as at Leighton Buzzard,[47] it was simply a matter of form for most or all of the customary tenants to be given copies, a matter of convenience for tenant and lord alike. Copies might be given for tenures of any length: at Willington they were for a term of years or for life, at Englefield for life, at Leighton Buzzard for indefinite hereditary tenure.[48] The vagueness or inconsistency of the terminology used at Cuxham can be found elsewhere. On the Westminster Abbey estates copies were demonstrably given to customary tenants, possibly regularly and commonly, from the second half of the fourteenth century on, but their tenure is practically never said to be

---

[44] Raftis, *Tenure*, p. 202; above, p. 134.
[45] MM 5923, m. 7; 5932; 5940.
[46] Above, p. 203.
[47] Above, p. 233.
[48] Above, pp. 203, 151, 233; cf. pp. 192-3.

'by copy' before the sixteenth century.[49] It follows that early references to tenure by copy may be an inadequate guide to the spread of the practice of giving tenants copies of court roll. For what it is worth they suggest that the process was a slow one; we have seen the earliest references to copies at Woolstone in 1372 (of an admission in 1349), at Willington in 1383, at Leighton Buzzard in 1413, at Coleshill in 1528-9.[50] But they can be found much earlier. In a careful and perceptive study of the procedures recorded in manorial court rolls J.S. Beckerman has shown how in the second half of the thirteenth century the practice arose of calling the court's own rolls in evidence in questions arising over particular holdings, this being one aspect of an increasing tendency to refer to written records as proof rather than to manorial juries. Then, in the early fourteenth century, we find not the court's original rolls but tenants' own extracts or copies being used for this purpose—by 1311 on the St. Albans Abbey estates, by 1315 on Earl Warenne's manor of Wakefield (Yorkshire).[51] By 1500 the copy of court roll had already a long history behind it, but copyhold, as the legally recognized tenure to which it gave rise, was only starting to come into being. It is in no way surprising, and may not even be significant, that the fifteenth-century records of south-east Durham do not refer to tenure by copy.

2 LAND MARKET, LORD, AND TENANT

We have seen that townsmen would often acquire lands either in the fields of the town and its hamlets, as at Leighton Buzzard, or in neighbouring manors, as at Speenhamland and Eastrop, where the land market was all but dominated by tenants from Newbury and Highworth.[1] Earlier in Bedfordshire, in 1297, men of Dunstable were prominent as sub-tenants in Caddington and Kensworth, a couple of miles away.[2]

---

[49] Harvey, *Westminster*, pp. 280 n, 284-5; cf. above, pp. 140-1.

[50] Above, pp. 130, 203, 233, 156. On the adoption of written copies cf. pp. 130, 138-9, 148.
Court Rolls of the Manor of Wakefield, ed. W.P. Baildon and others (Yorks. Archaeological Soc., 5 vols., 1901-45), iii. 149).

[1] Above, pp. 232, 142-6.

[2] A. Jones, 'Caddington, Kensworth, and Dunstable in 1297', *EcHR*, 2nd ser., xxxii (1979), 324-6; cf. Hatcher, *Cornwall*, p. 248, and Searle, *Battle*, pp. 128-32.

Townsmen might go a little farther afield. A Hartlepool merchant had land at Wolviston, while men of Hitchin had lands at Arlesey and also at Knebworth and Offley—all of them places between 3 and 6 miles from the town.[3] Some of this land may have been acquired by town butchers for grazing; at Adisham (Kent) butchers from Canterbury and Sandwich, both about 6 miles away, would buy land which they would sell again after. a short period.[4] But mostly it must have been either to supplement a living gained from a trade or craft or simply as an investment to sublet to local husbandmen. We can see the fifteenth-century Londoners who acquired land at Leighton Buzzard and other places in Bedfordshire in the same light;[5] the city's size and, presumably, the strong competition for lands closer at hand led them to look for investment to more distant centres that were linked to London by trade or direct routes.

With these exceptions it was the local inhabitants who took part in the local land market. In south-east Durham, the one area where we have looked at a complete block of land, tenants do not even seem to have acquired lands in neighbouring vills to add to their holdings.[6] The scattered places investigated in Berkshire and Bedfordshire cannot give us such clear evidence, but deeds of 1350-1500 from both counties give the impression that tenants' lands were mostly in the vills where they lived; typically both parties are described as belonging to the place where the lands lay. This of course could well have differed a good deal from one region to another, but at least it seems likely that the rural land market of this period was mostly intensely local. But this was a time of new or increased mobility; those who were acquiring land may already have been living in the vill or they may have been newcomers, moving in from outside.[7] Conversely, of course, the land may have come on the market because it had been given up by those who had moved

[3] Above, pp. 280, 221; Roden, 'Chiltern Field Systems', p. 276.

[4] Campbell, 'Adisham', pp. 291-2.

[5] Above, pp. 189-90, 234-5.

[6] Above, pp. 314-15; work on the Huntingdonshire manors of Ramsey Abbey mostly points the same way (Dewindt, *Holywell*, p. 203 n; Raftis, *Warboys*, pp. 132-3, where no land transactions appear).

[7] Raftis, *Tenure*, pp. 129-82; Dewindt, *Holywell*, pp. 109-10, 152-5; see above, pp. 184-5, 288-90, 314-15.

away. Again we have been given a fairly consistent picture by
our last three chapters. Even in south-east Durham, where
there was relatively little movement, we find that particularly
the larger holdings in a vill tended to be taken over by
newcomers.[8] In Berkshire and Bedfordshire there was more
mobility: Brightwalton, South Moreton, Englefield, Coleshill,
Blunham, and Arlesey all show many changes of family names
between one list of tenants and another, pointing to influxes of
newcomers, mostly throughout the whole period.[9] This fully
accords with other local studies of the fourteenth and fifteenth
centuries, though in detail there may be significant variations;
thus the apparent rush of newcomers to Englefield in 1348-9
contrasts with Halesowen (Worcestershire) where, although
there was much immigration throughout the fourteenth century, vacancies caused by the Black Death seem to have been
filled from among the surviving inhabitants.[10] But in looking at
the immigration into these villages we should bear in mind the
evidence from Arlesey that the newcomers mostly came from
places quite close at hand,[11] and the evidence too from Zvi
Razi's family reconstructions at Halesowen that many of those
coming from outside to take up holdings were in fact, despite
differing surnames, related by blood or by marriage to people
already living there.[12]

In 1946 R.H. Hilton showed how local landholding on the
estates of Leicester Abbey underwent 'a sort of polarization
process' in the late fourteenth and fifteenth centuries: some
tenants built up large holdings, while others were reduced to
very small holdings or none at all, so that the difference
between the richest and poorest increased, and few or none
were left with middle-sized holdings—a virgate or half-
virgate.[13] The same developments have since been reported
elsewhere with occasional variations; thus Christopher Dyer

---

[8] Above, p. 314.

[9] Above, Ch. III, section 2, Ch. IV, section 2.

[10] Above, p. 150; Razi, *Life, Marriage and Death*, pp. 30-2, 110, 112-13, 117-20. In the
Chilterns too the vacancies of 1348-9 seem to have been filled mostly from within each
manor (D. Roden, 'Changing Settlement in the Chiltern Hills before 1850', *Folk Life*,
viii (1971), p. 66). This may reflect differences in the pattern of deaths in each area.

[11] Above, p. 221; cf. p. 289 and Dyer, *Lords and Peasants*, pp. 366-7.

[12] Razi, *Life, Marriage and Death*, pp. 120-2.

[13] Hilton, *Leics. Estates*, pp. 100-5.

found that on the bishopric of Worcester estates, while large holdings grew, the number of small as well as middle-sized holdings shrank, corresponding rather to the picture of general 'economic promotion' drawn by M.M. Postan.[14] But the accumulation of large holdings and with it an increasing gap between rich and poor tenants has seemed a normal consequence of the workings of a local land market. Edward Miller found this even in the mid-thirteenth century on the East Anglian and other estates of the bishopric of Ely.[15]

In the four studies here we have seen rather more varied developments. In particular two of the three places in thirteenth-century Norfolk present a picture quite different from the Ely estates: the division of holdings and the operation of the land market, combined clearly with population pressure and heavy demand for land, increased the number of tenants and reduced not only the average size of holding but the median as well—the largest holdings became smaller, not bigger. This is what probably happened at Gressenhall and certainly at Martham, but at Sedgeford the land market led some tenants to accumulate large holdings.[16] It is very interesting as it shows that we need still more work on individual vills before we can assess the overall effects of the land market on the tenantry of thirteenth-century East Anglia; it confirms too what John Hatcher found in early-fourteenth-century Cornwall,[17] that a local land market did not in fact always lead to engrossment, the building up of extra-large holdings by a few individuals. This, however, is the consistent pattern given by all three of our later-medieval studies: everywhere we see some tenants using the land market to accumulate holdings on a scale that must have placed them in a dominating position within the local community. On the other hand we see a good deal of variation in what happened to the rest of the tenantry. At Cowpen Bewley we have a very clear case of economic promotion: the largest holdings got larger but so did the smallest ones too.[18] Brightwalton presents an equally clear case of

---

[14] Dyer, *Lords and Peasants*, pp. 299-301, 312; at Holywell (Hunts.) and Battle (Sussex) the pattern was similar (Dewindt, *Holywell*, pp. 113-15; Searle, *Battle*, p. 377).

[15] Miller, *Ely*, pp. 133-5, 148-51.

[16] Above, pp. 59-60, 70, 95, 101.

[17] Hatcher, *Cornwall*, pp. 56, 100, 229.

[18] Above, pp. 309-11.

simple polarization by the early fifteenth century, and at Blunham an increase in the number of small holdings in the late fifteenth century was a prelude to polarization in the first half of the sixteenth, when large holdings were built up and some of the smaller tenants probably lost their lands altogether.[19] At Sotwell Stonor the growth of five large holdings was accompanied by the virtual disappearance of the standard half-virgate tenants whereas at Shillington, although there too some large holdings had been built up, the middle range of tenants, holding basically a virgate each, still predominated in the first half of the fifteenth century.[20] It is easier to point to these and to other variations than to assess their significance. The trouble is that we know very little about the poorest people in each community; the disappearance or continuance or enlargement of the smallest landholdings is only part of the story. The less successful families may have left the manor altogether, as in fourteenth-century Woolstone.[21] Alternatively they may have been employed on the new large holdings: Hilton points to the significant number of labourers and servants in the Leicestershire poll-tax returns of 1380.[22] Then again, the tenants of the largest holdings may have sublet them instead of tilling them themselves; we have seen this happening at Speenhamland and Eastrop.[23] There is some reason too to suppose that the late fourteenth and fifteenth centuries saw a small but significant influx of craftsmen into many village communities; they would be tenants of no more than a dwelling with little land or none at all, but this would be no guide to their economic status or possible local standing.[24] All this suggests that at the lower end of the scale the realities of village life may have differed a good deal from the formal tenurial picture. What we can be certain of is the accumulation of large holdings in so many places; there are very few communities with records full enough to enable us to go beyond

---

[19] Above, pp. 130-1, 199-200.

[20] Above, pp. 139, 211.

[21] Above, p. 129.

[22] Hilton, *Leics. Estates*, pp. 100, 163-4.

[23] Above, pp. 143-4, 148-9.

[24] P.D.A. Harvey, 'Non-agrarian Activities in the Rural Communities of Late-medieval England', forthcoming in the proceedings of the 14th Settimana di Studio (1982), Istituto Internazionale di Storia Economica Francesco Datini, Prato.

this. It could, for instance, be misleading to draw a sharp distinction between places of economic promotion, where all holdings got larger, and those of polarization, where the smaller ones declined; similar local conditions could produce either phenomenon, but equally either might be produced by quite varied actual circumstances.[25] It is interesting that at Halesowen, where polarization was increasing the gap between rich and poor tenants after 1350, life expectancy of all tenants increased and the difference between rich and poor in this respect diminished—perhaps a result, as Zvi Razi suggests, of generally raised standards of living.[26]

After the mid-fourteenth century, then, the formation of some large holdings seems to have been a consistent feature of the local land market. But the units from which these holdings were built up were mostly quite small. Where the land market was active it was based not on the transfer of standard holdings or of substantial areas of land, 10 or 20 acres at a time; such transactions there will certainly have been, and they were increasing in number and significance,[27] but far more will have been concerned with much smaller parcels, 2 or 3 acres or less. We saw at Arlesey that 'the scale of the market as a whole was probably linked to the scale of the market in small parcels'; it is likely that this comment can correctly be applied to the medieval local land market in general.[28] Some of these small pieces of land will of course have been free land in the first place; some will often have come from piecemeal reductions (permanent or temporary) of manorial demesnes. But some too will have come from the breakup, the fragmentation, of standard holdings. So much does this seem to have been the norm that we may even take the survival or disintegration of the standard holdings on a particular manor as a rough index to the activity of its local land market. Where there was a really active land market the standard holdings disappeared altogether, as in fifteenth-century Leighton Buzzard, or else they survived

[25] Dyer, *Lords and Peasants*, pp. 300-1, similarly urges caution in interpreting limited evidence on these points.

[26] Z. Razi, 'Family, Land and the Village Community in Later Medieval England', *P&P*, xciii (1981), 31; Razi, *Life, Marriage and Death*, pp. 128-31.

[27] Above, pp. 119-20, 184-5, 238.

[28] Above, p. 220. Harvey, *Westminster*, p. 328, reaches a similar conclusion over the market in free land on parts of the Westminster Abbey estates.

only as spectral relics in administrative documents, as at Martham in 1292.[29] At Arlesey, where there was a moderate land market (four or five transfers a year, on average, between 1377 and 1536), some standard holdings had disintegrated but many remained.[30] Where nearly all the standard holdings survived as intact units, as at Eastrop or Willington or in south-east Durham, there were relatively few transfers of land.[31] We must of course always allow for particular local circumstances. But it looks very much as if in places where the standard holding disintegrated at an early date—as at Halesowen, or on Westminster Abbey's manors at Aldenham (Hertfordshire), Hampstead (Middlesex), and South Benfleet (Essex), or in East Anglia and Kent—we would expect to find a land market already active in the thirteenth century.[32] Where the standard holding survived to the sixteenth century—as at Banbury (Oxfordshire), or on Westminster Abbey's manors at Islip (Oxfordshire), Turweston (Buckinghamshire), and around Pershore (Worcestershire), or in Durham—we would expect that there had been no effective medieval land market.[33] At the same time, even where the standard holding survived we often still find that individuals will have formed large holdings simply by taking over two, three, or more of them. The conditions of the late Middle Ages favoured the formation of large holdings whether this was done through the operations of a local land market or by simple accumulation of tenancies.

We have seen how manorial lords such as Winchester Cathedral Priory at Woolstone or the Grey family at Blunham could, with prudent management, make substantial profits from the local land market.[34] R.M. Smith has even estimated that the fines paid on land transfers provided some three-quarters of the income from one manor in Suffolk between 1259 and 1300.[35] But if the development of a land market involved the fragmentation of standard holdings the manorial

---

[29] Above, pp. 234, 67-9, 75.
[30] Above, Ch. IV, section 3; Ch. II, section 3.
[31] Above, pp. 146-9, 203-4, 304.
[32] Razi, *Life, Marriage and Death*, p. 8; Harvey, *Westminster*, pp. 206-7.
[33] *VCH Oxon.*, x. 53-4; Harvey, *Westminster*, pp. 286-7, 323-7.
[34] Above, pp. 111, 183.
[35] Macfarlane, *Eng. Individualism*, p. 109 n; cf. Hatcher, *Cornwall*, pp. 87-9, and Bean, *Percy Estates*, pp. 52-4, 60.

lord might lose more than he gained. Where the rents from
these holdings were paid entirely in money he would run no
risk, for they could be as minutely subdivided as the holding
itself and the lord would suffer no loss; thus at Shillington in
1306 a virgate had been divided, through sale, among twelve
tenants in unequal portions, but as the service due from it was
simply a rent of 5*s*. 8*d*. a year there was no difficulty in sharing
the obligation in portions as small as ½*d*. and as precisely
defined as 1*s*. 1¾*d*.[36] But harder problems arose where rents
took the form of labour services and renders of produce, and we
can see why Worcester Cathedral Priory, as manorial lord of
Stoke Prior (Worcestershire), took back into its own hands a
half-virgate that had been so much split up that the services due
from it could not be fully and properly performed.[37] Various
solutions were possible. One was to maintain, on paper so to
speak, a continuing structure of standard holdings which might
bear no relation to the existing pattern of tenures but which
served as a basis for allotting obligations to rents and services.
This was very common in Kent (as at Gillingham[38]) and in
East Anglia (as at Gressenhall[39]), but occurred elsewhere too;
on two Hertfordshire manors of Westminster Abbey rents and
services were still based on the full virgate at the end of the thirteenth century, but on one, Aldenham, these virgates had
entirely disintegrated and bore little relation to the actual
holdings in the vill, while on the other, Stevenage, an intermediate stage had been reached, for the tenants all held half-
virgates while their obligations were expressed in terms of full
ones.[40] A simpler way to meet the problem was for the
manorial lord to abandon all attempt to keep track of the
fragmentation of each standard holding and simply to make
one tenant responsible for all its customary obligations—a
method adopted on parts of the bishopric of Ely estates by the

---

[36] Raftis, *Tenure*, p. 88.

[37] Hilton, *Medieval Society*, p. 163. At Weston (Hunts.) Ramsey Abbey in 1308 required all 14 tenants between whom a 30-acre holding was unequally divided to render
the whole of the very light services due from the entire holding (Raftis, *Tenure*,
pp. 88-9); on the archbishopric of Canterbury's Kent manors special juries might be
empanelled to find how a yoke had been divided so as to allot the rents and services
proportionately (Du Boulay, *Canterbury*, pp. 152-3).

[38] A.R.H. Baker in Baker & Butlin, pp. 394-8.

[39] Above, Ch. II, section 2.

[40] Harvey, *Westminster*, pp. 206-7, 210.

early fourteenth century.[41] But the simplest solution of all was
to stop the holdings from being split up. We can deduce
manorial lords' opposition to dividing customary holdings from
the fact that on certain estates free holdings were the first to
disintegrate, even if (as on the Peterborough Abbey estates)
they tried to restrain even their free tenants from dividing their
holdings.[42] The 1297 extents of the St. Paul's Cathedral
manors of Caddington and Kensworth (Bedfordshire) are particularly interesting: they show that standard holdings held
freely for money rents were divided between many sub-tenants,
but those held by customary tenants for labour services have no
sub-tenants named. It may be that the customary holdings
remained intact, or alternatively that the extents did not record
their subdivision.[43] In the long term manorial lords were
remarkably unsuccessful in preventing any holdings, free or
customary, from disintegrating, but from the thirteenth century onwards we find them making more or less vain attempts
to stem the tide. We have seen how at Gressenhall the Foliots
may have succeeded in this until the early fourteenth century;
the bishops of Ely abandoned the struggle on their manors at
about the same time.[44] A fairly effective method used on some
Westminster Abbey manors was to impose a new rent on any
land subtracted from a holding while still demanding almost
the whole of its customary obligations from the original
tenant.[45] At Blunham we saw the earl of Kent in his Charter of
1471 regulating his tenants' alienation of customary lands and
trying to prevent the complete dispersal of the standard half-
virgates and quarterlands.[46]

One reason why the standard holdings at Gressenhall survived as long as they did may have been the persistence of
labour services there.[47] It is easy to see how difficult it must
have been either to divide labour services, especially week-
work, in such a way that they would be efficiently performed,
or to exact them in full from the tenant of only part of a divided

---

[41] Miller, *Ely*, pp. 133, 138-9.
[42] Harvey, *Westminster*, pp. 212-13; King, *Peterborough*, p. 119.
[43] Jones in *EcHR*, 2nd ser., xxxii (1979), 322.
[44] Above, p. 56; Miller, *Ely*, pp. 138, 146-7.
[45] Harvey, *Westminster*, pp. 301-3.
[46] Above, p. 198.
[47] Above, pp. 36, 56.

holding. We might thus suppose that the decline of labour services was a prerequisite for a local land market, and that its
spread followed the abolition of week-work. This is possible;
and it should be said at once that the detailed chronology of the
disappearance of week-work in the thirteenth and fourteenth
centuries is less clear than might appear at first sight.[48] But
labour services by the thirteenth century were, for lords as well
as tenants, an inconvenient and inefficient anachronism, kept
in being more for legal than for economic reasons; they were
not a strong, buoyant institution.[49] Probably, therefore, we
should look at it the other way round, and say that labour services (like the standard holding) could survive only where no
local land market developed. What happened at Gressenhall
and Blunham and on the Ely and Westminster Abbey estates
suggests that manorial lords were less powerful than one might
suppose in the face of local pressures for an active land market.
This is borne out by the differences we find between one manor
and another on a single estate—between, for instance, manors
of Bec Abbey in the thirteenth century: Ogbourne St. George
(Wiltshire) where standard virgates, half-virgates, and 4-acre
holdings all rendered week-work and other labour services, and
Blakenham (Suffolk) where the wholly disintegrated holdings
rendered money rents and a very few boon-works.[50] If the
manorial lord chose to keep labour services on the one manor,
why not keep them on the other? The regional pattern is too
strong to allow us to suppose that the difference arose from the
simple choice or initiative of the manorial lord. It is argued that
it was the labour services at Martham that led Norwich
Cathedral Priory to retain there throughout the thirteenth century the standard tenements that it had wholly abandoned at
Sedgeford,[51] but even at Martham it was only the notional
structure that remained—the holdings themselves had been
split up between many tenants in the course of the thirteenth
century.

[48] Because although a holding's obligation might include labour services, these
might be 'sold' (i.e. replaced by payment in cash) either occasionally or regularly (this
is usefully illustrated by Kosminsky, *Studies*, pp. 164-5, and Raftis, *Warboys*,
pp. 197-8). Thus to discover the actual incidence of labour services on any manor we
need to have not only a custumal but also a substantial series of annual accounts.

[49] P.D.A. Harvey, 'The English Inflation of 1180-1220', *P&P*, lxi (1973), 22-3.

[50] *Bec Documents*, pp. 29-36, 92-6.

[51] Above, Ch. II, section 5.

Christopher Dyer has suggested that one way the bishops of Worcester tried to prevent the disintegration of standard holdings was by insisting on impartible inheritance—on primogeniture in fact—for all customary holdings; he shows that partible inheritance (or rather, joint tenure among brothers, a point we shall return to) seems to have operated on parts of the estate in about 1170 but had vanished by 1299.[52] This raises the question of the part local inheritance customs may have played in breaking up standard holdings, a question that has already arisen, particularly in looking at our Norfolk manors. That partible inheritance could rapidly split a holding into many fragments is of course obvious; we have seen this happening at Martham.[53] That partible inheritance was widespread in East Anglia and Kent makes it easy to explain the early decay of standard holdings there, and Rosamond Faith's demonstration that it occurred also, though much more patchily, in many other parts of England as well[54] might make us wonder whether it may not have been a widespread cause of disintegration of standard holdings and therewith of the early development of a local land market. But here our three Norfolk manors are instructive. At Gressenhall standard holdings were still intact units at the end of the thirteenth century, whereas by then at Martham no more than a formal structure remained; yet both were manors of partible inheritance. At Sedgeford on the other hand the local inheritance custom was primogeniture, yet here holdings were scarcely less fragmented than on the other two, any slight difference being best explained simply by its being in an area of poorer soils.[55] Nor is it difficult to find places outside East Anglia where, despite impartible inheritance, standard holdings had collapsed and a vigorous land market had developed before the end of the thirteenth century. The manors in the Chilterns investigated by David Roden, especially Codicote (Hertfordshire), are examples of this; Halesowen (Worcestershire) is another.[56]

[52] Dyer, *Lords and Peasants*, pp. 86, 106; cf. King, *Peterborough*, pp. 117-19.

[53] Above, pp. 71-5.

[54] 'Peasant Families and Inheritance Customs in Medieval England', *AgHR*, xiv (1966), 93-5.

[55] Above, Ch. II, section 5.

[56] D. Roden, 'Inheritance Customs and Succession to Land in the Chiltern Hills in the Thirteenth and Early Fourteenth Centuries', *JBS*, vii (1967), 1-11 (but the point is made more clearly in Roden, 'Chiltern Field Systems', pp. 161-2, 165-7); Razi, *Life, Marriage and Death*, p.8.

It seems, then, as if the standard holdings did not simply disintegrate in the wake of the decline of week-work, nor yet in response to local inheritance customs. What in fact generally underlay the phenomenon was the land market itself—the demand for transfers of land not just on death but *inter vivos*, from one living person to another, whether by sale or by lease or by any other arrangement. Historians sometimes assume that the standard holding in the thirteenth and fourteenth centuries was a strong institution, firmly rooted in past history and basic to current agrarian and tenurial practice, so that its disappearance is viewed with mild surprise. In fact it was a very fragile thing. Once the individual tenant's lands and rights had been precisely defined, as they came to be defined in the twelfth century, the standard holding had lost most of its point and became little more than a historical relic; where it survived to the fourteenth or fifteenth century or later this could only be because no pressures had been brought to bear on it in that particular locality. Conversely the peasant land market is sometimes viewed as a frail, almost alien, growth, springing up as it were in the interstices of the medieval agrarian system in places where 'manorialization' was weakest; whereas in fact all the evidence suggests that by the thirteenth century it was already a very strong force indeed and that wherever it arose it created pressures that manorial lords were powerless to resist.

Why did this land market arise? Although in two of our vills in thirteenth-century Norfolk, probably an area of extreme land shortage, the land market seems to have reduced the size of all holdings, in all other cases we have seen it consistently led to the enlargement—the substantial enlargement—of some tenants' holdings. Engrossment of this sort seems generally to have come about only through the workings of a local land market, though in some places after the Black Death population losses led to tenants acquiring extra holdings simply by taking them over as they fell vacant. We should not dismiss the exceptions as insignificant. All the same it looks as if the land market normally led to the enlargement of some individuals' holdings and as if the land market was the way such enlargement was normally achieved. Essentially it was those who acquired lands who brought the market into being and

almost certainly the main prerequisite for this was local prosperity: the means of building up enough resources in money,
enough capital, to pay whatever was needed for the purchase or
lease of the extra land and to find the stock, the labour, the
equipment, to work the enlarged holding. This explains why
the land market dealt in small pieces rather than complete
holdings: the resources of those acquiring lands were inadequate to cope with substantial additions unless they were
acquired piecemeal. It seems unlikely that a land market could
develop in places where the level of prosperity was low.
Significantly, there were unusually uniform holdings on those
villages on the bishopric of Worcester estates that came to be
deserted in the late Middle Ages—and we have learned from
M.W. Beresford and others that desertion and impoverishment
went hand in hand.[57] Of the four Chiltern vills investigated by
David Roden Ibstone (Buckinghamshire) was the poorest and
was the only one to have no local land market—even though
free tenants predominated there and labour services were light,
consisting of boon-works rather than week-work.[58] Different
levels of prosperity are surely one reason for local and regional
variations in the land market. But they are far from the whole
story; we have been rightly warned, in looking at Coleshill,
that an active land market cannot be taken as a simple index
to local prosperity.[59] In some prosperous vills or regions
seignorial demands in heavy rents, whether in cash or in labour
services, high entry fines, and the like might effectively stop a
local land market from developing by the indirect means of
preventing tenants from collecting sufficient funds; it is significant here that we find an early land market in Kent and East
Anglia, where seignorial demands were mostly fairly light, and
that in many places a land market quickly developed after the
Black Death had led to reduced tenant obligations.[60] And

[57] Dyer, *Lords and Peasants*, p. 263; *Deserted Medieval Villages*, ed. M. Beresford and
J.G. Hurst (London, 1971), pp. 21-6.

[58] Roden, 'Chiltern Field Systems', pp. 236-42; D. Roden, 'Field Systems in
Ibstone, a Township of the South-west Chilterns, during the Later Middle Ages',
Records of Buckinghamshire, xviii, No. 1 (1966), pp. 43-4.

[59] Above, p. 156.

[60] Thus Roden, 'Chiltern Field Systems', pp. 115, 117, notes how at Kings Walden
(Herts.) the character of the local land market changed in the mid-14th century: values
declined and larger units came to be transferred. Hilton, *Eng. Peasantry*, pp. 196-205,
shows how difficult it was for the peasant to accumulate capital in the 13th century and

although neither partible inheritance of customary lands nor a predominance of free tenures was a prerequisite for a land market which could perfectly well develop without either, yet each could serve to prime the pump, giving the market an early impetus in particular places.

Why should the peasant wish to enlarge his holding? The answer is not necessarily self-evident, though simple ambition must often have been the explanation. From available evidence we might well suppose that this was why, say, John Pope of Sotwell Stonor or William Taillour of Leighton Buzzard or William White of Cowpen Bewley was buying land in the fifteenth century.[61] It is interesting that on several of our Berkshire manors families that built up extensive holdings in the fifteenth century failed to maintain their position—a peasant aristocracy that came to nothing.[62] The same thing happened in south-east Durham but at an earlier date: families prominent in the late fourteenth century had disappeared by the mid-fifteenth, though some of their late-fifteenth-century successors prospered throughout the sixteenth.[63] Similar patterns of transient peasant wealth in the late Middle Ages have been reported elsewhere.[64] This may simply reflect the mobility of the late-medieval population, or it may be that the conditions of the time made it difficult to sustain the consistent degree of investment needed for farming on this particular scale—as we have been reminded by the evidence of harvests in Durham,[65] small-scale farming was still a chancy business in the late Middle Ages. In some places, indeed, there seems to have been opposition to any accumulation of lands; it was stated as local custom at Ombersley (Worcestershire) in 1415 that a composite holding should be divided on the tenant's death between his children of both sexes.[66]

how the difficulties eased in the 14th and 15th centuries. Royal demands will have contributed to the difficulties in general, and some areas suffered particularly from purveyance; interestingly, however, it was eastern England that was most affected in the early 14th century (Maddicott, *Eng. Peasantry*, pp. 17-18, 67-70).

[61] Above, pp. 141, 231, 245, 310.
[62] Above, pp. 145, 157-8, 167-8, 173-6.
[63] Above, p. 316.
[64] e.g. *VCH Oxon.*, vi. 226; Harvey, *Westminster*, pp. 289-90.
[65] Above, Ch. V, section 4.
[66] Hilton, *Eng. Peasantry*, p. 41.

But sheer economic ambition need not have been the only reason for acquiring extra lands. Particularly since 1966, when the work of A.V. Chayanov was published in English,[67] historians have been looking in medieval England for the pattern he describes from Russia: as a family itself expanded, producing more mouths to feed or more hands to till the soil, so it would enlarge its holding accordingly, but when the children left home or took up lands of their own the parents would no longer need so much land and would reduce the holding. There are not many places in late-medieval England with records of peasant families full enough to tell whether this was happening or not. Halesowen (Worcestershire) was one, however, and there Zvi Razi has found nothing to suggest that lands were being acquired or disposed of on this basis.[68] On the other hand there may well be some cases of this happening on the estates of Ramsey Abbey and the bishopric of Worcester, and although we have no clear evidence it would at least fit very well with what we have seen at Arlesey, with its pool of marketable pieces of land that moved fairly rapidly from one holder to another.[69] Yet another distinct but related reason for acquiring extra land was to provide for children, especially for those who under local inheritance custom would get no part of the basic holding on the parent's death. We have seen this happening at Sedgeford and it has been found elsewhere too in the thirteenth and fourteenth centuries—at Halesowen and in the Chilterns for instance.[70] Where inheritance customs came to be less strictly applied in the late Middle Ages—as at Sotwell Stonor, or as at Adisham (Kent)[71]—there will not have been the same need to buy land for children who would otherwise be landless, but land might still be acquired to provide adequately for all the children if there were several in the family.

These three reasons why the peasant might wish to enlarge his holding—and thus why the peasant land market grew

---

[67] *The Theory of Peasant Economy*, ed. D. Thorner, B. Kerblay, and R.E.F. Smith (Homewood, 1966); cf. Hilton, *Eng. Peasantry*, pp. 6-7.

[68] Razi, *Life, Marriage and Death*, pp. 144-6.

[69] Dewindt, *Holywell*, pp. 116-22, 129-33; Dyer, *Lords and Peasants*, pp. 306-8; above, pp. 217-19, 222-3.

[70] Above, pp. 92-4, 100-1; Razi in *P&P*, xciii (1981), 6-8; Roden in *JBS*, vii (1967), pp. 6-7.

[71] Above, pp. 139-40; Campbell, 'Adisham', pp. 251-2, 266.

up—are not mutually exclusive: all three may well be correct. It is not just that one may have operated in one village or region, another in another; all three could perfectly well be found in a single place or in a single individual. The late-medieval peasant may well have been no more capable than his historian 500 years later of analysing his motives when he set about acquiring more lands; economic ambition, immediate provision for an expanding family, provision for non-inheriting children after his death might all have played their part in any one purchase.

The part played by the land market in providing for the landless members of the tenant's family, either immediately or on his death, raises the question of the rôles of the family and the individual in the rural society of medieval England—a question that has been especially to the fore since Alan Macfarlane argued in 1978 that the basic unit of this society was essentially the individual not the family, that the members of the peasant family were, as he put it, ego-centred rather than ancestor-centred, and that the peasant tenant should be seen as a landholder in his own right, not as his generation's trustee for property which belonged to the family as a whole, past and future.[72] It is indisputable that the inhabitants of the medieval countryside were viewed as individuals by royal administrators, as we see in tax assessments, by estate administrators, as we see in manorial court records, and very likely by each other too, though of this we have practically no evidence. Certainly if either the king or the estate owner wished to treat with any part of the rural community corporately it was to the vill, the manor, or the tithing group that he would turn, not to the single family. Throughout this book we have seen peasant tenants buying and selling, leasing and bequeathing land, all as between one individual and another. None of this need imply, however, that a very strong sense of family commitment and of family responsibility was not widespread among these same peasant tenants: there is overwhelming evidence that it was. In the four studies here we have seen this over and again: in the way families provided for all their members in despite or even in defiance of local inheritance customs;[73] in the way a

[72] Macfarlane, *Eng. Individualism*, pp. 80-164 *passim*.
[73] Above, pp. 44-5, 92-4, 100-1, 103, 300-1.

holding, technically divided by partible inheritance, yet remained intact;[74] in the reversions and other devices that were used to keep lands in the family.[75] All this can be paralleled and expanded from other work on the rural society of late-medieval England.[76] Admittedly this sense of family may have been declining by the fifteenth century: one strikingly consistent feature of the late-medieval land market in Berkshire, Bedfordshire, and Durham is the declining proportion of land transfers made between relatives.[77] But Zvi Razi, from his detailed reconstruction of family relationships at Halesowen, has shown that this may be illusory: the records from less well-documented manors are just not full enough to show that people of different surnames might still be related.[78] He is careful to stress that what happened in one place did not necessarily happen in another;[79] but if we can correctly draw analogies from Halesowen it could be that we see a very stable balance in the conflicting claims of the individual and his family throughout the thirteenth, fourteenth, and fifteenth centuries.

Whether we can carry this same stability back into the twelfth century is open to question. Particularly since Rosamond Faith's work on inheritance customs in 1966[80] historians have tended to think that in late Anglo-Saxon England there was widespread partible inheritance among the peasantry, a custom generally changed for impartible inheritance (mostly primogeniture) following the example of the upper ranks of Anglo-Norman society.[81] This may be so; but an ancient

[74] Above, pp. 40-1, 43-7, 74-5.

[75] Above, pp. 140, 142.

[76] e.g. Dewindt, *Holywell*, pp. 133-4, 185 n. For the higher ranks of 12th-century society cf. Milsom, *Legal Framework*, pp. 121-2, 132-7.

[77] Above, pp. 132, 136, 150, 156, 217-19, 237, 248, 296-90.

[78] Razi in *P&P*, xciii (1981), 16-22.

[79] Ibid., p. 36.

[80] In *AgHR*, xiv (1966), 77-95.

[81] Thus, e.g., Harvey, *Westminster*, p. 210. Partible inheritance among the peasantry would accord with the partible inheritance found in the upper ranks of late Anglo-Saxon landowners (T.H. Aston, 'The Origins of the Manor in England' and 'A Postscript', in *Social Relations and Ideas*, ed. T.H. Aston and others (Cambridge, 1983), pp. 20-1, 27-9), as well as with contemporary Welsh customs (G.R.J. Jones, 'Multiple Estates and Early Settlement', in *Medieval Settlement: Continuity and Change*, ed. P.H. Sawyer (London, 1976), pp. 16-17, 35). Cf. the comment of Hyams, *King, Lords, and Peasants*, p. 77 n, that manorial custom was Anglo-Saxon law that 'slid down society with those who used it' after 1066.

custom of joint tenure by all sons who stayed at home is by no means impossible.[82] We have seen how in the twelfth century a change in emphasis in the relations between lord and tenant led to the tenant's rights being viewed more strictly in territorial terms and to a more precise definition of his holding.[83] It would be entirely consistent for this to define not only exactly what each man held, but also exactly which man held it—in other words the introduction of precise inheritance custom to make it perfectly clear who was answerable for every parcel of the rights and obligations that made up a holding: the eldest son, or the youngest son, or all the sons, not jointly but each taking a specific share of the divided property. Which of these customs was adopted may well have made less difference in practice than might appear: Rosamond Faith argued in 1966 that the practical effects of ultimogeniture and partible inheritance were much the same,[84] and we can see that, where a local land market enabled younger brothers to be separately provided for, primogeniture too need not be so very different. The crucial difference was not between one or other inheritance custom, but between defined inheritance custom and undifferentiated joint inheritance. This, of course, is no more than speculation, but it is a possibility that needs to be taken into account in assessing what few facts or hints we have about the succession to peasant holdings before the thirteenth century. It is possible, even likely, that the position varied a good deal from one part of the country to another; it may be that what happened was at most a move towards defined inheritance in places where it was not already established custom. But certainly development on these lines would help to explain why in areas of partible inheritance standard holdings could still be basically intact in the early thirteenth century;[85] it is a problem to which slow

---

[82] It is interesting that Aston, op. cit., p. 28, suggests the possibility of just such joint tenure in particular circumstances in the late Anglo-Saxon period, and that Rees, *S. Wales and March*, p. 157, refers to it in later medieval south Wales.

[83] Above Ch. I, section 2.

[84] In *AgHR*, xiv (1966), 83-4.

[85] It might also help to explain, on the assumption that joint tenure gave way to partible inheritance, the division of standard holdings in many places, so that virgates became half-virgates, etc. (Rees, *S. Wales and March*, p. 153; Raftis, *Tenure*, p. 17; Harvey, *Westminster*, pp. 299-300). But this is to advance still further into mere speculation.

population growth and the availability of new land for colonization are not very convincing answers.

But if this occurred it cannot have been more than a shift of emphasis. If peasant families in fact held jointly there will normally have been a recognized head of each household: eleventh- and twelfth-century manorial surveys generally name individuals, not family groups, as their local tenants,[86] though, significantly, some obligations lay on the entire peasant household, not on the individual tenant.[87] Inheritance customs may have simply extended, or even just made explicit, the local arrangements governing the family group. Alan Macfarlane hints that the origin of what he sees as very distinctive English individualism lay in the depths of Germanic antiquity; this may be so, but it is at least possible that the twelfth century saw a significant step in local tenures away from the family group and towards the individual as an aspect of the process of definition of tenure, of land, and of law. At the same time it was a shift of emphasis at most. The sharp distinction that Macfarlane draws between family and individual may be helpful in contrasting England's rural structure with that of other parts of Europe;[88] it is less clear that it assists our understanding of that structure in England itself. Throughout the Middle Ages in England we see family and individual playing distinct but interdependent rôles. It is with the family made up of individuals and with the individual within his family that the historian of the medieval English peasantry is concerned.

[86] The joint tenure on the bishopric of Worcester estates *c*.1170 (above, p. 348) is thus exceptional in being so recorded.

[87] e.g. the frequent obligation to perform certain harvest works with the entire household, as on the Burton Abbey estates at Appleby (Leics.), Cauldwell, and Findern (both Derbs.) and on manors of the bishop of Durham (C.G.O. Bridgeman, 'The Burton Abbey Twelfth Century Surveys', *Collections for a History of Staffordshire 1916* (William Salt Soc., 1918), pp. 245, 243, 235; *Boldon Buke, passim*).

[88] Macfarlane, *Eng. Individualism, passim*.

Index

Englefield (Berks.) 107-9, 149-52, 160, 161, 168, 330, 333, 337, 340
Englefield, family 150
engrossment of holdings: as basis of land market 340-4, 349-53
entry fines 25, 334, 344, 350; in Norf. 43-4, 46-8, 105; in Berks. 111, 112, 113-18, 124, 128, 132, 138, 148, 157; in Beds. 186, 201-2, 204, 205 n., 211-12, 216, 220, 233, 234, 237, 244-5, 334; in Durh. 261, 307-8, 313, 327
Erl, —— 36 n., 37 n., 45
eruingmen, eruings 8, 17 n., 64-6, 68, 69, 74, 78, 83
Escelyn, Beatrix 87
escheators 213-14
Esgoer, John 233
Eton College 225
Etonbury (Beds.) 215
Eversole, William de 131 n.
Everton (Beds.) 196
exchanges of land 24, 41, 76-7, 83, 94, 169-70
exchequer land 14, 270, 273, 277
Eynsham Abbey 332
Eyston, family 168
Eyworth (Beds.) 189

Faber, Edmund 50
    Jordan 50
    Thomas 46
    see also Smith
Fairjon, —— 284, 292
fairs 228-9
Faith, Rosamond 4, 296, 348, 354, 355
Faldgate, Robert 71
families: intra-family, inter-family, land transfers, in Norf. 75-6; in Berks. 132-3, 136, 142; in Beds. 188-9, 200-1, 203, 207-9, 216-17, 237-8; in Durh. 295-9; family and individual 351-6; *see also* joint tenure
farmers, lessees of manorial demesnes 26; in Berks. 109, 110, 135, 141, 154, 165-7, 174; in Beds. 182, 191, 205, 216; in Durh. 303-4; *see also* accounts
farmland (form of tenure) 268-9, 273, 277
Fauconer, Thomas 213
Fawkes, family 316
    Gilbert 322

Fayrey, family 190
Fenne, *see* Atte Fenne
Fermour, Richard 190
ferries 298, 310 n., 311, 323-4
ferryland 310
Fery, William son of Richard de 276
Feryman, family 292
field systems 6, 13, 16, 180; in particular places 17, 79, 80, 84, 99-100, 196, 226-7; location of holdings in fields 54, 68, 76-7, 240-4, 248; *see also* names
Finberg, H. P. R. 273
Findern (Derbs.) 356 n.
fish 55, 290
Fish, family 100 n.
    Peter 90
Fisher, family 292
Fite, —— 37 n.
Fleg, Bartholomew of 79
Flegg, East and West, hundreds (Norf.) 62, 82
Fleote, *see* Atte Fleote
Fleta 283
Flitton (Beds.) 246
Foliot, family 33-6, 38, 41, 56, 78, 81, 346
    Jordan 34
Fontevrault Abbey 224, 225
Fordham, John, bishop of Durham 262
forges 231, 309, 311
Forncett (Norf.) 53 n., 66 n.
Fortescue, Sir Adrian 175, 176
Fortey, Nicholas 163
Fowkes, Thomas 229
Fowler, Alice wife of Thomas 301
    John son of Thomas 301
    Richard 230
    Thomas 301
Fox, H. S. A. 6, 13
Foxton, John 128
Francis, Sir Adam 189
freeholders, free holdings 19-22, 331-2, 346, 350-1; in Norf. 31, 36, 38, 41-2, 61, 79, 81, 85, 87-92, 94, 97; in Berks. 108, 112, 126, 130, 135, 147, 149, 154; in Beds. 186-7, 196, 197, 234; in Durh. 259, 266, 272, 276, 278-84, 286-8, 299, 302; *see also* burgesses, drengage holdings, molmen, sokemen
Freeman, Richard 235
Fring (Norf.) 85
Fristerlyng, Robert son of Eustace 284